WOULDN'T IT BE NICE

My Own Story

BRIAN WILSON

with Todd Gold

■■ HarperCollins*Publishers*

FIRST EDITION

Designed by Cassandra J. Pappas

Library of Congress Cataloging-in-Publication Data

Wilson, Brian, 1942-
    Wouldn't it be nice / Brian Wilson with Todd Gold. — 1st ed.
        p.   cm.
    Includes index.
    ISBN 0-06-018313-6
    1. Wilson, Brian, 1942-   . 2. Rock musicians—United States—
Biography. 3. Beach Boys. I. Gold, Todd. II. Title.
ML420.W5525A3   1991
782.42166′092—dc20
    [B]   90-56403

91 92 93 94 95 CC/RRD 10 9 8 7 6 5 4 3 2 1

To Dr. Eugene Landy—
without you there'd be no music
—Brian Wilson

To Beth, Abby and Eliza,
the girls on the beach
—TG

Contents

Acknowledgments

To the best of my ability, this book is how I remember my life up until this point. A lot of people have helped me live it, some helped me destroy it, and quite a number of people generously contributed their time, support, and love to saving it.

I want to thank several longtime friends for their help and contributions to this book: Danny Hutton, who graciously contributed his recollections of a past both of us have long put behind us; Van Dyke Parks and Tony Asher, soldiers from heroic times, who also assisted by remembering details that might've been overlooked; the late Gary Usher, to whom I said goodbye but have not forgotten; also Roger Christian and David Marks.

It's worth noting that of my family members and the Beach Boys, only Al Jardine and Bruce Johnston shared their memories with me for inclusion in this book. For that, they have my appreciation.

I want to thank Hubert and May Everly for the use of their beautiful Hawaiian home over the years.

In addition, I want to thank some of my friends who have helped me so much, among them: Dr. Solon Samuels, a wise man indeed; Dr. Murry "Buzz" Susser, one of my original healers; Dr. Arnold Dahlke; Bill Flaxman; Dr. Gerald Wall; Dr. Steven Zax; Henry Edwards; Cliff and Gypsi De Young; Don Tringali; Kirk Hallam; Lin Bolen; Lynne Turner; Dr. Arnie Horwitz; Don Engel; Mike Rosenfeld; Dr. Arnold Ross; Dr. Leroy Perry; Mark Meador; Prem Nagar; Dr. David Allen.

Thanks also to these other close friends who stuck with me through thick and thicker: Pam Thomas; Gordon Forbes; Carlos Booker; Scott Steinberg; Chad Einbinder; Sally Steinberg; Sandy Friedman; Greg Dahlke; Nikki Simon; Deirdre Courtiney; Sean Corrigan; Chris Rogerson; David Berlow; Michael Whitis; Cynthia Rubenstein; Tanya Oliver; Dr. Ray Corsini; Leslie Moore Dahlke; Caroline Henning; Michael Eames; Jeffrey Lee; Angela Otto; and Gloria Perez.

Thanks to the girls who make the spring eternal, and the summer endless, Mary Kay Reynolds and Sidney Gray.

Evan Landy has been a special friend, taking me to my first A.A. meeting and accompanying me on many other adventures; and Frances Morgan has been truly special.

Michael Bernard, the programmer on my solo albums, doesn't get the credit he deserves, but here it is in writing: Michael, your work doesn't go unheard. And hey, Frankie Schubart, supplier of all the nuts and bolts, take a bow, man.

My friend, collaborator, and ocean swimming buddy Alexandra Morgan, who has become the sister I always wanted, has given my life the harmony of a beautiful duet, and my personal assistant Kevin Leslie has always been there for me, on land, sea, and in the air. Both of you deserve my special and heartfelt thanks.

I also want to acknowledge the professionalism and support of my HarperCollins editor Tom Miller, his assistant Jim Hornfischer, and my William Morris agent Dan Strone. All three can play in my band anytime.

I often think of the one family member who would've stood on my side and helped me fight my current battles. Dennis, I miss you.

Unfortunately, others in my family and so-called friends, people who've regularly professed the most concern about my happiness and well-being, were also among the most unwilling to contribute to this project.

It's been difficult to communicate with my daughters Carnie and Wendy. I know you girls wish I were a better father. I do, too. Hopefully you realize that, in my own way, I love you, think about you, and am proud of all your successes. I wish you could feel the same way about me.

This autobiography was written at a time in my life when I felt better and stronger than ever. But I wouldn't have gotten to such a place if not for Dr. Eugene Landy, my closest confidante and most trusted friend. He and I have come a long way since we started working together back in 1983. We've climbed mountains, walked shoulder-to-shoulder into battle, and dared to try things others have called impossible. In a life that hasn't been too kind, he provided a shoulder to lean on. As a doctor, teacher, parent, liberator, songwriter, and manager, he's been an invaluable master-of-all-trades. But most of all, he's been my friend. While many have misunderstood our relationship, we have always seen it clearly.

If not for him, I would not have been able to write this book, which I hope you enjoy. It took a while.

Love and mercy,

Brian Wilson
Malibu, California

It's impossible to write a book of this scope without the support and assistance of many people, and in an effort to acknowledge that fact, I want to thank and express gratitude to my family, who worked as hard and sacrificed as much as I did in writing this book; my boss, Landon Y. Jones, the managing editor of *People Weekly* magazine; Cutler Durkee, who always knows when the surf's up; Lisa Russell, a good ear; Jack Kelley for understanding; Peter Castro; Monica Rizzo and Florence Nishda for taking care of business; Dina's Flying Fingers; Fine Printing in Westwood; Michael Eames and Caroline Henning, unsung heroes; Brad Benedict; Neal Preston; David Rensin; Kevin Leslie, the dude of all dudes; Tom Miller; Jim Hornfischer; Dan Strone, who began and ended this book a fan; Dr. Eugene Landy; and Brian.

Todd Gold
Westwood, California

Fired!

I imagined the headlines. *Brian Wilson. Beach Boys Genius. Fired From Group.*

Fired.

The word was absolutely foreign to me, impossible to understand or accept. I sat motionless, speechless, impassive.

"Listen to what we're saying," said Mike Love, the Beach Boys' lead singer and my first cousin.

The Beach Boys were seated around a large conference table, watching my reaction to the letter they had given me to read. I read it several times, then glanced at each of my band mates—stone-faced Mike, my bearded baby brother, Carl, and my friend since high school Al Jardine. The words "terminated" and "effective immediately" resonated in my syrupy brain. In shock, I didn't know what to think, or how to react.

"I'm fired?" I asked. "Is that what you're telling me?"

"That's right," Mike said.

"Fired." I still didn't believe it. "What the fuck?" I *founded* the Beach Boys!

It was November 5, 1982. The day began with gray afternoon skies, a murky consciousness, and an oversized mug of extra-strength instant coffee—my usual eye-opener. Holding my coffee mug still with one hand, I used the other to heap half a dozen scoops of instant crystals into my cup.

Then I added sugar—lots of it. My hands trembled so violently an equal amount spilled on the countertop. By the time I finished filling the cup, there was barely room left for the water.

In those days, I was a zonked-out zombie, a star-crossed Sixties rock star who took a drug trip and never returned. I lived in a dense fog. Fear permeated my thoughts and determined my actions. I was schizoid, my behavior constantly veering. The perceptions and pictures that entered my head were translated into codes only I understood, distorted and fractured into cubist interpretations of reality.

It's only now, after nearly a decade of nontraditional, much publicized and much misunderstood therapy that I've been able to piece together and understand what I was like. In those days I was content to live inside myself, a withdrawn mass of misery and confusion and fear.

I didn't leave the house much and I didn't go out if the sky was cloudy. That was one of my rules. Why bother if it wasn't sunny out? I preferred the sky to be blue. Baby blue. Clear blue. A blue that offered hope. Despite the weather, I rarely saw that color sky. It wasn't that color this particular November afternoon, and I didn't want to go out. Unfortunately I had no choice in the matter.

Going out wasn't going to be easy. Every little movement was hard: getting off the sofa, getting dressed. I sat upright on the couch and flicked my cigarette onto the hardwood floor. The red tip burned into the varnish and the wood, adding to the pattern of black marks I had created. There were thousands of them, covering every square inch of floor space. Now there was one more.

"Carolyn!" I yelled.

Carolyn Williams, an ambitious black woman, was my former mental hospital nurse-turned-live-in companion. I was like a dependent child, overgrown and demanding. She catered to my helplessness, fulfilling the motherly needs that had been handled over the years by my ex-wife Marilyn, her older sister, and assorted groupies.

"My pants!" I called. "I can't find my pants."

Carolyn, having started out as my caretaker, had become emotionally involved with me, much more than I was with her. Although she might've legitimately cared for me, many thought she had long ago stepped out of bounds. Nursing was one thing, insisting on attending Beach Boys meetings was another. As was smoking pot with me.

But the relationship worked. She took care of the house and left me alone.

"Look around," she hollered from another room.

I scanned the living room haphazardly, surveying the gross wreckage of a night—perhaps longer—that had been spent consuming unthinkable quantities of junk food, booze, and cocaine. I didn't see any pants. Then, a few minutes later, I realized why. I was wearing them. That struck me as funny. I laughed. I got a case of what I called the laughs, and I let out a loud, from-the-belly guffaw. Ha! Ha! Ha! I couldn't stop laughing. It was all so funny.

Then I remembered. I hadn't changed out of my pants before crashing on the sofa the night before. The shirt I wore was also the same one I'd worn the previous night. That was par for the course. I'd long ago given up worrying about changing clothes or personal hygiene. Washing, showering, brushing my teeth, combing my hair—the stuff people take for civilized behavior. My hair was greasy. I stank. I was dirty.

But in the scheme of day-to-day survival, clean clothes and a hot shower were the least of my concerns. I was convinced that I could die at any moment. I told myself that over and over until all I did was wait, expectantly, for the moment to arrive. It scared the shit out of me. It also paralyzed me with excitement. Almost as if I was strapped into the front seat of a rollercoaster. It didn't leave much time to worry about clean pants.

My addled mind was able to handle but a single thought at any moment, and then that thought had to do with attending a Beach Boys band meeting. The clock was ticking. I had a few hours to go. I had to face the inevitable. A meeting, hmmm. A meeting, hmmm. I repeated those words over and over until they became something of a mantra.

How did this meeting manage to intrude on my mostly sedentary, extremely isolated life? Wary of everything, I retraced the chronology, looking for a clue that would signal danger. I remembered Carolyn telling me she'd taken a call from the Beach Boys' manager's secretary. The group was having a meeting the following afternoon. I absolutely *had* to attend. No arguments. No excuses. It was a command performance.

Still: Why were they calling a meeting?

I sighed and focused my attention on eating breakfast. A man of my size and thought production needed energy. Fuel to stoke the fire. Breakfast consisted of two, sometimes three, extra-thick, marbelized New York steaks broiled till the fat sizzled on top and served with a bottle of steak sauce. That was the morning routine. My megacoffee, a couple of steaks, some more coffee to get me going again, and cigarettes.

I smoked five or six packs of Marlboros a day. I was surrounded by smoke. The cigarettes ruined my voice, but they gave me something to do with my hands between meals. I had priorities.

After breakfast, I labored into the front yard and began to walk. At more than 340 pounds, I waddled more than I walked. But that was part of the routine. Waddling back and forth across the front lawn, flicking cigs and sparking new ones.

From the outside, my three-bedroom house appeared ordinary, no different from my Pacific Palisades neighbors, who were wealthy doctors, lawyers, and celebrities. The itnerior was a different story, done in the style of a junkie's crash pad. A fetid odor greeted visitors at the door. Dirty clothes, food, and cigarette stubs littered the floors. Carolyn's three kids ran around at will. Their dogs frequently relieved themselves inside the house. These days I get sick to my stomach thinking about it.

I spent most of my waking time in this smelly cave, splayed on the living room leather sofa like a walrus, thinking. I let my brain go by itself, pedal-to-the metal. My mind was a hyperactive house of thrills vacillating between numbness and panic, paranoia, and terror. Thoughts rolled through me like unrelenting seismic waves.

Years earlier I thought of music, nothing but music. Now I thought of death. I waited for it. It scared the shit out of me. But knowing any breath could be the last also made life exciting.

I couldn't relax. Not ever. Not for one second. My mind sped on automatic—out of control.

I was insane.

"Brian, are you ready to go?" Carolyn called.

"Almost," I mumbled.

"We're gonna be late," she said.

So what? I had gotten the urge to get high. A blast of coke would make me more sociable and better able to communicate. The prospect of squaring off with the Beach Boys made me anxious and scared. I felt like a guppy in a tank of sharks. I needed something to make me forget the fear.

My breaths were short and heavy as I trod through the house, looking for leftover cocaine. My pulmonary system felt the strain of an undersized engine pulling too much weight. Beads of sweat rolled off my face. The search was futile, a wasted effort. No matter where I looked, I couldn't find any coke from the previous night. That shouldn't have come as any surprise. My brother Dennis, the Beach Boys' drummer, had been over the previous night. The way we snorted coke, if there had been any remaining we'd have still been doing it.

There was one last chance though. The mirror Dennis and I had used was on top of the piano. I lunged toward it. As I suspected, there were a few specks of residue on the surface. It wasn't much, but it was enough to kick-start my heart into a jackhammer beat as I anticipated the rush. Coke was the key that unlocked my shackles, stood me atop mountains, let me see above the clouds. It gave me the courage I ordinarily lacked.

"Brian!" Carolyn's high-pitched voice snarled.

I was hunched over the piano, licking the mirror.

"Don't you be doing any of that," she said. "You can smoke a joint. But no coke."

Carolyn stood beside the front door, holding the car keys. No way was I getting out of this meeting. Not only had the Beach Boys stipulated that, but Carolyn had also laid down the law. She'd let me know that she was going to drag me to this Beach Boys corporate meeting even if she had to hire a tow truck. Her street sense made clear to her the meaning of this tribal gathering. At stake was the lifeblood of our wretched existence together—money.

What can I say about money? If music was the root of all happiness in my life, money accounted for most of the evil. My father had abused and beaten me during childhood and had made me afraid of people, but nothing twisted me like money. I'd made a million dollars before I was old enough to vote. I rarely thought about the stuff, only when I needed to buy drugs, and even then it was a fleeting thought. Songwriting royalties and Beach Boys touring revenues gave me a large enough cushion that I never worried about affording any kind of life-style.

If I wanted cash, from $100 to $1,000—whatever I needed—I called my accountants and asked for an amount. Theirs was a number I could dial from a comalike state. At that time, I went through about $10,000 every couple of weeks, an astronomical sum for which there is only one explanation—drugs.

But a couple of weeks before this meeting, the money flow stopped. Suddenly and without warning, the cash well ran dry, like Old Faithful refusing to erupt. It wasn't just that the accountants were refusing to meet my requests. They had informed Carolyn, who then told me, that there simply was no more money to be had. I was broke and in arrears to the IRS. I freaked at the news.

With Carolyn's help, I figured the purpose of this meeting was to straighten my financial situation out. My life had operated like that for the past twenty years. I'd fuck up and then someone with a clearer head would rescue me and patch things up. It was easy being a rock star.

Carolyn aimed my large white Caddy past the beautiful Pacific Palisades homes and their postcardlike front lawns. Following Sunset Boulevard, we headed toward Beverly Hills. I puffed on a joint and assumed that by nightfall I'd be problem-free.

"Now what're you going to say to them?" Carolyn asked.

I didn't hear the question. The pot was working. My head rolled lazily back in a cloud of blue smoke, a planet in its own solar system. "Huh?" I said from deep within my daze.

"I want you to go over how you're going to get our money back," she said.

"Oh yeah," I muttered. "I don't know."

Carolyn coached me during the drive about what I should say, carrying on several dialogues by herself. The words drifted right past my one good ear and out the window. After the twenty-minute drive across town she had to wake me from a half sleep.

I led the way into our manager's office building. Carolyn stayed a few steps behind me, careful not to overplay her position. She was tolerated by the band, not liked.

A secretary motioned us toward the familiar conference room. I'd been inside hundreds of times to discuss group projects, albums, contract negotiations. This time, though, I sensed something different, a vibration that made me wary of the situation into which I was walking. I was used to controlling situations with my behavior. I hated being controlled myself.

As I opened the door and looked inside, paranoia swept over me. I wanted to turn and run. It seemed as if I was interrupting something. Everyone was seated around the table—Carl, Mike, Al, the band's manager Tom Hulett, and their attorney John Branca. Suddenly, all eyes shifted from whatever they'd been doing onto my corpulent figure, which filled the doorway. I turned sideways to get through. The large room seemed crowded and airless. I failed to notice that Dennis was missing.

It took every ounce of strength to shuffle forward and drop into one of the two empty seats. Carolyn sat in the other one. I braced myself for some cataclysmic, horrible, life-ending disaster to occur. What that might be I could only imagine. I actually thought there was a possibility someone might shoot me. At least hit me. I was also scared I might lose control and hit one of them. I didn't know what to expect. What to think. I couldn't think. I could only react. Anticipate and react.

"We have a letter for you, Brian," Mike said, pushing an envelope toward me. "Would you please read it?"

"Sure," I said and started to put it in my pocket.

"Now," he commanded.

I opened the envelope and removed a piece of paper, which had several typewritten paragraphs. I fumbled for my reading glasses. "This is to inform you that your services as an employee of Brother Records Inc., and otherwise, are hereby terminated, effective immediately." As I read more, my confusion changed to anger, and by the time I got to the point stipulating that this action was "not reversible" I was boiling mad. Everyone, the final sentence trailed off, "wished me the best of health." It was signed by Carl, Mike, Al, and Dennis.

I slammed the letter to the table. Carolyn grabbed it. "What the fuck?" I shouted. "What the fuck is going on?"

"You're fired from the group," Mike said.

I'd read that in the letter, and now I'd been told that same thing. It still took a moment to register.

For Christ's sake, I thought, they can't terminate me. The Beach Boys was my group. How many times had Dennis said that? How many times had I heard him even onstage proclaim, "Brian Wilson is the Beach Boys. We are his messengers." Sure, Mike was the front man, the only one of us who had the ego for that job. He sang lead, but no matter how strongly he believed he was the group's guiding light, it just wasn't true. The same went for Carl and Al.

The credits argued the point better than I could. Between 1962 and 1968 I wrote and produced fourteen albums, more than 120 songs, including the hits "Help Me, Rhonda," "California Girls," and "Good Vibrations." I had kept the Beach Boys competitive with music's leading innovators, Phil Spector and the Beatles. It wasn't a one-man effort, but it was darn close. I'd played mother hen to a bunch of guys, multimillionaires now, who would've been pumping gas or selling dental floss without me.

I'd paid a price too. I'd lost my mind.

Fire me? That was a joke.

"It's for your own good, Brian," Carl said in an even voice. "Believe me, it's not something we like having to do."

"We're really sorry," Al seconded.

Panicked, desperate, and furious, I scanned the table for an ally, a friendly face. I wanted someone to rescue me, tell me this was a sick joke, a nightmare. But help wasn't forthcoming. Instead I was met by the sober stares of serious, coldhearted businessmen. They masqueraded as rock and rollers, but they were actually board members of a multimillion-dollar corporation. At the moment they were turning on their chief executive officer.

Although my insides screamed "Help!" I was having a hard time finding anything to say. Every insecurity and fear was rushing toward the center of my nervous system. "What the fuck am I going to do if I'm not in the group?" I asked. "What in Christ's name am I going to do for money?"

"That's not our problem," Mike snapped. Mike's gun-barrel blue eyes bore two holes straight through me. "Listen, Brian, to put it bluntly, you've exhausted your share of fuckups," he continued. "You're a fucking mess. You weigh more than three hundred and forty pounds. You smoke more than enough cigarettes to choke a goddamn elephant. You can't sing worth shit anymore. You can't even play your own fucking songs. And ninety percent of the time you commit to a gig, you don't show."

"You've been wanting to say those things for years," I yelled at the group. "It's all jealousy, right? Jealousy because you can't write a fucking song to save your life?"

"Shut up, Brian," Mike answered. "You're committing slow suicide. Do you expect us to pay you for it?"

"Okay, okay, so that's it," I said. "I can lose the weight. Is that what you want?"

"Right," Mike said. "How?"

I didn't know how and thought hard. "Richard Simmons," I blurted. "The diet guy."

Laughter erupted throughout the room. I didn't see the humor then.

"Brian, I don't think you get it," said Tom Hulett, who'd once worked for Elvis Presley and his manager, Colonel Tom Parker. "I kick myself every day for not stepping in when Elvis was heading in the same direction that you are. I'm not about to let you become the next headline in *Billboard*. And that's what's going to happen if something isn't done to stop you from killing yourself."

The words sank in. The room turned dead quiet. My back against a wall, I looked around in a herky-jerky manner. Someone integral to the formula was missing, someone who gave the scene credibility. Dennis. He wasn't here!

"Where the fuck is Dennis?" I demanded.

I'd snorted coke with Dennis the previous evening, not even ten hours ago. Where was he? Dennis was my hero, my truest friend and staunchest admirer, the one person who treated me like a human being. Everyone else saw me as either a money machine or a sicko, but Dennis would toss his arm around me, write a song, drink a beer with me, and make me feel okay. Where was my one friend?

"Yeah, where's Dennis?" Carolyn added.

"Not here," Mike said. "He's not the point. He can take care of himself. You can't."

Bullshit. Dennis was no better than me. In lots of ways, he was worse. Both of us had been scarred by our father, indelibly scarred. But while I'd withdrawn from the world, too fragile to fight for myself, Dennis lashed out, violently, angrily, intent on destroying anything and everything, including himself. We understood each other.

"So what do I have to do?" I sighed. "What do I have to do to get money?"

"You have to get help," Hulett said. "That's all. You have to get help. You have to get well."

"We want you to start seeing your old psychologist," Carl said. "Dr. Landy."

The name unsettled me instantly, shook me hard. I'd spent most of 1976 under the care of Dr. Eugene Landy. We knew each other well. He was an unorthodox, clinical psychologist who'd done what more than twenty psychiatrists before him couldn't—he got results. Although I knew he was caring and loving, he was also a tyrant. His twenty-four-hour-a-day therapy was mental health's equivalent to army boot camp.

I knew what would happen if I saw Dr. Landy, and it scared the shit out of me. Dr. Landy would take away my drugs. Then he'd force me to confront the world. I'd done that once. I didn't want to go through that again.

"Look," Mike said. "You see Landy, you'll get the money. That's the deal."

Fuck the deal. I wasn't about to give in to their demands. There was no need for any more discussion. Frustrated, pissed off, I pushed away from the table, knocking over my chair with a loud crash, and stalked out of the office. To hell with the money. They couldn't dictate to me. I didn't need them. It was the other way around. They needed me, and they could find me at home.

Although I was inches from death, I didn't see what everyone else couldn't help but see. Despite having the figure of the Goodyear blimp and an appetite for drugs and booze rivaling that of an entire rehab hospital, I was blind to my self-destructiveness, content with my death wish. I just wanted to be left alone.

The hell with fame and stardom and the Beach Boys. I'd done my work. Now I wanted to slip into the peace and quiet and darkness of nonexistence.

2

Money for Drugs

*A*fter the meeting, Carolyn flew into a tantrum that lasted for days. "They can't do that to you," she ranted. "They owe you. My man made the Beach Boys." If she wasn't outraged at the Beach Boys, which she was pretty much all the time, she focused her anger on the man who had been thrust into the center of our seemingly insurmountable troubles, Dr. Landy.

"Those Beach Boys are gonna get you to Dr. Landy, Brian," she warned repeatedly. "They're gonna get your ass to Dr. Landy, and then it's going to be over. That doc's gonna hurt you. He's gonna scare you. He's gonna break us up."

Carolyn said everything she could think of to scare me into fighting back. She toyed with my basest fears. I was resigned to waiting, though. Even I knew something had to give. It was only a matter of time. I didn't see any reason to fight. Anything to fight for. What did I have to fight for?

Truth was, I'd fucked up. Royally.

The halcyon days of entertaining pop luminaries like Paul McCartney and Elton John in my Bel Air mansion, of receiving visitors and journalists like a king granting an audience to his court were long gone. All I had left were the cold facts: my fifteen-year marriage to Marilyn had ended in 1979. The affair I'd had with my wife's older sister was over too. My two .

daughters, Carnie and Wendy, were like strangers. I had few, if any, friends. And I regarded the Beach Boys as a monster I'd created only to have it turn on me, like Frankenstein.

It was all gone: the mansion, the Rolls-Royce, the people, the laughter, the frivolity, the creativity. Nothing remained except my reputation and the music I had made in a day when I was more a visionary than a vegetable.

From early childhood on, music defined my life. It was the core to my existence, the way I communicated, thought, worked out my troubles, shared my happiness. I heard it in my head, a twenty-four-hour radio station that played even in my sleep. If I didn't work at the piano once a day, I felt sick.

Now my life had deteriorated to the point where I rarely sat down at the piano.

If I did, it was late at night, and then only after guzzling a gallon of wino quality Hi-Lo wine. As I played, the tears streamed out of my eyes. My playing skill hadn't diminished, but I found it impossible to write. There was too much sadness and pain inside me.

Carolyn was outspoken in her resolve not to alter our living situation, despite our apparent lack of money. I said nothing. I was prepared to ignore everything said at the Beach Boys meeting. See no evil, hear no evil. "Brian, you know they can't do anything to you," she argued. "You wrote the songs they sing." Whatever she said was fine with me.

In the midst of this dope-clouded effort at denial, the only Beach Boy who had not been present at the fateful meeting suddenly appeared on my doorstep: Dennis. True to form, my irascible, fun-loving, take-the-shirt-off-my-back, stoned brother was drunk and broke and in desperate need of a place to sleep. I kept a bed for him in an uncompleted back room that didn't even have insulated walls. He didn't care.

Like me, Dennis was also having trouble with the Beach Boys. But we shared more than that in common. When Dennis showed up that night I was pacing the house, mumbling, as I was apt to do, to imaginary beings. Dennis ignored my craziness. Ordinarily, Dennis came looking for money to buy cocaine, but this time he'd surprised me by showing up with a gram in his pocket.

He dumped the coke on the kitchen table, separated it in two halves with his finger, and inhaled his portion. Then I did mine. Both of us were past enjoying any sort of rush. Before the initial burst even began to fade, Dennis and I looked at each other with the same thought. More! The fire had been started. We had to get more cocaine. Dennis said he could get more. He had a connection. He just needed money. I told him I was strapped.

"Right, I believe that," he laughed. "Brian, you're as rich as fucking God."

Instead of taking no for an answer, Dennis poked around the house, yanking open drawers, upending sofa cushions in the other room, looking very much the part of a burglar. "There's got to be a check or two lying around here," he ranted. "I know you, Brian. You've always got a royalty check tossed someplace."

Indeed, royalty checks, some as high as $50,000, that my accountants missed turned up constantly—under sofa cushions, in drawers. But Dennis wasn't having any luck. In desperation, he finally stuck his hands in my bathrobe pocket and pulled out a tiny slip of paper. Our eyes bulged. It was a thousand-dollar check. I couldn't believe it. Money, just when we needed it. Dennis did a little jig and babbled "party," while I signed it over to him. Then he disappeared out the door, promising to bring back the ten grams the money was going to buy.

Several days passed before Dennis returned, and by that time both my $1,000 and the coke it bought were gone. He'd brought his fourteen-year-old girlfriend instead. Both of them were strung out and wired.

I was no better. I was snorting a gram one of my regular dealers had fronted to me. It was just enough to get us crazy.

Dennis watched with uncontrolled outrage as his teenage girlfriend inhaled the last line of coke, which he had obviously intended to take himself. He flipped out. Calling her a bitch, he whacked her across her head. "Goddamn coke whore," he hollered. "I ought to kill you." The girl yelled back. Dennis reared up and punched her. She screamed. Then he kicked her hard, and she went flying across the room. Before she landed, he was on top of her, beating her in the face with his fists.

"Dennis, get off her," I yelled.

Although it was completely out of character for me, I took hold of Dennis, lifted him off the girl, and tossed him against the wall. He recoiled like a rattlesnake and pounced on me, throwing punches right and left. Despite a size advantage, I wasn't a fighter. But Dennis was. I covered my face and screamed, "I quit. I quit. No more, Dennis. I quit."

"Fuck you, Brian," he said. "Keep fighting."

"Please, Dennis, please, don't hit me anymore," I pleaded.

He had no interest in fighting if I wasn't going to fight back. Disgusted, Dennis stopped hitting me, grabbed his girlfriend by the arm, and walked out.

Dennis only added to my craziness; he didn't create it. I remember discovering some cash in a drawer one afternoon and immediately had four grams of coke delivered to the house. Later that night, while Carolyn was watching television with her cousins in the master bedroom, I stood over the kitchen counter and snorted all four grams as quickly as possible.

It was an experiment. I wanted to see what would happen if I inhaled four grams at once. If one gram made me feel good, I reasoned, four would no doubt make me feel in-fucking-credibly great.

My mad scientist's brain took off like a rocket. My heart raced triple-time, pumping blood into vessels that were exploding. My shoulders stiffened; my jaw clenched. The pressure inside my head built up so much I put my hands on either side and pressed tight to keep it together. I felt there was a chance my cranium would rip apart. My breathing was labored. I was terrified. Something was wrong. Very wrong.

Suddenly, everything went black. Before I could summon help I passed out on the kitchen floor.

I awoke the next morning in the same spot where I'd passed out.

From ground level, I saw Carolyn feeding her children lunch. Rising to a sitting position, I flicked aside a dog who had turned from picking trash out of the garbage to sniffing me. Carolyn looked me over, saw I was ambulatory, and asked me to call the accountant for some money.

"This is Brian," I said. "I need five thousand."

"I'm sorry, Brian," she said. "I can't give it to you. You're cut off until the boys say otherwise."

"Fuck!" I slammed the receiver down. "No money."

I couldn't remember the last time I'd gotten up before noon, but early one morning Carolyn shook me out of a deep, troubled, drug-laden sleep. I'd slept through earthquakes. But she wasn't going to let me sleep through whatever was bothering her now. "Get your fat ass out of bed," she shouted, punching me. "Brian! *"Brian!"*

"Wa-woa," I opened my glazed eyes. "What? Where?"

Carolyn grabbed my arm, rolled me out of bed, and guided me to the front door, which was wide open. She pointed outside to the lawn. I saw a large FOR SALE sign that was planted so prominently in the middle of the yard that not even I could miss it. Carolyn demanded an explanation. I shrugged; I didn't know.

She put me on the phone with my accountants, who told me that indeed my house was for sale.

"Why?" I asked.

"You need the money," they said.

Carolyn fumed as realtors began ushering prospective buyers through our disheveled quarters. I sat passively on the sofa and watched the sorry parade go by. Then the gas was turned off. The following day it was the electricity. By early December, my house had turned into a half-million dollar tenement and I didn't care. If I had cared, I would've done something to help myself. But reversing the situation, I knew, was beyond me—beyond anything I was capable of.

Unable to sleep at night, I lay on the sofa in the cruel grip of wild hallucinations. Permutations of my dead father's voice filled my head. They told me horrible things. That people were going to invade my home and harm me. They told me to harm myself. Scared shitless, I screamed at the top of my lungs. Loud, blood-curdling, frightened screams that echoed through the house, filling the hallways with horror.

Days became as tortured as the nights. The paranoia was unrelenting. I was a grown man who functioned with the emotional capacity of a deeply disturbed six-year-old. In desperate need to escape but unable to, I withdrew even further into my shell, a catatonic mix of flesh and fear. Things were falling apart. I knew that. The ceiling was caving in, collapsing—literally and figuratively.

Outside, as I plodded across the front lawn, chain-smoking, my chest heaved with pain. I prepared myself for a heart attack. I envisioned dropping dead in my tracks. I knew it was going to happen. Day after day, I felt the pain in my heart. As it increased, I stopped whatever I was doing and waited for death to tap me on the shoulder. I'd just wait, frozen with fear. Sometimes I wouldn't move for half an hour, sometimes longer.

That was the worst. Knowing death was coming soon, but not knowing exactly when.

By that point, more than a month had passed since the Beach Boys had issued their ultimatum and the war of attrition Carolyn had been waging was just about lost. Our utilities were off. We had no gas or electricity. We were out of money and nearly out of a home. Carolyn, who had been selling my furniture and possessions to pay for food, was at last out of options. She then did what the Beach Boys knew was inevitable, the only thing she could do in order for both of us to survive: She phoned Dr. Landy's office.

The call lasted less than thirty seconds. I watched her hang up in disgust. Dr. Landy's receptionist had told her that if I wanted an appointment, I had to call myself. I'd gone through this before with Marilyn, but had forgotten.

"The bitch says it doesn't matter if you're a bank president or a bank robber," Carolyn explained. "Dr. Landy says each patient has to call for their own appointment. It's a goddamn rule."

Carolyn considered our options. Then she dialed the number again and handed me the phone.

3

The Glass Eye

I've always thought my dad never should have had kids. Not that I'm not happy to be here. But Dad was a tyrant, possessed by an explosive, unpredictable temper. He yelled at his three boys constantly, especially his oldest, who happened to be me.

Although he saw himself as a loving father who guided his brood with a firm hand, he abused us psychologically and physically, creating wounds that never healed. My mother often drank I suppose, to ease her pain; my brother Dennis is dead; my brother Carl is remote and uncommunicative. Dad instilled in me a predisposition to mental illness that left me a cripple.

I've come to understand him as a man who, despite words to the contrary, hated himself, resented the world, and took out terrible feelings on his family. He was an enigma who, even during the happiest of times, had to be approached gingerly. I never knew what to expect from him, and I don't think he always knew what to expect from himself either.

Dad's early years were difficult. Born in Hutchinson, Kansas, on July 2, 1917, he was the third of William "Bud" and Edith Wilson's eight children. The large family was a financial strain that caused my grandfather, a plumber, to move constantly, which eventually brought the clan to Los Angeles.

My grandfather, who died alone, was despised by his family for his hard drinking and even harder temper. Descriptions consistently painted the portrait of a man no one wanted to be around when he ran out of whiskey. At the dinner table, he sat with a bottle on one side and a spitoon on the other, and everyone ate as quickly as possible, trying to leave the table before the violence started. His beatings were brutal, continuing until blood broke through the skin and cries echoed throughout the neighborhood.

Most families are ashamed to speak about such atrocities, and mine was no different. I was a teenager before I heard my dad mention anything about his upbringing.

One evening he came into the kitchen while my mother was straightening things. I was at the table. He started shouting at her for no apparent reason, but that's how he was a lot of the time. Praying he wouldn't turn on me, I watched as his face turned red and the veins in his neck stood out. Threatening my mother, he seemed more out of control than I usually saw him.

That's when I jumped into the fray. I thought he was going to strike my mother. "Don't hit her," I pleaded. "Don't hit Mom."

Although I was bigger than my father, he was a more intimidating physical presence, and I knew that if I interfered I was risking a painful beating. I couldn't help myself, though. My mom had been drinking. She looked helpless and frightened, more frightened than I was.

My mom and dad wheeled around and looked at me, startled by my interruption. Something in my dad snapped and he stormed out of the room. My mother patted me on the back and fixed me a snack.

There were few hugs and kisses in my family. The only succor my mother offered was food. I loved to eat and, I suppose, I also ate to find love.

After dinner the next night, my dad said he wanted to talk. I got up from the piano, the place where I spent most of my waking hours, and followed him into the kitchen. I thought he was going to bawl me out, but he had something else on his mind. "Son, I want you to know that I'll never hit your mother," he said. "I'm not the type of man who would ever knock a woman on her ass." I didn't believe him.

Then he confessed that as a kid he had been knocked around pretty hard by his father. I asked what his father had been like. Silent for an uncomfortably long time, he told me how his dad had come home one night staggering drunk, which was not uncommon, except for the fact that my dad was still awake, and that put him in danger. Indeed, not five minutes passed before my dad was being used as a punching bag. He ran and hid under his bed, hoping his dad wouldn't find him.

But his father found him and repeatedly jabbed him with a broom handle. The more my dad screamed and pleaded for his father to quit, the harder his dad speared him.

After my dad finished this story, I wanted desperately to ask if he saw the parallel between the way his dad treated him and the way he treated us. I wanted to scream, "Why the hell do you beat us?" But I didn't. Too scared, I remained silent as my dad closed his eyes and made me sit through another long silence, which ended with another eerily familiar tale.

My dad recounted how, at nineteen, he was sleeping in the upstairs attic of his parents' home, listening to his mother and father battle. The yelling and screaming was suddenly punctuated by the sound of a struggle, then the sound of furniture being pushed and tossed. Hearing his mother in pain, he dashed into his parents' bedroom just as she was taking a punch to her breast.

My dad stepped in and knocked his old man on his ass with a single shot to the chin. He then hightailed it to his room.

Later that night the door to my dad's attic bedroom burst open. His father stood in the doorway, holding a lead pipe. A moment later, before my dad could even move, his father was clubbing him over the head with the pipe like a slab of beef. Despite my dad's screams, the beating continued until blood splattered everywhere and a piece of his ear had been whacked off.

My dad never forgot that punishment, and he made sure his own family never did either.

Two years after his ear was hacked off, my dad married his high school sweetheart, Audree Korthof. He was twenty-one, she was a year younger. From her blond hair to her effervescent personality to her protected upbringing, my mother looked as if she would have nothing in common with her new husband. However, both loved music. It gave them a passion.

My dad was an aspiring songwriter and had taught himself how to play the piano in his early teens. My mother was an accomplished pianist by the time she started high school. Inspired by her, my dad began entering songwriting competitions, with little success. After they were married, he worked on the Goodyear assembly line, but both still believed Murry Wilson's songs would one day find a wide audience.

Several of his songs, including "Fiesta Day Polka" and "Hide My Tears," were recorded (to little money or acclaim) by the time I was born, June 20, 1942, at Centinela Hospital in Inglewood. Whether or not I was a welcome addition has always been a matter of debate in my mind. I've always believed that I was dropped shortly after birth, since almost everything that's happened to me afterward has been painful.

My mother remembers being nervous upon bringing me home to the tidy little apartment that was near downtown L.A.

My dad once said that becoming a father turned him white as a ghost inside—scared the shit out of him. He yelled constantly, especially at me, which is my earliest recollection of him. He even dropped me in my infancy on the concrete sidewalk outside our apartment. The large welt that appeared disappeared after a few days, but it's possible I suffered some brain damage as a result.

According to my mother, I was a skittish toddler. A more accurate description might be shell-shocked. My dad's tirades were unrelenting. One explosion followed another, and in our cramped quarters there was no room to escape. The effect these outbursts had on me was severe. By the time I started elementary school, I was nervous and high-strung, withdrawn and frightened of almost everything. I expected everyone to yell at me or threaten me.

It didn't help that I was deaf in my right ear, something that made me even less outgoing. Whether the deafness was a result of a birth defect or one of my dad's early beatings has been lost and buried among my family's many skeletons. Nevertheless, I grew up asking everyone to repeat himself. It got on people's nerves quickly. My dad had little patience for repeating anything. Others, thinking I was totally deaf, yelled at me, causing me to recoil in shock. Either way, I decided early on that it was a lot easier just to let things pass.

Consequently, I missed a lot.

But there was already a lot going on in my head. As far as I can remember, I've always heard music, faint strains of melody floating in the background, the volume vacillating according to my mood. Early on, I learned that when I tuned the world out, I was able to tune in a mysterious, God-given music. It was my gift, and it allowed me to interpret and understand emotions I couldn't even articulate.

My aptitude for music surfaced before I could walk. At eleven months, I supposedly hummed the "Marine Corps Hymn," which delighted my dad. At two, I was visiting my grandmother's when I first heard "Rhapsody in Blue." The Gershwin masterpiece left an indelible imprint on my soul. I still hear every emotion I've ever experienced in that piece, which became seminal to my life.

But it wasn't the year's only milestone. On December 4, 1944, my middle brother, Dennis, was born.

With the apartment filled to overflowing, my dad took a big step and bought a new house in Hawthorne, California. The down payment of $2,300 was more money than he'd ever spent in his life, but my parents could stand on the green lawn outside their newly painted home on the corner of West 119th Street and Kornblum Avenue and see themselves as part of an expanding nation.

Hawthorne was a working-class community of characterless tract homes that sprang up on the barren landscape like weeds as the defense industry took off in the 1930s. It was advertised as the City of Good Neighbors. When they bought the house, my parents were buying into the American Dream and all it stood for—hope for a better life. It should have been cause for celebration.

My parents seemed on track. They owned a car, a home, had two kids, and the prospect of a bright future. There was no reason to think otherwise when my youngest brother, Carl, was born on December 21, 1946.

My father continued to work at Goodyear, but he still believed songwriting was going to be his ticket to the good life. He parked himself every night at the upright piano in our living room and played songs he had composed. His simple, sweet music was in sharp contrast to his temper, which faded when he played. I had a difficult time understanding the two sides of his personality, but there was no question which one I preferred.

I was five years old when I showed an initial interest in songwriting: I asked my dad who wrote a particular song he was playing.

"Brian," he smiled proudly, "that's a Murry Wilson song."

I was impressed. One day my fourth grade teacher at York Elementary School told the class a story about lumberjacking and Paul Bunyan. At the end of the day, the teacher asked us to create a project at home related to what we had learned. Something creative, she said, like a collage, a poem, a painting, or a song.

I spent hours looking around the house for anything to do with lumberjacking. Then inspiration struck. I raced to my bedroom closet and pulled out a toy ukulele my dad had given me. I knew four chords and gave the uke a couple of strums. It was an epiphany. My dad wrote songs; I told myself that I could write songs too.

I started to write my first one that afternoon. By bedtime, I was still at it. Although I tried to play softly, my out-of-tune uke was heard throughout the house, and it got the reaction I feared most.

"Brian!" my dad bellowed from his bedroom. "What the hell are you doing?"

"Nothing," I said.

"Then get your ass in bed."

"In a minute, Dad."

The song wasn't quite finished, and I couldn't bring myself to quit until it was complete. I'm the same way today. I knew the risk I was taking. One major whipping. But I continued to strum.

Several minutes later, my dad was standing over me in his pajamas, puffing a cigarette. He ran his hand through his hair and shook his head with displeasure. "I told you it's time to quit," he said, grabbing my arm and lifting me up.

"But listen," I said. "I'm writing a song for school."

Then I played him what I had done so far.

"That's all I got right now," I said.

My dad took a drag off his cigarette. He was making up his mind about something. I wasn't sure if he was going to hit me. I braced for a licking. At the least, I thought he might smash the uke against the wall. Instead, he acknowledged my effort with a slight smile and returned to the bedroom, giving me a few minutes more to work.

"But that's it," he warned. "Or else I'm gonna splinter that thing across your ass. Understand?"

That was about the nicest he ever was to me.

In contrast to the violence, there was always music filtering through our house. During the day my mother kept the phonograph spinning with records by Gershwin, Rosemary Clooney, Les Paul and Mary Ford. At night, she and my dad played duets on the piano and organ in the converted garage everyone referred to as the music room, which was two steps down from the living room. My brothers and I always thought it was so cool to say, "Let's go downstairs."

In these family jam sessions, my dad played Murry Wilson originals on the piano and my mom accompanied him on the organ. My mom played the chords, while my dad ran away with the melody. I was impressed by how the songs always ended softly, the music spiraling up to the heavens. Neither Dennis nor Carl ever showed much interest in these sessions, but I watched with rapt attention, memorizing every word and every note of every song.

"Brian," my dad would say. "Come on, sing a little."

It didn't take much coaxing. Ever since I'd hummed the "Marine

Corps Hymn" my dad had been impressed with my voice, but my mom was an even better audience. She asked me to sing every time we got in the car. Particularly high on her request list was my imitation of her favorite singer, Rosemary Clooney. I had Rosemary down pat. In fact, it got to the point where my mom would just say, "Brian, do a little Rosemary Clooney for me, will you?"

At home, my dad called out the titles to his songs: "His Little Darling and Me." "Two Step Side Step." I'd sing enthusiastically: "Two step side step/and a world away/Two step side step/took my girl away/Two step side step/at the dance last Saturday night . . ."

Watching my dad at the piano, it was obvious he had taught himself to play. His face was a picture of intense concentration as he picked out the melodies seemingly by force of will. After writing a song, he performed it immediately for my mother and then talked excitedly about which famous singer it would be perfect for. The money he imagined making from royalties after it became a smash got bigger as his success rate went the opposite way.

My dad's songwriting career peaked when I was ten years old. A semi-well-known singing group called the Bachelors released his song "Two Step Side Step" on an album, but my dad believed the song had more potential than they gave it. "If one of those crooks at the record company gets behind it," he said repeatedly, "it's gonna be a smash!"

Convinced that "Two Step Side Step" was going to sweep across the U.S., he even invented a little side-step shuffle dance to accompany it. He played the record constantly, obsessed by it, until it seemed as if we were waking up and going to sleep with the song in the background.

"What's he doing?" Dennis asked me one evening as we watched my dad prance around the music room.

"He's practicing," I whispered, adding, "The song is going to be a smash."

"Yeah, well I think it stinks," Dennis scoffed. "I also think the old man is cracked."

One day the publisher called and told him that the song was going to be performed by Lawrence Welk on live radio, and my dad flipped. He was happier than I'd ever seen him. He felt he was finally getting some long-overdue recognition. That suited the rest of us fine. With my dad enjoying a little satisfaction, the entire week leading up to the Welk show was as pleasant as I can remember. No screaming or yelling.

Then the big night arrived.

"Do you know what this means, Audree?" my dad asked over dinner. He didn't wait for an answer. "Exposure," he said. "Doors are going to open. Opportunity is going to knock. People are going to know the name Murry Wilson."

I believed him. Just as his temper was terrifying, my dad's spirit and enthusiasm—when it got going—was infectious.

A good salesman, by this time he had quit Goodyear and borrowed money to start ABLE Machinery, selling heavy equipment to the airplane industry. He was often a hard sell, inevitably pushing customers too far, but when he got charged up about something, he was a force most people found irresistible.

The night of the Welk show the entire family gathered around the radio, abuzz with excitement. Both the live broadcast and Welk's fame made us feel party to an enormous event, something much larger than our sedate suburban existence, a happening that seemed to shine a beacon of light upon our otherwise anonymous house. My dad was too excited to sit. He smoked one cigarette after another, pacing around the room.

"Why don't you quit pacing and practice your dance?" Dennis suggested.

"Quiet," my dad growled. "I don't want to miss anything."

The room hushed just in time for the entire family to cling to every word of Welk's intro.

"I want to play a tune now," Welk said, "written by a talented Californian whose name is Murry Wilson. It's called 'Two Step Side Step.' A one and a two—"

"Murry—" my beaming mom started to say before getting interrupted.

"Hey, that's Dad's song!" Carl screamed.

"Dad, they're really playing it!" I exclaimed. "I don't believe it."

Neither did he. My dad was overcome by emotion. His grin disappeared and tears ran from his eyes. He took off his glasses and wiped his eyes with his handkerchief. But he couldn't suppress the emotion. It was strange to see this bear of a man reduced to blubber. In the biggest moment of his songwriting life, he suddenly left the room, holding a hand over his face, too embarrassed to cry in front of his family.

I was blown away too. It was hard to imagine that a song my own dad had written on our own ordinary upright, a song I had sung countless times, had found its way onto radio and into thousands of homes, entertaining countless people, making them feel good, perhaps even good enough that the dance my dad had invented might be practiced in places outside our own house.

The impression was a lasting one.

It wasn't the only impression that's lasted. I remember standing in the backyard. A nine-year-old boy. Helpless. Screaming.

"Ouch. Stop, please. Ouch!"

I was doubled over, lying on the ground in a fetal position, trying to shield whatever part of my skinny little boy's body I could from my father. With a splintered two-by-four, he delivered blows to my back and midsection, standing over me, a giant with a giant weapon, swinging it over and over as if truly delighted by the dull thud it made against my torso.

"Stop, Dad. Please. You're hurting me."

Why was he doing this?

Moments earlier I had been playing with our neighbor's puppy, which my dad had volunteered to watch while its owner was out of town. He kept it chained in our backyard. Wanting to play fetch with the dog, I untied the little critter. But no sooner did I loosen his collar then the dog ran off into another yard.

Although I called him, my dad and not the dog came flying around the house. The expression on his face told me what was coming. He asked what the hell happened, but didn't wait for me to answer. That was obvious. Looking for something with which to strike me, he picked up the nearest implement—the splintered two-by-four—and began swinging full force into the center of my back.

With the first blow I let out a cry and doubled over, but he kept swinging.

"I thought I told you not to unleash the dog," he said.

"Ouch!"

"Buck up, ya namby-pamby," he said.

"Ouch!"

One more shot to my leg and he tossed the board to the side. I didn't dare look up at him as he went back to the house.

"And bring the mutt back," he called.

He wrote lovely music, simple, uncomplicated, and soothing melodies. His songs gave the impression of a nice, pleasant gentleman, a peaceful soul, and I suppose deep inside him there was a tiny bit that resembled such a man. But we only saw that part of him when he played the piano. The rest of the time he was pure danger, a land mine waiting to be detonated. The day would be going along fine, then suddenly and without any warning, KABOOM!

One evening he called us all into the kitchen. Dinner, which had been uneventful, was long over. Dennis was about to go outside and ride his bike. Carl and I were watching television. My dad called and called, his voice vehement. What the hell could he want? I wondered. All of us hurried into the kitchen to find my dad standing on top of the table, totally naked and pounding his chest like Tarzan.

"I'm king of this family," he roared. "I'm king of this goddamn family. Is that clear?"

No one dared answer him. We all stood around in too much shock to speak.

"Is that clear?" he asked.

"Yes, yes, yes," we nodded, then tentatively filed out of the room.

He continued ranting. "I'm king of this family. I'm the goddamn king."

None of us dared question him. Oddly, Dennis, Carl, and I never discussed my dad's aberant behavior. We were too busy avoiding him. Dennis escaped the house whenever he could. Carl spent a great deal of his childhood hiding under the bed. The closest we ever came to talking about the violence was when Carl would crawl out from under the bed and ask Dennis, "Did it hurt?"

This question always followed some kind of fight between my dad and Dennis, who was forever on the short end of my dad's extremely short fuse. Dennis felt the need to beat up the world. By the time he turned fifteen, Dennis smoked, drank, had been jumped by a gang of Mexican hoodlums, and had been accused of getting a neighborhood girl pregnant.

I didn't like Dennis much at that point, probably because I was intimidated by his damn-the-world nature. He was so angry at everything he didn't give a shit what happened to him.

I hung out with Carl, who was the opposite of threatening. Carl was fat—so fat that Dennis nicknamed him Porky, which Carl hated as much as Dennis delighted in calling him that.

Babied and protected by my mom far more than either Dennis or I was, Carl's vice was eating. He found affection in food. Even when he watched Dennis working out with weights, Carl snacked. Afterward, Dennis used to laugh, "Brian, you should've seen Porky working out. His stomach's getting bigger with every bite."

Carl was sensitive and showed an interest in music long before Dennis. That was our bond—music and dodging our dad's fierce outbursts. Whenever trouble broke out, Carl hightailed it out of the line of fire as fast as his fat, short legs would take him and squeezed under his bed.

Later, he'd find me. "Did it hurt, Brian?" he'd ask.

"Hurt like a motherfucker," I said.

We didn't know why our dad was so volatile, unpredictible, violent. We didn't think about asking why. He just was that way.

My mother was no help. She almost never opposed my father, almost never rose up and defended her children. Not that we saw, anyway. Who knows? She might've been abused herself. I often saw her pour a drink in the afternoon and continue sipping throughout the evening. She was passive and aloof by the time my dad came home, a bystander who refused to intercede in the flagrant child abuse going on in front of her.

She once looked on as he tied me to a tree as punishment. Another time, while the rest of the family was eating dinner, my dad barged into my room and caught me masturbating. Discovering sex had been confusing for me, since it caused me to be attracted to other people, which ran counter to my withdrawn psychological makeup. My dad led me to believe I was doing something wrong. Not hiding his disgust, he shouted to my mom, "The boy's not to have dinner for two nights."

My mom complied.

Those incidents are modest compared to the worst. I've blanked out most of the details leading up to it. I remember being in the kitchen with my mom and dad. It was just the three of us. My dad started berating me for something, I can't recall what, while my mom looked on passively from the sidelines, gripping her ever-present tumbler.

Suddenly, my dad threw a folded newspaper on the floor, opened it, and ordered me to take a shit. Right there. On the paper. I was petrified and began heaving with rasping sobs. I looked up toward my dad's menacing face with red eyes that pleaded to be forgiven whatever misdeed I'd committed. I wanted to be excused. Hit. Anything but what he was asking me to do.

"Now!" he commanded.

Afterward, he forced me to look. He made my mother look too.

Satisfied, he left the room. My mom hurried out right behind him. I was left alone, given the task of disposing of the excrement. It took me a while to get up, to stop crying, and even then I couldn't direct my eyes toward what I'd been forced to do. I felt beaten, abused, soiled.

I'd been humiliated, no question. But more than that, while my mother had looked on, my own father had robbed me of my self-esteem; he had raped me.

I've never forgotten this incident. After years of therapy, I am able to understand my father and my mother better. But I was scarred for life, and I've never forgiven my mom for not rescuing me. No matter how much understanding I've been able to acquire, the anger has never gone away.

When I was fourteen a friend who lived next door insisted that my dad had a glass eye. I refused to believe it. He was older than me, which gave him some credence, but what he was telling me was so improbable, so horrendous, that I simply couldn't fathom it. I told him so.

"You're lying," I said.

"Don't believe me," he shrugged. "See if I care if your pop has a glass eye."

A glass eye? I started to cry and ran home.

I couldn't wait for my dad to get home that night. But all through dinner, and then while everyone watched television, I stared at my dad's eyes. I figured if I looked long and hard enough, I would detect a difference. He'd blink funny. The light would reflect in some weird way. I didn't know what to look for but thought I might see something that would tip me off.

I thought I was being discreet, but my dad must have noticed. After dinner the next evening, he told me to follow him into the bedroom. "I want to show you something, son," he said.

I didn't know what to expect. My dad stood with his back to me and fidgeted for a moment. His hands were doing something. Then, all of a sudden, he turned around and thrust out his hand so that it was just below my chin. I had to quickly inch backwards to see what he was showing me. Then, just as quickly, I got sick. Resting in the center of his palm was what looked like a shiny marble.

"This is a glass eye," he said in a matter-of-fact voice. "Any questions, son?"

I was too unnerved to think of the obvious, so he told me. He was just twenty-five and working at Goodyear, where he was stationed beside a heavy-duty machine that conditioned rubber with sulfuric acid. During one shift, a metal brush loaded with acid accidentally fell on a spinning conveyor belt and flew into his face, shattering his glasses and obliterating his left eye. In the hospital he was fitted with a glass substitute.

I couldn't move my gaze from his palm, equally repulsed and fascinated. Then I wondered what he looked like without the glass eye, and slowly I looked up to where his eye was supposed to be. The socket was empty, a pit of scarred, cherry-colored, raw flesh.

"See that," my dad pointed. "That's flesh."

I freaked and ran from the room, screaming and crying as if I'd just witnessed a murder, hysterical. I wondered, What is this guy trying to do to me?

Later, I heard that my mom had run into the bedroom, where she saw my dad holding his eye in his hand like a lucky charm and chuckling to himself. In one of the rare instances where she braved his wrath by speaking up, she asked what he was doing.

"I just wanted him to see what his old man is made of," he replied.

4

Girls

By the time I was eight years old, my young life was already being shaped and influenced by music. While other boys my age followed baseball or football, arranged play dates with friends, or watched television, I thought about music. I was an oddball. The part of me that related to music was advanced far beyond my years.

Whatever music I heard affected me. None affected me more than the music I heard when my father played the family piano. When he played I crept as close to the piano as possible without disturbing him and studied his technique. I watched how his fingers made chords and memorized the positions. I noticed how his left and right hands complemented each other, and I visualized my own hands doing the same thing.

I dreamed about playing the piano myself. I desperately wanted to try. If I could make music, perhaps my dad would show me the love I craved. But I was petrified to ask him permission. If he said no, I would've been crushed. The piano was his throne. Along with his pipe, which had replaced his Chesterfields, and slippers, it was something that was clearly his and not something the rest of us could tamper with without his approval. I was so frightened of how he'd react that I didn't dare touch the piano even while he was at work. That's how much I feared him. I had good reason.

My dad yelled at or beat me so often that all he had to do was look at me and I'd flinch. I was always looking over my shoulder, expecting the worst from everyone.

After he quit hiding his glass eye, he began keeping it at night in a water glass beside his bed. The first time I saw that I wanted to puke, and from then on I rinsed all our drinking glasses till wrinkles formed on my fingers. To this day I prefer to drink out of a bottle.

It was easier to avoid my dad if possible, which was why I held out asking him if I could try my hand at the piano. But the attraction proved too strong for me to ignore and I began sneaking time while he was at work. After school was best, because then my mom was busy with Dennis and Carl and I could do whatever I wanted as long as it didn't create a problem.

I don't remember the first time I sat down at the piano, but I remember the sensation of playing. It was pure happiness. For the first time, I was in touch with the deep waters of my soul. It was as if I discovered my native tongue. I never had instruction on reading music, though from the start I was able to put together notes. I took accordion lessons for six weeks, playing a little baby accordion. But the teacher complained to my mother that I wasn't reading.

"He just hears it once," the teacher told my mother, "and he plays the whole thing through perfectly."

After six weeks, I was supposed to get a new, larger accordion, but my dad couldn't afford it and my formal education ended right there. I was on my own. It didn't matter. I watched my dad form chords, and gradually I began picking out bits and pieces of songs.

I was a natural.

It wasn't long before my mom heard me playing. As I grew more confident of my ability, I played louder. I wanted her to hear me. It was a test. If she didn't reprimand me, I figured it was okay to play, and soon I played all the time, including after my dad got home. Realizing he wasn't going to scold me, I concentrated on practicing, especially my dad's songs. I spent an entire week working on an instrumental he wrote, which surprised him when he finally heard me play the piece through.

"Brian, get your ass in here," he called from the kitchen.

I stopped playing and prepared for the worst. My dad was seated at the kitchen table, cleaning his pipe. He didn't look angry, a good sign.

"How'd you learn to do that?" he asked.

"What?" I said.

"Don't give me that. I want to know how you learned to play my song."

"I don't know," I shrugged. "I just kept trying, I guess."

"Hmmm," he grinned. "Not bad for a kid."

What a relief!

The piano in our music room quickly became my refuge from the uncertainty that plagued my home. I thought of it as a private sanctuary, the one place where I was immune from my father's temper, didn't have to worry about my mother's drinking, and could forget about my lack of confidence and my fear. At the piano, I was left alone. I practiced constantly, endlessly, abnormally long for a child.

Playing the piano provided me safety and solitude and literally saved my ass. I recall playing one time while my dad flung Dennis against the wall, slapped him around, and then cursed him as Dennis stormed out of the house. That was just one of many incidents where I didn't miss a note, supplying background music to the hell that often substituted for a family life, knowing full well that I could just as easily have been on the receiving end of my dad's blows.

If I wasn't playing the piano, I was listening to the radio or the phonograph. I was obsessed. Music was a compulsion, as necessary to my health and well-being as food and sleep. It provided harmony in my life. It nourished me with everything I lacked, like love, care, and stability.

Rock and roll is nothing if not liberating. At age fourteen I discovered the key that unshackled my fragile soul. My piano playing had matured rapidly. I no longer pecked out melodies; now my hands worked together, complementing each other like dance partners. Playing a strong right-hand rhythm and a creative left-hand bass, the music sprang out of me, a torrent of adolescent emotion begging to be explored.

It was the same as discovering sex, except that instead of rushing home after school, throwing down my books, and locking my bedroom door, I sat down at the piano and thought, Whoa baby, let's get it on! My mom literally had to drag me to the dinner table. Not a day passed without me playing for hours. I'm no different now; I still *have* to play at least an hour or so every single day.

One afternoon my mom was carting me, Dennis, and Carl around on errands. The car radio was tuned to a popular station. My mom had pretty hip taste. Then a song I'd never heard before came on and she turned it up. The first note caught my ear and I bolted forward.

"Day by day, I'm falling in love with you," a voice sang, "and day by day, my love seems to grow . . ."

The song had a jazzy rhythm, modern vocal sound. That's what got me—the vocals. I'd never heard anything like them before. I flipped. "I love it, Mom," I screamed. "I love that sound. What is it?"

She smiled and told me to sit back. "That's the Four Freshmen, Brian," she said.

"The Freshmen?"

"The *Four* Freshmen," she corrected me. "They're a singing group."

I couldn't get the song out of my head. Within days I was begging her to take me to a record store. I was incorrigible since that afternoon, talking nonstop about the Four Freshmen and their unbelievable sound. It would have been amusing, even annoying, had I not been so serious and passionate. I gave my mom little choice but to take me to the store.

The local music store had a sampling booth in the back, a claustrophobic, stuffy cubicle for listening to records before buying them. I made a beeline for the door. The album I placed on the turntable was *The Four Freshmen and Five Trombones*. My mom waited, smiling as I snapped my fingers, and when I emerged with what I imagine was a glassy-eyed grin, I had only one thing on my mind.

"Can we buy it?" I asked. "Please, buy it for me, Mom."

My mom couldn't resist, and that was the last anyone saw of me for a week. I didn't care about anything else—food, friends, girls, sports, nothing. Outside of attending high school—and only because I had to—I just listened to that record. Some people have religious experiences. Others experience births or deaths. For me, that record was life-changing, triggering something in my brain. It started a year-long obsession with the Four Freshmen.

I couldn't get enough. I bought every album and single I could find. I played them till the grooves wore out. Transfixed. Fascinated. I absorbed every note of every song, figuring out how the lush, intricate harmonies were woven together, discovering on my own how to do it myself. I sang with the record. I imagined myself adding parts, redoing the productions, wondering if the songs couldn't have been done in a different manner.

Then I heard about a Four Freshmen concert. I had to see them! They were playing at the Coconut Grove, and I pleaded with my dad to take me to the show. It was the first concert I ever attended, and I sat through the hour-plus performance with a Gee Whiz look plastered on my face. Afterward, I could hardly believe it when my dad said he knew someone who could get us backstage to meet them.

The Freshmen themselves. I stood in awe, mouth agape. They were in various stages of undress, changing out of their stage clothes. They were probably on their way to have some drinks at a bar. My dad approached them. I couldn't believe it. He was going to speak to them.

Offering a handshake, he introduced both of us. "Hi, I'm Murry Wilson," he said, "and this is my son, Brian. He's a big fan."

"Cool," one of them said. "You got our records, man?"

"All of 'em," I grinned.

The next evening I persuaded my family to gather in the music room, where I taught them a Freshmen song. Although Dennis couldn't concentrate and split, I got a good four-part harmony going using my mom and dad, Carl, and myself. We tried again the next night, and though they never entirely learned the Freshmen song, my first attempt at creating a modern harmony sound—the lush sound that would become a Beach Boys trademark—was still, in my opinion, a success.

Until I was sixteen, I shared a small bedroom with my brothers, which was crammed with possessions, including my baseball mitt, the surfboard my father had bought Dennis for his ninth birthday, toys, clothes, and books. But nothing filled the room as much as the psychological wounds we shared, particularly at night when the house was still. Carl liked to eat; Dennis, angry and rebellious, always wanted to argue; I turned into a clown, parodying my favorite comedian, Jonathan Winters. I told wild, animated stories that sent the three of us laughing to sleep.

One night I decided to teach them a favorite song of mine, the song, "Ivory Tower." It had a spiritual feel and began, "Come down, come down, off your ivory tower. . . ." I taught Dennis and Carl background harmonies, and then I sang the lead. We practiced night after night, singing softly, hoping we wouldn't wake our dad.

Secretly, I always hoped he would catch us. I wanted him to say, "Sounds nice." I coveted his affection. A single compliment would have sufficed, but it never came, no matter how hard I tried.

I went all out too. At six-two, 165 pounds, I developed into a well-coordinated, pretty good athlete. I played center field on the Hawthorne High School varsity baseball team and quarterback on the junior varsity football team. During games my dad stalked the sidelines, yelling at me to play harder, tougher, even though I was usually the star. I used to sing to myself in the outfield as a way of ignoring him. Afterward, his opinion of me rarely varied.

"You're no good," he said. "You're lazy. You don't concentrate. I see you out there. You look like you're singing. You gotta be more aggressive. You gotta learn to fight. Otherwise, you might as well quit now. Might as well face up to being a loser."

For my sixteenth birthday my parents gave me a tape recorder. I'd barely opened the box before I snapped at Carl, "Don't touch it."

He backed away immediately, and I hit the rewind button. We were fascinated. Both of watched the tape spin backwards. Before it rewound all the way, I hit Stop. Then Play. A moment later, Carl's and my voices came out of the round speaker, accompanied by me playing piano on a half-baked rendition of "Rock and Roll Music."

"That's so cool," I said in awe.

It was a Wollensak, a large, bulky two-reeler. I thought of it as the most valuable possession in the entire house. I used it like a science kit, experimenting daily. I recorded myself singing a cappella, replayed it as I played piano and sang live, allowing me to harmonize with myself. Then I added Carl. Then my mom and Carl. Little did I know I was imitating, however crudely, a studio technique called "overdubbing."

That December Carl got a Rickenbacker guitar and a neighbor taught him how to play it. He practiced every day and his interest appreciated along with his skill. Soon I was adding his guitar playing to my tapes. Between listening to the Four Freshmen and another group called the Hi-Los and experimenting with my tape recorder, my life was complete. At least it seemed that way until my senior year of high school.

High school was confusing, a struggle to fit in and seem normal. I knew I wasn't. I might've looked like anyone else in my V-neck sweaters and polished shoes, but inside I was always on edge, trying to balance the fear I'd grown up with against my desire to fit in. Awkward and goofy, I hung out with the jocks but was more comfortable around the intellectuals, including the thespian club to which I belonged. The girls thought I was handsome but hard to talk to, which I compensated for by always joking around. Humor was a way to hide my awkwardness and lack of self-confidence.

Then I fell in love and really got screwed up. Her name was Carol Mountain, and she embodied what I considered perfection. She had long, sandy brown hair that fell to the middle of her back, big, beautiful eyes, and a laugh that floated in the air like a sweet perfume. I couldn't look at Carol without getting butterflies in my stomach. If she looked at me, I got lightheaded.

Sex was the ultimate mystery to me. A few years earlier, my dad, in his own sensitive manner, had sat me down in the kitchen and explained the basics to me.

"Brian," he said, "I'm going to teach you about sex now."

Great. I already knew what was what from hanging around my buddies. Still, there were areas about which I wasn't exactly sure and I hoped my dad would shed light on the subject.

"Have you ever seen two dogs fuck?" he began his discussion.

I shook my head no.

"The male dog mounts the female," he continued, "sticks his penis in and has sex. That's how babies are made."

It was like listening to a butcher describe open heart surgery. There was no delicacy, no feeling, no passion, or emotion. But that was my dad. I weighed what he said and knew for sure that his explanation of sex wasn't even related to the way I felt when I thought about Carol. He talked about something physical; I was twisted in knots by emotions I couldn't begin to understand.

It was love and I had never been more upset. Days and weeks passed when I thought of nothing but Carol. She assumed a position that was larger than life. Even after I got to be friends with her, she remained an icon. Beautiful, unattainable, utterly perplexing. She dated a basketball star named Gordon Marsh. Gordon knew I had a thing for Carol, and to tease me he coaxed me into a double date.

Carol knew something funny was up because the afternoon of the date she stopped me outside Spanish class.

"Brian, I have to talk to you," she said.

She was standing inches from me, which caused my heart to pound. "Yeah?"

"Don't let Gordon push you around," she said. "You don't have to go on this date if you don't want to."

I didn't know what to say. I wanted to be with her. Just near her was okay. But I also sensed that I was being used to stroke Gordon's ego. "Okay, I won't go," I said and walked away dejected.

I'd just blown a chance to spend an evening with the girl of my dreams. It didn't matter that were were going to have separate dates. I would be with her. I should've told her how I felt about her—or hinted at it. But I didn't. I lacked the self-assurance to go after something I wanted that badly, frightened of going out on a limb and risking being rejected.

Oh well. I may not have gotten Carol, but that year I got a two-tone '57 Ford Fairlane for my seventeenth birthday. I was cleaning it one day when I accidentally knocked over a tiny bottle of perfume that I was using to freshen the interior. I was upset at first, but the perfume smelled so nice I ended up not minding. It was a fragrance that reminded me, every time I got in the car, of one special girl.

"Hey, Bri," Carl said one afternoon. "I want to know if you like this kind of music."

Carl was a pudgy fourteen-year-old who looked up to me, particularly when it came to music. Just home from school, he was anxious to turn on the radio. We had different tastes in music. I liked classical stuff, Gershwin, and the Four Freshmen. Carl was heavily into R&B, Chuck Berry, and Little Richard. But in his eyes my opinion was important.

He flipped on the radio and sat down on my bed. After each song, he provided commentary on the artist.

"Oh man, Carl," I said. "This is it. I really like this. Who's singing?"

"Johnny Otis," he said.

Little more than two minutes—the length of a song—and I was hooked. I was finished with the Four Freshmen. I'd learned as much from them as possible and was ready for new influences. Johnny Otis, an R&B mainstay and L.A. club fixture, had a popular radio show on station KFOX. Carl and I stayed up countless nights listening to Otis's nine-to-midnight show, talking about what we were hearing and adding the new songs to our musical vocabulary.

What got me were the vocals. Instrumentally, the records were simple, nothing sophisticated in terms of music or production. But the singing was a groove. There was a flair to the leads. I picked up on it right away and injected more oomph and punch to the way I played piano. My playing got more soulful, more powerful, and a lot more fun. I found that I could say things through music that I couldn't say otherwise.

I started writing songs, a skill that came as naturally to me as falling off a log, and in the process I discovered something I found nowhere else, the thing that had been missing from my life—a feeling of joy and happiness.

Capturing that feeling became my single-minded pursuit. I tried explaining that to my twelfth-grade piano and harmony instructor, Fred Morgan. Mr. Morgan liked me. Because of my deaf right ear, he let me sit closer to the piano. He even indulged some of my rock and roll ideas, even though they often strayed from the more serious classwork.

But he had no tolerance for poor work habits, which was a problem that year. I had a bad case of senioritis. Between the varsity baseball team, music, and hanging out at Foster's Freeze at night, I didn't put much effort into my studies. Mr. Morgan didn't hide his displeasure.

"I wouldn't mind so much if you were an average student," Mr. Morgan told me. "But you have a quick mind. You have superior talent, especially for arranging. I'm expecting you to show some improvement on your harmony exercises."

I didn't. The exercises consisted of blocking in additional harmonic parts around a given vocal part in a piece of music. I failed to finish. When Mr. Morgan asked why, I explained that my head was somewhere else. He didn't understand.

A few weeks later, I screwed up on the biggest requirement of the entire course, writing a piano sonata. The assignment, handed out the first week of the term, was in lieu of a final exam. I didn't do it. Mr. Morgan gave me an "F" for the project and a "C" for the course.

I did hand in an original composition, though. Just not a piano sonata. It was a pop song called "Surfin'."

"I've got nothing against the song," Mr. Morgan said. "It's kind of nice. It's just not what I asked for."

It took me a whole year before I could muster up the courage to ask Carol out. It was during the summer after graduation. I was eighteen and thought, Well, it's now or never. When Carol said yes, I went into an immediate panic. What should I do? Where should I take her? What should I wear? What should I say? I felt like I was about to short-circuit.

Finally, I settled on a movie, and took her to see Jack Lemmon in *The Apartment*. She liked it. But then I blew it. On the way home, I drove like a total jerk. I either hit the gas too hard or I braked too suddenly. I peeled out of one intersection as if I were a drag racer. The tires screeched, and I left behind a cloud of smoke and a trail of skid marks.

Carol didn't appreciate my driving. What did I know? I was only trying to act the way I thought macho guys acted. I was trying to act the way I thought Carol wanted a guy to act. I didn't have enough self-confidence to just act myself. Insecurity makes you do the dumbest things.

Like when I walked her up to the door. She said good night and wanted to go inside, but I didn't want the date to end yet.

"I've got you cornered now," I said with a sly chuckle.

Carol gave me a queer look, and I knew I was acting stupidly. The words hadn't yet left my mouth and I knew it. I couldn't help myself. I didn't know how to act with girls, especially girls I liked. I pushed Carol up against the screen door and kissed her on the lips. My mind had played out this passionate scene so many times, I was startled when Carol pushed me away.

"Brian!" she exclaimed. "What are you doing?"

"I . . . I . . . I'm . . ." I started to say.

But I realized there was nothing to say. I had blown it. My heart sank like an anvil dropped overboard at sea. I couldn't figure out why I didn't get on with girls.

What I came to realize years later—too late—is that I didn't have a clue to the subtleties of love. How could I? There was no love at home.

Leaving Carol standing on the doorstep, I quickly turned and ran toward my car.

"I gotta go," I called. "Thanks."

After the debacle with Carol, I threw myself back into music. If I had a spare moment, I spent it sitting at the piano. By this time, I'd moved my bed out of the bedroom and into the music room. I slept right next to the piano. I could play until I dropped, then roll straight into bed. It was a comforting setup during a directionless period.

After graduating from high school, I spent the summer working odd jobs and waiting for my first semester of college to begin. In the fall, I started El Camino Junior College, taking history, Spanish, and psychology. I planned on spending a couple of years at El Camino and then transferring to a larger local university. In the meantime, I was content to live at home. I was still childlike and immature in many ways and the future seemed so far off, though I remember telling the school's vocational counselor that I was thinking about becoming a psychologist.

"Any special reason?" he asked.

"People confuse me," I said. "I'd like to understand them a little better."

5

The Pendletones

I both envied and felt intimidated by my cousin Mike Love. Tall and blond, he exuded confidence and swagger. He had a big ego. He wasn't especially nice. I looked at him and knew I couldn't measure up. I'd hear my dad's voice remind me, "You're a loser."

Looking as if he stepped out of an ad for sun-kissed health products, Mike was the oldest of my Uncle Milton's and Aunt Emily's six children. Uncle Milton had prospered in the sheet-metal business he inherited from his father. They were the wealthiest people my family knew, their large three-story home set on a hill overlooking the affluent suburb of View Park.

Every Christmas our extended family gathered at the Loves' for a traditional holiday feast, which always included my aunt organizing a group of us to sing carols through the neighborhood. Mike and I, the oldest of the cousins, were always among the carolers, but for different reasons. I enjoyed singing. He wanted to stand in front of the group and be noticed. He made sure his voice was heard above everyone else's.

Mike was a lot like his dad: physically imposing and very aggressive. Uncle Milton was the life of any party, a real joker who would raise his voice until everyone was paying attention to him, and if he wasn't around, Mike moved in to take his place. Like father, like son.

Showing an interest in music whenever we got together, Mike and I carried on long, intense discussions about what groups we admired, which songs on the radio were good, and what radio stations were best. Typical teenage stuff. He was always much more adamant about swaying my opinion than I was his. He not only enjoyed getting his way, the don't-cross-me look in his eyes said he had to get it.

We'd been singing together seriously since the start of my senior year of high school. I was sixteen and Mike almost eighteen when I got together with him, his oldest sister, Maureen, and their friend John Stewart and taught them how to sing harmony, like the Four Freshmen. We practiced "Bermuda Shorts," a popular song. Mike dug the song and the sound we made. At his suggestion, we put on a little performance for our families before everyone went outside to carol and got a standing ovation.

"Man, that was a gas," he said afterward. "We gotta do that again, Brian."

It took almost a year for us to get together again. One of us got the idea of performing at a student assembly at my alma mater, Hawthorne High School. With two of my friends, we spent weeks rehearsing "Hully Gully," a song by the Olympics.

In our matching buzz haircuts, T-shirts, and jeans, we drew tremendous applause, which went straight to our heads. Especially Mike's. Like me, he reveled in the attention, but for different reasons.

Throughout his life, Mike had gotten everything he wanted. He was his family's golden boy, spoiled rotten. Yet after graduating from Dorsey High School, his life turned into one big disappointment.

He worked at his dad's sheet-metal company during the day and pumped gas at a Standard Oil station at night. He needed the money, having gotten his high school girlfriend pregnant. Although he constantly bragged to me and Dennis about his expert cocksmanship, it suddenly became a nightmare for him. Dennis had a big laugh at Mike's expense, but I didn't find any humor in the situation.

Mike's solution was typical: he planned to spirit his girlfriend to Tijuana, where she could get an abortion, ironic considering Mike is now a conservative Republican. His mother convinced him not to follow through and to marry instead. Soon after the ceremony, he became the father of a girl, Melinda.

Somehow he kept his head together and whenever we spoke he was always thinking about a way to make music together. One evening I was out cruising and pulled my Ford into his gas station. We exchanged small talk as he filled my car up with gas, cleaned the windows, and checked the oil. As he closed the hood, Mike leaned around the side and flashed me a smile that was full of ideas.

"Hey, Bri," he said, "maybe we can get together soon and make"—then he slammed the hood down, producing a hard crash—"some sounds."

"You bet," I said. I looked forward to it.

Al Jardine and I were high school classmates, members of the football team, and music nuts. Al had sung and played guitar in the Islanders, a folk group that had recently broken up. We didn't share the same taste in music.

But I felt as if I owed Al. He had been the fullback on the football team I quarterbacked for, and during a game I'd called a pitchout, a forty-nine flip left, but after taking the ball from the center, I'd flipped right instead, leaving Al waiting for the ball alone and unprotected. The defense smashed into him and broke his leg. The sight of him splayed out on the mottled turf, screaming in agony, was a picture I couldn't shake no matter how many times I apologized.

I was still apologizing when we ran into each other on the El Camino College campus. Both of us were walking away from the athletic field.

"I'm really sorry about what happened to your leg," I said.

"Brian, I've told you a thousand times—forget it," he laughed.

Although I didn't know him well, I admired Al's outgoing nature. It turned out he thought I was a clubby, confident, high-brow thespian who was smart, talented, and came from a storybook family. Like everyone else, he had no idea of the fear that had burdened me since childhood, of how my life was one endless round of shadow boxing, maintaining and pretending to be the type of guy he thought I was. He saw me as a good athlete and great piano player. That was enough.

Standing on the edge of the El Camino football field, Al and I might've been two college freshmen, but our conversation was exactly as it had been during high school. Sports, cars, chicks, and my forte, music. He wanted to get together to play.

"Okay," I said. "When?"

"How about right now?" he replied.

We ended up walking into the nurse's room, which doubled as the football team's training room, and there we collected a couple of pals, forming a crude group of hatchet singers. A football player sang bass, a big fullback guy; Al's singing buddy Gary Winfrey; Al and me. Desperate to get something going, I tried arranging all these voices in some kind of harmonious fashion right there.

But the bass singer was flat, and the fullback, who had just sprained his knee during the afternoon's football scrimmage, was flat on his back in bed, which made it hard for him to sing. Then the nurse booted us out. It wasn't clear whether she needed the room or hated our singing. Undeterred, we moved to an empty music classroom. We were soon kicked out of there by a professor who brought in his class. It was obvious we needed a more private rehearsal space.

"Hey, Al," I said, "why don't you come over to my house and I'll put us together with my cousin Mike and my brother Carl?"

"They sing?" he asked.

"Yeah. Mike sings really good bass, and Carl can play the guitar and sing great."

Al looked puzzled. He didn't know Mike. But Carl had been only twelve the last time Al had seen him play guitar at a high school assembly when he filled in for a friend of mine who had epilepsy.

"You sure Carl can play?" he asked. "I mean, he's not even four foot tall, is he?"

"Don't worry," I assured him. "Just come by."

I was already confident about my music. Hungry too. I had been singing nearly every weekend with Mike and his sister at their house. With me playing piano and doing background harmonies and Maureen and Mike singing lead, our sessions were enthusiastic, daylong affairs, during which we banged out every hit from that summer, including Ricky Nelson's "Travelin' Man," the Shirelles's "Mama Said," and Gary "U.S." Bonds's "Quarter to Three."

Adding Al to the scene was one of those fortunate accidents that changed the chemistry for the better. Maureen dropped out, and Mike began coming over to my house. Al's and Carl's playing complemented each other, affording us both a rhythm and lead guitar. But the real magic occurred in the blending of our voices. The four-part harmony sounded rich and wonderful from the start. Even Dennis, who floated in and out of our rehearsals without being part, was impressed enough to say, "That sounds decent. Really good."

Little did the five of us realize that in my bedroom we had formed the Beach Boys. The same lineup would become an institution, outlasting the Beatles and the Mamas and the Papas, Three Dog Night, and every other big sixties group. With the exception of Dennis, we'd grow old alongside the Rolling Stones, prospering well into our third decade.

There was a spirit to those jams that allowed everything to jell. Everyone contributed something. Carl kept us hip to the latest tunes, Al taught us his repertoire of folk songs, and Dennis, though he didn't play anything, added a combustible spark just by his presence. But the most important byplay occurred between Mike and me. His cockiness was the perfect foil to my reserve, and Mike could spit out choice slang like a short-order cook flipping flapjacks.

Mike was the one who constantly urged me to write songs. "Come on, Brian," he was always saying, "we can write songs as good as the stuff on the radio."

"You think so?" I asked.

"Brian, the stuff you play when you're screwing around is better than three quarters of what's on the radio."

That was the prod I needed, the excuse to cut loose. Someone only had to believe in me. For that I'll always be grateful to Mike. I had the need to kick ass and draw some positive attention to myself. Playing was as much ego as escape.

Two ingredients are necessary to write—stick-to-it-iveness and confidence. Writing a hit song is a little like trying to catch a rainbow. You have to be lucky.

My method of writing hasn't varied much since those early days. I start by banging out chords, searching for catchy rhythms, usually beginning with a run of boogie-woogie. I play until all sense of time and place is overcome by the music, until I'm lost, until the left, logical hemisphere of my brain slows down. From within those trance-inducing rhythms spring notes, then snippets of melody that seem to jump out of thin air. If I'm lucky, I catch 'em.

Mike gave our fledgling band its first name, the Pendletones, a play off Pendleton shirts, then something of a fad.

It was Al who got us on the track leading to the recording studio. One day, just after we had all started singing together, he and his friend, Gary Winfrey, stopped by the house to see if I was home. They wanted to see if I was interested in helping out on a folk song they wanted to record, "Sloop John B."

Although I wasn't home, Al and Gary spoke to my dad about finding a publisher who might be interested in recording the song. A few days later, Dad called Al's house and talked with his mom. He wanted to see if the guys were really serious. He was the music industry veteran. If something was to happen that included me, he wanted a cut of the action.

By the beginning of September 1961, Gary Winfrey dropped out of the picture and my dad arranged for the Pendletones to meet Hite and Dorinda Morgan, social acquaintances of his and my mom's who operated several small labels out of the Stereo Masters office in Hollywood. The Morgans had published my dad's song "Two Step Side Step."

"You'll have the guys sing background," he said to me. "Al can't carry a song by himself."

The five of us arrived at the Morgans' Melrose Avenue office on an overcast afternoon. We should've been nervous—this was our break—but we too young to know any better. As we filed into the office, polite, clean-cut kids, carrying our instruments like a bunch of Boy Scouts with knapsacks, I had the distinct feeling that I was exactly where I should be. I *knew* I belonged around music.

"I'm Hite Morgan," the older man said, sticking out his hand.

"Hello," I said, and then turned to his wife. "Mrs. Morgan, I'll bet you don't remember me. I'm Murry Wilson's son. We met a few years ago when my dad brought me around to an audition."

The Morgans were my parents' age. Sitting on the edge of his desk, Hite looked weary and distracted; his wife was straightening papers. We spoke briefly about the time I'd gone to their house with my father as the lead singer in a group that was trying out for Art Laboe's Original Sound record label. I barely remembered. They reminded me that Laboe thought I was too young at ten to front a group and rejected us.

"So let me hear this song of yours," said Hite, trying to sound enthusiastic but ready to go home.

The Morgans ran a mom and pop publishing business. Their small, cluttered office was home to two labels, Deck and X records. The floor was littered with papers and boxes; we played in the clear space that doubled as a recording studio. Hite spoke in a slow monotone, except when he heard something that caught his attention.

Unfortunately, our straight forward rendition of the traditional folk song did not elicit a positive response. Hite barely moved. Dorinda braved a nice smile.

"So, do you boys have any other songs?" he said diplomatically.

"We weren't good enough?" I asked.

"No, no, not at all," he said. "You boys did a fine job. You have real fine voices. But these days you need something original. You've gotta have an angle. The music business is all about selling a product."

There was a long, awkward moment of silence that caught us looking at our shoelaces. The Morgans' obligation to my dad was fulfilled; the next move was clearly ours. We just hadn't thought that far ahead. We never considered what to do if they asked for another song. That's when Dennis opened up his mouth, taking the rest of us by surprise.

"Yeah, we got an original," he said. "It's called 'Surfin'." The one thing Dennis never lacked was balls. I had been writing the song, but I was nowhere near finished with it.

"Surfin'?" Dorinda puzzled.

Dennis surfed. He was the only one of us who actually knew how to surf. I hated the ocean; its murky vastness and power frightened me. Dennis explained that surfing was a big craze with all the kids. He told a few stories about his own surfing exploits, about waxing a board, about the girls—especially the girls—who came out in droves to watch guys surf, and he mentioned surf guitarist Dick Dale.

His enthusiasm got the Morgans excited, and Hite asked to hear the song. That's when I cut in.

"Well, it's not finished," I said. "We've got the song, and it's original. But it's not done yet."

Hite didn't seem to mind. In fact, I think he was somewhat amused by our boyish bravura. Five teenaged guys, what else could he expect? Sure we had a song. Everybody had a song. Still, he told us to call when the song was completed, and I said we would. Already, my mind was spinning, riveted on the song, like a marksman taking aim. Hite issued an invitation. I saw it as a challenge.

There's a point when everyone decides to follow a specific path in life. You decide to be a doctor, an artist, an accountant, a ballplayer, a reporter. You may not tell anyone. But you know in your heart. Walking out of the Morgans', climbing into my Ford, and then later that night as I played the piano, I accepted Hite Morgan's challenge. I decided I was going to write songs.

I knew I could do it. I had been born with a special gift. The time had come to put it to use.

"You guys ought to write a song about surfing," said Dennis. "It's getting really big."

It was afternoon. Dennis had just come back from the beach. His surfboard was leaning against the front of the house. Mike and I were in the music room, where we had been trying to write a commercial-sounding song. We'd been there several hours, but nothing was working. Then Dennis had mentioned the latest fad, surfing. Right away both Mike and I recognized the potential in writing about a fad.

I began noodling around the piano and singing "Surfin', surfin', 'surfin'." It sounded stupid. But then Mike sang "ba-ba-dippity-dippity-ba-ba." He was fooling around, trying to spark a new idea with the same bass sounds he'd sung countless times before. From some reason, though, this time when he sang I pounded out a few chords to accompany him and then he took up the chant I'd been singing, "Surfin', surfin' . . ."

"Do it again," I said.

Twenty seconds later, I had the opening for the song that would become the Beach Boys' first hit single. A couple of hours later, I finished the song and called it "Surfin'." It still needed lots of work, but the timing couldn't have been better. My folks were going to Mexico City on a three-day vacation with one of my dad's business associates from England. The house would be ours! The refrigerator was stocked, and my dad slipped me some extra cash, $150, in case we ran low on food.

"Brian, you're in charge now," he said.

I called the guys. The rehearsal hall was open for business. With Al adding another $300, a loan from his mom, we rented a stand-up bass, a drum set, an electric guitar, amps, and a couple of microphones. Properly equipped, we proceeded to spend three inspired, virtually sleepless days and nights rehearsing my new song, "Surfin'." That Saturday we even threw a party that was our first gig.

By Sunday night, I had flipped for "Surfin' " in a big way. It had a good groove and, I thought, sounded very commercial. I couldn't wait to play it for the Morgans.

My dad's eyes bulged as soon as he stepped through the front door and spotted the instruments and extension chords strewn across the music room. His face turned bright red with anger; he kicked at an electrical chord, pushed the stand-up bass, screamed about the mess, and then stalked over to me, putting his face inches from mine.

"What the hell is going on?" he demanded.

"We rented some instruments," I said.

Without missing a beat, he threw me against the wall like a sack of potatoes. There was the dull, thudding bang of my body hitting the wall, then a loud grunt, my lungs straining for air. Berating me in front of the guys, handling me roughly, he was making me feel like a pussy, his favorite pastime. I stood there, humiliated.

"Where the hell do you get off disobeying me?"

"I'm sorry." My head was lowered, my eyes focused on the floor. "It was my idea. I'm sorry."

"Sorry. Shit."

"I just wanted to fill out the sound, see how my song would sound with instruments."

He stalked off, irate, muttering threats under his breath, and continued his tirade in another room. My mother listened passively, as always, refusing to take either side in the matter. Later, when Dad had cooled off some, Dennis suggested we play him the song. He agreed to listen.

"I don't know," he said afterward. "It's not professional quality. But it's not bad."

Several days later we saw the Morgans again. My stomach churned as if I were about to play in front of 35,000 people without having rehearsed. I'd spent hours teaching the guys how to harmonize. I very much wanted the Morgans to like the song. This had become more than an audition. For me, it was a matter of validation.

Midway through the song I noticed Hite was smiling and tapping his foot. The stoic face had disappeared and been replaced by bright, enthusiastic eyes. By the time we finished playing, Hite was on his feet, wriggling like a fish out of water.

"That's a smash!" he exclaimed. "That's a smash!"

I couldn't believe it. "Wow!" and "Really?" were the only words that came out of my mouth.

"I'll call your dad with the information. Congrats, guys. Go home and practice."

6

Goin' Surfin'

My dad's wide eyes gave him away. The good news threw him for a loop. Then he caught himself and returned to the role of seasoned veteran. He bit on his pipe, wiped his glasses, affected a nonplussed attitude. He reminded us that he had been in the same position, though no one pointed out that he'd never sung his own material. But we still listened to his warnings to be wary and go slowly as if they were gospel.

Using his experience, he was going to lead the way. He said he would speak to Hite.

"If there's any talk of contracts, let me do the talking," he said. "Otherwise, they'll steal your shorts."

Our first session was done in the Morgans' office on October 3, 1961. Hite and Dorinda wanted to hear what we sounded like on tape. Hite explained his "living room" setup, actually an Ampex 22 recorder, and I watched him mark the tape box "Pendletones Surfing Song."

With Carl on guitar, we did "Surfin'," "Luau," written by the Morgans' son, Bruce, and "Lavender," a pleasant song Dorinda wrote. ("Lavender" was the second one we sang that afternoon. The recording was lost until early 1991 when some collectors digging up old Beach Boys lore discovered the tape in an unopened dated box in Bruce's closet. The song is notable because it shows that our harmonies, the sound that was to become the Beach Boys' trademark, were already developed.)

By experimenting with the boys, I had come up with the idea of putting three-part harmonies against a lead vocal and a groovin' Chuck Berry type of rhythm. It turned out I was right.

But that didn't make it any easier to get the songs on tape. A few days before our session, I decided Dennis wasn't a good enough drummer to play on record. He still needed about six more months of practice. My dad agreed, and I recruited a drummer from a local country and western band. Dennis found out at the Morgans' office and understandably blew his lid. I thought he was going to beat me up.

As it turned out, the Morgans didn't think my country and western drummer had the right feel for rock and roll and they let him go before any recording started. That gave Dennis his opening.

"Why can't I play?" he protested. "Why?"

"Because you don't know how to play the goddamn drums good enough," my dad answered. "That's why."

"But it's not fair. Al's never played stand-up bass. And Brian's never played drums before."

Dennis had a point. Carl was the only one of us playing a familiar instrument.

"It doesn't matter," my dad said without regard for Dennis's feelings. "This is a professional record we're making, and you're not good enough."

Hurt by the put-down, Dennis kicked a guitar case, slammed his fist into the wall, and stomped out of the room. There was a long, uneasy pause, after which the air settled. We grouped around one microphone and got set to play and sing live. My dad settled back in the chair next to Hite, puffed his pipe, and gave us a lone instruction.

"Boys, try to play and sing on key."

We were at the Morgans' all day: twelve takes of "Surfin' " and ten takes of "Luau" tried everyone's patience. I was to blame. I wanted the songs to sound perfect. After Hite played "Surfin' " back, the final version he marked "X-301," we broke out in mile-wide grins. I can be heard playing the trash can, a drum substitute, and there are background noises from the street. Even Dennis, who'd wandered back into the studio, couldn't hold back a smile.

Hite announced that he was going to turn our demo into a record, press up a small quantity, and see how it did on local radio. I was too naive to question the difference between demos and master. Even my dad was in over his head. We were overwhelmed by the excitement of being in a recording studio and hearing someone say they were going to get our song on the radio. Whatever else happened would be a dream.

*　　　*　　　*

Then there were records. We heard they were being shipped. Then we saw them in boxes, which were delivered to our house. Gathering around, we lifted them out carefully, handling them more delicately than anything we'd ever touched. It was the five of us on that record. Our music. Our voices.

There was only one problem. The label read "Surfin'," by the "Beach Boys." We were the Pendletones!

"That's not our name," fifteen-year-old Carl said.

"What the fuck?" Mike added.

Dad called the Morgans. There was an explanation. After the session, the Morgans struck a distribution deal with Candix Records, a small, independent label, to release "Surfin'," and between then and the single's release on December 8, 1961, Russ Regan, a young promotion man, lumped us in with Jan and Dean and other young Southern California surf bands and rechristened us the Beach Boys. The only problem was we didn't find out until we read the label.

"Well, change it back," my dad bellowed into the telephone. "Change it back to the Pendletones. That's what the kids call themselves."

"No dice," he was told.

The records had already been pressed, the labels printed, and the whole kit and kaboodle shipped. It was a small-time operation. Low budget. Reprinting the labels was too costly, my dad was informed.

There was nothing we could do except shrug it off. That was easy. We had a record out. That was a considerable achievement by itself, far more important than a silly name.

Within days of its release both KFWB and KDAY, two of Los Angeles's most influential radio stations, started playing "Surfin'." I was lying in bed one night with the radio on, having just quit playing the piano. I'd gone through our songs, and the music was still fresh in my head. I was getting sleepy. Suddenly, "Surfin' " came on. The sound hit me like an injection of adrenaline and I bolted upright.

"Hey, everybody!" I shouted louder than I thought possible. " 'Surfin' ' is on the radio! 'Surfin' ' is on the radio!"

The entire family—my mom and dad, Carl, and Dennis—rushed into the room, gathered around the radio, and listened with dopey grins plastered on our faces. Except for my dad. He cocked his head to the side and listened with pursed lips while the rest of us fell apart. My mom danced around the room; Carl went straight to the kitchen, ate handfuls of food, and then threw up; Dennis and I thought the whole thing was cool.

"That was 'Surfin' ' by the Beach Boys," the DJ yelled. "This week's Pick to Click."

My dad wasn't enthusiastic. "It's not good enough," he said to me.

"What?" I shuddered. "Dad, the song's on the radio. 'Surfin' ' is on the radio."

"It's weak, Brian," he said. "You can't hear Al's bass. You can't hear you or Carl singing in the background. It's not good enough."

Typical. Nothing but criticism from my dad. Either my writing was weak or I didn't play right. Or my singing was weak. Or I was a loser. Or I should listen to him. Or I should do things his way. Or all of the above. He had been around. He knew.

From "Surfin' " on, my dad was so goddamn jealous of what I was able to achieve and he wasn't that he was unable to utter a single compliment. Nothing was ever good enough for him, and as a result nothing was ever good enough for me. I've spent a lifetime trying to prove him wrong, but it's been impossible to escape his stinging criticism.

But his was only one of many opinions. Not the least of them belonged to my first real girlfriend, Judy Bowles, who loved the music I created. A pretty, outgoing blonde with the bluest of blue eyes, she was inspiration personified, looking like the kind of California girl stereotyped in later Beach Boys songs. We had met in Little League. I was helping a friend coach; her younger brother played center field.

Judy caught my eye one afternoon from her seat in the bleachers, and the next time she showed up I sat beside her. We kissed a few weeks later and were inseparable for the next year and a half. Aggressive in ways that I wasn't, Judy's lightheartedness was a perfect match for my goofy shyness. She taught me a lot about sex, but like all the girls with whom I was involved, she constantly asked, "Brian, why are you always putting yourself down? Have a little confidence."

No one person has ever been able to give me the feeling I got from music. By the end of December, "Surfin' " was a local hit—Top 40 and climbing. The song caught on and became everything my dad had wished for one of his own songs. Despite how he felt about it, he smelled money to be made and jumped on the promotion bandwagon, calling every radio station in the area, then the state. Unprepared for success, everyone tried to maintain a sense of cool, but it was extremely hard.

The excitement grew tenfold when we got our first paying gig as the

Beach Boys at the Ritchie Valens Memorial Dance in Long Beach. Ike and Tina Turner, who headlined a handful of acts on that night's bill, went on before us, though I recall Ike wasn't there. Just Tina, who was something to marvel at. She burned up the stage, dancing as if she had fire under her feet and singing in a voice that was hot enough to singe the front row. I'd heard R&B on the radio, but I'd never seen it in person.

Intimidated, I should have wondered what the Beach Boys were doing there, considering we were five clean-cut, unworldly white boys from a conservative white suburb, in an auditorium full of black kids who wanted to cut loose and groove. There was barely a white person in the place—not that it mattered, but the crowd looked anything but fans of surf music. We performed our well-rehearsed twenty-minute set, which included "Surfin' " and "Bermuda Shorts."

That night was an education. In one show we discovered what the world of music was about—R&B, rock and roll, and money. Afterward, the five of us walked outside to the ticket window and got fifty dollars apiece. We held out our hands and felt the weight of the bills. It was a big deal.

All we talked about on the way home—or most of the way home—was how we had actually gotten paid for playing rock and roll. We were crammed into my Ford, the five of us and our instruments. Suddenly, Mike noticed it was roomier in the car than it had been on the way over. We spend a few minutes wondering why and then realized the answer, which put a damper on our triumphant night.

"Dennis's drums," Carl said. "Where are they?"

"Who packed 'em up?" Mike asked.

Dennis shrugged. We'd run out so fast to collect our money that he'd forgotten to go back and pack his drums. They were rented too.

"We gotta turn back and get 'em," Al said. "We gotta get 'em or else we lose my mom's deposit. That's three hundred bucks—more than we made tonight!"

We went back and got the drums.

By mid-January "Surfin' " charted on *Billboard,* the industry's official yardstick, at 118. We were national. It seemed bigger than life. Suddenly, we didn't feel like five anonymous, unimportant guys sitting in a godforsaken suburb. My brothers, who were just seventeen and fifteen, turned into egomaniacs, especially Dennis. Al said he wanted to see some money before getting too excited. Mike and I alone grasped the big picture.

We were the most desperate to break out of our lives, the ones most in need of ego-massaging rewards. Mike immediately talked of quitting his job. I began to think about quitting El Camino and devoting myself full-time to the Beach Boys, knowing that "Surfin' " represented only the tip of my talent. The attention it received whetted my appetite for more as it gave me the approval I hadn't gotten at home.

My dad saw the Beach Boys as a chance at realizing some glory too. There was never a formal meeting or discussion between any of us, but from the time the Morgans made the deal with Candix, my dad simply assumed the managerial reins. No one objected. It made sense. After "Surfin' " was released, he had official Beach Boys stationery printed up, which listed me as leader and Murry Wilson as manager.

My dad deserves credit for getting us off the ground. He was relentless, probably because like me he was looking to validate himself. Determined, energetic, driven, he hounded us mercilessly, making us work harder than we would have on our own. But my dad also worked hard himself, aware that what went on behind the scenes was as important as the music. Every night he sat on his bed in his pajamas and called radio stations, schmoozing with DJs and record stores. After "Surfin' " hit the charts, he was the first one to begin clamoring for a follow-up.

"If you don't deliver those crooks in distribution another song," he lectured, "they'll never cough up the money they owe us for the first one."

It's always been assumed that my girlfriend, Judy Bowles, was the blond role model for "Surfer Girl." Blond and blue-eyed, she fit the bill. But it's not so. There was never one specific "surfer girl." I wrote "Surfer Girl" while driving around Hawthorne one afternoon. The melody popped into my head as clearly and nearly as complete as it later sounded on record. I heard everything and rushed straight home and finished it on the piano. Because I had heard the melody in my head, independent of sitting at the piano, I figured I really did have a flair for writing.

If I could do that . . .

I taught the arrangement to the guys, none of whom had ever learned anything as complex as "Surfer Girl," but they were still knocked out by it. We were reluctant to play a ballad for the Morgans, though. With Hite and my dad planning to take us back into the studio in early February, we figured they wanted something similar to "Surfin'," upbeat and fun. Still, "Surfer Girl" was our best song, so we took a shot.

"Oh, there's nothing wrong with that," Hite grinned after we finished playing. "Singing a pretty song about a surfer girl. That's a smash if I ever heard one."

"Surfin' " had already peaked at seventy-five by the time we ventured back into the studio again. We recorded four more original songs, including "Surfer Girl," "Karate," "Judy" (which *was* written about Judy Bowles), and "Surfin' Safari," a silly song with a simple-but-cool C-F-G chord pattern that I came up with one day while trying to play the piano the way Chuck Berry played his guitar. The session was going along glitch-free, four songs in three hours.

When we were almost finished, my dad pulled me aside and strongly suggested we record several of his songs too. How could he, I thought? It was insulting. He was muscling in on our action. First as manager, now as songwriter. I didn't want to get into it. Not here. Not when we had finished a long session that had us all excited.

He didn't leave me any choice. "I don't think that would be a good idea," I said.

For a moment, he didn't say anything. He just turned his back on me. Then he whipped around, pissed. "You're going to record my songs or the group breaks up," he shouted.

The other guys heard us arguing, and I tried to take control of the situation before it blew up by talking sense to my dad. "You don't want to break us up, Dad," I said. "Look, everything is fine. We're just getting going. Why are you doing this to me?"

"I don't give a damn if you're going or coming," he said. "My songs are better than yours. You should record 'em."

At that point, I didn't have the nerve to take a swing at him, but I was that angry. Instead, I begged and pleaded, told my dad that I didn't want to argue, that I liked his songs, loved them, in fact, but that I wanted to do my own original material. "Try to understand. They're our songs. They're what we want to play. We've worked hard for this."

I don't know if what I said got through to my dad, but without saying a word, he walked back around the glass and took his place next to Hite. An uneasy stillness fell over the crowded studio as we reassembled by our instruments for a final take. Then my dad turned to Hite and said, "The boys are ready to do another song."

7

Songwriters Against the World

My dad examined our first royalty check, which amounted to less than $1,000.

"That's it? That's all the money we got?" I asked.

"What have I been telling you about the music business?" he answered. "Crooks. All of them."

The meager sum was a disappointment to everyone. "Surfin' " had sold upwards of 50,000 copies, an amount that seemed enormous, and all of us were expecting the royalty payment to be a windfall. But $1,000? After it was split five ways, our disappointment was impossible to hide. It seemed that we really had been hoodwinked just as my dad had warned.

"I'll draw blood before I let 'em get away with this crap," he promised.

My dad confronted the Morgans, who blamed the discrepancy on our distributor, Candix Records. Candix was having money problems, Hite reluctantly admitted. He said he was shopping for a new distribution deal. My dad, who was already mad, was not interested in a new deal. Candix's difficulties gave him the loophole he needed to break his agreement with the Morgans and shop around for a more lucrative deal for the Beach Boys.

"Screw 'em," he explained. "I can get more money myself."

"You can?" Mike said.

"Do it then," I said.

"Yeah, yeah," he said. "I'll book time in a studio, produce a professional-sounding demo, and make a deal with one of the major labels. No more of this fly-by-night crap."

We rehearsed in the music room every afternoon, the sounds drifting through the neighborhood, occasionally drawing complaints. But about the same time my dad began searching for a new label, one of our rehearsals attracted a skinny guy whose uncle lived across the street. Gary Usher was a go-getter. One day he knocked on the front door and asked for me.

"I've heard you guys on the radio," he said.

"Yeah? What d'ya think?" I asked.

"Cool. Really cool. Can I listen to what you're doing?"

Gary came inside. Then during a break, he told me he knew a thing or two about the music business, which immediately made me want to know everything about him. Gary, five years older than me, played guitar and sang. He'd recorded two singles on a small label, and though the sales didn't approach ours, Gary was lots more confident, savvy, and experienced than me, and that made him the most fascinating guy I'd ever met.

Gary and I spent all that afternoon and evening exchanging thoughts about music and life, discovering in our opposite personalities kindred souls. Late that night we wrote the first of many songs. "The Lonely Sea" was a dreamy, sophomoric elegy about the enormity of life, reflecting the feel of our discussion. It appeared on the second Beach Boys album. The song took only a few minutes to write, but in that brief time we became the closest of friends.

The friendship was fast and fiery. We told things to each other that we wouldn't share with our families or our girlfriends, secrets we wouldn't discuss with anyone else. We understood each other without having to explain. Both of us felt an urgent, panicky need to prove ourselves, believing that the acclaim of success would heal our wounds or at least make us forget them.

"You know anything about Carole King or Gerry Goffin?" he asked one day.

"Who?" I asked. "What do they sing?" I'd never heard their names before and thought they were a new group, a husband and wife knockoff of Jan and Dean.

"How about Barry Mann and Cynthia Weil?" he asked.

I shook my head no and asked who they were.

"They're songwriters," he said. "In New York. They're *the* songwriters. They're the ones we're up against. The competition. If we're going to be great, we've got to go after them."

"That's what we have to aim for, right? That's what you're telling me?" I asked.

Gary nodded. He described the frantic-paced songwriting that went on in the Brill Building in New York, the music factory where writers like King and Goffin and Mann and Weil churned out single after single as if they were on an assembly line. He explained how they competed against each other for chart position. They didn't merely try to write good or great songs, Gary told me. They aimed for the top. They wanted every song to be Number One.

I got it instinctively. It had to do with ego; it had to do with proving your self-worth.

"So, brother, what we have to do is write a number one song," Gary said.

"No sweat," I said.

Gary and I wrote as if our lives depended on it, turning out dozens of mediocre songs, including "The Beginning of the End," a truly terrible ballad. But out of that initial writing frenzy came our first good song. Gary drove a white 348 Chevy, but what he really wanted was a hot rod 409. He talked about it constantly, and one night as he dreamed out loud, I provided some fast-paced background music. With his eyes closed, Gary reeled off the lyrics and I pounded out the music. Suddenly we finished "409," the Beach Boys' first car song, a theme that became as much an emblem for us as surfing.

Averaging a song a day, Gary's and my next creative triumph was titled "In My Room." Gary recognized that the music room served as a sanctuary to me. He never got over the fact that I slept there, right beside the piano. We wrote the song at the organ, because I happened to be sitting there, playing in the key of B. Gary was eating, half listening, gossiping about something. As we talked, my fingers absent-mindedly skipped across the keyboard and stumbled across the now famous melody.

"Wait!" Gary said. "Do that again."

I did. I played those same dozen or so notes, and Gary sang lyrics. The first words out of his mouth were:

"There's a place where I can go and tell my secrets to . . ."

The song was finished in less than an hour.

When it came to demoing our songs, Gary was a willing foil to my anything-that-works whimsy. Wanting the sound of real waves on "The Lonely Sea," I convinced Gary to help lug my bulky Wollensak to the ocean in the middle of the night. For the rest of his life, he laughed about knocking on someone's door at 1:00 A.M. and asking to plug in our extension chord.

"This isn't music," he said as we laid the electrical chord on the sand. "It's madness."

No, it was the beginning. When demoing "409," I wanted the sound of a real car. Gary raised his eyebrows; my brothers laughed, anticipating an exciting night. It didn't matter to me that it was 2:00 A.M. We positioned Gary's powerful Chevy in the middle of the street, strung together several extension chords, set the tape recorder beside his engine, and revved it up. He gunned it over and over, until it sounded as if the Indy 500 was getting set to start.

Lights flickered on in houses up and down our sleepy street and bleary-eyed, angry neighbors opened their doors, wondering what was going on. Finally, my dad came out.

"Goddamnit, what the hell are you boys doing?" he said.

By then, we had Gary's car on tape and were just screwing around. Later when I produced the Beach Boys and started adding what were then unusual sounds for records—people eating, trains, dogs barking, or hammers hammering—critics were astonished. They raved. But I was only trying to get the songs to sound the way I heard them in my head.

It wasn't long after Gary and I started writing that my dad announced he was ready to take a demo around town. At Western Studios, which would eventually become home to the Beach Boys, we recorded four songs: "Surfer Girl," "Judy," "409," and "Surfin' Safari." Western's house engineer, Chuck Britz, a brilliant man who later became our regular engineer, presided. I thought we did pretty well. All I remember is my dad standing next to Chuck, yelling.

"Give it more punch! Come on boys, give it more punch!"

That night I took more of his criticism:

"Brian, if you're ever going to amount to anything in this business, you're going to have to write a hell of a lot better. And play a lot better. You're going to have to put out. Right now, you're lazy. Too goddamn lazy for my book."

My dad's jabs never ceased. Not in the early days, not in the later days. At this point, though, there was no telling whether or not the Beach Boys were one-shot sensations. I certainly didn't think so. I'd already made the decision to drop out of school and pursue the group's future. Mike felt the same way and had quit his jobs. My dad supported our decisions.

But Al Jardine wasn't quite so sure. Dejected by the diminutive returns from "Surfin' " and the meager revenues from several live performances locally, he reconsidered his commitment to the band and opted to go back to school and continue his pre-dental studies.

"You don't understand, Brian," he told me. "It's not just the money. We just don't seem to be going anywhere."

"Sure we are," I argued. "We just made a demo. My dad's shopping it."

"But creatively speaking, we get onstage and no one knows our songs. We have to play other people's songs. I guess I expect something more."

"I've written a bunch of songs, good songs," I said. "You know that. You've heard them. Soon everyone will know them. You've just got to give it some time."

"No, Brian. I can't. You've got to understand. It's not working for me. The Beach Boys isn't working."

"Goddamnit, Al," I started yelling. "I can't believe you're doing this. I can't believe you're leaving. Leaving us in the lurch, that's what you're doing."

"Brian, I'm going to school. You can be a musician. All the luck—"

"All the luck?" I exclaimed. "Fuck you, Al. All the luck to you."

He didn't realize how seriously I had staked myself to the Beach Boys just as I wasn't able to understand his inability to do the same. I found security in the group, but Al was still searching for it.

I doubt he would've left the Beach Boys had he known that Capitol Records was about to sign us.

My dad knew Ken Nelson, Capitol's country and western A&R man, and through him he met Nick Venet, Capitol's rock and roll guy. At twenty-one, Venet was the record company's youngest executive. He also surfed. Accompanied by me and Gary, my dad cued up "Surfin' Safari" for Venet to hear.

"You don't have to play any more," Venet exclaimed after hearing just eight bars. "That song's a hit record! That song's going to change West Coast music!"

The Beach Boys were now Capitol recording artists! I was ecstatic. Capitol Records was home to luminaries like Frank Sinatra, the Lettermen, and, not the least, my beloved Four Freshmen. It was an honor just to be on the same label as those artists, and never would I have dared to dream that the songs I wrote would help push sales of Beach Boys albums past all of them.

Capitol wasted no time in releasing their first Beach Boys single, "409," which was delivered to record stores on June 4, 1962. The single's flip side was "Surfin' Safari." I was convinced that "409" was going straight to the top. It might've been unrealistic, but my naiveté and thirst for success gave me high expectations. The only thing I thought about was getting to the top. I was fanatic about it. Obsessed.

However, "409" did something none of us expected. It stiffed. I cried in private—that's how great my disappointment was. A few weeks later, though, Capitol began plugging "Surfin' Safari" and the single broke in, of all places, landlocked Phoenix. Then it scored in New York. From his bedside, my dad worked the telephone, calling DJs around the country. By August, "Surfin' Safari" was eighty-five on the charts; in October it reached a high of fourteen. The excitement returned.

"Brian," Nick Venet called one afternoon, "you're not going to believe this."

"What?" I asked.

"Sit down. "409" just charted too. You guys have a double-sided hit."

A double-sided hit! Sales would eventually reach 900,000.

Soon Capitol was hustling us into the company's Hollywood studio to record our debut album. Driving into the Capitol parking lot every day made me feel as if the group hit the big time, even though the record company regarded us as a teenage novelty. Everything was rushed. The *Surfin' Safari* album was done in a handful of long, tiring sessions between June and September. Nick Venet produced, counseled by my dad, who sat shoulder to shoulder with him behind the engineering board.

They drove each other nuts, arguing about sound, the surging of voices, and arrangements. But the final musical decisions already rested on my shoulders. I was consulted on every decision, and with what I contributed, I wouldn't have been out of line asking for a producer's credit—if I'd known what that was.

I'd just turned twenty. I couldn't even vote yet. It was my first taste of professional record production and I was overjoyed just to be a part of it. I learned something new every day, and though I held back my inclination to take over completely, I asserted myself through sheer stamina. Venet marveled at my drive. My band mates bristled at my stern leadership. I was tough, even mean. I didn't see any reason why we couldn't be the top dog among bands.

The *Surfin' Safari* album revealed our inexperience. Lacking the lush backgrounds that were to become my Beach Boys' trademark, it catered to the raw surf sound that was then the craze. Still, the songs showed our potential. "Chug-A-Lug" is one of the cutest little songs the group ever did, "Ten Little Indians" is a pretty hip play off the children's song, and it's clear that "Surfin' Safari" became the model for producer Phil Spector's hit "Da Doo Ron Ron." Same chords, similar melody.

Released on October 1, 1962, *Surfin' Safari* sported liner notes that introduced us to the world: "Last year when a group of sun-tanned youngsters recorded a song about their favorite sport, they had no idea that the tune was destined to ride a wave of popularity that would rival the sport itself." While that was correct, Mike was erroneously credited as the composer of "Surfin' "; I was described as the leader and vocal arranger, while Carl, Dennis, and our neighbor David Marks rounded out the rest of the group.

After Al's departure, I picked up the bass and David Marks enjoyed a short stint as the Beach Boys' rhythm guitarist. David was a wild kid who lived across the street from our house and had played with Dennis when they were younger. I didn't like him or the way he played guitar.

"He's too young," I argued. "And he's not good enough."

My dad didn't care. He also didn't listen.

"He can play rhythm guitar," he said. "He can't play lead, but he can play rhythm."

"I don't want David in the group," I said firmly. "I'm the leader. I don't want him."

"That's too bad," my dad snapped. "We need someone to play guitar. Now!"

By Thanksgiving the album had reached a high of thirty-two, while our egos rose even higher and ordinary life grew less ordinary. My dad was holding us back from the offers to perform that streamed in daily, thinking it best to let the public's desire to see us perform build. But that still didn't hold back the crowds. Every day dozens of kids would stand outside our house and look in the window while we rehearsed. They all knew our names. They were heady times.

But it was also a time of mounting tension between the two strongest forces in the Beach Boys, me and my dad. Both of us felt responsible for the group's success. With my songs gathering attention, I came into my own, finding success in a milieu where I could be everything I really wasn't: overconfident and egotistical. But my dad felt his input was responsible for the Beach Boys' success, and he began taking as much credit as he could.

Our biggest clash concerned Gary Usher. My dad didn't like him, and as Gary's and my collaboration intensified, so did my dad's antipathy. He had endless criticism: Gary was pushy, untrustworthy, an interloper who'd pushed himself on me. My dad hated coming home and finding me and Gray working in the music room. Gary listened to my dad's outdated ideas on songwriting and observed his iron-fisted control with disbelief.

"You ought to belt him," Gary once said. "Just haul off and hit the motherfucker."

Both of us knew my dad was jealous of the success we were having as songwriters, but Gary could go home at night while I had to tolerate Dad's crap. Even that became more and more difficult.

One night I was playing the piano, listening to my dad talk on the phone from his bedroom. He wasn't feeling well, the strain from running his machinery business, managing the Beach Boys, and dealing with the studio on top of maintaining the family was taking a toll on his health. He suffered from a stomach ulcer and intestinal problems as well as nervousness that came out as temper.

"Brian, wrong chord," he yelled from the bedroom. "Jesus Christ, that's the wrong goddman chord."

I ignored the comment and continued to play. A few minutes later, he was standing over me, a sick man snorting like an injured bull.

"Pick it up," he said. "Pick up the goddamn rhythm. You're playing as if you're asleep."

"What?" I looked up, shocked and angered.

"I said, you're too goddamn lazy," he answered.

For the first time in my twenty years I was unable to control my anger. Shooting up from the piano, I kicked the piano bench backwards so that it crashed against the floor. I had to grip the piano to keep myself from lunging at my dad.

"Fuck you!" I shouted. "Just fuck you, Dad!"

My dad looked shocked and didn't say a word. Carl ran into the room to investigate the commotion. He couldn't believe what I'd said. Neither could Dad, who hadn't moved. I didn't care what they thought. Collecting myself, I picked up the bench and started to play again, ignoring both of them. My dad finally returned to his bedroom, where I heard him instruct my mother to go back and club me with a board. She refused.

My dad couldn't help himself from meddling, criticizing, or just plain telling me what to write. Not long after that explosive incident, he interrupted me and Gary, telling us that we should write about something timeless, like love or beautiful flowers or a pretty day, instead of surfing and girls. He couldn't understand that we were doing just that, but in our own way.

"A pretty smile? A kiss? Springtime?" Gary said in a mocking voice.

My dad stared at Gary with undisguised hatred. He looked as if he wanted to pulverize him. I kept playing, even though I couldn't believe what I was hearing. My friend was saying things that I only thought but wouldn't ever dare voice.

"That's not happening," Gary continued. "You aren't tuned into what's hip."

"Shut up," my dad said. "If you knew a quarter of what you thought you did, Einstein would be out of a job."

Gary didn't let up until his chiding pushed my dad right over the edge. Spewing threats, my dad all but tossed Gary out of the house by the seat of his pants. More disputes followed, especially when Gary began asking for a fair percentage of his publishing rights. My dad berated me for working with Gary and allowing outside factions to splinter the family. Finally, one afternoon, he and Gary had an explosive shouting match in the parking lot outside Capitol.

Unwilling to give Gary one penny, let alone the potential gold mine of a number of hit songs, my dad organized the Sea of Tunes Publishing Company. Originally, I was the sole owner of both the publishing company and the song copyrights. After the Beach Boys had a couple of hits, my dad began pressuring me to turn the publishing company over to him. He claimed he was due money as manager and the father of the Wilson brothers.

I resisted, and he made my life miserable. After assuring me that I could own the copyrights to my songs, I relented and agreed to give him 50 percent of the publishing income generated by my songs. In exchange, he promised to administer Sea of Tunes. That satisfied him for a couple of months. But as soon as the big money started to roll in he tried grabbing an even larger share for himself, blind to the effect his demands had on me.

My dad found validation in money, but it wasn't the reason Gary and I wrote. We wanted acclaim. We wanted people to know we were great songwriters. After working at night, we often popped open a few beers, caught a buzz, and let ourselves dream of that day, never mentioning our common fear that it would never come.

One night my dad intruded into our private reverie and yelled at Gary for supplying me with beer. That did it. In need of more of an escape than a late-night beer, I decided to move out of the house. Quickly, I found a friend in need of a roommate and arranged to move in. Bob Norberg was an outgoing, athletic guy. I had met him at USC when the Beach Boys played a Sigma Chi frat party, and we quickly became buddies. He was a musician too, and with his girlfriend, Sheri, he had also performed at the frat party.

On moving day I stuffed my red-and-white 1960 Impala with my clothes and belongings and said good-bye. The two-bedroom apartment into which I was moving was only fifteen minutes away, but as I pulled out of the driveway, my dad stood in the center, waving and crying. As a young man, he had been known to cry if someone said a harsh word, but I'd rarely seen that side of him. The sight of his oldest son leaving home was more than he could handle.

It confused the hell out of me. One day he would beat me, the next I'd find him in tears. Such a troubled man.

It was a good move for me. Bob Norberg was a struggling songwriter who was working odd jobs. He surfed, had a girlfriend, liked to drink beer. Our apartment, at 108th and Crenshaw, in Inglewood, was strictly no-frills bachelor. Furnishings were simple—carpeting, two mattresses, and random junk—and the rent was a cheap $150 a month.

Norberg and I wrote a number of songs together, including "Your Summer Dream," which made it on the Beach Boys' *Surfer Girl* album. I wrote a song called "The Surfer Moon" for Bob and his girlfriend, whose act was billed Bob and Sheri. When we demoed "The Surfer Moon," Norberg and I recorded actual crickets chirping, a humorous late-night experience. My dad later sold it to Safari Records.

Norberg exercised his most profound effect on me when he began playing Phil Spector records. That changed everything for me. Spector was just emerging as the impresario of pop, a genius of unsurpassed magnitude. Norberg was hip to Spector long before I was. In fact, he went through a period when all he played on his record player was Spector's "He's Sure the Boy I Love."

Bob didn't just play the single. He also provided running commentary. "Brian, feel the groove Spector gets into," he hollered over the music. "Listen to the way Spector records his drums, the backgrounds. Those vocals are huge. The sound practically bowls you over."

"Yeah," I said. "I hear it."

I did more than hear it, though. I envied it.

8

Surfin' U.S.A.

*I*t was mid-December 1962, almost a full year since "Surfin' " had earned the Beach Boys nationwide attention. An awful lot had happened that year. We had a double-sided hit in "Surfin' Safari" and "409," an album, and a concert tour—actually just five shows. But they were spread across the West, requiring us to travel from home, and that was a big deal. Before leaving, I had an argument with my girlfriend, Judy, for whom I'd forgotten to get a Christmas gift.

"I wish you'd show me a bit more attention," she complained. "It's always the Beach Boys with you."

"I'm sorry," I said. "That's all I think about. I don't know if I can change."

Our relationship was rocky. My priorities were already intractable. Music came first. I didn't like to fight about it; that was something that had to be understood and accepted by anyone with whom I was involved. Judy tried, but the latest of our many spats made me look forward to the road trip.

My dad was especially anxious, since he was looking to prove a point to our booking agent. Although he kept control of promoting and managing the Beach Boys, he signed the William Morris Agency to handle booking live dates, which came in faster than he could handle. My dad had big expectations. The agency's twenty-two-year-old booking agent told him the Beach Boys would never make more money than Ruby and the

Romantics, who were getting $3,500 for seven days' work. My dad got mad. He called all the key radio stations in the cities where we were booked. Between December 17 and January 1, 1963, we grossed $26,684 for five nights' work. It was a staggering amount, especially since my dad, knowing what kids could afford to pay, insisted that ticket prices be kept at two dollars a head. The only place that didn't happen was Omaha, Nebraska, where the radio station KOIL charged $2.50. I remember that because of how miserable the show was there.

The venue was outdoors. We'd driven thirty-six hours without sleep in a station wagon crammed with our equipment. We played two shows. The high temperature was eight degrees above zero. We were so tired we made four false starts on "Surfer Girl," which we hadn't released yet. From the side, my dad yelled at me to keep on top of things, since it was my bass playing that kept the beat steady.

"Goddamnit, Brian!" my dad hollered from offstage. "Treble up! Stay interested!"

Stay interested? That wasn't the problem. I was trying to stay awake.

Back home, the record company was frantic to feed what they continued to think was a teenage fad. Pressuring us to make another album as quickly as possible, we no sooner unpacked than we began spending every day in the studio. Our second LP, *Surfin' U.S.A.*, took less than a month to record, which accounts for the number of instrumentals on it. The LP's first single, "Surfin' U.S.A.," owed itself to a number of influences, including Chuck Berry, Chubby Checker, and Judy Bowles's little brother, Jimmy.

Having come up with a melody inspired by that song, I thought, God, what about doing surf lyrics and mentioning every surf spot in the state? They're doing it here, there, in this city and that, like Chubby Checker's "Twistin' U.S.A." Jimmy was a surfer. I asked him to make a list of every surf spot he knew, and by God he didn't leave one out.

But that was about as smooth as it got for me. The balance of responsibility that would guide the Beach Boys wasn't completely defined yet. David Marks and Dennis weren't as devoted to music as they were to being popular and Carl was too young to be taken seriously. Mike, although devoted to the group, was limited by a lack of musical talent, leaving me at the creative helm, the position I wanted anyway.

The discovery I'd made as a child was being confirmed by the Beach Boys' success. I wrote and played music better than virtually anyone else, better than anyone I knew, and my brain naturally thought in six-part harmony, a pattern so complex not even my dad could understand it. I felt special. The fact that I was special became the only aspect of my life I cultivated. My family, friends, and business associates encouraged me to feel and act special, since my specialness also generated more money than anyone ever dreamed of. Eventually, such one-dimensional coddling would catch up to me and nearly do me in.

In the meantime, rock and roll was liberting. It allowed my fragile soul to soar.

While Nick Venet recognized my capability in the studio and allowed me increasing say in the production of the *Surfin' U.S.A.* album, my dad wasn't able to give up any authority. He couldn't help himself, and he horned in on every song we recorded, resulting in tiresome, time-consuming arguments.

"It's my song," I finally yelled during the session for "The Lonely Sea." "You don't know how I imagine it."

"Brian, remember who you're talking to," he said in a tone of disgust. "It's a crappy little boys' song. An Usher song, right? No different than the others you and he write. Listen to me. I know."

I tried not paying attention, but it wasn't long after that exchange that my dad returned to the studio and saw Gary, who had recently arrived, sitting beside me at the control board. We were listening to a playback of the song. My dad immediately ordered Gary to leave. He refused.

"No, I'm helping," he said.

"Out!" my dad ordered. "I'm the boss. I want you to get the hell out. Now!"

Gary stood up and seemed about to say something when my dad stepped forward and shoved him. Gary lost his balance and fell to the floor. Stunned, humiliated, and angrier than I'd ever seen him, my best friend got up and walked out of the studio. I wanted to follow, but my Dad blocked me. He was livid.

"I don't want you writing with that bastard ever again," he said.

Whether it was unconscious or coincidence, I began writing less with Gary at about the same time a kaleidoscope of influences entered my life. It was a hectic period, things happening one on top of the other as my reputation grew. Gary had been responsible for introducing me to a number of people who would assume an important role in my life, including his replacement as my collaborator, Roger Christian, and my future wife, Marilyn Rovell.

During this frantic month of recording our second album, Judy and

I broke up. As consolation, Gary orchestrated an introduction to a couple of vivacious teenaged girls, Diane and Marilyn Rovell, who were first cousins of his girlfriend, Ginger Blake. Gary brought Ginger and Diane to the Beach Boys' opening night at Pandora's Box, then Hollywood's most popular teen nightclub, where my dad had booked us for an entire week.

The Beach Boys were the hottest band in Los Angeles and the line to get inside wrapped around the block. Gary, Ginger, and Diane sat at a front table, staying for both shows. Diane screamed the entire evening; afterward she told me she had fallen in love at first sight. The threesome returned the next night and Diane brought her middle sister, Marilyn. I spent most of the first show making faces at Gary, trying to crack him up, until I spotted Marilyn.

She was a tad overweight, but her smile radiated warmth and light danced in her eyes. At intermission, I set down my bass, hopped off the stage, and approached their table. Nervous, I wanted to make a cool first impression. Gary stood up, prepared to make introductions, but before he said anything I stumbled over my feet and knocked into Marilyn, spilling her hot chocolate on her leg. She jumped up, startled.

I thought I'd blown it. But Marilyn took hold of my arm and laughed. "It's okay," she smiled. "It's okay. Don't worry about it. I'm all right."

There was a third sister, Barbara, who was younger. The Rovell sisters attended every show that week with Gary and Ginger. After the last night, I invited Marilyn and Diane to my parents' house, where the instruments were. I had feelings for both girls and couldn't decide which one I liked better. One day I'd lean toward Diane, and the next I'd think about Marilyn. When they showed up a few days later I learned that Diane actually liked Dennis, while Marilyn set her sights on Carl. Neither of their infatuations lasted as long as my confused feelings did for the sisters.

Roger Christian, one of L.A.'s most popular DJs, worked radio station KFWB's all-important nine-to-midnight shift, the time when everybody was cruising the town in their cars, listening to the radio. A laid-back fellow, Roger was bonkers about cars, a real zealot, especially about our song, "409." Somehow he knew Gary and asked if he'd have me look at some lyrics he'd written.

Our introduction took place after Roger's shift in KFWB's parking lot. He handed me a sheet of paper with lyrics typewritten like a poem. I scanned them quickly and recognized they were plugged into something cool.

"These are great!" I enthused. "Let me take them home and I'll see what I can do."

The catchy ode to hot rodding was titled "Little Deuce Coupe," and I began to work on it the next morning. Before lunch, I completed the music. Gary picked me up that night and took me over to the radio station. As soon as Roger went off the air, we drove over to Gary's. He had a piano. Roger was grinning foolishly when I finished playing it. He was a great guy who didn't hide his emotions.

I told him I thought it was going to be a monster hit and that I'd get the guys to record it as soon as possible. He mentioned that he had another set of lyrics that might also make a real good song.

"It's called 'Shut Down,' " he said. "It starts, 'Tack it up, tack it up, buddy going to shut you down . . .' "

"That's really hip," I said. "Real competitive stuff. Let me take that too."

For the next year Roger replaced Gary as the guy I turned to for lyrics if I wasn't writing by myself or with Mike. Gary's fate was sealed when a blowout between Dennis and my dad resulted in Dennis being kicked out of the house. When Gary heard that my brother had been sleeping in a friend's car he offered refuge in his apartment. My dad discovered that, decided that Gary might as well be dead, deemed him persona non grata, and said he should have nothing to do with the Beach Boys. Gutless, I didn't stand up for Gary, which got him upset with me and caused our friendship to dwindle.

I didn't mourn. There was so much flying my way, what with my popularity as music's boy wonder soaring. Everyone, it seemed, wanted to be my friend. I knew Jan Berry and Dean Torrence from having performed on the same concert bill several times. One afternoon when we weren't working on the album, I visited them at Aldon Music, Don Kirshner's company. They questioned me about the Beach Boys' album, so I sat at the office piano and played "Surfin' U.S.A."

"That's great," Jan said. "Why don't you let us record it?"

"No, that's for the Beach Boys," I said protectively. "But I've got some others. How about this?"

I pounded out another melody, singing the opening verse, "Two girls for every boy!" and the chorus.

"What's that one called?" Jan asked.

" 'Surf City,' " I said. "But I'm not done with it yet."

"Let me hear what you've got again," Jan said, sitting down next to me.

I played it several more times. Jan loved it and said he knew what needed to be done to finish it. Fine with me. I didn't mind letting Jan and Dean record my song. I thought Jan was a genius in the studio and watching him cut records was a righteous trip. He knew exactly what he needed and how to get it done. His records were clean, like the Four Seasons' records, but what I admired most was the way he mapped out everything that needed to be done in his head before he started.

My dad hated my admiration for Jan. He hated it more when he learned that I'd given them a song. He called them pirates and ordered me to stop hanging around with them.

"Jan Berry is just ripping off all your ideas," he snarled.

"Nonsense," I argued. "Jan and Dean are part of the same West Coast sound explosion that we are. There's nothing to worry about."

He didn't buy that, especially when "Surf City" zipped to Number One in July. It was my first chart-topper, but according to my dad the wrong guys were singing it. He wanted to wring my neck.

"You don't give away a number one song to the enemy!" he raged. "I don't believe you. You aren't satisfied that Jan and Dean steal your style. They have to steal your songs too. More troubling is that you even help them by singing backgrounds? Goddamnit, Brian, why don't you just give them your money, too?"

"Relax, Dad, there's plenty to go around," I said, though he was too insecure to believe me.

In May 1963 "Surfin' U.S.A." became the Beach Boys' first Top 10 single. The original pressing listed me as the sole writer, but once it became a hit Chuck Berry claimed the melody was his, an inadvertent copy of "Sweet Little Sixteen." There are plenty of musicologists who'd argue otherwise. Perhaps feeling pressured and wanting to avoid trouble, my dad gave Berry the copyright without ever informing me. But what I didn't learn for more than twenty-five years is that he also gave away my royalties for writing the lyrics, which clearly weren't Berry's.

Rather than enjoy the early success, I thirsted for more. In June, as "Shut Down" powered into twenty-third position, we hit the road in an overcrowded station wagon on a forty-date romp through the Midwest.

My dad, who stayed behind to run his machinery business, hired a road manager to maintain decorum, though he didn't let us pull out of the driveway without a few choice instructions. In pajamas and bathrobe, he stood beside the loaded car, already perfumed with the aroma of flatulence, and worked himself into a steamy lather:

"Brian, hold your bass and concentrate on the beat. Dennis, listen to Brian. Stay in time. All of you guys, I'm telling you, you better stay interested! If you don't play like the best goddamn group in the world, there's no way in hell you will ever be the best goddamn group in the world. Put out! Put out! Put out!"

The guys did, but not in the way my dad meant. Mike got laid in nearly every city, or so he said. David Marks contracted VD, and Carl lost his virginity to a hooker. In between endless fart jokes and discussions of the female anatomy, we also performed our asses off, playing one and two shows a night, perfect seasoning for a group whose ages ranged from Mike's twenty-two to Carl's sixteen.

While the other guys enjoyed the summer camp high jinks and freedom afforded by the road, I returned home hating it, a distaste that intensified until I later gave travel up altogether. My reason for not liking touring differed depending on whom I was talking to—my dad or a record company guy. The truth was I simply couldn't write on the road. I never learned how to write on an instrument other than a piano. And with ever-increasing pressure on me to turn out material at a rate of three LPs a year, I had to write.

It was a compulsion. If I didn't write, I didn't function properly. I was wracked with worry and anxiety. I didn't sleep. I suffered bad dreams. I was like a runner who refused to stop for fear he'd never regain his speed.

They didn't understand, but then I wasn't too good at explaining. The issue was too complex, personal, something I could only feel. I loved playing as a way of entertaining people, but I also played in order to separate myself from the world. As an abused child, I learned my playing kept my dad at bay. It drew people to me, made them like me, and at the same time I didn't have to deal with them.

But touring was part of the business. My dad greeted our return with news of several more bookings. Knowing how I felt about travel, I secretly called Al Jardine and told him I was having difficulty touring and wanted him back in the band. Al, who was between classes, had been suffering second thoughts about leaving the group ever since we had signed with Capitol. Now that we were a big success, he didn't need any persuading to dump dentistry for rock and roll.

I rushed him over copies of new material, including "Surfin' U.S.A.," "Shut Down," "Little Deuce Coupe," and "Surfer Girl," and specifics of the next trip. Carrying his guitar and bag, he met the group at the airport several days later. Poor guy. I'd failed to tell anyone, including my dad, that he was rejoining the band. I was too frightened they'd say no. As it turned out, no one minded, though my dad made one thing clear.

"I'm only paying him for playing live," he said. "No studio time. No royalties. Nothing."

Al hopped aboard, and it was a swell thing as the road turned rougher than I could handle. Playing on a bill with the Surfaris, a local surf band, I got beat up by one of the group members whom I reprimanded for dropping a bottle out a hotel room window. Before another show, Dennis shot Mike with a squirt gun, which caused Mike to take a swipe at him. Unfortunately, Mike missed and Dennis beat the crap out of him right before all of us walked onstage.

With my dad riding shotgun over the herd, the rules got more stringent. He had a system of fines none of us could ever remember: $50 for hanging out with girls, $100 for cussing, $100 for not setting up our equipment fast enough. I remember two shows, one in Sacramento and one in Michigan, where, in similar incidents, guys clubbed Dennis over the head with Coke bottles after catching their girlfriends flirting with him. That cost my brother $100 as well as blood.

David Marks paid perhaps the highest price. After one argument of several hundred he had with my dad, David threatened to quit. My dad was waiting for that. With Al back in the group, David was expendable. Holding back a grin, he asked David if he was sure he wanted to quit. He called my dad's bluff.

"Fine," Dad said. "That's what I've been waiting for. You got what you want."

The same nearly happened to Mike at the end of one roadtrip. My dad wanted him to help Carl set up his amp. Mike was the only one who didn't play an instrument; it made sense he should assist the rest of us.

"Carl's too fat to do it himself," my dad said.

"I don't want to help Carl," Mike protested. "That's his job. Singing's mine."

"Well, that'll cost you fifty bucks," my dad said.

"I'm not going to pay," Mike said.

"I don't want a hassle now," my dad replied. "But if you don't pay, you're out of the Beach Boys."

"The fuck I'm out of the Beach Boys," he scoffed. "The fuck I am."

"That's two hundred more for cussing," my dad bristled.

"The fuck it is!" Mike said.

Back home, my dad contemplated getting rid of Mike because he said fuck too many times. But someone at Capitol told him that was ridiculous, and Mike kept his job.

But I received more of my dad's abuse than anyone else. That, combined with the pressure to write new material, began taking a toll on me. I spent most days on the road locked in my hotel room, listening to the radio or trying to catch up on the sleep anxiety and uneasiness prevented me from getting at night. By showtime I was often wrapped so tight I had trouble leaving my room. In one northern California city, I guzzled an entire bottle of wine before going onstage. In another city, I sat on the bed tossing back so many drinks I just blew off the show.

My dad began eyeing me with a mix of distrust and disdain. On the same trip I remember being so exhausted from a lack of sleep that I couldn't unload my equipment from the truck. The other guys were all set up. My dad stalked up to me, our noses abutting, and demanded to know why the hell I was shirking my job. I apologized, but explained that I didn't have the strength or the desire to perform. Not that night anyway.

"The hell you won't," he yelled, and then with the sharpness of a spring, he backhanded me across the face. "The hell you don't feel like it."

I walked onstage that night with red eyes after having cried while he scrutinized me setting up my equipment and then was forced to listen to his criticisms from offstage. Look interested, Brian. Put out! Treble up! Pick up your bass! Try not to play like you want to be home with your mama. You're too lazy! Treble up! It was endless, torturous. And on those rare occasions when he wasn't standing beside the stage, I still heard him yelling at me. Treble up! Put out!

I just wanted off but felt like a prisoner, especially when I was trapped in the station wagon, crammed into the backseat with my arms wedged to my side, crippled by anxiety over not writing. On one such drive from Fresno to Bakersfield, my dad let me know he was tired of listening to me complain about leg cramps, not being able to sleep late, having to cart around equipment. We'd finished two shows in front of 7,000 kids. Riding in the front passenger seat while Mike drove, he turned around and told me to shut up.

"I've had it with your complaining," he said. "If you could play music half as good as you complain, then we'd really have something to talk about."

"I've been working hard," I said.

"You're working hard?" he laughed. "You call carrying your amps hard work? Playing bass is hard work? Let me tell you a little something about hard work. I lost my eye doing hard work on the assembly line. Acid burned the damn thing out. I'll show you what I've got in its place. How 'bout that?"

"No!" I screamed.

Without warning, my dad began whacking me across the head, swinging as hard as he could from his seat and telling me to shut my goddamn mouth. We had to shape up.

"All of you," he ranted, with a lifetime of resentment. "You're nothing but a bunch of little pussies, a bunch of pussies."

His slaps began turning into punches. This was a man who took pride in telling reporters, "I drove them up a wall. Being manager and a father can be pretty rough." Mike told him to knock it off, which distracted my dad from hitting me but turned his ire toward Mike.

"Shut up," my dad warned. "This is between me and Brian."

My brothers were laughing nervously, frightened they might be next. I was crying, tears matting my face, while trying to protect myself and pleading with my dad to stop. Mike finally pulled the car to the side of the road and shouted at my dad to stop. Seconds later, they were outside, trading punches. The three Wilson brothers watched this battle we could never fight ourselves from the car, horrified and secretly delighted that my dad might suffer his comeuppance.

The fight ended when Mike landed a punch to my dad's ample stomach. Dad doubled over, realizing the difference between an old man and a young man. After regaining his breath, my dad got back into the car and the group that would one day be known as America's Band drove the rest of the way in silence.

9

Marilyn, Diane, and Barbara

*I*n summer 1963, mine wasn't the biggest name in popular music, but it was the one on which the cognoscenti placed the greatest expectations. Based on what the Beach Boys had accomplished in only two albums, I was showered with accolades. But the surest benchmark was that my circle of acquaintances had rapidly expanded to include nearly everyone in the music business, or so it seemed, and they all told me how great I was.

However, none expected as much from me as I did. I felt a pressure for which there was no relief.

I spent hours confiding the ache to fifteen-year-old Marilyn Rovell, who listened with great sympathy. Over the past couple of months I had grown quite close to the Rovells, including the girls' parents, Irving and Mae. Their comfortable three-bedroom home was located in the predominantly Jewish Fairfax area of Los Angeles. The Rovells were the first Jews I knew well, and they introduced me to everything from matzo balls to mezuzahs.

The Rovells' warmth, generosity, and sense of family, symbolized by the pot of soup Mae seemed always to be simmering and her willingness to feed me at any time of the day or night, made me feel welcome. It was a feeling my family lacked. But it was Irving and Mae's dark-haired daughters who lured me back day after day. Unable to master my emotions, I fell in love with all three.

Initially, it was Diane, the oldest at seventeen, I liked most. She was the most effusive of the sisters and the one who most shared my taste in music. But the youngest, Barbara, also tugged at my heartstrings. She was the baby, the most illicit of my affections. As a gentle, fun-loving soul I was drawn to her as if she were a doll I wanted to cuddle.

But I ended up with Marilyn, because she had a maternal, caring, and giving side, which appealed to my sense of helplessness. I wanted nothing more than to be taken care of, to be mothered.

I moved into a little apartment in Hollywood, where I lived among my fears and worries. I often called Marilyn in the middle of the night, and I pleaded with her in a panicky voice to come over to my apartment. Please, please, please, I wailed, begged, cajoled. I told her I couldn't make it without her. At fifteen, she believed anything I said and, bundled up in a hat and gloves, climbed on her Honda motor scooter and drove over.

I didn't pursue a sexual intimacy as much as I did my desire for compassion and understanding. Throughout the night, I talked and Marilyn listened.

The Four Seasons' success had me concerned. Motown was coming on real strong. And then there was Phil Spector. I felt the chill of his long shadow. I didn't know how I was going to get the Beach Boys over the hump. Away from the blinding distraction of work and the studio rats who fed my ego during the day, I didn't think I could.

I aimed for the top, to sit on the throne, to eat the ambrosia served only to pop's gods. But the more I looked heavenward the more I felt dwarfed by Spector. I couldn't fathom his accomplishments, the unbelievable string of hits flying off his Philles label, including "He's a Rebel," "Then He Kissed Me," and "Da Doo Ron Ron." He had a Midas touch. In awe of his revolutionary Wall of Sound, I bought every single he put out and played them until the grooves wore out.

Although daunted and made insecure by Spector's genius, I was also inspired by it, and after listening to his records, I thought, by God, I'm going to try that too. But in order to do that I first had to acquire the same creative freedom that Spector commanded. He single-handedly changed the rules of record making; technically by overdubbing every instrument, which meant cramming as many musicians into a studio and getting as much sound on vinyl as possible, but also by elevating the producer's role, making his vision more integral to the process than the singer's talent.

I wanted the same power for myself. Heading into Capitol's studio that summer to make album number three, I recognized that the Beach

Boys were four-part harmony, but the vision belonged solely to me and I no longer wanted to siphon it through Nick Venet or my dad. I don't think anyone realized how rapidly I was growing or the magnitude of my intensity. All my thoughts concerned making the best goddamn records ever. How could I not take charge completely?

This wasn't the first time in the group's brief career that the producer's role was questioned. After *Surfin' Safari*, my dad and Nick Venet fought over which one of them discovered the group, each of them demanding the right to produce the next album; my dad relented. Then I got mad at Venet for not including me on the final mastering of the *Surfin' U.S.A.* LP, complained to my dad, and begged him to fire Nick for changing our sound. That led to more hassle.

Finally, Nick left, though Capitol still didn't buy the idea of me producing the Beach Boys. Artistic freedom in those days was a concept that ran contrary to the way the record industry functioned. I was a child to the company, too young at twenty-one to be granted so much autonomy and responsibility. But, Capitol, recognizing my value to the company as well as the fact that I had a pain-in-the-ass father, attempted to pacify me by letting me produce my pet project.

The group was called the Honeys, surf lingo for girlfriends, and the trio consisted of Marilyn and Diane Rovell and their cousin Ginger Blake, Gary Usher's old girlfriend. They were all great singers. Ginger had sung background on a few records and Marilyn and Diane had won prizes from numerous talent shows. Wanting nothing more than to be famous, the girls had hatched the idea of an all-girl surf group the previous Thanksgiving and I'd volunteered to produce.

I already had one production credit outside the Beach Boys. In September 1962 I produced two songs, "Revolution" and "Number One," for a black woman named Betty Everett. Released on tiny Dot Records as Rachel and the Revolvers, a background chorus consisting of me, Carl, and Gary Usher, the record disappeared quickly, becoming a footnote on my discography. But it whetted my appetite to produce more.

With the Honeys, I saw myself in the same role as Spector was with the Crystals and, before the summer was out, the Ronettes. I hired a bunch of Spector's studio musicians—the Wrecking Crew as they were known—including guitarist Glen Campbell, pianist Leon Russell, and drummer Hal Blaine. Between May and December 1963, the Honeys issued three singles, including "Surfin' Down the Swanee," a reworking of the Stephen Foster classic, "Shoot the Curl," "Pray for Surf," and "From

Jimmy with Tears." Nothing happened to any of them, and the Honeys were put on the back burner.

By then, however, my battle to produce the Beach Boys' third album was history, the victory mine. Soon after Nick Venet departed the scene, my dad and I had lunch with another producer Capitol wanted us to consider. Before any food was served, my dad told the man he didn't think it was going to work out. Asked why, since not a word had been discussed yet, my dad explained that the Beach Boys were a family thing. He knew how to get the best sound from his boys and how to mix the songs. It was silly to think anyone else could do the job better.

The guy got red-faced and left the table. I got sick to my stomach. Listening to my dad, I realized that with Nick Venet out as producer, my dad clearly planned to take over the job himself. That meant even more power struggles impeding my efforts. I didn't know what was going to happen.

At any rate, I told my dad I didn't think Capitol's studio had an appropriate sound for making rock and roll records. I wanted to record at Western Studios, which I thought had a better bass frequency and overall sound; I explained I could get a ballsier sound at Western. The records would sound better and do better because of it.

The story my dad told Capitol was slightly different from what we'd discussed. He explained that he and I wanted to be left alone to make hit records, which the Capitol execs didn't believe. Nor did they want to pay for outside studio time when they had studios right in their own building. But after some tense negotiations, my dad struck a deal. The Beach Boys would make a couple of records at Western, then let the power brokers at Capitol listen. If they approved, we'd continue at Western.

We set up at Western in Studio 3. I was officially listed as producer, though my dad sat at the board next to Western's engineer Chuck Britz and issued orders. We worked on four-track, recording in mono. The vocals were done live, one at a time, then overdubbed, each of us singing into old-fashioned tube U-47 microphones as we stood in a single-file line. In the booth, there might be four or five instruments plugged directly into the board.

It was crude by today's seventy-eight-track, high-tech standards, but I displayed a knack for making the instantaneous decisions four-track recording required, and by the middle of summer my dad and I played a handful of Capitol executives the two songs that determined whether or not we could stay at Western: "Surfer Girl" and "Little Deuce Coupe." The verdict was exactly the one I wanted to hear.

"Work at Western," Voyle Gilmore said. "It's no problem. Not if your songs continue to sound like those two."

With unmatched intensity I pushed myself and everyone else too. Sessions on the *Surfer Girl* album lasted nine and ten hours, unheard-of periods of time. But exercising an authority I hadn't enjoyed previously, I let perfectionism born out of my desperate need to be validated and loved guide me. My reputation as a tyrant spread fast, but so did word I was someone who didn't quit until a song was the best it could possibly be. That meant perfect.

Working with great material, I produced the Beach Boys' first really good album. I thought "Surfer Girl," with its Paris Sisters tenderness, was one of the sweetest little ballads anyone had ever recorded, especially the intro. "In My Room" sounded as comforting as the place where it was written. Having been perfected onstage "Little Deuce Coupe" smoked, and we got a lucky break the way "Catch a Wave" turned out.

The album, the group's second of 1963, was delivered to the record company in July, at which time *Surfin' U.S.A.*, the previous LP, was holding at number two. In September, the *Surfer Girl* album came out; a month later, it was number seven, powered by three Top 30 singles. As if that wasn't a frenzied enough pace, I had by that time already finished writing, producing, and mastering the *Little Deuce Coupe* LP, the band's fourth overall and the third of 1963. Released in November, it shows Capitol's bid to squeeze every note of music from me and the Beach Boys before what they perceived as the surf and car phenomenon disappeared. There was no rest. It was always more, more, more.

It's hard to describe how accelerated time was in those days. Entire months were seemingly compressed into a single afternoon. Everything was new, exciting, intimidating, and frightening. Within the span of a few months, I'd gone from a junior-college freshman to boy wonder rock star, moved out of my parents' house, moved out of my first apartment into my second, broken up with one girlfriend and started a new relationship with a girl whose older and younger sisters also turned me on, toured the country, and finished writing and producing three albums, including more than half a dozen hit singles.

But as easy as it was for me to function in Studio 3 it was the opposite when I drove out of the Western parking lot. Standing on top of the music world, a visionary at twenty-one, I was lost once I stepped outside its narrow parameters. I had difficulty sleeping at night; if I did drop off, it was often into a nightmarish world in which my mind tossed and turned, a stormy sea of stress and fears, ideas and pressures. The demons were lining up, waiting for me.

With my mind unable to rest, constantly occupied with doing better! better! better! I looked for an anchor, gravitating toward the only place of stability I knew, the Rovells'. A sixth sense took me there; I was in a survivalist mode. I spent nights on the sofa, showing up after I left the studio, often in the weest hours of night. No matter what the hour, Mae seemed prepared to feed me a nosh and both she and Irving wanted to sit at the table and kibitz.

I became such a permanent fixture of the household that the Rovells' became a semiofficial Beach Boys clubhouse. Often, dozens of kids in their dragsters gathered out front, hoping to catch sight of a Beach Boy. Next to me, Carl hung out at the house most frequently; Al occasionally did, and Mike almost never did. Dennis was the only one Mae and Irving didn't cotton to. He offended them once by bragging about how much money we were making and then, to prove it, ripping up a dollar bill.

Irving and Mae were aghast. He worked two jobs and she saved the loose change we accidentally left in sofa cushions and on counters. Ours were two different worlds. Irving and Mae encouraged my involvement with their girls. After a couple of months of my sleeping on the sofa, Mae offered me one of the two beds in the back bedroom. Marilyn and Barbara doubled up in the other.

It was an odd arrangement, but both Irving and Mae assumed I liked Diane best, since she and I still spent the most time together talking. Deep down I still harbored feelings for cute little Barbara, though I continually reminded myself she was too young. Which left Marilyn, the most solicitous of the sisters, the most practical, the most willing to mother me. Marilyn had a warmth the others didn't, and when my soul needed unburdening I sought her out.

"Don't worry, baby," she cooed. "Everything will work out."

I wanted to believe her, but at night I watched the two girls nestled in bed together and let my mind run wild, confused, and obsessed. I didn't know what to do, what to think. More than anything I wanted to be cared for, which made it easy for me to confuse Marilyn's willingness to nurture, tend to, and comfort me as real, true love.

We went slowly. The first time we were alone in the bedroom I leaned close and put my cheek next to hers. I felt her skin flush. Some time later Marilyn and I were kissing. She may not have been the most beautiful girl

I'd ever seen, but that didn't matter. I imagined Marilyn as an angel in search of wings; I was the wings. We were meant to be together, I told myself, destined to fly above all others.

The fable was romantic, convenient to believe in, though I'm still not certain whether what I felt for Marilyn was a normal adult love or a dire need to be cared for. It didn't matter. Stifling my feelings for Barbara and Diane, I began spending what little free time I had with Marilyn, filling her with my innermost dreams and fears.

One afternoon we were driving around in my new aquamarine Grand Prix when the DJ spun a brand-new Phil Spector–produced platter, the Ronettes singing "Be My Baby." I had to pull over.

"Oh my God!" I exclaimed. "This is great! It's the best song I've ever heard!"

Marilyn didn't know what to make of me. I really lost my head during the chorus. Listening intently, I was amazed by what I heard. The melody line remained constant, but the three chords kept changing around it. I started slapping the steering wheel, it was so unbelievable. Why hadn't I ever thought of something like that? Would I ever be able to think of something similar?

"What'd you think?" Marilyn asked when it finished.

"It blew my mind, that's what I thought," I said. "I mean, Holy shit! I can't do that. Not that great. Not ever."

"Don't worry, baby," she said, rubbing my neck. "You will. You'll do something that great."

I didn't know if any amount of encouragement could convince me otherwise. But that was the first stage of the cycle I ordinarily went through before writing: extreme depression, the feeling of being challenged, then the terror of possibly not being able to meet that challenge, and finally the inspiration that ultimately saved me. The rest was perspiration and perfectionism, plus the desire to prove to everyone, including myself, that I was competitive with the best.

I immediately bought ten copies of "Be My Baby" and played them incessantly. I learned every note, every sound, the pulse of every groove. Finally I called lyricist Roger Christian and told him I had an idea. He met me one afternoon at my parents' house, where, in one of our last collaborations, we wrote a lush ballad whose title and chorus came directly from Marilyn's comforting words, "Don't Worry, Baby." I knew the song was a smash before we finished writing it.

"I got an idea," I said. "Let's give it to Phil Spector and he can do it as a follow-up to 'Be My Baby.' "

I was second-guessing myself; I didn't really mean it and waited for Roger to talk me out of it, hoping he would.

"You're sure?" he asked. "It's a damn good song, Brian, and you might regret it."

"Okay, I'll keep it," I said, my voice rising to the occasion. "I bet I can do this song with the Beach Boys as good as Phil Spector."

Maybe better.

10

Meet the Beatles

*I*n the fall of 1963, Phil Spector asked me to Gold Star to watch a
session for his famous Christmas album. Spector and I had met
several times before and each encounter was decidedly odd.

The first time I was in Lou Adler's office, waiting to see Jan and Dean,
Spector walked in unexpectedly. I didn't know what to say. He was short
and scrawny, much less of a physical presence than I imagined by listening
to his immense Wall of Sound. Scared to speak, I told him I thought he
was a genius. He said thank you. Neither one of us looked the other in the
eye.

The next time I came into contact with Spector I was laying tracks for
"Be True to Your School" at Gold Star Studios, where he recorded in the
four-chamber Studio A. I was experimenting with the echo. In the middle
of a session, the door suddenly sprang open. Startled, I didn't see anyone
at first. Then a head emerged. Black hair, sunglasses, a thin face, and a
serious look. Spector.

"I hear everything," he snickered.

Then he darted out of sight and the door slammed. If he was playing
a head game with me, he was successful. I was unnerved and spent days
trying to figure out what he meant with that statement. A couple of days
later I peeked into Studio A, where he was recording. It was jammed with
musicians, more than I'd ever seen in a studio at the same time. After

listening several times to a playback, he left the room but stopped short when he saw me.

"Brian?" he said surprised.

Again I found myself tongue-tied.

"I think 'Be My Baby' is the greatest record I've ever heard," I blurted out.

He smiled, then without saying a word began walking out the door. In the hallway he halted as if stopped by a second thought, then turned around and looked at me.

"I think 'Then He Kissed Me' is better," he said, then swung around again and went on his way.

In the fall of 1963, Spector invited me to watch a session for his famous Christmas album. Unsure of what to expect from Spector's curious invitation, I went anyway. Marilyn had given me a pep talk beforehand, explaining that Spector probably admired me as much as I admired him. I didn't believe her. No one compared to Spector.

It didn't look like Christmas when I poked my head into the studio, though Spector had the presence of Santa Clause and everyone else crowded around in the role of his helpers. Singers Darlene Love and Ronnie Spector were on either side of the producer, who was sitting behind the board, brooding. A score of musicians, singers, and assistants floated through the studio. The place teemed with restless activity as this small army of performers waited for Spector to make a decision.

After some time, he decided to do another take on Ronnie's version of "Santa Claus Is Coming to Town." He listened to several takes, then shook his head and ordered up another song. He didn't like the first take of that one either. Then he walked up to me, looking like I'd understand.

"Brian," he said with his chin resting in his folded hands, "why don't you go over to the piano there?"

"Naw, I'm just watching," I said.

Spector tensed. Nobody, I realized, disobeyed or failed to do what he said. Leon Russell, who had been playing piano, sipped on a cup of coffee and stared at me. I didn't like being the center of attention.

"Like I said," he repeated a moment later, "why don't you go over to the piano and see if you can read the chord sheet for this song?"

I tried. But I knew I wasn't good at reading music, and that weakness was soon obvious to everyone. After the fourth take, Spector let me quit. Maybe next time, he offered. Rather than feeling hurt, I was relieved. I wanted to watch, and until late that night I studied Spector work in the studio, noticing that like me he was 100 percent hung up on creating an absolutely perfect song.

The other similarity, which I failed to notice, and didn't recognize until many years later, was that his aberrant personality was perhaps his best tool in making records, allowing him to manipulate people into doing exactly what he wanted. He didn't bend to the world; it bent for him. Like me, the moment he was no longer capable of pulling that stunt off, Spector bowed out of the music scene.

In fall 1963, the Beach Boys' balance wheel turned so that I found myself standing all alone at the ledge of a creative precipice. Dennis was still more interested in his skyrocketing popularity with girls than music. Carl, at seventeen, played good guitar but couldn't help me in the songwriting department. Al kept pretty much to himself. That left Mike Love and me to run the Beach Boys.

We were less in synch than ever before, though we still had our moments. In November, the day after John F. Kennedy was assassinated, Mike and I got together and wrote "The Warmth of the Sun," a plaintive, melancholy ballad that expressed our sentiments, beginning, "What good is the dawn that grows into the day? The sunset at night or living this way?" In December we wrote and recorded "Keep an Eye on Summer" and "Fun, Fun, Fun," a musical joyride that both of us thought was one of the best songs the band had put on tape.

Mike thought about how much money he was going to make if the song became a hit. Money didn't even enter my thinking process. I was only concerned whether or not KFWB radio station would play it and whether it would chart.

I saw the chance to grab the golden ring and, though I had to reach through barbed wire and booby traps to snag it, I thought of nothing except going for it. I felt as if I were stuck on a treadmill, doing everything I could to compete and to hold myself together. It was hard. I huffed and puffed. I battled fear and spiraling expectations. The demands were endless. I wasn't able to get any rest.

At night, I started to hear voices in my sleep. They weren't anything I could make out, but they sounded to me like screams. Loud, terrifying screams that darted past me like goblins in a haunted house. I used to lie in bed, waiting to return to the studio. The only way I kept the screams at bay and kept myself together was to work.

Work, work, work.

Marilyn, her folks, and sisters used to comfort me by saying I was merely fatigued. Too stressed. There was nothing to worry about. The Beach Boys' last two albums had both gone straight into the Top 10; in December "Be True to Your School" went to number six. I just needed rest.

"But what if I'm going mad?" I asked Marilyn.

She laughed and ushered me into the bedroom, where she pulled back the covers and instructed me to take a nap.

"You're not going mad," she said.

Barbara came in, stood next to Marilyn, and covered me up. I smiled at her. She was so damn cute. I asked for a small kiss on the cheek. She gave it to me and giggled. I told Barbara her kiss made me feel better, but it confused me even more. I loved Marilyn, I loved Barbara, I loved Diane. I had no answers to the questions I asked myself.

In January 1964 the Beach Boys flew to Australia in our first overseas tour. I had mixed feelings. As a vacation it made sense, but I wondered how I was going to keep it together while not being able to write. The Beach Boys were so hot, and I didn't want the flame to subside. I went with a reluctance I didn't mention to anyone and spent a few days taking in some sights. I noticed the girls didn't shave their legs, that the rooftops were all an orange-red color, that the beaches were magnificent.

But if we weren't performing or promoting, I was apt to be locked up in my hotel room. The other guys were intent on raising hell, roaming the cities, and taking advantage of a freedom they didn't have at home. I just wanted to be left alone.

I remember jumping up from my bed and racing down the hallway of one hotel after hearing Mike's loud voice calling us to his room.

"You've gotta see this!" he hollered from the open doorway.

Me, Dennis, Carl, and Al arrived simultaneously and found Mike wearing only a white bath towel. He was incredulous about something and wanted to share his discovery. Leading us into the bathroom, he pointed to the toilet. Carl and Al turned away, grossed out. Dennis and I were amazed.

"Fourteen inches!" Mike erupted in laughter. "I think it might be the world's largest turd!"

By then Mike and I were spending less time with each other than previously. He thought I was strange, while I was put off and frustrated by his single-minded interests in girls and money. Ours was the difference between church and state, art and commerce. As a result, I palled around in Australia with Al, who went with me one afternoon on a hike atop a hill that overlooked Sydney's beautiful harbor.

Looking down on the landscape and the boats and the ocean in the background, we played a tape of our next single, "Fun, Fun, Fun." After it finished playing, I decided that the song, contrary to my earlier opinion, wasn't happening. Al wanted to know in what way. I couldn't describe what was wrong, but something bothered me so much that Al had to spend several hours talking me out of calling Capitol and insisting they stop pressing the record. Something snapped in me; I was in the grip of an emotion that was inconsolable.

"You know, it's not fair," I said.

"What's not fair?" Al asked.

"It's hell for me to have to live up to my name," I explained. "I wish I was already there, over the hump and proven."

"But you are, Brian," he said. "Everybody loves the songs you write. They think you're the greatest."

"Really?" I asked.

"I'm not shittin' you," he said.

"But I just don't like what I have to go through in life," I said. "You know what I mean?"

"No," Al said, shaking his head

A week later, we were in Auckland, New Zealand, when I heard that a single by a new group had come out back home and was knocking everyone on their ass. The group was the Beatles, the song was "I Want to Hold Your Hand." It slingshotted straight to Number One, selling half a million copies in ten days. I desperately wanted to hear for myself what the fuss was about, and along with the rest of the guys I found a radio station that would play us the song and rushed over.

"The Beatles?" Mike puzzled. "What the hell?"

"I don't get it," Dennis said.

"I think they're a fad," Al added after the song finished. "The music is lightweight."

"Yeah, the song's real simple," I said. "Real simple. But it's catchy. There's something to it."

We flew back home several days later and began work on our next album, though none of us except me suspected that the ground rules had suddenly been transformed by those four mop-topped guys from Liverpool.

*   *   *

It was February 9, 1964. Like most Americans between the age of six and sixty, I was getting set to spend my Sunday evening watching television. "The Ed Sullivan Show" to be exact. The Beatles were going to be on. Following a large dinner at the Rovells', I was entertaining everyone with two new songs I'd written on their family upright, "I Get Around" and "Wendy," but the moment the show started I discontinued playing. I didn't want to miss one second of this much anticipated spectacle.

I was curious, but I also found the Beatles intimidating. My brother Carl, for God's sake, had pictures of John, Paul, George, and Ringo hanging in his bedroom, prompting my dad to call him "the traitor." That was lighthearted compared to the frenzied sales of "I Want to Hold Your Hand"—500,000 copies in less than a week! That easily erased the previous sales record, set by the Beach Boys' "Surfin' U.S.A." Worse, it dwarfed the release of "Fun, Fun, Fun."

"Oh my God, look at that," I said. "Look at those guys. I can't believe what a scream scene it is."

Indeed, with the audience out of control, screaming in hysterics, I barely heard a thing the Beatles played. However, what I saw impressed the hell out of me. They looked sharp, especially compared to the silly, juvenile striped shirts and white pants the Beach Boys wore onstage. I suddenly felt unhip, as if we looked more like golf caddies than rock and roll stars.

As Marilyn, Diane, and Barbara sat beside me and went as nuts over John, Paul, George, and Ringo as the in-studio audience, I was totally unsettled by what I'd seen. In the final weeks of finishing a new Beach Boys' LP, *Shut Down Volume 2,* I was concerned about the competition. I panicked that we were suddenly outdated. The next day I met Mike at a coffee shop to discuss what we'd seen.

"Did you see the Beatles last night?" I asked.

He did and was equally concerned. Both of us saw them as a threat, but we differed on what action to take.

"I want to toss the album," I said. "We'll start over and put out better songs."

"The songs are fine, Brian," Mike responded. "They fit into the Beach Boys' formula."

"That's the point," I argued. "We've got to grow, go beyond the formula. It's stupid not to."

"But, Brian, if you throw away the album, you're throwing away money in the bank," Mike said. "The songs have worked so far. They'll keep on working as long as we don't screw with the formula."

"You don't get it, do you, Mike?" I said, disgusted.

Against the way I thought, I decided to finish the album, but compulsive listening to *Meet the Beatles,* the Fab Four's debut album, caused me to worry that we wouldn't be breaking any new ground. *Shut Down Volume 2,* released in March, reached number thirteen on the album charts, but there was a disturbing sign indicating the changing landscape of pop music. "Fun, Fun, Fun," though a number five single, couldn't penetrate any higher. Why? The first four spots were occupied by the Beatles.

I was depressed, really low. Hearing really great material by other groups made me feel as small as the dot over an i. There was just one way to get over that depression. I had to create a new song. I had to look beyond what I'd already done, beyond the horizon, and find something new and better than anything I'd done before. I had to overcome my feeling of inferiority.

In March, I began an intensely personal writing streak, one that consumed every ounce of energy and thought. The songs welled up from the wound deep inside me. I played the guys "I Get Around," "All Summer Long," "Wendy," "Girls on the Beach," "Don't Back Down," and was given an enthusiastic review, except from Mike. Complaining that I wasn't writing with him anymore, he made a strong pitch to contribute lyrics. But it wasn't a good time for me.

"I'm so hot on these lyrics I've got I really don't want to work with anyone right now," I explained. "It's nothing personal."

"But we always wrote together, Brian," he said. "I don't think it's fair you do it all."

"I can't help it," I apologized. "I'm not trying to hurt your feelings, but I'm in such a groove that I don't want to stop. We'll get together again. Keep cool about it."

By the end of March I was putting the boys through arduous stints in the studio, expecting them to equal my effort. The pressure was greater than any of us had ever felt. Our relationships were tested. No one wanted to be the one to cave in. It was like playing a game of chicken. We were laying down the tracks to "I Get Around," which had grown from the simple, catchy melody I first played on the Rovells' piano to a complicated piece of music with alternating rhythms, car sounds, and Spectorlike production.

Aside from the myriad niggling problems that only I seemed to hear, there was one overriding impediment to our getting the song right—my dad. He created as much pressure and tension as the record company. The previous December, on his own, my dad canceled a "Fun, Fun, Fun" recording session I had scheduled. When the engineer, Chuck Britz, told me what my dad had done, I exploded. I was the producer, after all.

Racing from Hollywood to Hawthorne, I burst into my dad's house and found him on his bed, smoking a pipe and talking to his pet mynah bird.

"What the hell is going on?" I demanded. "What are you doing, canceling a session?"

"It wasn't ready," he said without looking up. "The song is weak. Too weak to waste your time and my money recording it. Do you know what they're billing you for studio time?"

"No, and I don't care," I fumed. "I think you're wrong, and I'm recording it."

My dad followed that scene up in Australia, where his dictatorial demeanor and constant fining pissed everyone off. He tried imposing prison-like rules on free men. It seemed we had to get permission just to breathe. After we returned, I played him rough cuts of "Wendy" and "I Get Around." He thought they were weak. During the sessions for "I Get Around," he sat beside Chuck Britz with a scowl on his face. It was intimidating and unnerving.

The music was good but something wasn't right, something was missing. That we all agreed. On a night when nothing was sounding good, I called a break and took the guys to dinner at Denny's. Ordinarily, when the waitress brought our food, I inhaled mine before anyone else had even grasped his fork, and then I exhorted, "Okay, back to the studio." This time, though, dinner turned into a band meeting.

"Something has to give," Mike said. "The problem is Murry. He's getting in the way of our productivity."

Mike's comments received no argument from anyone seated around the table. All of us felt the same, but I think Dennis, Carl, and I needed someone else to fire the first volley. Then it was open season. Everyone agreed my dad had done a good job in promoting us when the band was starting out. He called radio stations and fought the early battles. But he'd outlived his usefulness, turned negative. He offered more criticism than advice.

"He has a goddamn opinion about everything," Dennis chimed in. "From where we shit to who we fuck."

"Like I said," Mike added, "something has to give."

The only problem was how to sever the ties. The five of us debated that on the way back to the studio and for days afterward. Finally, Mike wrote a letter, informing him that he was fired. My dad ignored it and continued showing up as if nothing had changed. His voice seemed to punctuate every take; his comments were increasingly aimed at me.

"I don't like it, Brian," he said at one point. "Your arrangement stinks."

"I disagree," I argued. "I like it."

We finally had a version we liked, but when it came time to mix the song, my dad was wrapped around me tighter than my sweater. He couldn't control himself, couldn't sit back and let me do the work I was supposed to do. I tried ignoring his suggestions, which was like putting a match to explosives. Soon, his finger was jabbing me in the chest.

"Those guitars aren't loud enough. They don't have any drive."

"But I like it this way," I said. "I'm the producer now, and I don't want you telling me what to do."

My dad gave me a shove.

"Remember who you're talking to," he said.

"I know who I'm talking to," I snapped. "Tell me what you have done that makes you such an authority."

The other guys were watching in silence. They looked like wax figures, frozen in disbelief.

"I made this goddamn group," my dad bellowed. "I put you on the map. Without me, you'd be nothing. Zip. Nothing."

"Gee, I don't see it that way," I bristled. "If you want to know the truth, I think you're a jealous old man."

"Jealous of what?" my dad laughed sarcastically. "My son the loser? My son who—"

Something in me snapped. I couldn't take any more of his abuse. I wouldn't. Reacting with animal instinct, I jumped out of my chair and grabbed my dad by the shirt. I thought briefly about throwing a punch. I envisioned myself really laying him out. Instead, I shoved him. It was a hard enough shove so that he lost his balance and went stumbling backwards a step or two. Time seemed to freeze. Then, righting himself, my dad shot me the same kind of dark, hateful look he wore when I was a child and he had beaten me with a two-by-four. But this time I was the bigger, stronger one, and I stood my ground.

"What the hell?" he said.

"You're fired," I screamed. "Dad, you're fired. You're fired as manager of the Beach Boys."

He stood there, frozen, and looked as if I had thrown the punch that I restrained myself from doing. He was stunned, silent, confused, the picture of an old man who had lost his sense of time and place. Humiliated, he turned and walked out of the studio. I sat down at the board and drew a deep breath. I didn't want to hurt him, I just didn't want him getting in my way.

Then I turned to Chuck Britz and the guys.

"Let's get back to work."

My father drove home, lapsed into a severe depression, and took to his bed for more than a month. We didn't speak the duration of that time, but the next time I saw him I apologized for what happened.

"I just wanted the song to sound perfect," I explained.

But something had changed—forever.

Then my parents separated. My father had been unfaithful.

11

All Summer Long

*I*t wasn't the way a twenty-two-year-old should act. My train of thought drifted. I lost track in the midst of conversations. I counted things. I obsessed over tiny details, the number of tiles in a floor, dots in the ceiling, peas on a plate. I cried easily. I laughed too loud. I was always trying to compensate, to react the way I thought people wanted me to, since I was losing perspective on how I should act normally. But there was an easy rationale.

Oh, that's Brian acting like Brian.

It became a familiar refrain.

In early May, Spector called me at Western Studios. Some weeks earlier, I'd given him the demo to the song "Don't Hurt My Little Sister," which I'd written especially for him to produce and Darlene Love to sing. I'd been eagerly waiting for his response. Spector said he was at the Château Marmont, a Hollywood hotel famous for being a hideout for celebrities.

I went up that evening and Spector answered the door wearing pants and no shirt. Our conversation was friendly but very strained. There was too much ego between us. It might've been comforting to have had a friend of Spector's position and talent, someone who might've been able to understand me and what I was going through. But unfortunately he was as screwed up in his own way as I was in mine.

It's impossible to say how he would've responded if I'd told him the pressure was driving me crazy. No one else took me seriously. He probably would've applauded me for the fight I'd had with my dad, but I also might've scared the hell out of him if I'd confessed that my parents' recent separation—my mom finally tiring of my dad's well-known infidelity—left me feeling like a ship whose anchor had disappeared.

Instead, I kept the talk to something—perhaps the only thing—both Spector and I understood and were comfortable discussing, music. I asked this short, shirtless man with stringy hair if he had heard the Beach Boys' latest single, "I Get Around."

"Yeah," Spector nodded.

"What do you think about it?" I asked.

"I think it's dumb enough to do pretty good," he said. "Now why don't we play the piano for a bit?"

Spector motioned to the baby grand piano in the center of his suite, and I sat at the bench. Pulling up a chair, he instructed me to play "Don't Hurt My Little Sister." Then he suggested a few changes. I continued playing, incorporating the changes. After fifteen minutes, Spector got up from his chair, walked behind me, and said, "That's it. Keep playing that riff. Don't stop," and started singing. That lasted fifteen minutes.

"I think that's enough," he said. "I'll get an arrangement for it and see you at the studio."

Then Spector disappeared into his bedroom, the door slamming shut. Not even a good-bye or thanks. I walked out, wondering what was up. Several days later, though, I was notified of the session and showed up at Gold Star. For half a day, I watched Darlene Love stand in the vocal booth while Spector tinkered with every take. He asked me to try playing the piano on one take but didn't like it. Nothing pleased him, and suddenly he left to make a phone call.

It was his psychiatrist in New York. He yelled, gestured, and after about ten minutes he hung up and stalked out of the studio. One of his assistants told everyone the session was over and to go home. That was that!

So I kept the song, and a year later the Beach Boys recorded "Don't Hurt My Little Sister" for *The Beach Boys Today!* album. Spector eventually cut the song too, though his version, performed by the Blossoms, another one of his groups, was totally revamped and retitled "Things Are Changing (For the Better)." Oddly, the song was released as an instrumental on a public service record for equal opportunity employment.

In early July 1964, the *All Summer Long* album was released. I finally felt the Beach Boys had put out an LP that was competitive with Spector and the Beatles. The vocals were tight, the production was sharper and more inventive than anything we'd done previously. We were in a higher harmonic place and generally more exciting musically. On July 4, "I Get Around" became the first Beach Boys song to hit Number One. It stayed there for two weeks.

I was overjoyed, though the elation was short-lived as the strain of what to do next approached a dangerous point. I flinched and twitched noticeably. I stared at objects for unusually long periods of time, until I zoned out. People made me nervous, and I avoided contact with them. I heard voices—distracting, disturbing sounds that reminded me of my father's abusive criticisms. None of this was new. But now it was occurring with a frequency that should've been alarming to the people around me.

So was that refrain: Oh, that's just Brian being Brian.

Although I was paying a heavy toll for my ability to write songs people loved, by fall 1964, the Beach Boys were soaring and no one concerned themselves with my well-being. The *All Summer Long* LP was number four; we had several songs still on the charts; then yet another song, "When I Grow Up (To Be A Man)," was released in September and climbed steadily up to ninth place. I felt as if we were rock and roll's version of Cassius Clay, invincible, cocky, and distinctly American by the time we followed the Beatles on "The Ed Sullivan Show." Before going on, I urged the guys to kick ass.

"How'd we do against the Beatles?" I asked Marilyn by phone when we got back to our hotel.

"You were great," she said. "I could hardly hear you over all the screaming."

"Yeah," I chuckled. "I guess we showed 'em."

Returning home, my band mates began taking advantage of three years' worth of success. Mike filed for divorce, Carl and Al bought houses, and Dennis continued his playboy habits. Their heads soared. Looking ahead to a twenty-three-day tour of Europe, Mike and Dennis were more concerned about their social lives than the album that was due the first part of 1965, while I fretted about it day and night.

At one session, I berated all four of them for not caring as much as I did about making great music, then stormed out of the studio in a fit. The pressure was getting to me. But it was more than just writing and producing. My dad was playing a major head game with me. Over the past couple of months, he had decided to go after my 50 percent of income from the Sea of Tunes Publishing Company.

Toward the end of 1964, he demanded sole ownership of Sea of Tunes. Claiming I'd promised it to him the day the company was formed, he resorted to psychological torture, withholding my latest songwriter royalties, which were then a considerable $280,000.

It was like the movie *Gaslight*. Knowing the pressure I was under and exactly how to take advantage of me, my dad telephoned nightly, reminding me that I had promised to give him my half of the publishing income. I denied ever having made a promise like that. But he insisted I had, then explained how I'd still own the copyrights to the songs and could even pull them out of Sea of Tunes whenever I wanted.

"Brian, you've done a remarkable job in your writing and arrangements," he said. "We're all very proud of your leadership. But you should really try to temper your impatience with your brothers and those who don't have the same talent. Also, you need to keep your promises to your father."

"I didn't make any promises," I said. "Why do you do this to me?"

"Brian, I'm your father," he said. "I'm just trying to keep you on the straight and narrow. This is a business. I'm entitled. I've been your father all your life. I'm not doing anything that's unfair."

After months of daily calls, I finally relented and gave him 100 percent of the income from Sea of Tunes. Beaten and overstressed, I just wanted him off my back.

Straining under the pressure, I told everyone I needed to be excused from the European tour. I wanted to stay home and write, something I couldn't do on the road. I didn't get any sympathy, though. At the airport, Mike lectured me about responsibility. He called me a pussy. Considering everything I did in the studio, I shouldn't have felt guilty, but I did.

Grudgingly, I traveled to Europe, where I spent most of the time in bed or talking to Earl Leaf, the editor of *Teen Scene,* a Capitol Records Publication. Earl, a fun-loving beatnik, accompanied us on most of our early trips.

At the shows, I heard about everyone's adventures. Dennis and Mike each dropped more than a grand apiece in brothels. Mike even got beat up one night and claimed an angry proprietor stuck a gun in his face. Al and Carl, more sedate, ate up local museums and pastries respectively. Toward the end I finally loosened up. In Copenhagen, my luggage was stolen and I spent a thousand dollars on new clothes.

Otherwise, I agonized over not having written any new songs in nearly a month. One night Dennis, Carl, and I were drunkenly walking through the red-light district in Amsterdam, heading for a restaurant while Dennis tried talking me into sampling one of the local girls. I wasn't interested; I wanted to talk music. Ducking into a smoky, music-filled restaurant, where patrons were either strung out on opium or dancing on tabletops, I spied a piano, which I tried to play.

No sooner did I start than the barkeep jumped all over me, yanking me off the bench. I gave him a push and began playing anyway. A struggle ensued. The piano bench was knocked over, punches were exchanged, and before I knew it Carl and Dennis were dragging me out the front door and hustling me back to the hotel.

I spent the next several days calling Marilyn, complaining about being frustrated, depressed, frantic. I started drinking a lot. I'd always been a guy who liked a few beers, but I never drank to excess. Suddenly, the booze seemed to relieve the stress, and I drank heavily. Day and night. By the time we hit Munich, I was intoxicated all the time, unable to perform and growing edgier every hour. The guys thought I was finally shedding my nerd's skin and becoming one of them.

One night all of us went to a beer hall. The outing started off as fun. After downing a few, Dennis, Carl, and Mike hit the dance floor. I pulled Earl Leaf to the side. He saw I was crying and asked what was bothering me.

"I'm broken up about my mom," I said. "My mom and dad. Both of 'em."

"What about them?" he asked.

"I just can't stand to think about all the bad things they did to me," I cried.

Earl put his arm around my shoulder and comforted me. He told me not to worry while I blabbered on about various atrocities I'd suffered, none of which I'm sure made sense to him.

"Do you know what?" I said. "I wish I was still a kid, like when I was in my crib and my mom used to bring me soft-boiled eggs. That would always calm me down. Her delicious soft-boiled eggs."

It was a plea for help, but it came across as drunken blather, just old Brian being overdramatic. Still, I repeated myself, droning on and on about how great both of my parents were. It was pure fantasy, the opposite of how I felt. I managed to drape my arms around Carl and Dennis, who listened to me alternating between sobs and laughter and saw I wasn't joking.

"Are you okay?" Carl asked. "Brian, are you okay?"

"No, I'm completely fucked up," I cried. "I'm so fucked up, and it's all Dad's fault."

"You aren't all fucked up, Brian," Dennis comforted in the taxi that took us back to the hotel. "You're gonna be fine. You've just had too much to drink. You'll go to sleep and be fine in the morning."

"I'm never going to be fine," I slurred. "Want to know why? Because Dad made me take a shit on the newspaper."

As soon as we returned home, I got into a bad argument with Marilyn because her mother wouldn't stop talking to me. In months past, I'd enjoyed talking to Mae for hours. Now I didn't want to be bothered. Not a word unless I was in the mood. I just wanted to sit at the kitchen table and think. Marilyn chastized me. It was her mother's house, after all. What did I expect?

I got my own apartment, in Hollywood, not too far from the Rovells'. It was a two-bedroom place, big enough to put a piano and to wander and think. In my own apartment, I was freed of inhibitions and could obsess on songs in any manner I chose—pacing, staring, or lying on the floor.

Such obsessing was integral to how I made records. The songs might've sounded simple, but the complex weave of backgrounds and textures were all thoroughly thought out before I ever got into the studio. Only after I heard the finished song in my head did I begin building the tracks in the studio. I knew exactly what instruments I wanted, the arrangements, and the vocals. Everyone learned his part individually, a process that made perfect sense to me because I knew how the final version would sound. But it left the other guys in the dark till the end, infuriated.

The downside of living alone was that I hibernated, withdrew, and grew lonelier than ever. I didn't have the slightest clue of how to live on my own, how to care for myself. Nor did I have any inclination to learn how. I pleaded with Marilyn to ditch school and stay with me. I begged her to come over in the middle of the night and waited anxiously by the window until I heard her little Honda putting up the street.

Sometimes, instead of calling Marilyn, I drove to the Rovells'. Although it was late at night, I let myself inside. Mae was usually up. I walked down the hallway and into the girls' bedroom, where'd I'd once slept. I stared at Marilyn and Barbara as they slept in their twin beds.

Quietly, I knelt down beside Barbara and gently put my head on her stomach or shoulder. I breathed in her scent. I took her hand in mine, softly, like a baby bird, and stroked it as she slept.

One night she opened her eyes and smiled. I tried kissing her, but she turned away.

"No, Brian," she said.

"Do I have to leave?" I asked.

"No," she said softly so as not to wake Marilyn. "You can stay."

I didn't climb into bed with Barbara very often, but it was enough that my feelings for her should have been known. Even as Marilyn and I grew more serious about each other, I still wrestled with my attraction to her younger sister. Later, it would be her older sister, Diane.

But there was never any question that I was going to be with Marilyn the most. She was my angel. I needed her, and she needed to be needed. That was the basis of our relationship and the reason it lasted. She was patient, understanding, and motherly. Gently, she pushed me into giving more than I thought I could, physically and emotionally.

To me, intimacy and sex were two different things. One had to do with the body. The other dealt with the far more sensitive issue of baring the soul.

In November, only a few weeks after having returned from the European tour, the Beach Boys left for a second trip to Australia. In the airport, Mike and Dennis laid bets on who was going to lay the most girls. That kind of talk always made me uneasy, especially around Marilyn. Not that I was prudish, just vulnerable. It reminded me of my dad's unfeeling explanation of the birds and the bees.

Aware that I was uncomfortable, Mike buddied up to me in the airport and promised to get me a few dingo dollies. For some reason I played along, wanting to fit in with the guys. Marilyn heard that and glared at me, irate.

"I hope you guys have a good time," she said. "Because I'm going to have a good time too."

Marilyn wasn't particularly precocious. She merely wanted to hurt me, and she did. I demanded to know what she meant by having a good time. Was she going to screw around like Mike and Dennis?

"I mean I'm going to have a good time," she threatened. "If you don't understand, Mike can explain it to you."

I boarded the plane shaking. I had no intention of fooling around with other girls. All I could think about was losing Marilyn. After barely an hour in the air, I convinced the pilot to radio a message to Marilyn. When I called her the moment we touched down in Sydney the following morning, she relayed her astonishment over my telegram, which had told her, "Please wait for my call. I love you. Brian." Crazed with passion, jealousy, and fear, I told her how interminable the flight was, how I thought I wasn't ever going to get off that airplane.

"Honey, I need you so badly," I said. "I never want to lose you. The mere thought of losing you was like an arrow shooting straight through my heart. It made me realize how much I love you, Marilyn. Even more than I thought possible."

"I love you too, Brian," she cooed. "I never really thought of leaving you."

"I'd die," I said. "I'd fall apart if you did. That's why I thought up a plan."

"What?"

"We'll get married," I said. "When I get back, we'll make all the arrangements and get married."

Marilyn, at sixteen, was surprised and unsure how to respond. I called her dozens of times a day, every day, trying to convince her to say yes. She constantly parried my proposals, insisting that she first had to consult her parents. Mae and Irving adored me, but they also worried their daughter was growing up too fast. Even though I was like family, it was a dilemma. As soon as I returned from Australia, they realized I was serious about marrying their middle daughter. It was only a matter of time until my doggedness proved victorious.

My biggest battle was with my dad. Recently split from my mom, he was sour on the institution. But that's not why he objected to my marrying. He said I was too immature and cited as proof the difficulties he and I were having with Sea of Tunes and the hundreds of thousands of dollars he was refusing to pay me.

"Brian, this idea only proves everything I've ever said to you about your being irresponsible," he said. "If you can't follow through on promises you've made to me, I don't know how you think you can handle marriage."

"I can, Dad," I said. "I need Marilyn."

"Ha!" he laughed. "You've got your whole life ahead of you. What the hell do you want to get married for? You're a kid!"

"But I love Marilyn," I said. "I love her, I don't want to lose her, and I want to marry her."

"Listen, Brian, Marilyn is okay," he said sternly. "But have you thought about this? She's a Jew. If you marry her, your children will be little Jewish children. How does that sit with you?"

"It's absurd to think like that," I answered. "I don't even like hearing that kind of talk. I love Marilyn, and that's all I care about."

Finally, December 1 was set as the date. Arrangements were made at the Sands Hotel in Las Vegas. Mae and Irving, Marilyn and her sisters and

I all flew to Vegas in the morning. I was gung-ho with excitement. Marilyn was on pins and needles. But in order to obtain the marriage license, I needed my birth certificate, and I'd forgotten to bring mine.

Remembering that I'd left it in my desk drawer at home, I called Carl and Dennis in L.A., but they couldn't find it. Marilyn cried all night in her suite. It was a disaster. We flew home the next morning. As I apologized, Marilyn and her mother worked out another date a week later. On December 7, Marilyn and I were married in an intimate ceremony by a rabbi who wished us a long and healthy life together.

The first couple of months were rocky. One night Marilyn and I were in bed, snuggled up in a prelude to lovemaking, and I whispered, "I love you."

But then a horrible thing happened. I whispered the wrong name. I said "Barbara."

"Barbara?" Marilyn screamed.

She bolted upright and flipped on the light.

"Barbara? What do you mean, Barbara?"

"I love Barbara," I answered, my eyes still closed.

"You love Barbara?" Marilyn screamed. "You love my little sister? Why did you marry me?"

"No, I don't love Barbara," I said, realizing my grave mistake and trying, unsuccessfully, to get out of it. "I don't know why I said that."

After spending the night on the sofa, I returned to the bed and kept track of what I said. We were kids playing adult. We were governed by emotions rather than reason. One night Marilyn said she didn't like the apartment. I was insulted. One thing led to another and I shoved her. She called the cops. I yanked the phone out of the wall. The place destroyed, we decided the next morning to move.

12

Fasten Your Seat Belts

T here was a fire station across the street from the duplex apartment Marilyn and I rented on Gardner Street in West Hollywood. Marilyn decorated the two-bedroom place comfortably, but it was hard for me to relax. I blamed the sirens that blared throughout the night, punctuating the whirring of my brain, but there were other factors. Capitol had released two albums, *The Beach Boys' Concert,* which became our first Number One LP, and *The Beach Boys' Christmas Album;* and the company was clamoring for another album to release after the New Year. The Beach Boys were heading off on a brief tour before Christmas, and no one was taking my pleas to stay home and write seriously. Marilyn and I were having a tough go learning how to live together. .

Everything was a hassle. My mind wasn't able to settle down. It was as if I heard a constant clicking. Click, click, click. It set me on edge.

In the midst of this I began hanging out with a sharp young guy who had introduced himself to me outside Western one afternoon. His name was Loren Schwartz. He appeared to me as cool, glib, confident, and hip—the kind of guy whose confidence I liked to be around and feed off. An assistant at the William Morris Agency, he seemed to know a lot of people in the music business, names that impressed me, and as it turned out Loren lived close to my new apartment.

Accepting an invitation to hang out with him, I showed up at his place one afternoon and walked straight into another world. Loren's apartment was vintage sixties, a black-lighted psychedelic haven. The walls were plastered with Day-Glo posters; the bookshelves overflowed with metaphysical tomes Kahlil Gibran, the *I Ching*, and the *Bhagavad Gita;* conversation soared about my head, disappearing into a holding pattern in air that was scented by a sweet, pungent odor.

"What's that?" I asked one night, referring to a baggie of green stuff Loren was sprinkling into a cigarette rolling paper.

"Marijuana," he said earnestly. "You know, pot," he said, when I looked confused.

Everything about Loren, from the way he lived to his friends, was new to me. I entered the most fascinating kind of culture shock. It was the end of 1964 and the color-coated thinking that would define the sixties was changing the hue of the cultural landscape, but I was oblivious to almost everything that was going on. Neither my suburban Hawthorne upbringing nor years of single-minded pursuit in the studio prepared me for expansive, open thinking.

My newest best friend, Loren, changed that rather suddenly. "Try this," he said, offering me the brownish-colored cigarette he'd rolled.

I'd heard of marijuana before. My father had warned me and my brothers of the evils of smoking it. But I'd never been around the stuff. I'd never seen anyone actually smoke marijuana before, and from what I saw it didn't look that dangerous.

"No, no thanks," I said.

"Come on," Loren urged. "Just a couple puffs."

Skeptical, I asked what it was like. Loren explained that it would make me high, sensitive, open. Music would sound better, denser; food would taste great; *I'd even be able to relax on it* without the drunken feeling of booze.

He didn't need to say anything else. I took the cigarette, inhaled, and held my breath as Loren instructed, then let go. I coughed uncontrollably and asked if I'd done something wrong. No, that's supposed to happen. He told me to repeat the procedure.

"Is anything happening?" Loren asked after a couple more puffs. "Do you feel anything?"

"What?" I asked.

I didn't hear. I was listening to music, my mind adrift in the wash of sound.

"Do you feel anything?" he asked.

"Real groovy," I smiled, enjoying the light-headedness. "I feel great. I mean, funny."

"No, you feel high," he said.

It was late when I returned home. Marilyn took one look at me and decided something was wrong. My eyes were distant, glassy, more remote than usual. She assumed I was drunk and wanted to know where I'd been. I explained that wasn't the situation. I might've looked drunk, but I was actually tripping out on marijuana.

Marilyn freaked. She knew only what she'd been taught, that marijuana was dangerous, illegal, something only weirdos and addicts used. She stormed into the bedroom and slammed the door. Later, she came out and demanded to know where and how I'd managed to get it. I told her more about Loren, that others who hung out there included young musicians David Crosby, Roger McGuinn, and Van Dyke Parks, guys like me, and that the scene was extremely cool. Marilyn didn't buy it. My behavior was strange enough without adding drugs.

Marilyn forbade me to see Loren again, but I ignored her. I liked Loren and I liked how pot made me feel. It unlocked a door to new perceptions and I eagerly entered.

The next week was rocky between me and Marilyn. The strain of not seeing eye to eye caused one argument after another. Added to that were the problems I was having with my dad as well as another Beach Boys tour I didn't want to go on: a breakneck swing through the Southwest in support of our latest Top 10 single, "Dance, Dance, Dance." The day before departing, December 22, Marilyn and I tried to hash things out over breakfast at Tiny Naylor's coffee shop, where I shoveled in eggs, potatoes, and three different desserts.

It seemed as if I lived on sugar and caffeine, running on auto pilot and fighting constant fatigue. I'd put on forty-five pounds in the past two years and appeared to others as more scatterbrained than ever. It's obvious to me now that what I needed was rest. The other guys only had to sing their parts, but in two years I'd written, produced, arranged, sung, and played on eight albums. I was exhausted.

In what was becoming a familiar chorus, I wanted off the tour. But the response was the same as always. I was told the tour was booked, the tickets were sold, and the band was depending on me to play bass. Marilyn sympathized. She tried convincing me that being away from everything would do me good. It was only two weeks.

That night I got a call from my dad. He wanted to tell me that the money he was withholding was increasing, more than $300,000, and whenever I wanted to complete the deal making him owner of Sea of Tunes, I could get paid. I hung up and went to bed feeling as if I'd been sentenced to prison. Every night, I tossed in bed as Marilyn slept soundly, attempting to dodge the troubling thoughts and voices that darted through my head. It was more like war than sleep.

The next morning I complained to Marilyn of a terrible sense of foreboding, but she treated me with the sensitivity of a mother whose child doesn't want to go to school for the third day in a row and drove me to the airport, where we joined the sizable Beach Boys' entourage of wives, girlfriends, lovers, and hangers-on collected in a corner. With Christmas on everyone's mind, spirits among the group were high, except mine. I sat beside Marilyn, a blob of depressed, preoccupied, high-strung, unsmiling flesh.

As everyone talked, I drifted off into my stare modes, a blank gaze covering my face, while my mind sorted through the various fears disturbing me, including competing with the Beatles and a new Spector-produced single, the Righteous Brothers' "You've Lost That Lovin' Feelin'," which I'd just heard. I still consider it the best ballad ever. As always, I wrestled with the fear that if I didn't hold myself together, despite how I felt, my dad's haunting criticism would be proved right: I *would* be a loser.

Then I saw something that fed right into my insecurities, something that snapped me back to consciousness. It was Mike and Marilyn. They were looking at each other affectionately, gazing into each other's eyes. I thought Mike wanted to fuck my wife. And the way Marilyn returned his look, she appeared to want him too. That's what I told myself, anyway.

"What is it with you two?" I asked, disturbed. "You want to fuck each other, right?"

"Don't be silly," Marilyn said. "Michael's not my type."

"I'm not?" Mike asked, puzzled but aware that he had found a way to get to me. "What's wrong with me?"

Marilyn attempted to explain and calm me while Mike kept up the joke, but I didn't hear a word. I was too busy escalating this imaginary love affair in my mind, worrying how it would affect me. I'd lose Marilyn. Mike would end up fucking both Diane and Barbara. I would have no one to take care of me. I'd be all alone, miserable and helpless. By the time I returned to the real world, I was devastated.

"Is it because he has a big cock?" I asked bluntly.

"Brian!" Marilyn gasped. "Don't talk like that. There's nothing going on between Mike and me."

Dazed and depressed, I said good-bye to Marilyn and boarded the plane. I took a seat in back. My mind sputtered, my eyes couldn't focus. Al sat down beside me. I was counting the number of stitches in the seam of the pouch on the chair in front of me. The hum of the plane's engines starting down the runway sounded like the screams of a terrified animal. My mind went blank—a snowy screen, bad reception on a television. I knew I was losing it.

Minutes after we were airborne, I turned to Al. Tears were streaming out of my eyes. My face was red. My hair felt as if it were standing, about to fly out of my scalp strand by strand.

"What's wrong, Brian?" Al asked, alarmed.

"I'm going to crack up any minute," I said.

"Cool it, Brian," he said. "Pull yourself together."

It was impossible. I was already over the edge. Ravaged by pain and drenched by a flood of tears, I buried my face in a pillow and let myself go, hurtling over the brink of sanity. I cried. I screamed. I pounded my fists in the back of the chair.

Al called a stewardess back. She place her hand on my back.

"I want to get off this airplane," I ranted. "I want off. Right now."

"But we just took off, sir," she said.

"I don't care. I want off this fucking airplane!"

"I'm sorry." She tried soothing me. "But before you can get off, we have to land. Once we land, then you can get off."

That didn't cut it and, like a rubber band snapping, I erupted in a tower of anger. Struggling for something that would insure my survival, I stood up in a bearish show of strength, forearmed the stewardess to the side, stepped over Al, and bounced down the aisle, out of control, scared, utterly mad. I yelled at anyone who attempted to restrain me. I told everyone to leave me alone, to go and fuck themselves.

I had a full-scale breakdown. Within minutes, my brothers wrestled me into submission and ushered me into a seat. Dennis and Carl each held a hand until we landed in Houston that afternoon, reassuring me that everything would be okay.

But once we landed, I'd changed my mind.

"I'm not getting off," I insisted. "Turn the plane around and fly back to L.A."

"No, Brian, they can't," Carl said. "Let's go to the hotel. I'll help you get to the hotel."

"Please," I pleaded, "I want to go back home. I want to go back home and see Mom."

I said "Mom." But I meant Marilyn, who had become the caring, loving mother I never had.

"We'll call her from the hotel."

I was taken to a hospital and told a doctor what happened on the plane. He told me not to worry, gave me a tranquilizer, and sent me back to the hotel. I rested for several hours and regained enough composure to perform the entire show that night. Afterward, I went directly to the hotel, took another tranquilizer, and fell asleep.

The next morning I woke up sick. My stomach was full of knots, my head was spinning out of control, and all I did was cry into my pillow.

Carl visited. So did Dennis. But I wanted to be alone and begged them to let me rest. Later, the phone rang. I picked it up and threw it against the wall. I double-bolted the door. I didn't want to see anyone. Finally, the Beach Boys' road manager pounded on the door so long that I answered. He said he was escorting me home on a flight leaving that night. I couldn't wait and sat beside the clock, watching the seconds turn into minutes and the minutes turn into hours.

I sent word that I wanted my mom to pick me up at the airport. Not Marilyn. Not my dad. Especially not my dad. Just my mom. I craved mothering.

My mom greeted me at the gate, concerned. She was rising to the occasion. Seeing her, I couldn't hold back the tears any longer and let myself cry in her arms. We stood there for at least ten minutes, hugging and crying.

"You know, Dad always told me I was a failure," I lamented in the car. "He was right. Look at me."

"Nonsense," my mom said. "Just relax and tell me where you want to go. Home with Marilyn? To my house? Where?"

"I want to go to our old Hawthorne house," I sputtered.

No one had lived there for several years. My parents still owned the house, though since their separation it had stood vacant. The front door opened with an eerie whine, the unlocking of an old memory chest, and we stepped inside the empty house. Standing in the entryway, I breathed in the familiar smell of my youth. I remember feeling strange back in that house, but it was strangely comforting.

In the darkness, I walked down the hall, directionless, in pursuit of traces of myself. I turned the doorknob to the closet where I'd once hidden from my dad. I glanced into the empty kitchen, where my dad had stood naked on top of the table and screamed he was king of the family. I looked in his bedroom, where he had showed me his glass eye, where the glass of water on his nightstand held the eyeball every night.

With tears flowing in silence, I crept into my old bedroom. My mom followed right behind. *In my room.* These empty four walls, the place it had all begun, where I had discovered the soul-satisfying pleasures of music and written my earliest songs, was quiet and empty, a skeleton of faded sounds. Still, with my eyes shut, I had no trouble imagining my bed and the piano and organ in the space that was two steps down. I wanted to slip back into that special time and place but couldn't find the way.

I sat down in the middle of the room.

"You know, one of my songs is number eight," I said to my mom. " 'Dance, Dance, Dance' it is."

She sat down beside me.

"I know," she said.

"But I'm so tired," I sighed. "I'm so tired, and I'm so scared."

For the next three hours I sat on the floor and exposed my scarred soul to my mom. She didn't have any answers for me. Nothing that was able to mend the wounds. But she was my mother. She listened, quietly and patiently and without judgment, as I told her about the demons and fears that vexed my life. My dad. The beatings. The humiliation of my youth. My failure with Carol Mountain. Judy Bowles. My confusion over Marilyn and her sisters. The pressure of the Beach Boys. Spector. Smoking pot. My jealousy over Mike and Marilyn.

It all came out in swells of tears, upsurges of rage, anger, and fright. I was like a kid reaching for his security blanket. Throughout the ordeal, my mom kept her cool. She held my hand, she patted my back, she listened, and then when I was all talked out, she helped me up and drove me home.

"Could you do something for me?" I asked before getting out of her car.

"I'll try," she said. "What is it?"

"Do you remember when I was a little boy, you used to make me soft-boiled eggs?"

"Tomorrow I'll make them. For lunch."

13

Lava Lites, Acid, and Seeing God

Marilyn didn't have the vaguest idea of what it was like to be scared all the time, but she finally reacted to my scream for help. Carl had explained everything to her from Houston, assuring her that though I was fragile, I was okay. Still, Marilyn was a wreck when I walked into the house. She had begun panicking after hearing Carl's description of what had happened on the plane. *It seems Brian's had a breakdown.*

That's all Marilyn needed to hear. She scheduled an emergency appointment with a psychiatrist. I went willingly. It was my first time seeing a psychiatrist and I didn't know what to expect.

If madness is an inability to adjust to the way people are supposed to act, then I was on my way, since except for functioning in the studio, I was increasingly unable to get in step with the rules. I was driven by obsessions, extreme behavior, demons, and fears; I was an oddball with a deadpan delivery, so out of it I was hip. Everything I did or thought was aimed at creating music that would make people happy and also keep them away from me, and because I was successful, my weirdness was accepted.

That's just Brian being Brian.

Even the psychiatrist bought that. I visited several times in quick succession, each time relating my concern that Marilyn was falling in love with Mike. The doctor, who never picked up on the delusional quality of my worries, told me I shouldn't dwell on it and then discussed the meaning of infatuation. The incident on the airplane he chalked up to exhaustion, said it wasn't unusual for talented people to be different in temperament, and advised me to rest before going back to work.

Pressured by Capitol to deliver a new album in the first quarter of 1965, I took a couple of days off, spent most of the time smoking pot, and started recording *The Beach Boys Today,* the band's ninth LP, during the first week of January. I appeared fine, strong, the same determined leader as always. Only Marilyn knew about my smoking pot. Only a couple of months since I'd first tried it, the dope was already exerting a not-so-subtle influence on me and the music I wrote.

In three hectic weeks, I produced the boys doing a number of new songs: "Please Let Me Wonder," a lush, moody introspective ballad as well as the first song I wrote high—its title is a plea to the others to let me pursue my own creative path; "Do You Wanna Dance"; "Good to My Baby"; and the first version of "Help Me, Rhonda."

Initially spelled "Ronda," I wrote "Help Me, Rhonda" one night when I was fooling around on the piano, imitating Bobby Darin singing "Mack the Knife." I wanted to come up with a cool shuffle beat. After several hours, I'd done it. There's never been a correlation between the time it takes to write a song and how well it does saleswise, but for me the studio is where the hours pile up and a song either becomes a hit or it doesn't.

"Help Me, Rhonda" was no exception. It took two long, tedious sessions. Al, singing only his second lead vocal, was having trouble getting it right, and I was experimenting with ukuleles, harmonicas, fluctuating volumes, and all sorts of odd backing vocals.

In early February, Gary Usher asked me if he could record the song with his group, and that motivated me to kick butt and get the damn thing done. At the end of February, we finished the simple track that became the single in April 1965. It hit Number One—the Beach Boys' second Number One.

But during those February sessions, the pressure to write, the dope I was smoking nightly, and my breakdown all combined to effect a major shift in the Beach Boys' formula. The calendar was full of tour dates. Three days here, five there, a couple back at home. I knew that I couldn't handle that and had to disengage from the road once and for all. The stakes had gotten that big; there was just too much pressure.

Though I was back at work, the symptoms of the malaise that had caused my breakdown were still apparent. They were camouflaged by the fact that I was working in the one area where I could function better than everyone else, but I was extremely skittish, obtuse in thought, and obsessed with meeting the extraordinary demands heaped on me by both the record company and my own insecurities. I had to keep pushing the envelope, competing, proving that I wasn't the loser my dad said I was.

Then it dawned on me. Through the sheer cleverness of being crazier than anybody else, I consciously realized for the first time that I could use my instability to my advantage. I could manipulate people to get my way. I could use my craziness to insulate and buffer me from dealing with a world that caused me problems, including the Beach Boys. I could get off the road. Though fragile and unreliable, I was still the only one who wrote hit songs and was indispensable to the band. They had to listen to me.

In my mind, there was only one option. I was going to devote myself solely to making music in the studio. Nothing else interested me. The level at which I was thinking, creating, and working required obsessive, uninterrupted concentration and focus, which experience had taught me was impossible on the road.

A short tour was scheduled in the midst of those sessions. Before it started, I summoned the guys to the studio for a meeting. They were used to getting sudden demanding calls from me. They were like visitations from a phantom, unexpected and unpredictable. One, two, three in the morning, it didn't matter to me. If I had an idea, I wanted the guys at the studio, pronto.

Hating confrontations, I'd gone out to dinner by myself and gorged on junk food, knowing the meeting was going to be an emotional one. I was playing the piano by myself when they began showing up. Mike, Carl, Dennis, and Al thought I wanted to record before the tour started. They had no idea what I was going to say. Then I said it. I wasn't going to perform onstage anymore. They didn't take me seriously at first, but as I continued their jaws dropped.

"There's no need to worry, though," I said. "I foresee a beautiful future for the Beach Boys. But the only way we can achieve it is if we all do our separate jobs. You guys will tour. I will stay in the studio and make music."

The silence evinced their astonishment and shock, but the surprise lasted only a moment before the emotions surfaced. Dennis picked up an ashtray, threatened to hit anyone who got in his way, and stormed out of the studio. Al, tears in his eyes, complained of stomach cramps. My mom, whom I'd asked to the studio as well, placed a comforting arm around Al and told him not to worry. Carl and Mike both kept a cool head, though Mike tried to change my mind.

"Goddamnit, Brian, you're acting rash, as usual," he said. "You're babying yourself. You can write songs on the road."

"No, I can't," I said. "I feel much more comfortable at home. Plus, if I write a song and want to cut it the same day, I can't. It's impossible."

"Okay, but what the hell are we going to do about the Beach Boys?" Mike asked. "If you aren't onstage, then what? What's the status of the group?"

"It's unchanged," I answered. "We're still the Beach Boys. I'll just be in the studio and you guys will tour. Nothing else is different."

Despite the upset, I went home feeling relieved, and the next day the guys were more accepting. Only my dad remained unforgiving. He called the next afternoon as I was leaving for the studio. That screwed up the day good. We'd had little to do with each other since his firing. Business meetings mostly, but even then we hardly spoke.

Right off, he let me know he was furious. "I hear you're a goddamn traitor to the band," he said. "Is that what I'm hearing?"

"I'm not getting into it, Dad," I said. "I made my decision. My mind's made up."

"I know you're weak," he said. "That's no surprise. All I've got to say is, if you can't cut it, you might as well get out of the business altogether."

"No, Dad, I'm not going to do that," I said. "The Beach Boys is my band. You were fired. Remember?"

A couple of days later the Beach Boys took off on their first tour without me. A string of fourteen one-nighters, it was the type of grueling road trip that would've destroyed me. Guitarist Glen Campbell, who, along with drummer Hal Blaine, was one of the many studio aces I borrowed from Spector's Wrecking Crew, was hired as my replacement. A country boy joker, Glen was a nice guy, a hell of a musician; his falsetto was good enough to cover my parts.

The guys were gone less than two weeks when Capitol, on March 1, 1965, released *The Beach Boys Today* album. It charted immediately. By May it was number four on the album charts, while at the same time "Help Me, Rhonda" was Number One. It seemed business as usual.

Except that there were some subtle but noticeable changes in the music. The whole second side of *The Beach Boys Today* had been written and arranged while I was high. Compared to previous Beach Boys albums, the music was slower, more plaintive, and emotional. The chord patterns were more complex, the productions denser, richer in sound, and my thinking with regard to making records was different. Able to break down songs to precise little increments, I began to deal with each instrument individually, stacking sounds one at a time.

The catalyst was marijuana. With the guys on the road, I felt free to explore the boundaries of my creativity, and that meant smoking pot. I thought creatively when high, in ways I'd never done before. I began smoking every day. I loved being high, loved being in the place it put me. Alone. Out there. In touch with the inner machinations of my emotional epicenter. It altered whole frames of reference, mellowing me out, making me more cerebral, spiritual, increasingly analytical of how I was feeling and what I was thinking.

These were complex feelings and emotions, beyond my ability to express them verbally, except to say that I was in a very creative state of mind. But the shift in thought gushed out of me when I sat down at the piano. Before smoking grass, I was an aggressive piano player, an attacker. I leaned into the keyboard, hard and fast, a balls-out show-off with a teenage soul. But stoned, I didn't want to impress others as much as I sought to express and explore what was going on inside of me, the anxiousness, the fear, the insecurity, and my work began to show this new part of me.

The change, though in its infancy, didn't please everyone. Mike, who'd begun complaining before the road trip that slower songs, like "Please Let Me Wonder" and "In the Back of My Mind," weren't "Beach Boys enough," picked it up when they returned home. Marilyn also griped that there seemed to be a wall growing between us. Close to Carl, she complained to him about friends of mine like Loren, though she kept quiet about the drugs.

Meanwhile, after three months of touring, Glen Campbell quit the band to pursue a solo career. He had too much talent to remain in the background. As thanks, I produced him doing "Guess I'm Dumb," an outtake from the upcoming Beach Boys album. The Honeys—Marilyn, Diane, and Ginger—sang background. It wasn't the breakout song Glen was looking for, but he went on to have a great career anyway.

In May, Marilyn reached her limit of tolerance and informed Carl that I was using marijuana on a regular basis. Alarms sounded. Assuming that pot was the source of all my troubles, Carl immediately told my dad. He decided to straighten me out real quick.

Here I am at three months old, waiting for my big break. *Courtesy Audree Wilson*

With Grandpa at eight months. *Courtesy Audree Wilson*

Two years old.
Courtesy Audree Wilson

Two faces of my dad, Murry Wilson.
Courtesy Capitol Records

Eating apples at age seven with my neighbor. *Courtesy Audree Wilson*

At age 12. *Courtesy Audree Wilson*

This is what rock stars looked like in 1963. *Courtesy Capitol Records*

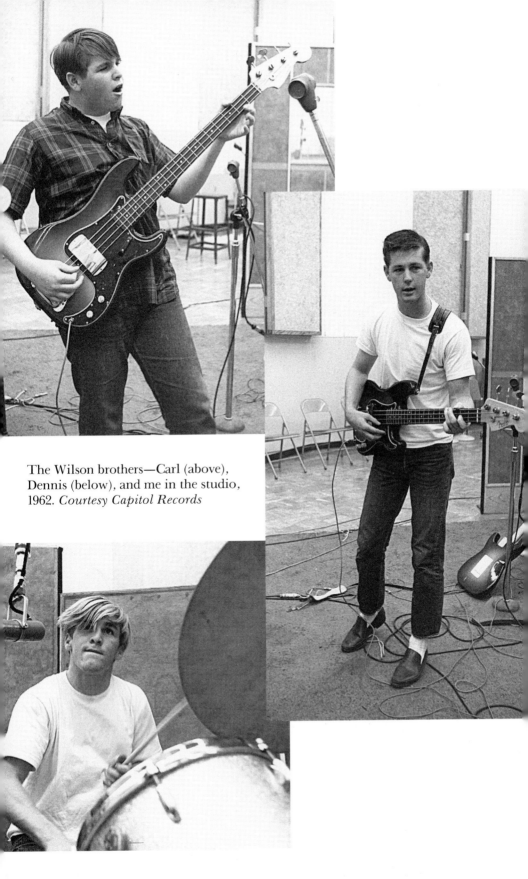

The Wilson brothers—Carl (above),
Dennis (below), and me in the studio,
1962. *Courtesy Capitol Records*

At Western Studios:
This is how we did it. I
was bossy even then.
*Courtesy Capitol
Records*

Let's go surfin': An outtake from the *Surfin' Safari* album cover. David
Marks, who substituted for Al briefly, is between Dennis and Carl.
Courtesy Capitol Records

Arriving in New York to appear on the Ed Sullivan Show, 1963. *Courtesy Capitol Records*

Flexing our muscle inside the airport. *Courtesy Capitol Records*

Flippin' the bird and passing the time during a 1964 photo shoot. *Courtesy Capitol Records*

The Beach Boys in their habitat. *Courtesy Capitol Records*

Rising to the occasion in Paris on our first major European tour in September 1964. *Courtesy Capitol Records*

Tasting ice cream and coffee at a café in Paris on our 1964 tour. *Courtesy Capitol Records*

Aw shucks, fellas, it was nothing. Accepting a gold record from Capitol president Voyle Gilmore for the Beach Boys' *Concert* LP. *Courtesy Capitol Records*

Quenching our thirst in a Munich beer hall; later that night I fell into a deep depression. *Courtesy Capitol Records*

Outtake from a publicity photo for the group's *Christmas* album. *Courtesy Capitol Records*

With my dog, Banana, in 1965. *Peter Reum Collection*

Al Jardine and Dennis on the road with my replacement after I decided not to tour anymore, young guitarist Glen Campbell, 1965. *Courtesy Capitol Records*

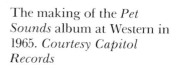

The making of the *Pet Sounds* album at Western in 1965. *Courtesy Capitol Records*

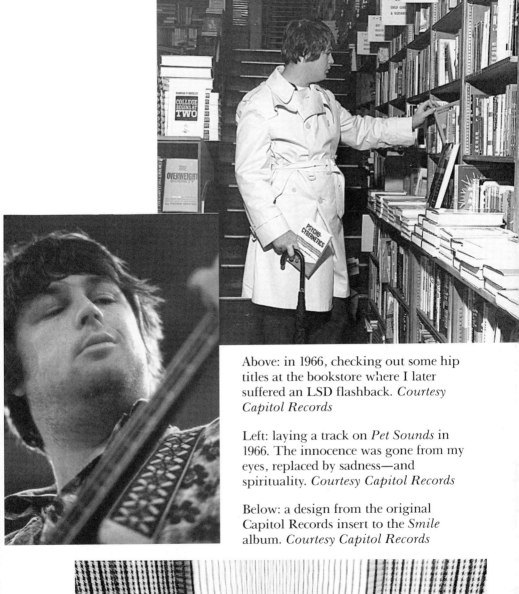

Above: in 1966, checking out some hip titles at the bookstore where I later suffered an LSD flashback. *Courtesy Capitol Records*

Left: laying a track on *Pet Sounds* in 1966. The innocence was gone from my eyes, replaced by sadness—and spirituality. *Courtesy Capitol Records*

Below: a design from the original Capitol Records insert to the *Smile* album. *Courtesy Capitol Records*

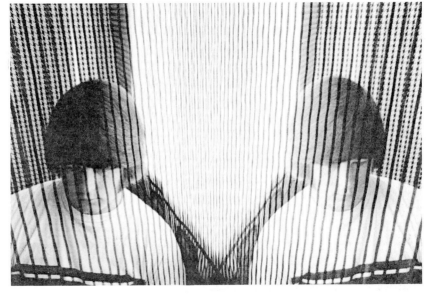

With Marilyn, who was pregnant with Carnie, at our Bellagio home in 1968. *Peter Reum Collection*

On the beach in 1967. *Peter Reum Collection*

Writing lyrics with Van Dyke Parks in 1967. *Peter Reum Collection*

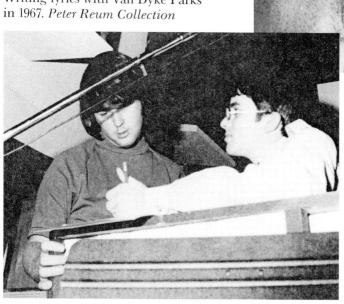

Playing Hawaii in 1967.
Peter Reum Collection

With my mother in
Hawaii, 1967. *Peter Reum
Collection*

At home with Marilyn in late 1967. The fun has faded. *Peter Reum Collection*

Celebrating the release of *The Beach Boys Love You* LP in April 1977, our final album with Warner Brothers Records. From left: Carl, ex-wife Anne, me, Marilyn, Dennis, and Dean Torrence of Jan and Dean. *Courtesy Capitol Records*

With Marilyn, Carnie, and Wendy in the mid-1970s. *Peter Reum Collection*

The Love brothers. From left, Steve, Mike, and Stan. *Peter Reum Collection*

On tour with the Boys in September 1979; I was smoking on stage and getting fatter and fatter. *Beach Boys Archives*

Jammin'. *Courtesy Capitol Records*

The mad genius producing at the board, 1981. *Courtesy Capitol Records*

One day when I wasn't home, my dad rounded up Mike and Al and drove to my apartment. Marilyn let them in, and they searched for drugs, which I kept hidden from Marilyn. They turned everything upside down until they finally discovered my stash. Then they sat on the sofa and waited for me to walk in the front door. I stopped dead in my tracks.

"What's this?" my dad asked, pushing an old shoebox across the living room coffee table.

"Where'd you get that?" I demanded.

"I asked what is this shit?" my dad repeated.

The confrontation seemed to confirm what I was beginning to fear—they were all against me. I'd had those thoughts but had always talked myself out of believing them. With all of them on one side and me on another, it was going to be impossible not to think that way.

"Well, let me see," I said.

In the box, I saw a red light bulb I liked to put in a lamp and turn on when I got home, some rolling papers, and a baggie containing about half an ounce of pot. I didn't say a word.

"Cut the crap, Brian," my dad yelled.

Marilyn started to cry. My dad, whose temper had run out, began yelling. Looking as if he wanted to hit me, he flipped the box off the table, spilling everything onto the carpet. I got angry. Supported by Mike and Al, my dad threatened to call the cops, though when everything was said and done, the only concrete thing said was that no one wanted my new friend Loren to have access to me anymore.

"What the hell does he have to do with this?" I asked.

"He's your goddamn pusher," my dad snapped.

"How do you know?"

"I know."

Marilyn had returned to the room. Knowing she was the one who had told my dad about Loren, I gave her a nasty look. No one was going to tell me what to do.

"Go near him," my dad warned, "and I'll call the cops."

Bullshit. I saw him anyway. Loren had certain qualities I wanted to absorb, just as Mike, Gary Usher, and Roger Christian all had something about them that attracted me, qualities like confidence and strength I knew I lacked and sought through companionship. Loren possessed knowledge, hipness, a line to some mysterious trove of ideas I wanted to know more about. He had unlocked the doors of perception for me, and I wanted to continue the trip.

Marilyn and the guys thought the few descriptions I shared with them of being high were nothing but gibberish, but Loren understood when I explained that pot made music grow in my head, made it more accessible, easier to grasp.

One night he asked me if I'd like to actually hear music in a way that would blow my mind. I could hold it, mold it, juggle the sounds like a circus performer.

I thought he was joking.

"No, I'm serious," he said. "Brian, you're unique. An artist. Very bright. Very talented. I know of something that can really expand your vision. Really open you up to music. In a way you've never experienced."

"What are you talking about?"

"LSD," he said.

"What's LSD?" I asked.

"It's a drug that's twenty times more powerful than grass," he said.

Wow! If something was twenty times stronger than grass, then it made perfect sense to me that it would also be twenty times better than grass. It was spring. *The Beach Boys Today* album was in the midst of spinning off five hit singles; it was the band's most triumphant LP yet. But motivated by deadlines and my constant desperation to achieve even more, I was willing to experiment with anything that promised to take me to an even higher plateau, never mind the price I'd have to pay later.

Stupidly, I told Marilyn I was going to try LSD. She already despised Loren. Now she was convinced that he was turning me into a drug addict. Livid, she pleaded with me not to take it.

"I've read that people ruin their brains on LSD," she said. "Don't do it, Brian. Please."

I told her I had to. Loren said it would help the way I wrote music.

"Loren says!" she cried out, frustrated. "Loren says! It's always Loren says! I'm your wife. Listen to me before you listen to him."

"I can't, Marilyn," I said. "I have to do it."

There was an evangelistic quality to Loren, an exotica that was hard for me to resist. He spoke of the mind-expanding benefits of drugs with the smoothness of one of my songs, and once I heard the message I couldn't get it out of my head. There was truth in what Loren said too. Pot helped me write better songs. It also allowed me get inside myself and withdraw without having to disappear. I could only imagine LSD.

The night arrived. Loren set a scene at his apartment: low lights, Lava Lites, music, something to drink. There was a sacredness to it all—from the way we said hello to the way Loren handed me a small paper stamp and told me to swallow it. There was always some story to the drugs Loren had. The hash was from Turkey, the grass Jamaica, and the LSD was from up north. Some chemist named Stanley Owsley. Its intensity was unrivaled, Loren said.

Within fifteen minutes I felt myself stirring. It began with a tension in my neck, like little gnomes grabbing onto my shoulders, and became an all-encompassing fuzziness. Loren suddenly realized I wasn't listening to him. As my guide, he came to my side.

"Are you okay, Brian?"

"A little uptight," I replied.

"Just relax," he said. "Try to relax."

I couldn't. Chilled and higher than I'd ever been, I stood up and didn't move for what Loren later told me was almost an hour, doing nothing more than stare at the undulating liquid in the Lava Lite until I had absorbed its slow rhythm. My brain was a morass of rubber thoughts.

Suddenly, I clicked into the music blasting out of Loren's stereo speakers. As I had been promised, music had never sounded so full and tangible, denser and heavier than any music I'd ever heard. I imagined wading through it like a river, until I felt consumed by it, and just as suddenly as I'd checked into the sounds I had to play Loren's piano. I sat down in front of the keyboard—but when I looked down all the white keys appeared fused together into a single note. The chords I'd been poised to play moments ago vanished in my confusion. My mind went blank. I tried to play anyway, but only one finger had the ability to work.

I hit an A.

Boing!

Then I hit it again. Over and over again for half an hour. That's all I was able to play. It freaked me out. What if I couldn't play anymore?

"Oh my God, Loren, I can't play the piano," I wailed.

"What?" he asked. "I'm too high to understand what you're saying."

"I've got to get out of here."

Loren followed me out the front door. I felt as if I was coming unglued. We walked up the street. I spotted a house with a FOR SALE sign in front and shouted, "I have to buy this house! I have to buy this unbelievable house!" Loren convinced me otherwise, and as we continued walking, like a lunatic, I shouted whatever thoughts came into my head. Seeing a strange-looking man turn a corner, I convinced myself he was God, leading me on a journey of my entire life, showing me the tiny seed I'd once been and taking me to the place where I'd finish my life.

Then he vanished. I was lost.

Some eight hours later I woke up on Loren's couch, scared of everything. It was the next day. I had vague recollections of what had happened in the interim, but mostly I felt exhausted, shaky, and frightened.

Returning home a bewildered mess, I was immediately chastized by Marilyn. She didn't mince words in telling me how angry she was at me for having gone through with the LSD. She was also concerned by the dopey state of mind I was still in.

"But please don't frown at me, baby," I said. "Don't frown."

"I'm not frowning, Brian," she said. "You're still on that LSD."

Unable to control her upset, Marilyn ran out of the room in a fit of tears. I followed, trying to explain. She wouldn't even look at me. I pleaded with her to talk. I tried explaining the trip. The drug was powerful. Awesome. Frightening. My heart palpitated. My brain did somersaults and cartwheels. Panic had shot through my system. I was scared and needed her to take care of me.

I promised never to do it again.

"I saw God, Mare," I said. "I blew my fucking mind. I saw God. I actually saw him. Felt him. I realized God."

"And that was good?" she asked.

"No. Yes. I don't know," I stammered, confused. "It scared the shit out of me."

Marilyn shook her head. She started crying again. "What's happening to you, Brian?" she sobbed. "I feel as if I don't even know you."

14

The Beach Boys' Party!

T hat night, in the afterglow of the LSD, I sat at the piano, lit a joint, and tried to forget how weird and unpleasant everything was. I was scared, fatigued, wishing Marilyn wasn't angry at me. But within the miasma I began to feel the simmering of a change in consciousness. Grass had given me added creativity, but LSD, though I didn't know it yet, was giving me new colors to paint with.

I tried to write a country and western shuffle that night, and before turning in I had something catchy. The next morning I began singing about girls, comparing the girls in California to those in other parts of the country and I latched onto the concept of naming those regions, like I did surf spots in "Surfin' U.S.A." The song was finished within the week, and it took another week of playing around before I plunked out the symphonic lead to "California Girls."

In the first week of April I started recording "California Girls," which was the first Beach Boys session to include keyboardist Bruce Johnston. Bruce, a singer-musician-producer from Beverly Hills, who, with Columbia Records producer Terry Melcher, had formed the Rip Chords, a Beach Boys knockoff, was originally asked by Mike if he knew anyone to take Glen Campbell's place. After trying several people, Bruce flew to New Orleans for a weekend gig and stayed.

The "California Girls" sessions began two weeks after he did, though while the boys were back east I laid the instrumental tracks at Gold Star with Spector's Wrecking Crew aces, including drummer Hal Blaine, guitarists Glen Campbell, Ray Pohlman, bassists Carol Kaye and Lyle Ritz, and pianists Don Randi and Leon Russell. The vocals were done at Western, but I still caught hell from engineer Chuck Britz for not doing the entire song at Western.

"Why the hell didn't you give us a chance?" Chuck asked. "You let 'Help Me, Rhonda' get away. Now 'California Girls.'"

"I didn't think Western was big enough to hold all the guys I wanted," I said, referring to the large number of musicians I was starting to employ.

"Shit," Britz said. "The next time you do a big orchestral production, I want you to do it here."

"I can only do what I feel is right," I said.

I've never liked the way I sound on that record and would've redone the song had there been time. But there wasn't. Summer was approaching, and there hadn't been a summer for the past three years that didn't include a new Beach Boys album. In addition, we had unexpected competition from, of all people, our ex-manager, Murry Wilson. After being fired, my dad vowed to form a new group that would teach a lesson to "those ungrateful little bastards," his term of endearment for the Beach Boys.

The group was called the Sun Rays, and they were a Beach Boys imitation, four teenage musicians from Hollywood Professional School who allowed my dad to cowrite and produce most of their songs. In March 1965 their first singles, "Car Party" and "Outta Gas," both Murry Wilson originals, were released. My dad demanded the Beach Boys sign the Sun Rays as their exclusive opening act.

"No way," I said.

"Hey, after all I did for your careers," he said. "You're going to shit on me like that?"

I didn't hear from my dad again until June, when the third Sun Rays single, "I Live for the Sun," which he cowrote, charted. He wanted to gloat. I congratulated him, but I also let him know that his songs were rip-offs of mine.

"What the hell do you know?" he bristled. "You've gotten where you are only because of my hard work. Both of us know that I'm the writer in the family. The real talent. You'll always be second best. You should listen to a few of our records. Maybe you'll learn something."

"Oh, come on, Dad," I said. "You're copying me. I recorded a song, "California Girls," that's going to blow you out of the water."

"The hell it will," he said. "Like I told you months ago, the Sun Rays are going to kick your ass."

They didn't. After several more singles, the Sun Rays faded into the background. But that didn't stop my dad from still trying to kick my ass. He had his ways. On June 9, I received a letter from him, reminding me that I had promised three years earlier to make him sole owner of Sea of Tunes. He even claimed that my mother had witnessed it.

Enclosing the documents to make the transfer official, my dad emphasized that it was time I made good on my promise to him and my matter to release any and all interest in the Sea of Tunes Publishing Company, except for the songwriter's royalties due me. He spent several more lines trying to convince me, then laid on a guilt trip about how our family could've been so close, but. . . .

He was unrelenting. As always, I denied ever having made such an agreement. I complained to my mom, who told me to discuss the matter with my father. He knew what was right. But there was no talking to my dad. I tried.

"Sea of Tunes is my company," I explained. "I've given you everything. All the publishing money. But the songs are mine, and so is the company. I've created those songs."

"Brian, I'm your father," he said. "I know what's right. I remember the handshake. In our living room. That's a verbal agreement."

"But, Dad, that never happened," I argued.

"Son, when you grow up—"

I hung up the phone, disgusted. When I grew up! I can only wonder what my life would've been like had I grown up in a nurturing environment. Instead, I had to fight every day, not for my sanity—that was already going—but for my life.

By summer 1965, my chief concern was to stay atop the field of artists, like the Beatles and Bob Dylan, who were influencing and changing pop music. On June 28—eight days after my twenty-third birthday—the *Summer Days (And Summer Nights)* album came out. The band's tenth album in less than three years, it went to number two in August. The top album was *Beatles VI*, the latest from our nemeses across the Atlantic.

But I wasn't disappointed. Not only did the album include one bona fide hit, "California Girls," it also had two of my favorite Beach Boys songs, "Let Him Run Wild"—a tribute to Burt Bacharach, one of my favorite songwriters—and "Girl Don't Tell Me," which I originally intended to submit to the Beatles. Also, the second side was full of slower, richer, increasingly introspective ballads, songs that marked the beginning of a creative tear that peaked with *Pet Sounds* and self-destructed with *Smile*.

In most music magazine polls, the Beach Boys were neck and neck with the Beatles as the world's most popular group, but our personal lives prevented us from similar acclaim at home. Carl and Al maintained pretty low-key lives, while Dennis and Mike chased every skirt they saw. When Mike got slapped with a paternity suit following the birth of his daughter, Shawn, Dennis confided that he could just as easily have been in the same predicament, but was lucky.

My home life was the most tumultuous. Marilyn complained that LSD had changed me. Her griping was like a tape that wouldn't quit playing. I didn't see it then, but she was right. The change was gradual, like a slow, allergic reaction. I slept later. I was subject to wider, more unpredictable mood swings, crying one minute, laughing hysterically the next for no reason. I ate tremendous amounts of sweets. I refused to be sociable. Marilyn wanted to live a normal existence. I wasn't close to normal.

My drug use added to our problems, luring me farther out into the abstract world than all but the farthest out, most patient, and intellectual characters could handle. Marilyn certainly wasn't among that group. But my friends were, especially Loren. Marilyn hated him even more than she did the drugs.

Finally, Marilyn issued an ultimatum—it was either her or Loren. I couldn't handle that and ignored her. Frustrated, exhausted, and downright mad, Marilyn packed her belongings and moved into an apartment of her own. I ignored that too, since it was easier to do that than deal with it. But Carl, who sympathized with Marilyn, was troubled by it. He pleaded with her not to divorce me. Marilyn told him divorce wasn't in her plans. She was at wit's end and needed not just a separation but some time away.

Between the roiling emotional currents inside me, the heavy place I was at spiritually and musically, and my nightly experimentation, I let nearly a month pass before I found the *need* to deal with the fact that Marilyn had left me. I was too absorbed with myself. I didn't require affection as much as I did care and babying.

One night toward the end of our separation, a friend asked if I wanted to trip. He had some acid. Strong stuff. Something like twenty-five micrograms, which I understood to be an extremely potent dose. Despite the lingering sense of fear and confusion the first dosage had left me with, I was game to experiment again.

Why? I told myself that it had also given me the inspiration to write and produce "California Girls." I was willing to take the risk to find more of that kind of inspiration.

As the LSD kicked in, I remember hearing fire trucks from the station across the street rumbling out of the driveway, their sirens wailing louder and louder. I got scared, more profoundly, deathly scared than ever in my life. Paranoid. There was nothing to be scared of. Just noise outside that was dissipating in the distance. But I sensed danger. I imagined flames consuming me. The firemen breaking into the apartment. Getting hurt. Dying. I couldn't stop.

Sitting on the sofa, I struggled to keep my tenuous grasp on reality. But my imagination was betraying me, serving up a horror movie instead. Finally, I was bathed in flames, dying, dying, and then the screen inside my brain went blank. I visualized myself drifting back in time. Getting smaller and younger. I saw myself as a teenager, then a young boy. I relived arguments I'd had with my dad. I wanted to run and hide but couldn't move. I continued getting smaller. I was a baby. An infant. Then I was back inside the womb. An egg. And then, finally, I was gone.

I didn't exist.

"You better not drive," my friend called as I ran out the front door, keys jangling in my hand.

I can't imagine how I managed to navigate a car, but I drove straight to Marilyn's parents' house. I walked in the front door, expecting to find Mae and Irving. But they weren't there. Only Barbara lying on the sofa, watching TV. I took a moment to stare at her, the object of so many of my fantasies. Then, acting on impulse, I jumped on top of her and began to kiss and paw her, finally blurting, "I love you, Barbara. Oh, I love you."

She let loose a frightened scream that penetrated my ear with the sharpness of a butcher knife, then punched and kicked me. I got off her instantly. Her yell had scared me too. Barbara beat me with a pillow as I stood over her, a dumb, drugged-out gaze on my face as she ordered me to leave. I was too high to understand her. The messages my brain was sending were fucked up.

Thinking Barbara was upset and not knowing I was the reason, I reached out to hug her. That was the last thing she wanted. She dodged my grasp, clawed my arm with her long fingernails, and grabbed my hand so hard that she tore a big wart right off my finger. It hurt like a mother-fucker, and the pain caused me to beat a hasty retreat out of there. I went home. Somehow.

*   *   *

It took several days to come down. I sat around the house, watched television, and stayed in bed. I wasn't sick, but I sure wasn't well either. My brain fizzled, a fire smoldering in the rain.

I sank into a dark, lonely depression and wanted someone to comfort me and tend to my hypersensitive, childlike wants. I went to Marilyn's apartment. Not knowing what to say, I stood outside crying. It wasn't planned, but still it was manipulative on my part. I knew that if Marilyn saw me hurting bad enough there was no way she could resist me. It was past midnight, and her lights were off. I knocked at the door anyway. After a minute or so, Marilyn answered wearing her nightgown. I felt like a child coming home to mother.

"Are you alone?" I asked.

"Of course, Brian," she said testily. "What do you want?"

I wanted in. But Marilyn refused to open the door. Eventually, she gave in to my pleadings. I wasted no time and apologized for everything—the drugs, the lack of attention I showed her, the incident with Barbara.

"I miss you so much, baby," I said. "Come back with me, please. We'll do it right this time. We'll buy a house. I know you want a house. A family."

"I don't know, Brian," she said.

"Think about it, Mare. We have enough money now to do anything. We'll get a house and start a family. We can have a normal life. Everything you want."

"I don't know," she said. "I really need more time to think about it."

Two weeks later Marilyn and I went shopping for a house and purchased the second one the realtor showed us. It was up a windy road, on Laurel Way, in the Hollywood Hills, and had a panoramic view of the San Fernando Valley. Marilyn was ecstatic. In deciding to stick with the marriage, she must have taken a long and hard look at exactly what I was capable of giving her as a husband. If not a normal relationship, it was at least enough money to support any life-style she wanted.

She plunged into decorating our new house. The living room featured multicolored Lava Lites. The dining room was consumed by a long, monstrous Spanish table. The kitchen was wallpapered in black and white. A kitschy plastic Jesus with movable eyes hung in the bathroom. The bedroom was dominated by an enormous four-poster bed; angels were carved onto the headboard. In the orange-and-blue den was a jukebox stocked with Spector records.

My favorite room was my office. It had cork walls, my piano, and an inspiring view. I referred to it as my "piano laboratory." I bought a monkey and kept it on top of my black desk. The monkey was eventually replaced by two dogs, a weimaraner named Louie, and Banana, a friendly beagle who was famous for playing fetch.

In November, Capitol released "The Little Girl I Once Knew" as the follow-up single to "California Girls." The single stiffed. Radio programmers didn't know what to make of it. After "Help Me, Rhonda" and "California Girls," back-to-back top fives, they were confused by changes in tempo and several breaks in the music that caused dead air. I caught hell from the record company and Mike, who warned me again not to fuck with the formula.

The Beach Boys represented sun, surf, and cars. Up-tempo good spirits. Not moody ballads. Not artistic growth.

Capitol demanded another album right away. Wanting a guaranteed smash, they suggested another live album that could be crammed with surefire hits. I balked. The Beach Boys had released a concert LP the previous year. Then I got the idea of doing something similar, yet different. We'd throw a party and record it. Not only would it be quick and low-budget, the concept was original. Plus, it would give the album a unifying theme.

The theme of *The Beach Boys' Party!* album was obvious. The story released with the LP described the band and their friends getting together at Mike's house. He always wanted to be at the center of things.

It was actually recorded over two fun-filled evenings in Studio 2 at Western.

The first session was scheduled to begin at five o'clock, but people didn't show till six. By then, the studio looked like a giant, messy picnic area—food and bottles littered everywhere. The guys brought their wives or girlfriends or friends. Carl was with his fiancé, Annie Hinsche, whose brother, Billy Hinsche, of the group Dino, Desi & Billy, was also among the merrymakers. Dennis showed up with bronchitis and left early. Mike and Bruce tried on new suits they had bought in New York.

At seven, the party finally got to a point where I could corral everyone into thinking about doing some work. In one especially spirited take, we zipped through some of our favorites, including "Hully Gully" and the Beatles' "Tell Me Why." Afterward, we listened to the playback and finished the food. I'd never been party to such a relaxed session.

The following night everyone arrived on time and tossed out suggestions. Mike sang "Alley Oop"; I offered up two Beatles songs, "You've Got to Hide Your Love Away" and "I Should Have Known Better." I then ravaged our own "I Get Around," singing, "We never get turned down by the girls we pick up on." Al plucked out "The Times They Are A-Changin'," which the rest of us, acting as his background choir, destroyed by shouting "Right" or "Wrong" at the end of each chorus.

Midway through, Dean Torrence of Jan and Dean wandered into the studio. He and Jan were recording their own album down the hall. They'd gotten into an argument. Jan called a break and Dean came to visit.

"Any suggestions?" I asked.

" 'Barbara Ann,' " Dean replied after a moment of thought.

The Regents had done it first. Then Jan and Dean. But our three-minute, semi-serious take—half the people in the room were singing while the other half were munching on potato chips, swigging sodas, and laughing—was an out-of-the-box smash. The single, forty-six seconds shorter than the album's version, shot to number two on the charts and became an even bigger international hit. Our biggest ever.

Dean wasn't credited on the record, though. Lou Adler prohibited them from singing on other artists' songs, threatening to withhold royalties from their own work if they disobeyed him. But it was no secret that Dean was singing, especially when at the end, Carl said, "Thank you, Dean." Of course, that sort of inside political nonsense made it even cooler.

Released in October 1965, *The Beach Boys' Party!* album shot into the Top 10, spending six months on the charts. I was alone among the group in not celebrating the triumph. The party-time music, while fun, was a throwback to the Beach Boys' old material. It might not have been out of step with the times—not yet anyway—but it was definitely out of synch with what I wanted to do. I was heading in a much different direction and, whether the Beach Boys liked it or not, I was taking them with me.

I'd forgotten that only four years earlier Gary Usher and I had sat in my bedroom and dreamed about going head to head with the Brill Building songwriters. I'd since become one of them, racking up an impressive share of chart numbers, making a reputation for myself that put me among the likes of Lennon and McCartney, Dylan and even Spector. But now that wasn't enough to satisfy me.

In the waning weeks of 1965, the Beach Boys departed on an ambitious tour of Asia, Japan, and Hawaii, leaving me alone to write the next album.

My real intention was to redraw the entire map of pop music. With the next album, I wanted to move off the charts and onto a higher plateau. I wanted to take the lead.

Music was exploding. There was an urgency to compete. It was a heady time.

It scared the hell out of me.

15

Better Than Everything Else

S everal days before Christmas 1965, I pulled my Corvette out of the garage, wound down Laurel Canyon, and, twenty minutes later, parked in front of Pickwick Bookstore in Hollywood. In the parking lot, I found myself unable to remember how I had driven there. I tried retracing the path I'd taken, but my mind was completely blank. I couldn't remember what songs had been on the radio. I couldn't even remember why I'd gone to the store.

It was spooky.

I walked into the store anyway. The clerk, who knew me, said hello and mentioned that he was crazy about "Barbara Ann," which was all over the radio. I heard what he said but didn't understand. My brain wasn't processing the information. I gave him a confused look.

He probably thought I was stoned. I was. But I hadn't done any drugs. Worse, I was getting higher and more out of myself with every heartbeat. That scared me. I didn't understand what was happening to me.

Moving slowly into the aisles, I concentrated on reading the book titles and their authors. In the philosophy section, I paged through books by Sartre, Camus, Kant. I tried the religion section and picked up the Bible, the *Bhagavad Gita,* and the *I Ching.* I stared at the pages, tried to read, but the letters all vibrated on the pages and I couldn't make sense of anything.

Suddenly, the inside of my brain undulated and sent a wave-like shiver through my body. A tremendous rush of anxiety poured through me.

Paranoia. An attack of some kind. I freaked out that there was too much knowledge confronting me. I was being overwhelmed by all the information contained in the books on the shelves. There was no way I could ever know everything. I panicked.

Oh my God!

The room began to spin. I was in the center of a giant spinning top. Turning, turning, turning. The moment was completely surreal. Then I saw the books melting down the shelves, dripping like wax down the side of a candle. I extended my arms, wanting to run my hands through the information, wanting to stain my skin with words written by mankind's greatest minds. But all I felt was air. The knowledge was eluding me.

It had been months since I'd taken acid. But I was having a flashback.

Hurrying outside, I fumbled for my car keys, unlocked the door, and slumped in the front seat, wondering how long the flashback was going to last. Several hours passed until I felt capable of driving. I didn't get home until dark. Avoiding Marilyn, I went straight to my office and locked the door, still high and panting with fear.

As the buzz subsided into a manageable burned-out sensation, I remembered Loren once explaining that hallucinations were comparable to Zen riddles, mysteries full of meaning. What had mine meant? I had driven to the bookstore, looking for what? Inspiration? Instead, I'd seen books melting, unable to grasp the knowledge contained in them. If that was a riddle, I wanted to know the solution.

In December, the Beatles' latest LP, *Rubber Soul,* hit Number One in Britain and the U.S. I heard individual cuts but didn't listen to the entire LP until someone from my expanding circle of friends, most of whom I'd inherited from Loren, brought it over to my house in early 1966 and insisted I listen and give my opinion, as if I were some kind of oracle.

Under a cloud of pot smoke, it was a ceremonial event. A bunch of us sat around the dining room table, gazing out the window at the expanse of city lights shimmering below, smoking joints as the album played. No one ventured an opinion until I expressed mine. That was easy. I was knocked out. Every song from "Michelle" to "Norwegian Wood" to "In My Life," and "The Word" was great.

"I'm flipped by it," I exclaimed. "I can't believe it."

"John and Paul, those guys are geniuses," Loren said.

"That album is just blowing my mind," I continued, excited by its amazing consistency. "They put only great stuff on the album. That's what I want to do."

"What?" he asked.

"I want to make a whole album a gas!" I said.

Suddenly, I wanted to share my idea with Marilyn. She was in the kitchen with her sister Diane and another girlfriend, making peanut butter sandwiches. After my attack on Barbara, I'd started spending more time with Diane, rekindling my dormant interest in her. She now worked as my secretary and spent a lot of time at the house. I spent a lot of time watching her, dreaming about what it would be like to make love to her.

Since our reconciliation, Marilyn had softened her position against pot to the point where I was able to get her to try a joint with me. Why the reversal? I was moving in more glamorous circles, and Marilyn didn't want to be left out. It also gave us something in common, which there wasn't a lot of. In addition, at this point among people our age, smoking grass wasn't looked upon as the worst thing in the world. Pot just naturally became a part of both our lives, not just mine.

"Mare!" I exclaimed. "I just finished listening to *Rubber Soul,* the Beatles' new album, and it's unbelievable. It's inspired me."

"That's great," she smiled, stoned.

"I mean it," I implored. "I'm going to make the greatest album! The greatest rock album ever made!"

Al Jardine, drawing on his folk background, suggested cutting the traditional song "Sloop John B" six months earlier, during one of the *Summer Days* sessions. He later confessed thinking that I had never heard him, but literally overnight I worked out an arrangement and recorded the basic tracks.

"Holy tomatoes!" Al declared when he heard the playback the next day. "I thought we'd collaborate, work out some arrangement."

"Well, I got an idea," I shrugged.

"No, it's great, Brian," he said. "A masterpiece. I'm just amazed how you developed it from such a simple and clear folk song into this big, Sousa-like production. You even kept the piano progressions I thought up. It's better than I ever could have done."

Now, during a break in the Beach Boys' winter tour schedule, we recorded "Sloop John B." With everyone lined up in front of a microphone, I tested Mike, Al, Carl, and Dennis singing lead vocals. But no one sounded right to me, and finally when no one was there I did it myself. With the guys on the road more often than not, that was happening more and more.

*   *   *

I had a lot of unfinished ideas, fragments of music I called "feels." Each feel represented a mood or an emotion I'd felt, and I planned to fit them together like a mosiac. But I didn't have a focus yet. I was searching for some kind of guidance and that search took me to an astrologer named Genevelyn. She lived in Hollywood, and her place was scented by cinnamon incense. I told her my birthday, June 20, 1942. I was a Gemini. She gazed into my eyes, did a bit of figuring, and told me that I had an abundance of Jupiter in my chart.

"What's that mean?" I asked.

"Jupiter is equated with wealth, money, and success," she explained. "Whatever project you are undertaking now is going to surpass your expectations."

"How do you mean?" I asked again.

"What I see in your chart and in your cards," she said in a solemn tone of voice, "is work that's not going to be merely successful—you've already had your share of success, don't you agree?"

I nodded.

"No, what I see happening is a great abundance of positive, spiritual warmth flowing from you."

I wasn't religious, but I'd definitely developed a spiritual awareness. Loren was always discoursing on spirituality, religious books, inspiring me to make music that would evoke such feelings. And now Genevelyn. I was on to something.

I then told the astrologer about the hallucination I'd had in the bookstore last December, presenting it as a riddle. Genevelyn thought about it for a moment, then explained something that made perfect sense to me. If I wasn't able to find inspiration for songs outside myself, as in books, then I had to look someplace else. I had to look inward. I had to write about the spirituality I felt in my heart.

Around January 1966 I had all these pieces of music, feels, and they needed lyrics. I remembered that five months earlier Loren had brought a friend of his to Western, where I was in the mist of laying tracks on the *Summer Days* album. Tony Asher was a bright young copy-and-jingle writer for Carson/Roberts, an advertising agency. During a break, I'd played them one of my feels and asked for an opinion. Then Tony played a little melody he had written.

"You like pretty music, don't you?" I asked.

"Yeah," he said.

Later, Tony admitted that he couldn't believe I'd asked what he thought about the music. I wasn't anything like what he'd expected, he said. He'd thought I would've had a rock star-sized ego.

"You don't even know me," he said. "And you're asking what I think of your songs."

"But I want to know what everyone thinks," I said. "I mean, maybe the music sucks."

"Trust me," Tony said. "Your music doesn't suck."

As soon as I thought of Tony, I sensed he'd be a great lyricist, the right voice for what I wanted to say. I asked Loren for his phone number.

"Is Tony Asher there?" I asked.

"Speaking," he said.

"Hi, this is Brian Wilson. I don't know if you remember meeting me, but"—

"Brian Wilson? You've got to be kidding," Tony said. "Who is this, really?"

"This *really* is Brian Wilson," I said, reminding him of our meeting at Western. "Listen, I was wondering, are you still interested in music?"

"Yeah. Why?" he asked, sounding surprised.

"I'm working on this new album for the Beach Boys and it's a real bitch," I explained. "We're already way behind schedule, and I need some help with the lyrics. Would you like to help me write?"

"I thought you wrote with Mike," he said.

"I don't think he's capable of what I have in mind," I said. "I need someone sensitive. Are you interested?"

"Am I?" he chuckled. "Are you crazy?"

At lunchtime the following afternoon, Tony drove his 356 Porsche to my house. I heard him coming and stood outside, waiting to greet him. We went straight to my office. He was impressed by the abundance of recording equipment I had set up next to the piano. Motioning for him to sit, I rewound a tape that I wanted to play for him. There were perhaps half a dozen songs on the reel.

"I like 'em," Tony said when the tape finished.

"It's spiritual music," I said. "But they need lyrics. I have some ideas."

I sat at the piano and started playing one of the songs. The richly textured chords resounded through the room, filling it so full of sound that sometimes when I was alone I imagined the sharps splitting air molecules and then the flats compressing them so I could still breathe. My eyes were closed; I was getting into it. Then I heard Tony raise his voice.

"Are we starting now?" he asked hesitantly.

"Yeah, of course," I said. "We've got to start right away. We're way behind."

"Shit, Brian," Tony said, "I'm on my lunch break. I have to be back at the office in forty-five minutes."

"Well, when can you start?"

Tony got a three-week leave from work, but I don't think he knew what he was getting himself into. He showed up the next Monday, at eleven sharp. I'd emphasized the importance of promptness. Marilyn let him inside and explained I was still in bed. Like songs, some days were harder to begin than others.

For me, the most difficult part of songwriting has always been the first ten minutes. It's a time of utter anxiety. Will anything come? Am I dried up? Am I the loser my dad said?

The same with every day. After opening my eyes, the first few hours were filled with fear. I awoke with the possibility that something dreadful was going to happen to me and fought the obligation I had to get out of bed. Conversely, the anticipation of something dreadful happening filled each day with great anticipation and nervous excitement. Over the next few years, the fear I woke up with got to a point where it never left.

After two hours I lumbered downstairs. Although I apologized, Tony couldn't help being a little wary. He watched as I scarfed down breakfast while sketching my initial plan for the album. It was going to be a competitive response to the Beatles. Every cut had to be great. I also wanted the songs to be bound by one unifying theme, though I had no clear idea of how that was going to work.

I just wanted the music to sound whole, to convey the timeless, emotional content inherent in great works of art—paintings, poetry, symphonies. What I've always described as the presence of God.

"The album has to be better than everything else," I said. "I want people to hear it and to say, 'Wow, that can't be the Beach Boys.'"

With completely different work habits, it's amazing we got anything done. Tony showed up on time every morning, never knowing whether or not I'd be out of bed. He'd just be hitting stride when I called a break to watch television shows. One minute I'd be fine, the next I'd be laughing manically, the next I'd cry inconsolably. He had a steady relationship. I was married but made no effort to hide the fact that I was falling in love with my wife's older sister, Diane. I explained that I needed Marilyn spiritually but still fantasized about her sister in a physical way. He didn't understand.

Although he thought of me as an amateur human being, Tony admired my musical talent enough to want to do great work with me.

Among our first songs was "You're So Good to Me," one of Tony's favorites. He thought it was a good pop song, light and hummable. I agreed but explained that those qualities were what I wanted to get away from.

"I want to show that the Beach Boys know *music*," I said. "I don't want to do the easy stuff."

"I understand," he said.

Our next song was done with the record company breathing so hard down my neck for a new single that I began every day by unplugging the phone. One of the prettiest, most personal songs I've ever written, "Caroline, No" concerned growing up and the loss of innocence. I'd reminisced to Tony about my high school crush on Carol Mountain and sighed, "If I saw her today, I'd probably think, God, she's lost something, because growing up does that to people."

But the song was most influenced by the changes Marilyn and I had gone through since meeting at Pandora's Box. We were young, Marilyn nearing twenty and me closing in on twenty-four, yet I thought we'd lost the innocence of our youth in the heavy seriousness of our lives. The lightness that had once been ours was fading. Subconsciously, I might've sensed that the power allowing me to do special things naturally might not last too much longer.

All that made me sad.

The first time I played the melody of "Caroline, No" he told me the song had single potential. He took a tape home, embellished on my concept, and completed the words. The Beach Boys were on the road when it came time to record "Caroline, No," though between the pressure Capitol was putting on me to get a single ready, the song's intensely personal nature, and the creative space I was in at the time, I didn't think about waiting for them to get back to town. Instead, I did it myself.

It took seventeen takes before the song sounded the way I wanted, perfect. At the end of the seventeenth take, tears were streaming down my eyes, and I knew I'd nailed it. But it still wasn't finished.

I played "Caroline, No" for my dad. Though our contact was minimal, for some reason I continued to solicit his opinion. He praised the song but suggested that I change the key from C to D. The engineer put a wrap around the recording head, a technique which sped up the playback, and the two of us listened again. My dad was right, and I took his advice.

As work progressed, I began to consider making the album a solo project. I kept the thought private, but it reflected my growing intuition that the guys, when they began hearing the music, wouldn't like or understand it. The songs were a telling self-portrait of my troubled psyche: "I Just Wasn't Made for These Times" was a lament about being too advanced and having to leave people behind; "Let's Go Away for a While," a Burt Bacharach tribute, was explained by the title. The track originally included lyrics but worked better as an instrumental and became one of the most satisfying of my songs.

It seemed Tony and I spent as much time simply talking as we did writing music, and one of those talks concerned my conflicting feelings toward Marilyn and Diane. Marilyn might've satisfied my emotional needs more than her sisters, but Diane and I always had the most in common. She was my secretary, and her constant presence fed my infatuation. It wasn't long before I let her know I loved her, and soon after that I was telling Marilyn the truth.

Nothing had happened between me and Diane yet, and, in truth, I wasn't doing anything more than verbalizing my fantasies by admitting I loved Diane. It strained Marilyn's and my relationship, but Marilyn was in for the whole nine yards and by this time knew that ours wasn't a normal marriage, that I wasn't someone of normal emotions.

"Did you see how beautiful she looked yesterday?" I asked Tony.

"Who?" he wondered.

"I was watching Diane, and God, she's so beautiful."

"Brian, you're married," he said.

"I know," I shrugged. "But wouldn't it be nice if I could lie down beside her and nestle myself in her long hair?"

"Come on, man," he said. "Do you hear what you're saying?"

"I'm in love with the idea of falling in love," I said. "I do it so easily. I can fall in love with a girl just by the way the light reflects on her hair. A sensation. A feeling. That's all I need."

"It's not that easy, though," he said.

"Yeah," I said. "But wouldn't it be nice if it was?"

After that discussion, Tony said that he had an idea for a melody that was on one of the tapes. I liked him to write lyrics at the piano with me. But Tony was adamant about working on that one at home. I gave him a tape, and the next day he arrived with a completed set of lyrics to "Wouldn't It Be Nice" and an apology.

"For what?" I asked.

"I thought maybe the words were too personal, too close to home," he said.

"No, that's exactly what I want."

16

"God Only Knows"

O ne day in late January or early February Lou Adler, who'd left Jan and Dean to become manager of the Mamas and the Papas, invited me to attend a Rolling Stones recording session. Things were at a standstill when I showed up at the RCA Victor Studio, but there seemed to be a hell of a party in progress. Tables overflowed with booze, drugs, and food. Girls were everywhere. Adler introduced me to Keith Richards and Mick Jagger.

They seemed nice, not like the hell-raisers I'd read about. But I told them I could never work in such a crazed atmosphere. To me, the studio was like a church.

"It works for us," said Mick, who told me he was a fan of the Beach Boys. "You want a drink?"

"No, thanks," I said. "I heard that you throw acid in people's Cokes." I wasn't joking.

Rather than take offense, Mick had a good laugh. He said they did get high and then pulled out a huge, fragrant joint from his shirt pocket.

"You want a hit?" he asked.

"Sure," I said, taking a puff.

Mick told me to keep it, as he had to go back to work. Then he rounded up the rest of his band, taking charge almost as I did with the Beach Boys, except that it took the Stones upwards of half an hour before everyone finished his drinks or did whatever and moseyed back into the studio. In the meantime, I'd settled back in the corner of a sofa and puffed at the joint Mick'd given me. It was potent stuff. Pretty soon I didn't know what the heck was going on.

"Where am I?" I asked a girl standing nearby.

"At a recording studio." She smiled.

"What am I doing?" I asked.

"You're listening to the Rolling Stones," she said, dancing.

"Oh yeah," I said. "What are they recording?"

"It's called 'My Obsession,'" she said. "Are you Brian Wilson?"

"Yes," I said.

"I love you," she said, kissing me on the cheek and dancing off into another part of the room.

Influenced by the pot, I thought "My Obsession" was the best fucking rock and roll song I'd ever heard in my life, and by the time I managed to make it home, a good several hours after spacing at the studio, I felt as if the Stones had knocked me on my ass. I just didn't see how the Beach Boys were going to compete. I canceled on Tony and stayed in bed for two straight days, smoking pot and licking my wounds.

Then, as always, I pulled myself out of bed, went to the piano to save myself, and resumed work with Tony. It was mid-February. I played him the song I'd written titled "Good, Good, Good Vibrations." I had the chorus but no lyrics for the verses. He loved the song but was a little weirded out when I explained why I'd written the song and what I wanted it to convey.

"My mom told me dogs discriminate between people," I said. "They like some because the people give off good vibrations. They bite others because they give off bad vibrations. I have a feeling this is a very spiritual song, and I want it to give off good vibrations."

He tried his hand at writing lyrics, and things were going so well that I put "Good, Good, Good Vibrations" on the preliminary list of songs I told Capitol would be on the album. Two weeks later, though, I changed my mind and took the song off. The time wasn't right. I couldn't produce it yet.

With plenty of other good songs needing work, Tony and I turned our attention to "God Only Knows," the song about which I felt the strongest and proudest. The melody was inspired by a John Sebastian record I'd been listening to, and the idea summarized everything I was trying to express in a single song. But it began with an argument. I hated the opening line, "I may not always love you." I didn't think it was the right way to begin a love song. It was too negative.

"Brian, that's real life," Tony argued. "People who are in love may not always stay in love with each other. But consider the next line."

Then Tony sang: " 'But as long as the stars are above you, you'll never need to doubt me . . .' "

" 'The love we're writing about will last until the stars burn out,' " he sang. " 'And that won't ever happen.' "

That made me feel better. Then we had another argument over the word God. No one had ever recorded it before in a popular song. I was concerned that with God in the song we wouldn't get any radio airplay. Tony understood, but he was adamant about not compromising the artistic integrity. I eventually agreed too. First, because God was a spiritual word, and second, because we'd be breaking ground. Both were good reasons to leave it unchanged.

People who were at the "God Only Knows" sessions still tell me that they were the most magical, beautiful musical experiences they've ever heard. I gathered twenty-three musicians in one studio, an extraordinary number for a pop record. Everyone played simultaneously, the different sounds bleeding into one other, producing a rich, heavenly blanket of music.

It wasn't like making records is today, with seventy-eight tracks and every instrument recorded individually and mixed later. Then, everyone had to play live. It either worked or it didn't. The ability to make the type of snap decisions a production of that size required was what separated Spector from the pack. I excelled there too, but I still did twenty takes before the tracks sounded the way I heard them in my head.

"Goddamnit, that was beautiful," Dennis said afterward. "How'd you write that?"

"I prayed," I answered. "I prayed to God."

"Well, I pray to God it sells," Mike interjected.

Indeed, not everyone appreciated what they heard. I played bits and pieces of songs to Mike and Carl over long-distance telephone, but by the time of the "God Only Knows" sessions they still hadn't heard any completed songs and didn't know whether they liked what they'd heard. Al complained that he spent three months singing the chorus to "Wouldn't It Be Nice" before he ever knew the verses. Then I decided not to use the guys playing instruments on the album, the first LP on which none of the Beach Boys does anything more than sing.

By March 1966, the time at which they began listening to the songs Tony and I had done, which was around the "God Only Knows" sessions, they were prepared not to like the music. And they didn't. First, they were put off by the fact that I didn't need them. The tracks and vocals were all well developed without them. I think their egos were bruised. But the guys also weren't prepared for how different the music was from the songs we'd done in the past.

Especially Mike, whose biggest concern was, Will it sell? He hated everything. He criticized it as "ego music." He complained that the songs were too avant-garde and didn't sound like the old stuff. He refused to sing on "Hang On to Your Ego" until the lyrics were reworked to "I Know There's an Answer." After one stormy vocal session, he let his disgust surface and snapped at me, "Who's gonna hear this shit? The ears of a dog?"

Ironically, Mike's barb inspired the album's title, *Pet Sounds*. It was quite clear that none of them, except Dennis, who was always my biggest supporter in the studio, and Bruce Johnston, who loved everything, understood the album's significance to me. I'd poured my soul into these songs. The pain, the joy, the conflicts, the sadness, the love. They were everything to me, my flesh and blood. They only knew the songs weren't about sun, fun, and bikini-clad buns.

But that's always been the core difference between me and the Beach Boys. To the guys, the group was a great gig, a terrific job. The pay was good, the fringe benefits even better. They just wanted me to crank out the songs like a machine. Stick in a nickel, pull the handle, take five dollars. Money never entered my mind when I wrote a song. Writing songs was what I did.

Pet Sounds represented the maturing of my talent, the single-minded pursuit of a personal vision. I wasn't just entertaining people, I was speaking directly to them, directly from my heart.

The clash of egos wasn't helped any when it was decided to release "Caroline, No" in early March, not as the first Beach Boys single off *Pet Sounds* but as a Brian Wilson solo. Despite protests from the group, Capitol supported the idea as a means of broadening our marketability. Lennon and McCartney were as widely known by themselves as the Beatles. Likewise, Mick Jagger and the Rolling Stones. Yet the Beach Boys were as bland personalitywise as the sand on the beach.

Having given up on my dream of making *Pet Sounds* a Brian Wilson album, I liked the idea of releasing "Caroline, No" as a solo record, but

I still made it clear to the guys that they didn't have to worry about me leaving the Beach Boys for a career of my own. That wasn't my goal. I'd worked too hard mother-henning the band to where it was. Besides, they were my family.

Unfortunately, "Caroline, No" got no higher than twenty-three, causing the record company to jump on Mike's side and ask, "What the hell is going on with the music?"

They immediately rushed out "Sloop John B," which was more in line with the Beach Boys' formula, and by May 1966 it was at number three. That was more like it.

In late April I brought home a dubbed-down acetate of the album to play for Marilyn. Her opinion was key to me. In our bedroom, we lit a joint and dimmed the lights, then started the album. The songs had been sequenced the night before, making this the first time anyone had listened to the album from start to finish, including me. After the last song, "Caroline, No" ended, concluding with the sound of a train vanishing into the distance and my dog Banana barking as it disappeared, Marilyn and I looked at each other. Both of us were crying. The album was all I had hoped it would be, beautiful, poignant, spiritual.

"Can't you see me on the back of that train?" I asked. "I can. Just going away."

The Capitol execs showed little enthusiasm when I previewed *Pet Sounds* for them prior to its release. Subsequent meetings failed to change their opinion. The music was a radical departure from the Beach Boys' formula; they didn't understand. It wasn't a Beach Boys album. They even talked of shelving the project. I felt misunderstood, hurt, and alienated. Rejected. But I didn't have the resolve to slam my fist on the table and argue. Instead, I got an idea that would illustrate how I felt without having to explain myself.

At the last meeting I attended concerning *Pet Sounds* I showed up holding a tape player and eight prerecorded, looped responses, including "No comment," "Can You Repeat That?," "No," and "Yes." Refusing to utter a word, I played the various tapes when appropriate.

Released on May 16, 1966, *Pet Sounds* was number ten after five weeks, though Capitol execs, adamant in their opinion of the LP, considered that a failure. As a result, they pulled the rug on whatever chance *Pet Sounds* had of matching in sales the critical acclaim it received. Eight weeks after *Pet*

Sounds came out, Capitol released the *Best of the Beach Boys* LP. They never would've done that to the Beatles. But they still considered the Beach Boys a surf band, nothing more. I took the lack of support very personally.

Pet Sounds drew widespread praise from fans, including Beatles John Lennon and Paul McCartney. Paul once told me he thought "God Only Knows" was one of the greatest songs ever written and told *Rolling Stone* magazine that he'd made *Pet Sounds* required listening for his children. But that didn't help sales. Even with "Wouldn't It Be Nice" and "God Only Knows" charting at numbers eight and thirty-nine, *Pet Sounds* was pushed into the background by the "best of" package, which raced into the Top 10.

Feeling burned, I told the guys we needed a different image to go along with the music. We had to keep up with the times. Bruce came up with the idea of hiring PR whiz Derek Taylor, a colorful, slick-talking Brit, who worked with the Beatles. He and I met in his Sunset Boulevard office. The discussion consumed several hours and several joints, while he told me about Lennon, McCartney, and the group's producer, George Martin. He was a great gossip, and I soaked it all up.

"And what about us?" I asked, finally. "What do you think you can do for the Beach Boys?"

"What do you want?" he asked.

"To be taken seriously," I replied. "I want people to take the Beach Boys' music seriously. As seriously as they do Lennon's and McCartney's. It's been a problem for us," I said. "The Beach Boys have neglected so many things—art on our album covers, a hip approach to the media—but now there's a cool thing happening with the music and I don't want to let that get away."

"Yeah, I see," Taylor said. "We can bring everything together in a real groovy way—the right kind of interviews, new pictures—"

"Without those stupid striped shirts," I interrupted.

Taylor understood and went to work on the press, especially in England, where the Beach Boys were the number one band ahead of even the Beatles. Pumping the papers with platitudes, he promoted the Beach Boys but concentrated most of his energy on hyping me as a musical wizard. My reclusiveness only added to the image.

My popularity skyrocketed. The initial press clippings sent back from London were all about me. "Brian Wilson! He's a Beach Boy and a Genius!" one headline read.

Suddenly, genius was the word everyone used to describe me. Every interviewer wanted to know, "Are you a genius?" I didn't know what I was, but soon after Taylor was hired it seemed clear that I better come up with an answer.

"I have a natural affinity for music, but I'm not a genius," I said. "I'm just a hardworking guy."

That's what I said. The trouble was, no one believed me. They wanted me to be a genius. That turned out to be too much to live up to.

17

Good and Bad Vibrations

I t was a hot afternoon, a pot bellied sun sitting straight up in the sky. I was driving around the William Morris Agency in Beverly Hills. The previous day I'd taken acid for the third and final time. After two bad experiences, this trip was the ultimate in LSD joyrides—everything it was supposed to be, four hours of enlightenment and spirituality.

Now Al Jardine was in the car with me, getting angrier every time I circled the block, which was up to twenty-five times.

"Stop the car and let me out," he demanded.

"Not until you promise me you'll drop acid," I said. "It'll change your life!"

"I think you're full of shit," Al said. "I'm not going to take LSD, and if you don't stop this goddamn car right this second, I'm going to make you."

I pulled the car to the side. Al hopped out and slammed the door shut. I called him back. One more thought.

"Al," I asked, "do you believe in God?"

"You know what, Brian?" he said. "You're full of a lot of weird ideas. You better stop taking drugs."

Indeed, I was full of weird ideas and I smoked too much pot, but I didn't give much heed to Al or any of the other guys whenever they tried telling me I was too far out. In summer 1966 the Beach Boys and I occupied two different worlds, merging occasionally in the studio. They were constantly on the road, while I was in the center of a creative scene that was just starting to discover itself.

The genius tag I'd acquired was like a magnet, attracting an eclectic group of bright, talented people who hung out with me, smoking pot and indulging my unbridled creativity. The main players included Loren, singer Danny Hutton, his manager, David Anderle, and Van Dyke Parks, a wiry intellectual musician. All of us were in our early twenties, and we approached life as a game, dreaming big, using ideas as toys and the studio as a playground. Everyone looked to me as the best guy on the team.

At the peak of a creative streak that had begun during the *Summer Days* album and found itself in the making of *Pet Sounds,* I talked about going further, breaking old boundaries and setting new standards, and I knew the song I began working on immediately after *Pet Sounds* was the one that was going to catapult me to that place.

"Good Vibrations" was going to be the summation of my musical vision, a harmonic convergence of imagination and talent, production values and craft, songwriting and spirituality. I'd written it five months earlier and imagined the grand, Spectorlike production while on the LSD trip I'd described so enthusiastically for Al. Instinctively, I knew it was the right song at the right time.

Written in three separate parts, "Good Vibrations" required seventeen sessions and six weeks—not six months as has always been reported—spread over three months, to record, costing a sum somewhere between $50,000 and $75,000, then an unheard amount for one song. I threw everything I could think of into the stew: fuzz bass, clarinet, cello, harp, and a theremin, a strange, electronic instrument. Chuck Britz, who worked the board on all seventeen sessions, always said the first session was the best. Glen Campbell, one of the nearly twenty musicians used that day, agreed, exclaiming, "Whew, Brian! What were you smokin' when you wrote that?"

A better question would've been, "What was I droppin'?"

I had asked Van Dyke Parks, whom I'd met in February at a party at Terry Melcher's Beverly Hills house, to take a crack at writing lyrics to "Good Vibrations." I decided not to use the original Tony Asher lyrics. Van Dyke listened to the track, liked the song, but declined the offer.

"No sense walking into someone else's problem," he said.

Van Dyke, a skinny kid with a unique perspective, spoke in funny, poetic, often beguiling torrents. Merely asking what he did provoked any number of answers. He was a piano player. Singer. Songwriter. The wearer of any number of hats. A functionary. The leper with the most fingers. He also had a fondness for amphetamines. After sampling some myself, I realized why Van Dyke talked so fast.

Van Dyke, a distant relative of the inventor of Raggedy Ann and Andy and poet James Whitcomb Riley, lived above a garage behind a small house owned by an old woman who spent all day working in her garden. His one tiny room was practically consumed by a large aquarium. The first time I visited him I took him some fish. The next time I took him forty white mice. Why? I thought he needed company, and since he lived like a mouse I took him some.

The first time Van Dyke came up to my house, he brought the police. It was close to 1:00 A.M., and he was stopped by a wary patrolman who followed his rickety Yamaha 80 motorbike up Laurel Way. Caught driving without his license, Van Dyke was in something of a jam. But he persuaded the cop, whose sister had a crush on Dennis, to follow him to my house, where I was able to trade an autograph for his pardon.

I couldn't understand why Van Dyke didn't own a car, though. Then he explained: he was broke. That touched me. I was rolling in it.

"How much do you need?" I asked.

"Well, a Volvo is regarded as the safest car on the road," he said. "I think they cost about five thousand dollars."

Fine. I called my accountant and told him to have a check drawn up and delivered to Van Dyke the next day. Unaccustomed to wealth, Van Dyke was wide-eyed, incredulous. He tried thanking me, but I was already heading toward the piano, where I played him a melody I'd written that afternoon. I repeated it, embellishing it with chords, and watched his face brighten. He said it sounded like a Marty Robbins ballad. Robbins was a country singer.

I told Van Dyke the title I had in mind, "Heroes and Villains," which he said was perfect, since the song evoked images of a Western town. He said the song should tell a story. I played it again, and Van Dyke, after pausing for moment to concentrate, spit out the lyrics as if he'd been thinking about them for weeks: *I've been in this town so long that back in the city I been taken for lost and gone and unknown . . .*

Although we completed the song that early summer night, like so many ideas it was put on the back burner so that I could concentrate without distraction on "Good Vibrations." In early summer, I began having second thoughts about the song. The song Spector thought was his crowning achievement, "River Deep, Mountain High," failed and took its producer along with it. Then one night I called Carl in North Dakota, where the Beach Boys were performing, and played him the track, holding the phone up to a speaker in the studio.

"Boy, that's really bizarre sounding music," Carl commented afterward.

"Huh?" I asked. "What do you mean?"

"I mean bizarre," he said. "It sounds bizarre."

I didn't know what to make of that. Between the pot I smoked, the pills I popped, and the lack of support I got from the guys, I began losing faith ever so slightly in my judgment. I began running around L.A., recording bits and pieces of the song at different places according to their particular acoustics. I put inserts at Sunset Sound and RCA; I recorded the opening bars—*I, I love the colorful clothes she wears*—and the drums at Gold Star. One evening Van Dyke suggested adding a cello, and the next day I was back at Sunset. I put the theremin on at Western. The *I'm pickin' up good vibrations* was done at Columbia. Then the guys returned from the road and added their two cents. Al didn't like it, Carl still thought it was bizarre, and Mike called it more avant-garde crap and too long.

Nonetheless, I finally handed "Good Vibrations" to Capitol in time to make it the first Beach Boys single of summer 1966. But the following week I took it back, pissing everyone off and rekindling the suspicion begun during *Pet Sounds* that I wasn't altogether there.

Tough. There's no one thing that says when a song is done or if it's right. That has to be felt, and I wasn't getting those vibes. At one point, I called Warner Brothers and inquired about selling it as a rhythm and blues record. I told David Anderle that I was going to bag the whole thing and maybe not ever release it. Of course, I often said things such as that just to incite a response, like, "Was 'Be My Baby' a big hit? Do you really think 'Good Vibrations' is a decent song?"

Anderle, who loved "Good Vibrations," raved about it to Danny Hutton. As soon as Danny heard it might be available, he urged Anderle to work out a deal. That was exactly what I wanted to hear. I needed someone else's enthusiasm to boost mine. If Anderle, whose opinion I valued, was that hot on the song, then I told myself that I better not give "Good Vibrations" away, and I had better wrestle the damn thing to an end.

In August, I finished the final edit, mixed the tracks down to mono, and knew, during the playback, that it was right. Throughout, I repeatedly thought, Oh my God, this is a real mindblower. I played it for Mike, Carl,

Dennis, Al, and Bruce the following day, and when the song finished they looked at me with bewilderment. They'd never heard anything like it, and they honestly didn't know whether or not it was any good. It was just different.

Finally, Bruce spoke up: "We're gonna have either the biggest hit in the world," he said. "Or the Beach Boys' career is over."

My band mates were not bothered because I hung around with strange people, took drugs, behaved in ways that defied convention, and had a marriage that was truly weird. Their problem was accepting what I was doing to the Beach Boys' music. They were afraid I was fucking up the formula that had made all of them wealthy and famous, and that wasn't kosher.

My defense was a stellar track record and the fact that none of the guys wrote songs. But it was just August. "Good Vibrations" wouldn't be out for two and a half more months. They didn't know what to expect.

I didn't know what to expect either, though I knew the direction I wanted to head with the next album. Up and farther out. Creatively, I was at the pinnacle of a streak that was heading into its third year. I'd climbed the ladder and stood at the top, all alone, imbibing on the thin air. But none of that satisfied my fundamental need to prove myself. I had to go farther. Now I wanted to jump off the ladder and . . . fly!

With "Good Vibrations" finished, I picked up work again with Van Dyke, to the disappointment of Tony Asher, who'd done a great job on *Pet Sounds*. But I chose collaborators by intuition, by the vibes I got from them, and Van Dyke's intellectual passion and esoteric way with words seemed to mesh with the way I was feeling. We were completely different individuals, yet with amphetamines pushing a freight train of ideas through our brains, Van Dyke and I enjoyed a compatibility that was inspiring.

I told him the new album was tentatively titled *Dumb Angel* and explained that my goal was to surpass *Pet Sounds*. Musically and philosophically. I imagined myself creating a whole new form of music, religious, white, spiritual music. In a phrase, I confided to Van Dyke, I was going to attempt to compose what I called "a teenage symphony to God."

Needing to put myself "out there" with God, I started the endeavor by purchasing a couple of thousand dollars' worth of marijuana and hashish, enough to keep me stoned and in the state of mind where I imagined myself being deeply creative and spiritual. Van Dyke added fistfuls of Desputols, popping them with me every night. The speed wrapped me tighter than a windup piano player, cranked me up with high-octane energy, pumped me full of the confidence I lacked. It made me a goddam visionary.

None of us had an iota of awareness that drugs were dangerous. No one thought for a moment that my usage was really my way of medicating the fright and terror and pain that motivated me to write in the first place. But the paradox of speed was soon evident. Although we talked and wrote all night, convinced that we were making important stuff, when it came time for the playback, Van Dyke and I used to look at each other with stupid gazes.

"I can't tell," I repeated after each song. "Man, I can't tell if it's good or bad."

"Well, neither can I," he said. "I can't tell either."

Except for the constant pressure of the recording company, which was disturbed that they didn't have a Beach Boys single throughout the whole summer, time was irrelevant. Days blurred. It was light, it was dark. With the Beach Boys touring practically nonstop, I worked and lived in a vacuum that isolated me from anything normal. Buffered by money, populated by hangers-on who encouraged any sort of creative indulgence, and skewed by drug use, I was Lord of the Manor, whose only rule was that life be a perpetual groove.

I got heavily involved with the idea of health and suggested to Marilyn that she turn the backyard into an organic vegetable garden and sell vegetables out a drive-through window we'd construct off the kitchen. Marilyn scotched that quickly.

But she went along with the sauna idea. After reading that a good sweat cleansed the body, I bought a portable sauna, set it in the bedroom, and drilled a hole in the wall beside it. Marilyn sat on the other side as I sweated. Every so often, I banged on the wall, which signaled her to take a hit off a joint, then blow the smoke through the hole and into my open mouth.

My obsession with the swimming pool began innocently. A dip a day. Then a slide was installed. I wanted everyone to get into the pool. Gradually, it became the only place where I felt comfortable talking to people.

I explained there was a possibility that the house was bugged. Marilyn refused to buy into that theory. But I was dead serious. The pot, the speed, the constant pressure nurtured the kernel of paranoia that had troubled me for years.

"Brian, tell me who'd do a thing like that?" Marilyn asked.

"I don't know," I said.

Marilyn thought I was ridiculous. I didn't care. I was beginning to interpret reality the way I saw fit. My brain distorted pictures and rearranged them. Slowly, surely, new meanings crept into everything. Rather than adapt or recognize I was losing it and get help, I was in a position where I could make the world bend for me. As a result, I began conducting business meetings in the swimming pool and refusing to speak on the phone.

Back then, the line between fun and frightening, healthy and hazardous was a thin one. When Loren told me at 3:00 A.M. that kaftans were the fashion rage and I couldn't find a store open at that hour, I vowed to start a clothing store that would stay open twenty-four hours a day. The same thing happened when I got the urge to play Ping-Pong at 2:00 A.M. and didn't own a table. Another night, Anderle, Van Dyke, and I were lying outside on the grass, hopped up on speed and looking up at the stars. Again, after wanting a telescope but being unable to find a place open that sold them, I looked Anderle in the eyes and exclaimed, "Let's buy a telescope place, man! We'll have it open around the clock!"

In the midst of this mayhem, Van Dyke and I managed to turn out songs for the *Dumb Angel* LP. At a dinner party one evening early in October 1966, I played a handful of acetates, including "Wonderful," "Holidays," "Cabin Essence," "Do You Dig Worms?," and a long, wild early rendition of "Heroes and Villains" that engendered such confused reaction I was forced to explain myself.

"The song is going to be a three-minute musical comedy," I said. "The whole album is going to be a far-out trip through the Old West. Real Americana. But with lots of interesting humor. I think it's going to be a big humor trip. There's even going to be talking and laughing between cuts."

Nothing entered my mind without being considered for the album. For instance, after clinking my fork on my dinner plate, I asked everyone at the table to tap their silverware on their plates and glasses, which produced a symphony of tones and sounds I decided to put on the album. I invited everyone to return for an encore performance the next night. But when people began calling Marilyn to see if I was serious, I was gone, the idea forgotten.

Not too long after, I asked most of the same people to go into a bar and engage in an old-fashioned barroom brawl, throwing *real* punches and breaking tables and chairs, so that I could record the sounds on tape. No one would, but everyone agreed it was an awesome idea.

With my mind constantly "on," there seemed no limit to what I could dream up, a sentiment not even the Beach Boys could deny when "Good Vibrations" was finally released on October 10, 1966. In the first four days, it sold 100,000 copies each day; within weeks, it became the Beach Boys' biggest single ever. Sales soared past one million copies, which satisfied the guys. It hit Number One and I savored the triumph.

On tour in the Midwest, the Beach Boys planned to debut "Good Vibrations" live in Ann Arbor, Michigan. For some reason, I quaked at the thought. I didn't think they were capable of reproducing my masterpiece, and I lost many nights' sleep because of it. Echoing the fear I'd been unable to silence since childhood, I repeatedly asked Marilyn, "What if they blow it in front of all those people? What if they blow it and everybody thinks I'm an idiot?"

With only one solution, I decided to join the group and put them through a rehearsal. I flew to Chicago, landing at O'Hare International at 1:00 A.M. On the way to my hotel, I began talking to the cab driver, who had quite a sense of humor, which I decided to record. Pulling out a portable tape recorder, I instructed him to drive around the hotel for an hour, while I got his opinion on everything from rock and roll to the confusing maze of highways that surrounded the airport.

"Now that is humor!" I exclaimed to the hotel bellman as I got out of the taxi. "That's what I want to get on my next album."

The driver laughed. The bellman looked at me as if I'd lost my mind. Neither man knew who I was or what I was talking about, and frankly, I was starting not to know either. At the moment, my identity was beside the point.

The next day I went to Ann Arbor and put the boys through a grueling daylong rehearsal of "Good Vibrations," which probably made them grateful I didn't tour regularly. I watched the following night's performance from backstage, and they played the song perfectly, not a single wrong note. Afterward, they literally dragged me onstage. I received a standing ovation from the crowd and the admiration of my band mates.

Oddly, within hours, I was freaking out on the plane taking me back to Los Angeles. Awash in feelings of loneliness and insecurity, I sat in my seat and grew extremely paranoid that no one liked me. I wondered, Are my friends really my friends? If not, why was I going back home? I summoned a stewardess.

"I have to make an emergency phone call," I said urgently.

"That's impossible, Mr. Wilson," she replied. "There are no telephones on the plane."

Distressed, I pleaded with the stewardess, then the pilot, who finally agreed to radio a brief message to an airport. Ground personnel then telephoned Marilyn with my message, which asked her to gather as many of my friends as possible at the airport. And a photographer too.

A couple dozen people met me at the plane, including Marilyn and her sisters, Danny Hutton, Anderle, Van Dyke, and Dean Torrence. It was such a relief to see that my friends cared enough about me to come out late at night. All of us posed for a photograph in front of a giant mural, the moment captured as a reminder to myself that I wasn't as lonely and alone as I imagined. Still, I remember whispering to Marilyn during the shot that I was so confused.

"Why?" she asked. "Isn't this what you wanted?"

"Yeah," I said. "The problem is I don't know whether I should be saying hello to everyone or whether it's time to say good-bye."

18

Psychedelicate

*T*he reception couldn't have been bigger. The first week of November 1966, the guys flew to London, where thousands of screaming fans greeted them in a scene reminiscent of the Beatles' first trip to the U.S. Some 600 city buses carried posters throughout London heralding their arrival. Their seven shows, including the opening November 6 concert at Finsbury Park Astoria, sold out in hours. "Good Vibrations" was the number one song in England. A review in the Sunday *Express* declared, "They've found a new sound at last." And readers of the influential *New Musical Express* voted the Beach Boys the number one group in the world.

The boys, reveling in the frenzy of being followed and doted on by breathless reporters and hysterical fans, called me regularly with updates and reports. One afternoon Dennis told me that he, Mike, and Carl had walked into a London Rolls-Royce dealership and bought four Phantom VII limousines. One for each of them, plus one for me. I didn't even need a car.

"Don't worry," Dennis laughed. "It was only thirty-two thousand!"

At first, it struck me as extravagant, but within thirty seconds I came around. The only problem was that delivery took three months. Unable to wait, I dropped another $20,000 on Lou Adler's Rolls, a move that illustrated what at the time were my two dominant traits, excess and manic, instantaneous gratification. Except for going to the studio, I used the Rolls mainly to get hamburgers at Dolores' Drive-In and take-out at Pioneer Chicken, though once, for a thrill, a bunch of us drove around the Beverly Hills Police Department while puffing on joints.

Offering no resistance to the tidal wave of attention that erupted as sales of "Good Vibrations" soared past 16 million copies, I slipped into the role of America's answer to Lennon and McCartney with as little thought as I did my bathrobe. Journalists by the dozen interviewed me as if I were the guru of hip. One reporter, Jules Siegel, music critic for *The Saturday Evening Post*, hung out with me and stayed as part of my entourage, fascinated by the fact that I was so out of it I was in the center of it.

Intoxicated by the attention, I enjoyed being recognized as the top dog and shot from the hip as I opined on an infinite number of topics, including the Watts summer riots, the moon, even Einstein's theory of relativity: "Time is fine," I said, "when it's in cadence." Once I offhandedly recommended to a reporter who was complaining about eyestrain that he go to the optometrist; the next week I saw it printed in *Melody Maker*. Most wanted to know the same things. How would I label my music?

"Contemporary American music," I said. "Not rock and roll."

Did I feel challenged by other U.S. groups?

"No," I said. "Right now it's kind of leveled off with the Beach Boys."

What did I think of Lennon and McCartney?

"Incredible songwriters," I said.

And Dylan?

"Great with words, but he might destroy music," I replied.

Did I ever think about the happiness I brought to so many people?

"Oh yeah!" I brightened. "But I'm thinking about the future, when I'll be in a position to really bring happiness to people."

Did I mean I wasn't satisfied?

"I'm never satisfied," I said.

Could I describe the word psychedelic?

"No, but psychedelic music will cover the face of the world and color the whole popular music scene," I predicted. "Anybody who is happening is psychedelic."

How would I describe myself?

"How do you mean?" I asked.

In a word. What are you like?

"Me," I thought for a moment. "I'm *psychedelicate!*"

* * *

A better description would've been delicate psyche. In the second week of November Van Dyke and I sat silently and uncomfortably in the backseat of my Rolls, which was parked in front of Gold Star. Inside, more than a dozen of the finest string musicians in Los Angeles were waiting for me to arrive and begin work on "Fire," a section of a longer suite titled *The Elements*. But for two hours I'd refused to get out of the car. Finally, Van Dyke lost his patience.

"This is embarrassing," he scolded me. "You're acting like a complete amateur."

"It's just not happening, and that's it," I said.

"Why?" he asked. "Why isn't it happening?"

"Bad vibes," I said. "Can you go in and tell everyone the session is off?"

Van Dyke was mad. He told me to make the announcement myself. Against going in the studio for whatever reason, I finally ordered the driver to take me back home. Van Dyke was mortified. He chastized me for being regressive and said he wouldn't be party to any more behavior like that. I didn't care what he said. I felt bad vibrations.

I'd become a creature of intuition, the manifestation of my increasingly aberrant mental condition, which caused me to manipulate people and situations to my liking rather than bend to fit them. All but a few individuals, Van Dyke and the Beach Boys among them, ever questioned me.

So when I walked into the rescheduled session at Gold Star two weeks later wearing a red fireman's hat, no one blinked. Had he been there, Van Dyke surely would've been disgusted, not just by me, but everyone else too. Marilyn, Diane, and my cousin Steve Korthof also wore red toppers. As I watched the musicians tune their instruments, I realized the picture wasn't complete and it needed to be in order to maintain the good vibes.

"Steve, where are the rest of those fire hats?" I asked. "Everybody has to wear fire hats. We've really got to get into this thing."

Steve ran out to the Rolls, then returned holding a stack of fire hats. A minute later, each musician was wearing a hat. Then I summoned the studio's janitor, Brother Julius, an older black man who lived in a bungalow behind Gold Star. At my urging, he reluctantly started a fire in a large metal bucket and placed it in front of the assembled players. Smoke began spiraling up and wafting through the studio. I was smiling. The tone was set.

"All right, let's go," I snapped.

Properly titled "Mrs. O'Leary's Cow" but better known as "Fire," the instrumental track was one long, eerie whine. It built slowly, like the beginning of a giant conflagration, and grew so intense it was possible to picture the kindling catching, spreading, and being whipped by the wind into a raging, out-of-control inferno. It created a disturbing picture that mirrored the screams that had filled my head and plagued my sleep for years.

The chords were weird, sick, not the straight eight. I ran the miniorchestra through twenty-four takes before I was satisfied. Still, during each version, I thought, Oh God, I'm flipping out to have written such stuff. The weirdest was the crash and crackle of instruments smoldering for the final time. Listening to the playback, I began to feel unnerved by the music, strange and eerie. I liked the music. But it scared me.

On the way home, I remarked, "You know, I think that music just might scare a whole lot of people."

No one was more scared than I was. The following day I learned that a building next door to the studio had burned down the night of the recording session. Several days later, I was told that since the session an unusual number of fires had broken out in Los Angeles. It was exactly as I feared. Instead of positive spiritual music, I'd tapped into a dark source, an extremely powerful fire music that emitted bad vibrations, which I decided were too dangerous to release into the world.

Roughly two minutes of "Fire" music still exists, locked in the Capitol vaults, where I hope it remains. Not because I still believe it possesses a negative power; that was merely a reflection of how disturbed I was at the time. I hope that segment remains unreleased simply because it's not good music.

Back then I was so scared of what I'd created I erased most of the tracks. I explained: "I was dabbling in some kind of musical witchcraft. I can't let it happen again. It's too scary."

At the end of November, Capitol scheduled *Smile* for a Christmas release and began applying the pressure. In the midst of the thirty-eight sessions that took place between October and mid-January, my teenage symphony was nowhere near finished and I began to feel my hold on reality grow more tenuous. The symptoms were indulged rather than treated.

One night, desperate for affection, I found myself unable to control my urges and made a play for Marilyn's sister Diane. My amorous feelings for her weren't secret. Marilyn had heard me fantasize about her older sister numerous times. She chalked it up to "crazy Brian." Diane also knew how I felt about her and didn't resist when I crept into her bedroom, which was next to Marilyn's and mine.

If it bothered anyone, I was oblivious. I was absorbed by my own concerns, which centered around the album being unfinished. It wasn't even close. The Beach Boys, traveling since October, hadn't listened to the material, and the arduous chore of adding vocals wasn't even being considered.

Just how far out of touch with reality I was drifting became frighteningly evident one night in early December. I returned home from seeing the movie *Seconds*. I walked into the house trembling. Marilyn was doing her nails. Anderle and *Saturday Evening Post* music critic Jules Siegel were visiting. As soon as they saw me, they realized I was terrified, in a kind of shock.

Siegel asked if something was wrong. I admitted to being strung out, adrift, and confused. I explained that I'd gone to the movies and asked if anyone else had seen the Rock Hudson movie. None had. But Siegel knew the story, which concerned a businessman who, frustrated by his life, undergoes reconstructive surgery and acquires a new identity. Despite the change, he still finds himself fighting the same conflicts. I found it most similar to my life, frighteningly so.

"I walked into that movie," I explained to everyone, "and the first thing that happened was a voice from the screen said, 'Hello, Mr. Wilson.' It completely blew my mind. You've got to admit that's pretty spooky, right?"

They didn't get it. They attributed it to coincidence and urged me to rid my head of such disturbing thoughts. I couldn't, though. I knew what was going on and I wanted them to see it too.

"It's Spector," I said. "He's really after me."

Just thinking about Spector activated a switch in my head. I felt intimidated, fearful. I kept thinking about the perfection and greatness I was striving for and the likelihood that I might never reach it.

My head was like a cauldron into which I'd been dumping a concoction of ingredients—the drugs I was ingesting, the pressure on me to write and produce, feelings I couldn't control. More and more, I was having paranoid, delusional periods. My interpretation of reality was fractured and weird. It made no sense to anyone but me. This was one of those moments and the more I tried to explain to Marilyn, Anderle, and everyone else what happened, the less sense I made.

"The whole thing was in the movie," I ranted as if I could make them understand by the force and volume of my explanation. "My whole life. Birth and death and rebirth. The whole thing. Even the beach was in it, a whole thing about the beach. It was my whole life right there on screen. Even the street number of the house was the same as my old address in Hawthorne."

I blamed Spector. I called him a mind-gangster and asked if they hadn't heard of people like that. They fuck with your mind. I was convinced that Spector had persuaded Columbia Pictures to make the movie just to screw with my head. Why can't all of you understand this? I demanded.

Frustrated, I left Marilyn and Anderle in the kitchen and pulled Siegel into the den. I'd make him understand. My jukebox, which sat in the corner, was stocked with Spector's hits as well as a few Beach Boys' songs. I punched up "Be My Baby," blasting out at full volume. After it finished, I played it again. Then a third time. I continued playing it until I began to drive myself mad with jealousy.

"Spector's always been a big thing with me," I explained to my journalist friend. "I heard that song three and a half years ago and I knew that it was between him and me. I knew exactly where he was at and now I've gone beyond him. You can understand how that movie might get someone upset under those circumstances, can't you?"

Siegel wasn't getting it, either. Perhaps, I thought, I wasn't explaining it clearly. I sat down at my desk and got out a piece of paper. I drew a diagram, a curved line, and then divided it into sections. At one end was Spector. I wrote down his name and then the word studio. He'd understood how to utilize the studio, the first one to really understand the magic of production.

"But I've gone beyond him now," I said. "I'm doing the spiritual sound, a white spiritual sound. Religious music. Did you hear the Beatles' album, *Rubber Soul?* Religious, right? That's the whole movement. That's where I'm going. It's going to scare a lot of people."

Indeed. But no one was more scared than me.

At the time, I had finished, or almost finished, a number of songs, the titles revealing the unfocused state of my symphony-in-progress: "Good Vibrations," "Do You Dig Worms?," "Wind Chimes," "Cabin Essence," "Wonderful," "I'm in Great Shape," "Child Is the Father of the Man," "Fire," "Love to Say Da Da," "The Old Master Painter," "You're Welcome," "I Ran," and "Prayer." Also in the works were "Heroes and

Villains," "Holidays," and "I Don't Know." There were a number of others too, some developed, some as brief as one minute, including "George Fell," "Barnyard," "Look," "She's Goin' Bald," "I Wanna Be Around," "My Only Sunshine," and "Been Away Too Long."

In early December 1966, Capitol printed album covers and took out ads for the much anticipated follow-up to *Pet Sounds* in *Billboard*. On the sixteenth, I notified the record company that I wasn't going to deliver the album before January 1, but I promised to get it in before the fifteenth. However, I knew that was impossible. Too much was working against me.

For starters, the drugs. Speed let me see farther than I'd ever seen, but I couldn't *get* anyplace on it. I found it impossible to make the connections as naturally as I once did. Then Capitol rejected as crazy my ideas for humor and sound effects albums, which led to the formation of Brother Records, an independent label I could use as an outlet for any brainstorm, commercial or not. Since it was Anderle's idea, he naturally was named president.

But the first order of business did nothing to ease my mind. Working with the Beach Boys' business manager Nick Grillo, and attorney, Abe Somers, Anderle found an error in Capitol's royalty payments to me and filed a lawsuit against our longtime label, alleging the withholding of $275,000. Right or wrong, I only knew the lawsuit caused acrimonious feelings between me and the record company, which was already upset that I was unable to deliver new material, and this added to the considerable weight I felt to finish *Smile* and make a hit.

On top of all that the Beach Boys returned home and began listening to the songs I'd written, their anticipation turning to anger with each cut. None of them liked a thing. Mike, naturally, was the most vitriolic in his attacks, accusing me of experimenting the group right out of an album. I'd committed the cardinal sin: I'd fucked with the formula.

At best, I was a fragile soul who needed nurturing. All of my close relationships were based on that fact, especially my marriage with Marilyn. But the guys didn't understand. They returned from months of touring, heard music that challenged the conventional approach of pop album making, song structure, and sequence, and they blew up. Their priority was getting radio airplay; mine was making art.

I was on a high wire, no safety net to catch me, struggling to keep my balance. With some kind of a support system, who knows, I might've been able to accomplish what I set out to do.

But there was no support system.

19

"Heroes and Villains"

*I*t started with a call to my business manager Nick Grillo. I explained that I needed a more creative atmosphere. The sheer force of my personality had already turned the Laurel Way house into a drug-addled, supercharged funhouse that manufactured whimsical ideas around the clock, a psychedelicate refuge where I walked the halls like the emperor in his new clothes. Everything I said was brilliant. Or so I was told. But for the work I wanted to do, it was stultifying.

It wasn't enough. I needed more. I had to get farther out.

That's when the carpenters arrived and began constructing a giant boxlike frame around the piano. It was gorgeous, two and a half feet high. A couple of days later, several dump trucks rumbled up the driveway and workmen emptied two tons of sand into the newly built box. Marilyn, who disapproved, reluctantly gave in to my search for inspiration.

"Who am I to argue with the creator?" she said, exasperated.

"You've got to understand," I said, with an undertone of desperation. "I want to play in the sand. I want to feel like a little kid. When I'm writing these songs, I want to feel what I'm writing, all the happiness."

I knew of no abetter feeling than the moment of creation, the instant when inspiration struck, when the idea exploded. It was then that I soared. It was as if I could fly. Nothing else mattered. I had no other thoughts. I felt like no other time in my life. I was happy.

I was chasing the experience of the moment. But turning the den into a giant sandbox wasn't my only renovation.

Soon after, a wooden playhouse was installed in front of the house so that anybody entering had to crawl through it. Then the den was tented with exotic burgundy fabric and decorated with overstuffed pillows and bubbling hookahs for smoking grass. It was a doper's paradise, but it turned out to be too claustrophobic for my taste. I only used it a couple of times before it was dismantled.

Clearly, these assemblages weren't an attempt to stimulate creativity as much as they were a camouflaged, cleverly rationalized and crazy efforts to escape the pressure and the people in my life. I was looking for places to hide from the escalating demands made on me. I wanted to be by myself and not have to worry about delivering a new album or competing with Lennon and McCartney or Spector. I was getting tired and needed a place to rest.

By placing the piano in the sand, I thought I was on to something creative. But the truth was evident when the regular piano tuner came over. The piano had been in the sandbox for a while. He took off his shoes, walked into the box, then raised the piano hood and looked inside. His face contorted in disbelief and outrage. The goddamn instrument was filled with several inches of sand. He had to vacuum it out.

Van Dyke was less appreciative of the sandbox. He took one look at me sitting at this grand piano set in the middle of a giant sandbox and immediately let me know that he found the sight disgusting. Juvenile, irresponsible, and sickening. Then he discovered that the dogs had taken to the sandbox more than even I had.

"What's that?" he asked, pointing in front of the piano.

I looked around the instrument. My dog Banana had relieved himself in the sand.

"It's dog shit," I answered.

Van Dyke smiled apprehensively. Then he pulled up a chair, refusing to walk in the sand. It wasn't the easiest of times between Van Dyke and me.

It was January 1967. The new year began when I told Capitol I couldn't deliver by the fifteenth as I'd previously said. I couldn't do much of anything, actually. Too much speed had whittled my power of concentration to a fraction of what it had once been. I couldn't pull songs together. I was tugged and distracted by the swirl of social confusion. Frustrated, I tried to blame Van Dyke for my problems.

"I'll have none of that," he snapped. "I'm engaged in the work of songwriting with you. But this process can't be completed if we aren't able to sit down in a room."

"We are," I argued. "We can."

"I mean," he said, "alone. We have to be able to sit down in a room alone."

"But these are my friends," I said referring to my entourage.

"They are hustlers with an eye toward potential wealth," he countered. "I am disappointed. The buzz is that you are creating something that is intensely personal. Yet you refuse to act remotely so."

One night while we were working, Dennis came to the house, complaining that the Beach Boys' stage outfits, the candy-striped shirts and straight-legged slacks that my dad had picked out in the band's infancy, had elicited ridicule in some of London's hipper circles. I sympathized, while Van Dyke immediately interpreted Dennis's tale on a much broader level. He saw it as a small example of the shame the U.S. was suffering throughout the world as a result of the Vietnam War.

"We should hit it head-on," he said.

"I like it," I said. "I don't know much about it, but my instincts tell me you're right."

Popping some speed, Van Dyke and I stayed up the rest of the night and wrote "Surf's Up," a song whose title we thought so utterly cliché and square that it couldn't be anything but hip. The music was haunting and beautiful, the lyrics complex and impressionistic. The first time Jules Siegel heard "Surf's Up" he thought the music was as brilliant as lines like "columnated ruins domino" were difficult to understand. He asked for an explanation.

" 'Columnated ruins domino'?" he asked. "What does that mean?"

"It has to with what's going on in the world today," I said. "Empires, ideas, lives, institutions, even popular songs—everything falls, collapses, tumbles, like a stack of dominoes."

I sat with Jules in my bedroom, playing the black acetate on my record player. The two of us listened in quiet, letting the words and music spiral around us. As my high voice floated softly out of the speakers, I supplied a running commentary that deciphered the lyrics.

"*Surf's Up!* It means hope! *Come about hard and join the once and often spring you gave.* Go back to the kids, to the beach, to childhood.

"*I heard the word*—God's voice—*Wonderful thing*—the joy of enlightenment, of seeing God.

"*A children's song!* And then there's the song itself. The music. The song of the children. The song of the universe, rising and falling in wave after wave."

After it finished, Jules and I went into the kitchen, where I grabbed a can of Reddi-wip whipped cream from the fridge and squirted a dab into my mouth. A moment later, I filled my lungs with nitrous oxide from the whipped cream canister. My eyes rolled back into my head and my lips swelled as the gas turned my face numb and my brain to putty.

Weak, I replayed the chorus in my head. "Columnated ruins domino." It was about to happen to me.

In early February, "Heroes and Villains," which had already gone through numerous incarnations, became my top priority. Depending on who was asked, it was already a month or two overdue. But sessions with the Beach Boys, who flat out no longer trusted me, were so rough that I began consulting my astrologer, Genevelyn, every week to see how they'd turn out. If I'd been stronger, I would've told them to fuck off and gotten four other guys to make the album. Anderle, in fact, was pushing me to do *Smile* as a solo.

But I wasn't strong enough for that and the guys tore at the music and the lyrics every chance they got. Desperate for support, I enlisted Van Dyke's help before one "Heroes and Villains" session. Ever since the "Fire" incident, he'd refused to go to the studio. However, I pleaded with him this time to make a rare appearance. I didn't explain why; Van Dyke just knew I needed help defending myself.

Van Dyke arrived late, walking into a particularly tense session at Columbia. The greeting he got from the others wasn't too friendly. They saw him as one of the corrupters. He watched several attempts to lay vocals, but then the confrontation that everyone knew was inevitable arrived. Calling a halt to the work, Mike approached Van Dyke and said he wanted to discuss "Heroes and Villains." He knew the song had something to do with traveling out west.

"But I want to know what the fuck 'Over and over the crow cries, uncover the corn field' means," he said.

Van Dyke thought for a brief moment. He tried not to appear as insulted as he felt inside. "I think it's great poetry is what it is," he started.

"Fine, it's great poetry. But what the hell does it mean?" Mike asked again. " 'Over and over the crow cries, uncover the corn field.' It doesn't mean shit, if you ask me. It's gibberish."

"Mike, if you are demanding a literal interpretation," Van Dyke said calmly, "I must say that, quite frankly, I have no idea what it means."

"No idea," Mike sighed in astonishment, then turned to the others. "He has no idea what these lyrics mean. And we're supposed to sing them? Brian, what the fuck is going on here? I mean, are you purposely trying to destroy the Beach Boys?"

Crushed, I walked out of the studio, and the session broke up. Van Dyke retreated a broken soldier, failed. I had summoned him as a diplomat, but he saw himself as a plumber. He didn't think it was his place to meddle. That left me alone and defenseless, unable to reconcile my vision with that of the other Beach Boys. I knew the album wasn't going to be. I just wanted to mop up and finish.

"I fear we've committed hari-kari," Van Dyke said on the way back to my house. "The only chore that remains is to drag out the carcass."

Van Dyke and I split up in late February 1967. In March he returned but left again a month later when Warner Brothers offered him a solo deal. Without him, the only thing left to do was begin tinkering with what was already in the can.

In April I started work on "Vegetables," a funky song Van Dyke and I had dashed out one night during my veggie obsession. Al, singing lead, was going through his second session of the night when we got word that Paul McCartney was dropping by for a visit. The Beatle had flown into Los Angeles aboard Frank Sinatra's Lear jet to visit his girlfriend Jane Asher. Paul was my favorite Beatle. Both of us played bass, and our birthdays were two days apart. I was thrilled.

Marilyn was pinching herself when Paul walked into the studio. In a white suit and red leather shoes, he epitomized cool. He chuckled. The studio was overflowing with different kinds of vegetables strewn across countertops, tables, amps, and instruments. I'd even played a game of pool with Hal Blaine using celery stalks for cues, cherry tomatoes and radishes as balls, and Dixie cups as the goal. McCartney raised an eyebrow at the sight.

"Inspiration," I explained. "We're doing a song called 'Vegetables.' So I brought a bunch of vegetables down here to get the right feeling."

McCartney and I got along famously for two people who only knew each other from our music and what we read in the newspapers. There was no sense of competition. He told me how much he loved *Pet Sounds;* I complimented everything the Beatles had done. Every so often, Al reminded me that he was still waiting to record his vocals. McCartney was amused by the silly song and enjoyed watching me produce. He even mentioned how impressed he was that I was able to wear so many hats as writer, singer, and producer, while the Beatles relied on George Martin to produce.

"How do you get the objectivity?" McCartney asked.

"It was always a matter of doing the songs the way I heard them in my head," I said. "I had everything all planned out. But it's getting harder to do that. The other guys give me shit all the time."

One newspaper, having got wind of the studio encounter, described our meeting as "like Van Gogh meeting Constable meeting Turner meeting Rembrandt in a time machine fueled by adrenaline and Dexedrine." I never understood what that meant, but the visit lasted a long time. It was nearly 2:00 A.M. by the time we finished "Vegetables." Then, prodded by Derek Taylor, McCartney sat down at the piano, mentioned that he'd just written this song a few days earlier, and started singing, *"Wednesday morning at five o'clock the day begins. Silently closing her bedroom door, she goes . . ."*

"It's called 'She's Leaving Home,' " McCartney said after finishing.

"God, what a beautiful song," said Marilyn, who had tears in her eyes.

"How 'bout your album, Brian?" Paul asked.

"I don't know," I said, staring at the ground. "I've got this song, 'Heroes and Villains,' that I think might be bigger than 'Good Vibrations.' I just can't get it right, though."

"Listen to him, the tormented artist," interjected Taylor. "Paul, Brian is the king of second thoughts, third thoughts, and so on. But it doesn't affect my job any. What he doesn't release makes nearly as much news as what he does eventually put out."

McCartney laughed. On his way out, he told me to hurry up. The Beatles had a new album due out in the summer: *Sgt. Pepper's Lonely Hearts Club Band.*

A month later, the middle of May 1967, I began to lose it. One session I refused to let Siegel inside to watch after convincing myself that his wife was a witch who was using ESP to confuse my brain. Days later I quit going to the studio. Capitol immediately canceled *Smile*'s release. For the next week, I sat in the house, closing the door on my family, my friends, and my music, and let myself begin to slip into the dark recesses of a depression that knew no bounds.

Previously, I'd always risen from depressions to meet the next challenge. Every song and every album had been like that. Besting my fears.

Proving to myself I wasn't a loser. Rising to the challenge. Music had always been my way of making sense of the world, but now not even the music was making sense anymore. Now I couldn't get up.

After smoking a joint one night, I played a tape of "Surf's Up." Its beauty nearly destroyed me. When it finished, I nearly destroyed the tape.

"Columnated ruins domino. Empires, ideas, lives, institutions—everything has to fall, tumbling like dominoes.

"The music hall a costly bow. Then even the music is gone.

"Canvass the town and brush the backdrop. He's off in his vision, on a trip. Reality is gone; he's creating it like a dream.

"Dove nested towers. The laughs come hard in 'Auld Lang Syne.' Then there's the parties, the drinking, trying to forget the wars, the battles at sea.

"A choke of grief. At his own sorrow and the emptiness of his life, because he can't even cry for the suffering in the world, for his own suffering."

I stayed in my bedroom and listened to the noises while Marilyn was supervising a slew of workmen who dismantled the sandbox. Hammers. Saws. Boards being ripped. Shoveling. Dump trucks hauling everything away. As I quit going to the studio, I might as well have been put in a dumpster and hauled away myself.

Anxious to clear both the craziness and the crowds out of our lives, Marilyn put the Laurel Way house up for sale immediately after the *Smile* album was canceled. A couple of weeks later, in April 1967, we paid $320,000 for a fourteen-room Spanish-style mansion in Bel Air that had once belonged to Tarzan creator Edgar Rice Burroughs. I loved the arches and the fountain in front, Marilyn liked the grounds and large rooms. We bought the place without ever seeing the upstairs.

Marilyn wanted a normal home. As if telling me that could reverse the chemistry that had been changing inside me since my first LSD trip. But I was all for a change of scenery too. The only remnants of our old place were my grand piano and oversized hand-carved bed frame. Reluctantly, she gave in when I wanted to paint the outside hot pink, but after receiving a threatening letter from the Bel Air Association, she repainted the exterior a more acceptable beige.

Since I'd stopped going to the studio, the studio was brought to me. A state-of-the-art recording studio was installed in the house, directly under my bedroom. The Beach Boys hoped that the close proximity would stimulate me to work. I wouldn't even have to change out of my pajamas.

I started out enthusiastic. With the guys helping, I began assessing the tracks that were finished before I stopped working on *Smile*. Then we began daily work on the handful of songs deemed salvageable, including "Vegetables," "Good Vibrations," "Wonderful," and "Heroes and Villains," which everyone still wanted as the single. With only one diversion—a session during which I convinced the guys to sing while stoned and lying on the floor—the album, now retitled *Smiley Smile*, was completed in two weeks and mixed in one marathon session.

But by then the fast-paced music world's interest in the next Brian Wilson release had been supplanted by other, bigger and hipper events. The Monterey Pop Festival promised to be the biggest event of the summer, perhaps of all 1967. The three-day concert, scheduled for June 16 through 18, included every prominent name in rock and roll, including Simon and Garfunkel, Eric Burden and the Animals, the Mamas and the Papas, Country Joe and the Fish, the Grateful Dead, Buffalo Springfield, and Jimi Hendrix.

With Lou Adler, Terry Melcher, and Derek Taylor on the organizing committee, the Beach Boys were one of the first bands invited to play. I also joined Paul McCartney, Mick Jagger, John Phillips, and Paul Simon in lending my name to the Board of Governors, a ceremonial position that showed my lofty standing in the rock community. But as the date approached, I began having second thoughts about the band's being on the bill.

Despite my personal problems, I still held a powerful sway over the guys. Studying the festival's lineup, I realized that rock and roll had undergone a radical change during the year that I was toiling on *Smile*. Next to the electric rock of Hendrix, Big Brother and the Holding Company, or Country Joe, the Beach Boys suddenly appeared out of it. I don't think the guys had caught on yet.

But they too had their doubts about playing. The festival was originally supposed to pay the band for performing. Then, suddenly, the show turned into a nonprofit event, and nobody was able to explain exactly where the money from tickets and television rights was going. Mike preferred getting paid when he sang. The other guys also thought the deal was shady. Everyone agreed to bow out.

Announced at the last minute, the band's cancelation was blamed on a number of circumstances: the record label was pressuring the group for a single and an album; Carl, who had some months earlier refused to enter the draft, had a pending court date on June 20; and I wasn't letting the guys play. It didn't matter. The decision was a disastrous one. The Beach Boys' absence was interpreted as an admission that we couldn't compete alongside hipper acts.

On Sunday, the last of the three nights, Jimi Hendrix, who turned the outdoor festival into a one-man showcase of his extraordinary talent, foreshadowed the hard times ahead when he hissed to the crowd, "You heard the last of surfing music . . ."

Hendrix's put-down became more of a prophecy as the summer rolled into July. Music was changed with the Beatles' new album, *Sgt. Pepper's Lonely Hearts Club Band,* which obviously wasn't responsible for my ruin, since I was already enfeebled and growing more so by the month. But July was equally notable for another important release. Genevelyn informed me that the latter part of the month was the right time to release "Heroes and Villains."

It's hard to remember exactly how I originally intended the song to sound. "Heroes and Villains" was my follow-up to "Good Vibrations." It was supposed to outdo that masterpiece and be the new masterpiece. The first version I did extended for seven minutes. The three-minute-and-thirty-six-second version the record company was releasing bore only a distant relation to the wild, rambling, roller-coaster rendition I'd once described as a musical comedy, but I continued to believe the song was special.

Wanting a debut commensurate with the importance I ascribed to this long-awaited, long-overdue single, I decided, on my own, to give KHJ Boss Radio an exclusive. After Genevelyn gave the word, I told the guys of my plan. Meeting at my house, we caravaned in our Rolls-Royces to the Hollywood radio station, our entourage numbering close to twenty, arriving outside the gates shortly before midnight. We were an army of anticipation. Then came trouble.

First, the security guard refused to let us pass through the gate. Then, once we talked our way into the station, the late-night DJ refused to play the song. "Heroes and Villains" wasn't on his playlist, and he wasn't allowed to deviate.

I was demoralized. New spiritual music from Brian Wilson didn't mean anything. It wasn't even on the playlist. But that was beside the point. Here I was, less than a year ago the biggest name in music, holding a new single above the turntable, offering an exclusive, and it didn't matter. It was obvious that my time had come and gone.

Someone in our entourage pushed the hapless DJ into calling his boss.

His boss chewed him out royally. The hell with the playlist, the DJ was told, play the damn song. Brian Wilson's in the studio.

Not for long. Before the dust settled, I retreated from the embarrassment of ignominity into the backseat of my limo. I ordered the driver to take me back home. The radio was playing. As we passed through the gates, I heard the DJ cue "Heroes and Villains" and begin his intro. It sounded forced. I pictured the guys standing around him, glaring.

That wasn't how I wanted my music to be played. Instead of listening, I flipped the radio off and sank into a deep, deep funk. I heard the rumble of the Rolls's motor. And over that I heard a voice. My dad's.

20

Fatherhood

I
t was August 1967. At the piano, I was teaching Danny Hutton and two other guys, Chuck Negron and Cory Wells, four songs I'd written, including "Time to Get Alone" and "Darlin'." From the first time I heard him sing, two years before, I loved Danny's voice. With Chuck and Cory, he now shared vocals in a group so new they didn't have a name yet. As the session broke up that night, I thought of a good one, Redwood.

"What?" Danny asked. "What kind of name is that?"

"It's like the trees," I said. "They grow extremely tall."

"I like it," Danny said.

With the Beach Boys on the road, making up for the financial disaster of *Smile*, I offered to produce Redwood. It was the first time in five years I wasn't frantically trying to prepare a new album for the Beach Boys, and I wanted to take advantage of that by doing something that excited me. Redwood was the hottest band I'd heard in years. I had big plans for them.

After speaking to Anderle about signing Redwood to Brother Records, I spent a day with the group recording "Time to Get Alone," a session during which I discovered I hadn't lost my touch as much as my desire. When we got together several days later at Wally Heider's recording studio, however, it was pretty obvious I wasn't the old Brian Wilson who'd once cracked the whip in the studio like General Patton.

*   *   *

This time the string section from the L.A. Philharmonic had come in after a performance, the members still wearing their tuxedos. They presented a sharp contrast to my jeans, T-shirt, and the oxygen tank I kept close by in case I wanted a quick blast of head-clearing fresh air. After Marilyn and Diane handed out charts, I listened to two takes. It wasn't working.

"Marilyn, you know what they need?" I said. "Breath spray."

"What?" she asked, confused.

"Breath spray," I said. "Binaca. Go out and get some."

Everybody took a short break until Marilyn returned. Then I had her walk up to each musician and give them a breath-freshening blast into their mouth. I'm sure they thought I was nuts. I don't know what I was thinking. In the meantime, though, I took a couple of blasts of oxygen, then went into the back alley and began doing wind sprints. I'm sure I had a reason that made sense.

On the way back in, I phoned Genevelyn—a bad move. She told me I was on a down cycle. Whatever I was involved in wasn't going to work out. After hanging up, I left the musicians, Redwood, Marilyn, Diane, and everyone else sitting in the studio and, without telling anyone, got into my purple Rolls and drove home. If it wasn't going to work out, there was no sense sticking around.

No one mentioned my queer behavior when work resumed a few days later. We were working on "Darlin'." Listening to Danny's voice attack the song, my enthusiasm charged back like gangbusters. The song was completed in days, as were the other two I produced. With four songs in the can, I began pushing Anderle, now Danny's ex-manager, to begin looking into making Redwood the first band signed to Brother Records.

The only problem, Anderle reminded me, was that each one of the Beach Boys had an equal say in Brother Records, and it turned out Mike had started expressing reservations about the group. Mike could quickly tick off all the reasons why he was wary of any idea that belonged to me; the twenty-three cuts from *Smile* alone used up all his fingers and toes. After the final session, Mike talked to Danny himself.

The next day Danny surprised the hell out of me by telling me Mike had killed the deal.

"About an hour after you left the studio, Mike took me up on the roof and started renegotiating the deal," Danny said.

"What'd he say?"

"Mike simply told me, 'Brian is not going to do an album deal with you,' " Danny recalled. "He said, 'There's not a chance in hell of it going.' He said the only possible deal was to release a single and then take it from there."

"And what'd you say?" I asked.

"I told him, 'Well, fuck that'," Danny said. " 'Fuck that shit. We're in this thing for a career. Not a goddamn single.' "

"The cheap motherfucker," I said, angered.

"Yeah, yeah, yeah," he said. "I know about him. See what you can do, will ya, Bri?"

"I'm sorry, but I can't do anything," I said. "I can't take on Mike. I can't. I won't win."

When the matter came to a vote, I sided with Redwood, while Mike intimidated Carl and Al, something he still does, into supporting him. Too bad. Within a year, Redwood changed their name to Three Dog Night, released their first album, a great success, and went on to become the most successful American group of the late sixties and early seventies. Mike's misjudgment cut the Beach Boys out of millions of dollars in royalties they would've shared had Brother Records signed the band.

The error was typical of the transition the Beach Boys were going through as the group tried to keep pace with the rapidly changing music scene. In September, *Smiley Smile,* the first LP to credit the Beach Boys as producer rather than Brian Wilson, was finally released. It peaked disappointingly at forty-one. Carl summed up everyone's sentiments when he described the album as "a bunt instead of a grand slam."

By then, the guys were already working on the next album in my home studio, though they seemed to spend as much time persuading me to leave the seclusion of my bedroom as they did recording. But as I lost touch with myself, I became even more distant from them. I stayed oblivious to Carl's problems with the draft; his case as a conscientious objector wasn't settled until 1969. I couldn't keep track of all of Dennis's girlfriends. I got scared of Mike when I heard that he'd beaten his second wife after finding a pack of cigarettes in her suitcase. And Al was so quiet I sometimes didn't hear about him for months.

I was amused, even proud, when Capitol released *The Many Moods of Murry Wilson,* my dad's first and only solo album. Though sappy and out of touch with the popular market, the songs carried my dad's melodic imprint as well as his peculiarities. The album featured several different singers, including Eck Kynor, a plumber who had done renovations on my dad's house, on the aptly titled "The Plumber's Song."

My dad and I hadn't spoken for close to three months, and it would've been nice if that silence had been broken by a call of congratulations. But it wasn't. Shortly after the album's release, my dad went to London on a promotional trip. When he got back, I was livid, having read one of the interviews he gave there. I demanded to know what he meant.

"Just a minute," he said. "What did I say about you? What the hell are you talking about, son?"

"Shit, I'll read it to you," I said, holding the clipping in front of me. "It's all right here."

"Read it then," he said.

In the rambling interview, my dad said that I hadn't written a good song since "Good Vibrations." He predicted I'd never write anything that good again. He chalked it up to luck. Brian had pulled one out of his sleeve. He boasted that his album would make people forget about Brian Wilson and the Beach Boys. They were monsters of his creation. Nice kids who got bigheaded. He was the real talent of the family.

I wanted to read it to him. I wanted to make him eat crow. But I couldn't do it. I didn't have the strength.

Instead, I hung up. Besides, what if he were right?

In December, *Wild Honey,* another Beach Boys–produced album, came out. It included the Top 20, finger-poppin' version of "Darlin' " and the title track, an R&B howler that was inspired by the big honey jar in our kitchen cabinet. Carl called the LP "music for Brian to cool out with."

Though the work was respectable, neither album matched the ground-breaking music of *Pet Sounds* or the daring I'd envisioned for *Smile,* and it was obvious that the Beach Boys no longer stood shoulder to shoulder with the Beatles but were falling out of step with the rest of rock. It was a disturbing fact that none of us wanted to admit. The guys, especially Carl, took over the production reins I'd relinquished. They were confident, even eager. Not that they were happy to have their big brother on the sidelines. But they didn't mind getting a chance to prove themselves.

Yet when all was said and done, they showed themselves to be excellent craftsmen, not visionaries, and at the time, late 1967 and early 1968, rock and roll teemed with artists who could see into the future: Hendrix, Dylan, the Who, Lennon, and McCartney.

The point was driven home in a scathing, downright nasty editorial written by *Rolling Stone* founder Jann Wenner, who months earlier had founded the magazine that became rock's arbiter of hip. Sounding the death knell, Wenner wrote, "Brian Wilson actually is an excellent writer and composer and a superb producer, however his genius is essentially a promotional shuck . . . The Beach Boys are just one prominent example of a group that has gotten hung up in trying to catch the Beatles. It's a pointless pursuit."

Wenner's editorial, the not altogether pointless rantings of a young man testing his power, had nothing to do with my decision, but it was clear to the guys that I had given up that very pursuit. I was just too darn consumed by my own difficulties to concentrate on music. I wasn't completely out of it, but every day I had less control over my mind. As I contended with the increasing nightmares, voices, and paranoia, each day became more devoted to merely surviving.

No one understood. Why should they? Marilyn, Diane, Carl, and Dennis, had all begun smoking marijuana over the past couple of years, but none of them experienced anything as remotely weird as I did. As a result they wrote me off as an over indulged child. My fears were interpreted as heavily dramatized ploys for attention. The convoluted theories of life I expounded, intricate plans I constantly devised in order to survive, like the meaning of fear and how to deal with it, were not even listened to.

Then again, everyone was getting far out themselves. On December 15, 1967, the Beach Boys were in Paris as part of a benefit concert for UNICEF that also involved a cross section of stars including Elizabeth Taylor, Marlon Brando, Richard Burton, and Ravi Shankar. Among the fans of sitarist Shankar was the Maharishi Mahesh Yogi, the figurehead of transcendental meditation, who was keeping company with two famous disciples, John Lennon and George Harrison. They were listening to Shankar rehearse when Dennis met them.

While in Paris, Dennis introduced the other Beach Boys—except Bruce, who was not interested—to the Maharishi, who spent the rest of the week starting the guys down the road to inner peace and enlightenment. He gave each of them his own mantra, told them never to reveal it, and meditated with them for hours each day.

Several days later, Dennis called to tell me that he'd met the Maharishi, whom he described as this tiny bearded guru who sat in a lotus position surrounded by flowers. He had bright eyes that seemed to dance and a squeaky laugh. He looked like a troll doll. It meant nothing to me, but the Maharishi sounded like a character. Dennis explained that the Maharishi was the prophet of something that seemed just my bag, meditation.

"This guy told me to live life to the fullest," Dennis said. "It made so much sense it blew my mind."

"Far out," I replied. "And what else did he say?"

"He asked me what my ultimate goal was in life," said Dennis. "And you know what I told him? I told him I wanted the whole goddamn package."

"And?"

"He laughed," Dennis continued. "Then we meditated. We're all gonna start meditating. The Beatles think it's real heavy. Me, Mike, and Carl have been doing it a week, and it's unbelievable, like drugs—but better. You gotta check it out."

It sounded good to me. I was for any emotional Band-Aid, pharmaceutical or otherwise.

Just after New Year's I traveled with the Beach Boys and an extended entourage to New York, where we had a personal audience with the Maharishi in his palatial hotel suite. Walking into his room, I was nearly bowled over by the sweet smell of flowers. The place overflowed with them. Assistants—handsome dark-skinned men and beautiful young women—scurried around doing absolutely nothing.

Dennis had described the Maharishi perfectly. A spry troll doll of a man, he wore a long white cotton robe and sat in the lotus position on a raised platform set in the middle of the opulent hotel suite. In a high-pitched voice, he spoke about spirituality, fulfillment, and inner peace. The guys were awed, believers. Naturally wary of people, I had mixed feelings. I sat on the floor and listened, though my 220-pound body twisted into an uncomfortable knot.

"So you are Brian, the big brother?" The Maharishi smiled at me.

"Yes." I nodded.

"What do you want?" he asked. "What path do you wish to wander?"

"I would," I said, pausing to think, "I'd like to wander the path to the nearest hamburger stand."

The room filled with uneasy laughter. The Maharishi was unfazed. He twinkled and twittered and without missing a beat said, "Ah, food for thought."

The Maharishi then gave me my mantra, which I wasn't ever supposed to reveal. It was eye-may-mah. Marilyn also received her mantra. Then all of us meditated. I felt some kind of charge, but meditation never really worked for me. The mantra was supposed to cleanse my mind of disturbing thoughts. Relax me. In practice, I was dealing with so many voices and pictures, twisted, unyielding, evil thoughts, that my simple eye-may-mah mantra was easily overwhelmed, and by the time I unlocked my thick legs I was so tense and riddled with anxiety that meditation became nothing more than a self-defeating exercise in futility and torment.

Mike was the opposite. He immediately became, and remains, one of the Maharishi's most evangelic disciples. But expanded awareness was only part of the attraction. Mike often said that one of the greatest things the Maharishi ever said was that wealthy individuals like him didn't have to give up their Rolls-Royces and forsake their material pleasures in order to develop inner spiritual qualities.

In February, Mike was pursuing those spiritual qualities at the Maharishi's ashram in Rishikesh, India, when the Maharishi became embroiled in a highly publicized scandal involving Mia Farrow's sister. The guru made a pass at her.

Mike's belief remained unaffected. Even after the Beatles dropped the Maharishi as a phony prophet, Mike intensified his support. He even returned to the U.S. and proposed that Brother Records make a film about TM.

When the movie came to a vote in the corporate meeting, I raised my hand no. Everyone else also voted against it. Defeated, Mike reared back from the table and stormed out of the room.

"I think he's taking his inner peace outdoors," Nick Grillo cracked.

Nonetheless, TM gave our disparate group of family and friends something in common, and we spent April and May recording what is my favorite Beach Boys album, *Friends*. Not that it's the best Beach Boys album. *Pet Sounds* is. *Smile* had potential. But *Friends* has been good listening no matter what mood I am in.

Made when the Beach Boys were learning to rely on me less than ever, the album is full of good, simply produced music, including Dennis's first songs, "Be Still" and "Little Bird." It came as a big surprise when he played them for me. I hadn't realized Dennis was so sensitive. I wrote only when the urge was impossible to ignore, infrequently. Only two songs were mine: "Passing By," a breezy instrumental, and "Busy Doin' Nothing," a catchy bossa nova whose autobiographical lyrics described what I did every day.

My biggest production of the spring had nothing to do with albums. On April 29, 1968, almost two weeks after finishing *Friends,* Marilyn gave birth to our first daughter. I'd thought about naming her Rose. Marilyn suggested Carnation, my favorite flower. We compromised on Carnie.

Marilyn had brought up the subject of children. I'd ignored her pregnancy. After taking Carnie home, I remembered what my dad had said about becoming a father—that it scared him shitless. I wasn't scared, though. In every photo of me holding Carnie, I appear confused and dazed, which was more indicative of how I felt. There was no question of whether I was going to be a good or bad father. Only why I had become one.

Marilyn wanted children because she wanted a family. That's the way she was raised.

Beyond that, I think children were Marilyn's way of staking claim to a territory whose boundaries weren't always clearly defined—me. She might've given up hope of stimulating any normal, adult intimacy between us. She might also have made peace with my relationships with her sisters. But by having my baby, Marilyn made it perfectly clear that she was Mrs. Brian Wilson and entitled to the status and power that came with it.

Since I didn't have anything to do with Carnie, I was never bothered by feedings or diapers and that sort of thing. But having a baby did produce a noticeable change in my life. Suddenly, Marilyn no longer tolerated the ploys and manipulations I'd used to get her to dote on me. Once Carnie came home, she scolded, "Stop it, Brian. I don't have the strength to deal with two babies."

Gradually, I discovered that being crazy was an almost foolproof shield from reality, enabling me to become a spectator to the Beach Boys' numerous setbacks. In April 1968, a swing through the South with the Buffalo Springfield and Strawberry Alarm Clock was derailed when Dr. Martin Luther King was assassinated. In early May, Mike came up with yet another idea indicative of his business acumen, persuading the Beach Boys to launch a seventeen-city tour with the Maharishi. Opening night in New York drew more police than audience and the tour was canceled halfway through at a loss of more than $500,000. In July the *Friends* album was released. Peaking at a disastrous 126, it was the Beach Boys' worst-selling U.S. album.

I was no help. The further inside myself I disappeared, the closer I got to a psyche paralyzed with fear. I couldn't tell up from down.

I was schizophrenic and didn't know it. Life began to resemble the distorted images of funhouse mirrors.

But there was a logic to that feeling of being scared twenty-four hours a day. If everybody was a threat, if everything was frightening, if strange voices were telling me Phil Sepctor wanted to kill me, if the devil was calling me, then it made perfect sense for me to protect myself, to walk around scared, to withdraw from contact with the outside world, to feel overburdened and depressed, to numb my senses and medicate my brain with pot and pills. Otherwise I would have had to confront the truth.

21

Cocaine and the Wizard

*I*t was winter 1968, as cold outside as it was in my heart. I was on the outs with both Marilyn and her sister Diane. I'd also made a play for Marilyn's best friend, Sherrie Champion, and been rebuffed. In need of an ally, I went to the Whisky-a-Go-Go nightclub, where Three Dog Night was playing to a packed house, and found Danny Hutton in the thick of backstage partying.

"Hey, Brian," he said.

He was up, alive, digging the chicks who were hanging out in the dressing room. I was feeling the opposite. Ignoring the party atmosphere, I stared out the window overlooking Sunset Boulevard. Cars whizzed by. A line of people waiting to get inside the club snaked around the block. I felt hot and opened the window and leaned out. Danny came up to me and asked what I was doing; people were cold.

"I'm going to jump," I said.

"Cut the crap, Brian," he snapped, slamming the window shut and pulling me away.

If I'd had a dollar for every time Danny told me to cut the crap, I wouldn't have worried about royalty checks, but this incident was different. I was actually bummed out enough to contemplate dying. I didn't think of it as suicide as much as not existing. Discarding the baggage. Silencing the demons. Losing the pressure. Straightening out the confusion.

"Cool it, Brian," Danny said. "Cool it."

"Let me jump, man," I argued.

Heads in the packed room turned in our direction as Danny ordered me to get a grip. He grabbed my shoulder and hustled me into a corner, where he introduced me to an acquaintance, a character who looked like the archetypal hippie. He took me into the bathroom and removed a tiny glass vial from his pocket. It was filled with cocaine. He spooned out a tiny amount and instructed me to snort it. Then he repeated the process into my other nostril.

Two quick blasts. I felt the powder rocket straight from my nose, up through my sinuses, and into my head. I smiled at Danny. In seconds, instead of being depressed, I was downright euphoric. A single thought filled my head—more. I wanted to snort more coke.

As the guy spooned out another helping, Danny slipped out and went onstage with Three Dog Night. Enveloped by the second rush, I forgot about the show, split the Whisky, and drove around town. The next afternoon I asked Danny whom I could get more coke from and made my first buy. That night I made my second buy. The next night I made my third. The high gave me mercy, relief, and escape. I got the same rush of clarity and invincibility as when I knocked out a great song. Except I didn't have to sit at the piano and confront the possibility of failure. I got to feel creative without having to do the work and began doing coke with the same single-mindedness that I used to write songs.

It was that way for the next five years. I spent three, four hundred dollars a pop. For me and for my friends. It was a treadmill. Here's the money, give me the coke. Every day and night the same. Snort more coke.

If there was a desperation to my excess, it was fueled in part by how desperately the Beach Boys needed a hit. In my downstairs studio, the guys worked on the band's latest LP, *20/20*. Described by Bruce as "a very un-Brian album," it represented the biggest group effort yet. Carl exerted himself the most. He produced a great version of the Barry-Greenwich-Spector classic "I Can Hear Music." I was proud of what he'd learned from me.

I wasn't completely out of it, though. With the studio directly below my bedroom, I heard the sessions through the floor—the thump of the drums and bass, the vibration of guitars, and the soaring harmonies the guys attempted without me. At best, my interest in recording was sporadic. I could go several weeks without doing a thing, staying out with Danny Hutton all night. But then I might hear something from my bed, run down to the studio, and give the guys a suggestion.

I also snuck down to the studio when no one was there. My engineer, Steve Desper, rented all sorts of instruments for me. Working furiously before I lost the motivation, I recorded countless songs, playing the guitar part, then the bass, perhaps an organ or harpsichord, then drums. I could pretty much play any instrument, except horns, for which I never had the lip. But after recording, I usually became dissatisfied and destroyed the tapes. Desper once complained that he erased more Brian Wilson songs than most people ever heard.

My involvement on the *20/20* album followed that pattern. Despite working on numerous songs, I contributed only one solo, "I Went to Sleep," which was left over from *Friends*. As for the other Brian Wilson songs, "Time to Get Alone" had been done by Redwood, while "Our Prayer" and "Cabin Essence" were both remnants from *Smile*. I produced Al singing the Leadbelly standard "Cotton Fields," a gem I treasured, but the guys later replaced my production with another version they liked better. By then, my feelings didn't count much anyway.

Dennis supplied the album's oddest cut, "Never Learn Not to Love." He's credited as writer, but the song owed itself to his strange new friend, a wild-eyed, long-haired guitarist-songwriter. It was originally titled "Cease to Exist," and Dennis liked the song. He pushed to record it as a favor to the vagabond musician he called the Wizard. At the time, the Wizard was trying to persuade Dennis to quit the Beach Boys and take up with his roguish "family."

One night when I thought everyone had left, I wandered into the studio. Dennis was still there, working on a song he intended to sing with the Wizard.

"What's so great about this guy?" I asked.

"His power," Dennis said. "He's so persuasive and full of power. And he's got these girls who do whatever he says."

"Why do you call him the Wizard?" I asked.

"Everyone does," said Dennis.

"But what's his name? His real name?"

"Charlie," Dennis smiled. "Charlie Manson."

I liked the image of a Wizard, but everything I heard about Manson gave me the creeps. Through the girls, he and his followers moved themselves into Dennis's large home off Sunset and helped themselves to his food, liquor, and grass. Dennis underwrote everything. In turn, he was waited on hand and foot by Manson's nubile, often seminaked girls and allowed to participate in the orgies Charlie orchestrated.

The tales Dennis told made it seem as if he were living the life of Riley, which was more than enough to interest Mike. Although he was always wary of Manson, the notion of easy sex once enticed Mike up to a dinner party at Dennis's house. Walking in with his date, Mike found the dining room table overflowing with food and the entire Manson family sitting around the table wearing absolutely nothing. They were stark naked.

"I've never been into group sex," he mentioned as he told me the story. "Well, maybe two women."

After dinner, according to Mike, the activity began to heat up and Mike slipped upstairs with his date.

"I was having a good time in the shower with this little chiquita," he continued. "We were getting into it, washing each other. Suddenly the shower door swings open and standing there is Charlie Manson. I didn't know if he was Jesus Christ or the devil, but there was fire in his eyes. Manson stood there, looking at us, and then said, 'You must come down and join the party.' Then he closed the door and left. Well, we finished up and split. Wasn't my kind of party."

Nor was it mine. Prodded by Manson, whose music and poetry he continually touted, Dennis brought Manson and a crew of followers up to my newly reconstructed studio to record songs. I never saw them; the bad vibes filled the house and I locked myself in the bedroom.

Marilyn detested them. They had weird names, they were dirty, they showed little respect for our property. Knowing that Dennis had gotten gonorrhea from sleeping with somebody in the Manson family, Marilyn had the toilets disinfected and scoured several times. One of them, Tex Watson, borrowed a car without asking permission. They ransacked our kitchen.

The idea of this Wizard filling my house and studio with bad vibrations freaked me out.

"You gotta get him out of here," I called down to Dennis.

"I can't, Brian," he said.

"I want him out, Dennis. Now."

"But I can't."

"Why can't you?"

"Because he's already here," Dennis said uneasily.

Manson and Dennis made a demo tape and split. Dennis was adamant about getting Manson a record deal.

In the meantime, the Beach Boys' business manager Nick Grillo, hired someone to look into Manson's background, and soon information came trickling in. The Wizard was a convicted thief on probation. That combined with the changes in Dennis was enough to frighten me. I became convinced the Wizard was experimenting in evil powers and immediately sent word to Dennis: neither Charlie Manson nor any of his family members were ever to set foot on my property again.

By April, their friendship began to sour. Manson listened to the band's recently released *20/20* LP, another bust, and hated Dennis's reworking of his song, "Cease to Exist." Manson had told Dennis he could alter the music to any of his songs in whatever way he wanted, but the lyrics were sacred; he was forbidden to touch them. That's exactly what Dennis had done, and Manson sought revenge.

That was one of many problems. Also in April, the Beach Boys sued Capitol for more than $2 million, alleging underpayment of royalties. The suit formally ended our seven-year relationship. The company fought back by not releasing any of our old records, a move that cut off royalties. I hated confrontations, especially those involving money, and sought to snort the problem away.

But no matter how far I drifted, there was no getting away from the monster I'd created. My dad, breaking a long silence, began calling every day, distressed that the royalties he depended on from his share in Sea of Tunes had dwindled to a mere trickle of what they'd been. In May, he forced me to write a song with him, convincing me that together we could snap the band out of its slump.

Sitting at the piano, we were a study in contrasts: my dad in slacks, a neatly pressed button-down shirt and tie, me in my bathrobe and bare feet, stoned but not telling him. In less than an hour, we finished "Break Away." Excited by the new song and anxious to be the hero again, I rallied the guys and took charge of the production, like in the old days.

But the support was short-lived. In the wake of the Capitol fallout, our accountant struck a deal with Deutsche Grammophon, then set up a European tour designed to impress the German record company. On the eve of the tour, I called a press conference that put the kibosh on the agreement, though my sole intention was to speak to our fans.

"I've always said, 'Be honest with your fans,' " I explained. "I don't see why I should lie and say everything is rosy when it's not." Revealing that the Beach Boys owed everyone money, I admitted, "If we don't watch it and do something drastic, inside a few months, we won't have a penny in the bank." I also confessed that much depended on our new single, "Break Away." "It's the kind of disc that will either be a smash or a miserable flop."

It wasn't a smash. In June, "Break Away" was released, hopes pinned to it like a tail on a kite. But it never got off the ground, stopping at sixty-three and failing to reverse the band's bad fortune. In the meantime, the guys made more investments: partnership in a studio that failed; signing Flame, a black South African group, to Brother Records; more real estate. Nothing worked. But then something happened that made everyone feel quite fortunate.

In August the entire city of Los Angeles was shaken to its mortal core by news of the gruesome, bloody Tate-LaBianca murders. Days after the bludgeoning, Manson appeared at Dennis's house. When Dennis asked where he had been, the freaky Wizard replied, "I been to the moon." Unnerved, Dennis wanted to distance himself from this strange man who'd become a nuisance, but it was difficult.

One afternoon, Manson showed up at his house brandishing a pistol. Dennis was on tour, and Manson left a message. Removing a bullet, he handed it to one of Dennis's friends and said, "When you see Dennis, tell him this is for him."

In November 1969, Manson and a group of his disciples were arrested for the Tate-LaBianca murders. Apparently, Manson attempted to reach Dennis from the police station, calling his house. When Dennis's friend wouldn't accept the charges Manson screamed, "You're going to be fucking sorry!" Upon hearing the news, Dennis freaked and spent days piecing together all of his eerie run-ins with Manson.

The last time I spoke to Dennis about the Wizard, he had few words. Just what a sick fuck Manson was. And what a lucky son of a bitch he was.

22

Sold Out

I wanted to meet Elvis. Why not?

It was late summer 1969. Bruce invited me and several of the other guys to RCA Studios, where Terry Melcher was producing a group doing a cover of "Why Do Fools Fall in Love?" Down the hall, Elvis was recording the sound track to one of his movies and word had been sent that he wanted to meet me. I was as big an Elvis fan as anyone.

After a couple of hours in the studio, word arrived: Elvis was ready. Several bodyguards preceded him, checked the place out, and drawled a few Memphis-intoned, "Hi boys. How yew'll doin'?" Then Elvis sauntered in, laid back, quiet, flashing a sheepish grin. He was introduced around the room, then to me. I seemed to impress him.

"I've heard a lot about you," he said, extending his hand for me to shake. "How yew doin', Duke?"

I wondered why he called me Duke, then figured Elvis was a joker. I knew he was a black belt. Hmmm. I decided to try some humor of my own out on him. Instead of shaking hands, I whipped around and feigned a karate chop and a kick, aiming both at Elvis's gut. Reacting with sharp reflexes, he raised a forearm to block and stepped backward. I broke up, but he didn't crack a smile.

"Hey, man," he said. "Don't do that."

"Just kidding," I smiled. "Nice to meet you. How're you doing?"

"Okay, I guess," he said. "But I'm a little concerned about you, Duke."

There was some nervous laughter, but it subsided as Elvis and I began talking about music. I told him about having recorded parts of "Good Vibrations" in this particular studio and he told me about recording in the South. After a few minutes, we ran out of things to talk about and I decided to fill the awkwardness with another joke. Jumping up from my chair, I threw another karate chop his way.

Elvis wasn't amused. He drew back in his chair, got up, and shook his head. I was the only one in the room laughing.

"I told you not to do that," Elvis snapped, motioning for his entourage to follow.

He was already out the door when he said "Let's go boys."

Maybe. But I was quite sane when, with regrets, I told Marilyn not to count on my being a father. It was September 1969 in the afternoon, a little more than a month after Marilyn had given birth to our second daughter, Wendy. I was still in bed, wrapped under a mound of blankets, when she came in glowing that sixteen-month-old Carnie had just leaned over her newborn sister's crib and said, "I love you, Wendy."

I saw how happy Marilyn was but couldn't share in the emotions and told her we needed to talk. In my heart I knew there was no way I could be a father to these girls. First off, I didn't know how to be one. I'd never learned from my own dad. More important, though, I had all I could handle keeping myself together. One hour I might be laughing, the next weeping inconsolably, and later on trying to stifle the voices in my head that threatened me with messages from the devil.

"You raise them," I said softly to Marilyn. "You'll do a great job, I know. Just as I know I'd screw up. There's too much weirdness in my head. I'll love them, but I don't know if I'll ever be able to show it."

It was one of the most difficult admissions I ever made, but the children only added to my many insecurities. Occasionally, I peeked into their bedroom late at night as I wandered the hallways and stared at their little bodies. They were an utter mystery to me, as much of an enigma as songwriting was to Marilyn. I related only to the way Marilyn felt about them, the love and closeness, the flesh and blood, because I felt the same way about my songs. I'd given birth to them.

If anything in the world comforted me, it was knowing I had my songs, the fruit of six years of being tapped into a mother lode of musical riches. I knew they'd always be there to protect me, as a cushion for any crisis, a reminder of who I was, perhaps a source of inspiration for what I might still become. In any event, those songs were my children and I treasured that I owned them.

Most of the time I was out of it, emotionally disturbed and intent on avoiding everyone and everything. In fact, I've recently been reminded through other people's testimony about the call I answered from the band's business manager Nick Grillo in November 1969. I was surprised to hear from him. There was no business to take care of. After asking how I was feeling, Grillo inquired if I'd been writing any songs. No. I'd been too scattered, too blue.

"Life's got me really down," I said.

"Brian, I've got some news to tell you," said Nick.

"What?" I asked.

"Listen carefully to what I'm going to say," he said. "It's complicated. But in a nutshell: your dad is going to sell Sea of Tunes. That means—"

"He what?" I exclaimed.

"He is going to sell Sea of Tunes. He is going to sell your songs."

Grillo then explained that my dad was going to sell Sea of Tunes Publishing Company to Irving Almo Music, the publishing arm of A&M Records. Although my dad collected the publishing royalties, I was still under the impression that I owned the company. I'd never given in to his demands and lies. Hysterical, I yelled at Grillo that my dad had no right. There was no way I wanted to sell my songs. It would've been like Marilyn selling Carnie. Unstable and trembling, I sat down and tried to catch my breath.

"Can he do that?" I gasped. "Can he?"

"He says he can, Brian," Nick said. "He says he's about made the deal. He's almost ready to sign the papers. Everything."

"Nick, man, you gotta come get me and drive me to his house," I pleaded. "Please, man. This is important. You gotta come get me. Now!"

Two hours later Grillo followed me up the walk to the front door of my dad's house in Whittier. I stood on the doorstep, pounding hard on the door. Blam! Blam! Blam! My dad finally came to the door. I saw his eyes peer through the window. Opening the door, he gave us a quizzical look, as uncertain about letting us in as he was about what we were doing on his doorstep. I bolted inside. My dad followed. Grillo brought up the rear, closing the door.

In the kitchen, I came down as hard as I could on my dad. I screamed he had no right to sell my songs. However, my dad insisted I'd signed the rights away and made him sole owner of Sea of Tunes. Then he brazenly told me to go to hell. It didn't matter that I'd never fallen for his lies. After years of telling me that I'd given him the company with a handshake, he finally believed it.

For the next half hour, we stood in the kitchen, battling, threatening, questioning, and accusing. The scene was violent. Years of unspoken, pent-up hatred and unrequited ambition suddenly clashed and exploded. I threw drinking glasses against the wall. Pots and pans were kicked and tossed, plates were broken, the silverware drawer was yanked open and spilled with an unsettling crash.

If there'd been a gun on the table, only one of us would've left the room. My dad was going to sell Sea of Tunes for $700,000. He might as well have given the songs away. Today, that catalog is valued at more than $20 million. But as far as I was concerned, there was not enough money in the world to buy those songs. They were my babies. My flesh. My soul. And now they no longer belonged to me.

Needing space, I stomped into the quiet living room. My head pounded. I heard my dad kick an unbroken dish and then the subsequent shatter. A moment later, he appeared in the room, huffing from the battle. Standing inches away from me, his jaw clenched, breathing as heavily as I was, he tried one last shot. He snapped off his glasses and popped out his glass eye.

"Look what I did for you," he yelled, thrusting the eyeball into my face. "Look at that, Brian. Look, will you."

I looked, then turned away. My dad moved along with me. We were doing a grotesque dance. I tried to hide my eyes.

"Look at this goddamn socket I've had to live with," he screamed. "For you I did it, Brian. For you."

He thrust the eyeball back in front of my face. Feeling its slick, smooth surface brush against my cheek, I got sick. My knees weakened and I crumbled to the ground. Tears were gushing down my face; I was crying out loud. Angry, confused, weak, dazed, frustrated, I pounded my fists on the ground and kicked, screamed, and cried like a little child.

"Why is he doing this to me?" I cried. "Why, why, why?"

The next day I told Grillo to talk to the Beach Boys' attorneys at the law firm of Mitchell, Silverberg & Knupp. I didn't know that Mitchell Silverberg was also legal counsel to A&M. If Grillo knew, he didn't tell me.

"Listen, Brian," Grillo reported back. "I talked to the lawyers. They said there's nothing you can do to stop it. The deal's as good as done. Sorry."

In the days that followed there was no question in my mind: I was beaten. Despondent, I muddled through the daytimes, struggling to drag my body out of bed but losing the struggle more often than not. At night, I dodged the voices that threatened me from behind and above and inside. *You're burned. Can't hide from the devil. Death is around the corner. Spector's pissed. No hiding from it. Brian. You're going to be killed. A bad death, bad death, bad death . . .*

The words resonated with a rhythm that put me into a trancelike state. There's nothing worse than hearing a solitary voice inside telling you to hide, hide, hide. You're going to die, die, die. But that's all I heard.

Late one day I stood outside the house of Hal Blaine, the Wrecking Crew drummer who had played on all the great Beach Boys records. I knocked harder than necessary. I made it sound urgent. Answering the door, Hal looked surprised to see me. We hadn't seen each other for a long time. I knew why I went, though. He represented the past, a time of glory and triumph. Hal glanced down at the oversized cardboard box that was sitting by my feet.

"What's going on, Bri?" he asked. "Whatcha got in the box?"

"Records," I said, picking up the box. "Got some records I want to give you."

"Okay, I'm curious," he said.

We walked inside, and I opened the box. It was filled with gold records, all the gold records I owned commemorating the numerous Beach Boys singles and albums that had sold more than 500,000 copies. Since the songs were no longer mine, I didn't want the records anymore. I'd decided Hal should have them. But as fast as I unloaded them, he packed the framed records back into the box.

"You can't just disassociate yourself from the past," he argued. "Brian, man, those songs are you. Whether or not you're in favor of the move your dad made. Whether or not you have those gold records. You wrote those songs, Brian. That's something nobody can ever take away from you, no matter how much money they're willing to pay."

"Yeah, I guess," I mumbled incoherently. "But I'm through, you know? There's no point."

"Oh come on, Brian," he said. "You can write more songs, a ton more."

"No," I said. "I did my work, man. None of it's mine anymore. I'm finished."

23

"Sail On Sailor"

*C*ustomers never failed to register their surprise after realizing it was me, the Beach Boys' genius and rock and roll's most famous recluse, running the cash register at the Radiant Radish. But from summer 1969 through July 1970, and especially in the months after Sea of Tunes was sold, I frequently showed up to work at the West Hollywood health food store. I often forgot to change clothes before leaving home and ended up talking to customers about vitamins while still wearing my pajamas, slippers, and bathrobe.

The Radiant Radish, like the twenty-four-hour telescope and Ping-Pong table stores, was the only one of my ideas to come to fruition. It was a partnership between me, the Beach Boys' road manager, Arnie Geller, and my cousin Steve Korthof, though the $15,000 of start-up money came from me.

The business was a mess. At night, I often put cash in the register from my own pocket so we could meet a certain total. I remember sticking in a fifty-dollar bill to give the store its highest daily take ever, $500. I was thrilled. None of us ever, however, figured out how to order, leaving the inventory in perpetual confusion, and almost a year after opening the Radiant Radish was closed.

If I wasn't writing or playing much music, I was still into listening. After touring England that summer with Three Dog Night, Danny Hutton called, excited about an English singer-songwriter he'd heard in London. The kid was in L.A., and Danny asked if he could bring him to my mansion. He was a great pianist, singer, and a huge fan of mine, Danny explained, not realizing he was depressing me, since this phenomenon sounded like he had everything I knew I was losing.

"He idolizes you, Brian," Danny said. "Come on."

"All right," I capitulated. "What's his name?"

"Elton John," Danny said.

Although I said no, Danny persuaded me to meet him and Elton at the studio where the Beach Boys were putting the finishing touches on the *Sunflower* album. It was the first album for Brother Records as a subsidiary of Reprise, a part of Warners. It also was late. The other guys had disappeared for the night, leaving me alone in the studio when Danny and Elton arrived. Elton wore a shiny silver suit made from material that was nothing like I'd seen before except on astronauts.

As a treat for Elton and Danny, I played the master tracks of "Good Vibrations" with the volume turned up and the sliders pushed down, which allowed the intricacies that are buried on the record to fly out. Elton was knocked out.

"So Danny says you write songs," I said. "Play some."

"Not after that," Elton said.

I pointed to the oversized black Boesendorfer grand piano in the center of the studio. Elton didn't move. He had released a handful of singles in England and was a veteran of session work, but he wasn't a star yet. He didn't have any aces that he could spin off to impress people as I had just done with "Good Vibrations." Or so he thought.

Reluctantly, Elton moved to the piano, gave Danny a here-goes look, and reeled off the most impressive string of new material I'd ever heard, including "Border Song," "Lady Samantha," and "Your Song." After each one, he looked at me expectantly, wanting a critique. I only said, "Yeah, that one was pretty damn good. What else?"

Elton's confidence wasn't yet on a par with his songs. After his minire-cital, he confessed he wasn't sure if he could sing well enough to be a performer as well as a songwriter. My theory about that has always been the voice doesn't have to be great as long as the sound it makes is memorable.

"Don't worry," I said. "You have a great sound, and that's what counts. Your music is very spiritual."

Shy and reserved and anything but the flamboyant showman he would later become, Elton asked if I were still writing. I said not much, which was hard considering how jealous I was of Elton at that moment. Listening to his songs, I knew he was hot, that he was tapped into the great source. I'd been there myself.

I sat down and played "This Whole World," a moody, relfective new song that came to me one night when I was at the piano, in the quiet of the big house, stoned and confused. A snapshot of where I was the moment I wrote it, the song begins, *"I'm thinking of this whole world, late at night . . ."*

It was my sole contribution to the Beach Boys' latest album, the soulful *Sunflower*, which also came out that same month, July 1970. Though critics embraced it, praising inspired cuts such as "Cool, Cool Water," which I'd written a couple of years earlier as a Coca-Cola commercial, and Carl's superb production of "Add Some Music," on which I played piano, the album was overlooked by record buyers. In October, it reached its highest chart position at 151.

After the guys returned from touring Europe, where they were still popular enough to sell out arenas, it became apparent to the Beach Boys that I wasn't the only head case in the band. On a swing through the Pacific Northwest, Mike suddenly went berserk. Coming off a three-week fast, part of his TM practice, his thinking became manic and irrational. He had to be hospitalized.

With Mike out of commission, the guys asked me to fill in on several dates, which I did. I toured for three days, a little-known asterisk to my reputation as a nonperforming recluse. I actually had a good time.

But I had a better time staying home, where I settled into a routine of sleeping late, eating immense amounts of fattening junk food, smoking pot, snorting coke, and spending almost every night at Danny Hutton's Laurel Canyon house. Protected by barbed wire and a television camera outside the front gate, Danny's house started jumping around 2:00 A.M., after the clubs emptied out. On any given evening John Lennon, Ringo Starr, Harry Nilsson, Lowell George, or Billy Preston would be there.

The place had a great vibe. Danny had several pianos in his music room, enough so that there was always an impromptu jam. An ample supply of stimulants fueled the creativity. It was the apogee of A-list hangouts. My M.O. was to arrive, look at everybody, and say, "Danny, call me when everybody leaves." I was too insecure to be around people.

"But they aren't leaving, Brian," Danny used to say. "They just got here."

I'd look around again. Step inside. Ask in a hush-hush way if there was any coke. That was the key. The cocaine filled me with confidence, after which I found it easier to park myself at the piano. I finished "Sail On Sailor" at Danny's pump organ. Playing all that I had written up to that point, I pounded away at the unfinished section and shouted to the roomful of musicians, "Does anybody have a few words? I could us a little help." About four guys dove toward me.

Not all of Danny's and my craziness took place at his house, though. One night he and I went to a popular West Hollywood nightclub. I can't remember who was playing that night, but we sat down next to Randy Newman and I decided to have some fun at his expense. I caught Randy's attention and exclaimed, "Look! Did you see that?" He shook his head no. "What?"

"Ghosts!" I screamed. "They're walking through the walls."

"What the fuck are you talking about?" said Randy. "Are you assholes high?"

Later that night, Danny and I decided to see the club's owner in his private room upstairs, knowing cocaine was done openly there. As we stood in line, waiting to get up the stairs, a couple of guys approached us. They pointed to a scary-looking black man sitting against the wall with a hat pulled over his face, looking like a vampire meditating over a cocktail. They told us his name. Miles Davis.

"You got any dope for Miles?" one of the guys asked.

Danny looked over at Miles, then at the guy who was doing the asking. Danny had steel balls.

"You tell Miles to fuck off," he said. "He ain't God, and we ain't room service."

If we didn't get killed then, I thought for sure I was going to die when Danny dragged me out to a party Alice Cooper was throwing in his suite at the Beverly Wilshire Hotel. The adventure began in the elevator of the posh Beverly Hills hotel when we got into the elevator with a Marine Corps officer. Glaring at our long hair and disheveled clothing, he tried to provoke something by calling us Commie fags. Danny smiled at him, while I hid in the corner, pulling my shirt over my head.

Then I walked into Alice's suite, and the party was even more frightening. The music was strange and loud. The people were worse. Some had makeup, others were in costume. I looked around, petrified, standing virtually motionless in the same spot where I entered. After about ten minutes, a skinny guy with a crazed look on his face bounced across some furniture and landed in front of me.

"Boo!" he said.

He scared me, and I turned completely around. He thought I was funny and laughed.

"You're Brian Wilson," he said.

"Yeah," I said, wanting him to go away.

"I'm Iggy," he said. "Iggy Pop."

Before meeting Iggy, I was ready to leave, and his boo accelerated my intentions. I found Danny, who was enjoying himself. Seeing me uptight, he tried to relax me by introducing Alice. Like Iggy, he was nicer than his getup led me to believe. But I couldn't handle the party and all the people and told Danny I had to get out as soon as possible.

That was okay. Somehow, though, in the process of leaving, both Alice and Iggy were invited to continue the party up at my house. They accepted. But my idea of a party was different from theirs.

Up at my house, I positioned everyone around the piano and began playing "Shortnin' Bread," the children's song. With me singing lead, I instructed Alice to repeat, "Mama, mama, mama" and Iggy to chant, "Shortnin', shortnin', shortnin'." Thinking something was up my sleeve, they enjoyed this bizarre situation for about fifteen minutes. But after about an hour of singing "Shortnin' Bread," they realized that either I really was as off the deep end as rumor had it or I was having fun at their expense. In truth it was a combination of both. Either way, they left.

"This is too much for us," Iggy said. "Too damn weird."

One night in early spring 1971 I drove to the beach, parked the car, and walked out onto the deserted sand. If Marilyn, sleeping in a separate bedroom that night, had known where I was going, she would've hidden the car keys, perhaps robbing me of the inspiration that led to one of my best and least-known songs. Of course, she would've had good reason. Lately, I'd been depressed, preoccupied with death. I'd ordered the gardener to dig a grave in the backyard and threatened to drive my Rolls off the Santa Monica pier.

Looking out toward the ocean, my mind, as it did almost every hour of every day, worked to explain the inconsistencies that dominated my life: the pain, torment, and confusion and the beautiful music I was able to make. Was there an answer? Did I have no control? Had I ever?

Feeling shipwrecked on an existential island, I lost myself in the blanket of darkness that stretched beyond the breaking waves to the other side of the Earth. The ocean was so incredibly vast, the universe so large, and suddenly I saw myself in proportion to that, a little pebble of sand, a jellyfish floating on top of the water, traveling with the current. I felt dwarfed, temporary.

The next day I began writing "Till I Die," perhaps the most personal song I ever wrote for the Beach Boys. In doing so I wanted to re-create the swell of emotions I'd felt at the beach the previous night. For several weeks, I struggled at the piano, experimenting with rhythms and chord changes, trying to emulate in sound the ocean's shifting tides and moods as well as its sheer enormity. I wanted the music to reflect the loneliness of floating a raft in the middle of the Pacific. I wanted each note to sound as if it was disappearing into the hugeness of the universe.

> I'm a cork on the ocean
> Floating over the raging sea
> How deep is the ocean?
> I lost my way
>
> I'm a rock in a landslide
> Rolling over the mountainside
> How deep is the valley?
> It kills my soul
>
> I'm a leaf on a windy day
> Pretty soon I'll be blown away
> How long will the wind blow?
> Until I die

I was vaguely aware of the shift in popularity the Beach Boys earned after playing with the Grateful Dead at San Francisco's Fillmore East at the end of April 1971. But their bravura performance, highlighting the band's trove of old favorites and crackerjack musicianship, won them a following among the counterculture for the first time since *Pet Sounds*, and they returned to L.A. with renewed confidence and a shrewd new manager.

I first met Jack Rieley at the Radiant Radish. When the Beach Boys hired him he was an ex-DJ who claimed to be a former journalist, who had won the Pulitzer Prize. Although he was later exposed as a liar, his cockiness and grasp of what the band needed to do to get out of the doldrums was perfect for the time. As the guys began recording their next album, *Landlocked*, Rieley seemed to have all the right answers.

However, it was equally obvious that I was out of synch with everyone when I played them a new song I'd written, "Till I Die." When I finished, Mike laughed out of disgust.

"What a fucking downer!" he said.

Carl and Al agreed.

"We make upbeat albums," Mike said. "That's what our fans like."

Crushed by the rejection, I walked out of the studio knowing the song was good but that I was unable to defend myself. Several days later, I went into the studio by myself and recorded "Till I Die" anyway. It was something I had to do.

Eventually, out of respect, but mostly because they needed material, the song was included on the album. While that was satisfying, I wasn't happy when Rieley told me the album was no longer being called *Landlocked*.

"What's it called?" I asked.

"*Surf's Up*," he said.

"Yeah. A couple of years ago Van Dyke Parks and I wrote a song with that same title," I said, evidencing how distanced I was from the Beach Boys' scene. "That's weird."

"No, it's not," he said. "We've redone the song and put it on the album."

Confused at first, I then got angry. I was superstitious about the *Smile* material. "Surf's Up" was a personal song, the centerpiece of that failed album. The guys had never liked the song or understood it. But, needing material, they lifted my performance from a 1967 Leonard Bernstein television special, layered it over the original track, and surrounded it with vocals that attempted to imitate a Brian Wilson sound.

I didn't like what I heard. But when it was clear that the song was staying on the album despite my protests, I gamely tried to help by singing the lead vocals myself. The lyrics were taped to a music stand in the studio. I tried a dozen times, maybe more. But I couldn't pull it off the way I had done originally, the way I heard the hauntingly beautiful song in my head.

Released in the early fall, the *Surf's Up* album climbed to twenty-nine in October, the Beach Boys' best commercial showing in a while. I was very moved by Bruce Johnston's song "Disney Girls," but I didn't have an attachment of any kind to the album. "Till I Die" was my postcard to the outside world. The song summed up everything I had to say at the time. *Surf's Up* gave me an eerie feeling of what might've been.

After that album came out, I played it nonstop for several days and then put it away until it was rereleased in 1990. *Surf's Up* bothered me. I made peace with the production and what might have been had *Smile* turned out, but I never got used to the way the haunting lyrics, written years before, forecast my deterioration:

> To a song dissolved in the dawn
> The music hall is a costly bow
> The music all is lost for now
> To a muted trumpeter's swan
> Columnated ruins domino

It was early spring 1972. Chronically high, depressed, and crazy, I was a cork on the ocean. I remember only snapshots:

CLICK: There was a fight. Drinking red wine one night with Marilyn and her best friend, Sherrie Champion, I fixated on Sherrie, then acted on impulse and grabbed her breast. She screamed and darted out of the room. Marilyn yelled, "Brian!" The three of us were drunk, and I didn't realize that I'd done something so wrong. But suddenly, Sherrie came into the room holding a large kitchen knife, threatening to kill me. I locked myself in the bedroom.

CLICK: More than a dozen suitcases and bags were piled by the front door, several beefy roadies carrying them out to waiting vans. Marilyn, Carnie, Wendy, and Diane were bundled up for the long flight to Holland, where the Beach Boys, in one of their most ludicrous ideas yet—this one stemming from Rieley—decided to build a studio and record an album. I'd trudged down from bed, still in my pajamas, to say good-bye.

"You're no better than the children," Marilyn said, resigned to that fact.

"Don't get mad at me," I said.

As the sole dissenter and the biggest problem, I was staying behind until Marilyn got the kids settled in Holland. Then she planned on fetching me. But once there, Marilyn didn't want to fly back again, and I was convinced to take the flight alone. Unaccompanied, I went to the airport three separate times before I actually boarded the plane.

The plane landed on time, but without me. Marilyn found my passport and ticket on my seat. But I wasn't anywhere in sight. She panicked. She knew I didn't like traveling, especially flying. She had someone call LAX. They had me listed as having boarded the plane. Security was notified. Finally, after searching the entire airport, a guard discovered me sleeping on a sofa in the duty-free lounge.

I had no idea of the activity and concern my disappearance had caused. I'd simply strolled off the airplane when it was delayed taking off. Marilyn made sure that I was put on the next plane and watched until it took off.

CLICK: Within the first month, I lost interest in the album and concentrated on smoking hash, which is prevalent in Holland. I began imagining the guys conspiring against me, instead of the truth: it was more comfortable to stay in bed and get high than it was to lie on the cold studio floor and feel incompetent.

I played Randy Newman's album *Sail Away* dozens of times a day. It put me in a meditative mood that I thought was creative. Listening, I stared out the window at the beautiful landscape, which appeared as if it had been lifted straight from the pages of a children's fairy tale. Inspired, I began writing my own musical fairy tale, *Mount Vernon and Fairway*, which, analyzed years later, reveals my conflicted feelings toward Mike, who not only resembled the blond prince in the story but grew up in a large house located at Mount Vernon and Fairway.

Carl hated it when I played him my original track. He said a single word—"What?" I'd thought I was creating a masterpiece, a work of genius. After it got roundly criticized, I fell apart. Later, Carl decided to put the fairy tale on a special bonus record that would be included in the album package. But I was beyond appeasing and let the rest of the trip slip past without doing anything, sinking into an ever bleaker depression.

CLICK: September 1972, Amsterdam. Everyone was gone from the house we rented. I nodded off and woke up in a living room chair, enveloped by depression. The depression had been spiraling downward for days, out of control, without letup. Opening my eyes, I couldn't remember a time when I didn't feel depressed or scared or paranoid.

Suddenly I felt very weird, straitjacketed, and then, with a massive quiver, saw the walls of the living room buckle and close in on me, like a giant accordian. I was flipping out. Tears streamed out of my eyes. Instinct told me to get up and go home. But I was in Holland. What the hell was I doing in Holland?

I got up and walked aimlessly through the house, gazing at the rooms as if I'd never been in them before, until I was standing in one of the upstairs bedrooms, the room where Diane and I last had sex. Looking around, I was drawn to a window that overlooked a pretty garden. I opened it, felt a breeze. Sticking my head out the window, I looked down. It was a large drop. If I fell, I'd surely die.

Then the thought hit me. There was a reason I was leaning out the open second-story window, looking down, measuring the distance from top to bottom. I didn't want to live anymore. It wasn't the first time I'd thought about suicide. I counted several times before: at the Whisky-a-Go-Go when Danny gave me cocaine, digging the grave, thinking about driving my Rolls off the pier. But I'd never had as good a reason for doing it as I did now.

Suddenly, it dawned on me. My brain no longer worked. I was fucked up, depressed, insecure, scared, and I wasn't ever going to get better.

I leaned farther out and tried feeling the air. I imagined falling. I wondered if there would be any resistance while I fell. Or would I drop like a piano. I concentrated on the ground and imagined myself falling, landing on the concrete, face forward, splat! I felt the finality of being dead. I closed my eyes. It was dark. I was dead. I knew I was dead. I saw my soul circling.

I was dead, dead, dead. I wallowed in it. I lay in it and felt death envelop me: soft, comfortable, peaceful, the end.

Suddenly, I pulled my head inside, shut the window, and took a deep breath of relief, realizing there was something drastically wrong with death.

There was no music.

24

Dad

*A*fter eight months and more than $500,000 in expenses, the Beach Boys finally returned from Holland, having left behind our manager, Jack Rieley, the brains of the Holland debacle, who wanted to oversee the group from there. The record company thought we should've left the album over there too. Warner Brothers took one listen and rejected *Holland* for not having a single. Then they debated on dropping the band from the label altogether, feeling burned that this album was no better than the previous LP, *Carl and the Passions—So Tough,* a flop I had no part of. They didn't need two bombs.

Enter my old collaborator Van Dyke Parks. Then holding a job at Warners as director of audio-visual services, he remembered having a tape at home of a song he had contributed lyrics to about a year earlier. In a meeting with Mo Ostin, chairman of the board of Warner Records, and his assistant David Berson, Van Dyke explained that "Sail On Sailor" wasn't completed, but it was a terrific construction. Then he turned on the tape, which began not with the familiar piano intro but with a creepy conversation between me and Van Dyke.

"Hypnotize me, Van Dyke," my voice crackled.

"Cut the shit, Brian," Van Dyke said. "You're a songwriter. That's what you do. And I want you to sit down and write a song for me."

"Hypnotize me, Van Dyke, and make me believe I'm not crazy," I pleaded. "Convince me I'm not crazy."

"Cut the shit, Brian, and play the tune."

"What's the name of the tune?" I asked.

"Sail On Sailor."

Finally, the music began.

Won over by the song, which showed single potential, Ostin and Van Dyke asked me to finish it. I made a feeble attempt to add shape but showed myself grossly incompetent. My concentration was shot. The rest of the Beach Boys finished the production. Released at the end of 1972, "Sail On Sailor" didn't go any higher than seventy-nine. The song was rereleased sixteen months later and hit forty-nine. In January 1973, *Holland* came out to mixed reviews, reached thirty-seven, and remained on the charts for seven months. It was the best selling Beach Boys album in years.

In May, as *Holland* was climbing up the charts, my dad called one evening. We hadn't spoken for a while, but Marilyn made me get on the phone. In poor health for the past year, he had battled diverticulitis and all sorts of irritations. Then in April, he suffered a heart attack, which confined him to bed. But true to form, he had a song he wanted me to work on.

" 'Lazzaloo,' " he said. "It's a smash."

My dad told me the song was about a guy who went to Turkey and fell in love with a Turkish woman. It was more than five minutes long. I didn't want to work on it but felt duty-bound to help. That was our relationship. We antagonized each other, yet we couldn't remain apart.

"This could be the last one," he said.

"What are you talking about?" I asked.

"I'm dying, Brian," he said. "I'm old and I'm dying and I'm scared."

I didn't want to face the fact, though Dennis had made amends during the past year. He sensed that Dad was nearing the end and spent more time with him. I was too involved in my own miseries to pay attention. But this time was different.

"We'll record the song," I said. "I'll come by and listen to it."

It took me about a month to get it together and visit my dad at his house in Whittier, but he was still intent on recording "Lazzaloo." Again, we were a study in contrasts. Weakened and tired, he sat on the couch while I circled the living room, manic, unfocused, nervous. There wasn't much to say. I let him know I had written *Mount Vernon and Fairway* for him and Dennis and Mike. Then I played the fairy tale, and he said it was pretty good. We discussed his idea for a few minutes but, looking at him, I saw only the pallor of a sick old man, defeated and sad, and it frightened me.

I had to get out. After starting for the door, I turned and went to the piano. I played a simple tune that had suddenly popped into my head.

"Dad, what's this song called?" I asked.

He laughed.

"That's my song." He smiled. "Remember? 'Two Step Side Step.' "

"Oh, yeah," I said. "That was a good one. I'll see you later."

"Okay, son," he said. "Good-bye."

Two weeks later. June 4, 1973. Marilyn walked into the bedroom where I was sleeping. By that time, we frequently slept in separate rooms. No one ever woke me in the morning unless it was important. Marilyn shook me hard until my eyes opened. Then her touch became gentler.

"Brian," she said softly. "Your father went today."

"What?" I said, sitting up.

"He's gone, Brian," she said. "He died."

"My dad died?" I asked. "My dad died? He's dead? Is that what happened?"

"Yes."

I buried my head in the pillow and cried.

My mother had gone over to my dad's house that morning. He'd been feeling okay, the best he'd felt since his heart attack in April. He'd wanted to go for a walk outside, which he hadn't yet done. Since he was feeling so healthy, my mom suggested shopping on Whittier Boulevard. She made breakfast while he dressed. Suddenly, she heard him call for help from the bathroom. He collapsed in her arms and never regained consciousness.

"You have to get dressed now," said Marilyn. "We have to go to your mom's house."

I didn't go to the funeral. Funerals aren't something I've ever believed in. By then, it's over. Why be reminded of the inevitable? To this day I've never been to a funeral, and I don't ever plan on going to one.

Instead, I took Diane and flew to New York, getting as far away from the funeral as possible. In New York, Diane was there to promote "Shyin' Away," the new single she and Marilyn made as a revival of their long-stalled singing career, though they called themselves Spring instead of the Honeys. I'd helped out on four tracks, co-writing two with Diane that offered insight into our relationship, "Had to Phone Ya" and "It's Like Heaven."

In the interviews I gave, I didn't talk about music as much as I did the effect my dad's death had on me.

"You know, since my father died, it's been a lot different," I said to a reporter from *Record World* magazine. "You know, I feel a lot more ambitious. It really does something to you when your father passes away. Takes a while to get over it too. I got a new perspective on life."

It all seemed unreal. Dad was dead. How weird.

25

Click Click

*W*hile I was in New York, Marilyn made a last-ditch attempt for a life approximating normal by dismantling the studio. Returning home, I bawled her out. The studio had been my temple, my emotional outlet, my diary. It was the only place on Earth where I found some kind of peace. But she stood resolute.

I realized there was no use fighting about it. The studio was gone. The room was barren. Ghosts remained.

It was over. I'd taken music as far as possible, and now it wasn't possible to go any farther. I went up to my bedroom, undressed, climbed into my enormous four-poster bed, pulled up the covers, stared at the intricately carved angels on the headboard, and stayed there, more or less, for the next two and a half years, from summer 1973 to late 1975.

All I have from that period are more snapshots:

CLICK: My routine. In the morning I watched "Mr. Rogers," the soothing children's show, while I had my breakfast, usually eggs and toast. At lunch, I wolfed down hamburgers, somewhere between three and six. At night I ate steaks, cookies, candies, anything that was left over from the day. Later, I watched Johnny Carson, and afterward I often went to Danny Hutton's, where I snorted coke.

CLICK: I heard Carnie, then five, ask Marilyn, "Why is my daddy like he is?"

Several days later, Marilyn told me she'd had a talk with the girls.

"I told them, 'Your dad has a drug problem. He is not like other dads. He is not normal. He is a genius. And you children are not living in a normal household. But you're good people. Believe in yourself and believe in what you want to do, and you'll be fine.' "

CLICK: Mid-1974. I woke up on Danny's couch after a night of cocaine. Suddenly, Danny leapt out of his bedroom wearing running clothes. He looked as if he were training for the Olympics. I asked where the hell he was going.

"Running," he said.

Twenty minutes later he bolted in the front door, dripping sweat but looking invigorated.

"I did three miles up and down San Vicente," he said.

"Oh God, that's exactly what I need to do," I said. "But I'm too fucking fat."

CLICK: The bathroom scale tipped past the 250-pound mark. I decided not to step on it ever again.

CLICK: I was talking to myself. You're fucked up. You can't cope. You experimented with drugs and experimented yourself right out of commission. You experimented yourself right into a prison of fear.

CLICK: My trips took me to the gates of consciousness, and then on to the other side. On acid, I saw myself stretched out from conception to death, the beginning to the end. Acid was everything I could ever be and anything I wouldn't be, and I had to come to grips with that. I tried coming to grips with the onslaught of information and knowledge, but what I discovered was an enormous insecurity about life. My life. I opened the Pandora's box in my mind and saw things that scared the fucking daylights out of me, and I decided to hide.

CLICK: Diagnosed as schizophrenic, I visited one gentle-voiced psychiatrist after another. More than twenty. So many they all seemed like the same person. Hmmm, Brian. Tell me about a typical day. I get scared. Of? Everything. You hear voices? All the time. The devil talks to me. And you know it's the devil? Most of the time it's the devil. What does he say? That I'm going to die. And what do you do?

CLICK: I put my head under the covers. I tapped my feet on the bed. I hummed tunes. I listened to the radio and watched television. I waited for something terrible to happen. On needles and pins every day. I was dead. I was also as alive as a scared cat.

CLICK: Late 1975. I had no control. I cried in front of the children. I screamed and yelled, terrorized by voices no one else heard. Marilyn found me in the hallway, incoherent, frightened, in need of more babying than the children. Sometimes we slept together, sexless. Many nights I roamed the house, sleeping in empty rooms, the chauffeur's quarters, anywhere I felt safe. But that was a hard place to find.

CLICK: Nearing Christmas 1975. I got hold of black heroin, an extremely potent drug. Wrapped in foil, I kept it hidden in my desk drawer, which was locked, and waited for a time when I was hurting and desperate. One night, I laid out a couple of lines and snorted them. I went numb. My head fell back, my body followed, tumbling out of the chair. Later, who knows how much later, Marilyn found me in the hallway, trying to get Carnie and Wendy to snort some with me.

CLICK: Marilyn was calling my cousin Stan Love, one of Mike's two brothers. An ex-pro basketball player, Stan was six feet, eight inches of frustrated muscle. Marilyn had hired him to do what she wasn't able to, watch over me.

"Come quick!" Marilyn screamed. "Come quick! He's in the kitchen."

Stan looked around. Carnie and Wendy were eating breakfast. Marilyn pointed down at the floor, where I was lying in a fetal position in front of the refrigerator, shaking, crying, semiconscious. A half-full vial of heroin was beyond my fingertips. I heard voices through the fog.

"Get him out of here!" Marilyn cried. "Get him the hell out of here!"

26

Shrink to the Stars

M arilyn was desperate.

She didn't know what to do with me. Depending on the hour, I was either an overgrown, self-destructive child or an uncontrollable basket case. She was freaked out by the voices I heard. She didn't understand my fears. She didn't have a clue what to do when I shut down. She was scared she'd wake up one morning and find me dead of an overdose. She was far too exhausted, drained, and helpless to go on.

At the end of 1975, Marilyn contacted Dr. Eugene Landy, a clinical psychologist and a pioneer in the treatment of drug abuse. She found him through a girlfriend who knew of his reputation for successfully treating celebrities and lost causes. But she was warned: he wasn't like normal psychologists. He was flamboyant, exceptionally smart, over-the-top in personality. Marilyn was at the point where she'd try anything.

Marilyn put a call in to Dr. Landy's receptionist and said she wanted to bring in her husband, Brian Wilson. The receptionist wasn't impressed by the name. She explained office rules stipulated that the patient call for his own appointment. There were no exceptions. Knowing I wasn't going to telephone, Marilyn scheduled an appointment for herself, the only way she was going to see this doctor who worked miracles.

On first meeting, Marilyn decided everything she'd heard about Dr. Landy appeared true. He didn't look anything like a doctor. He had long hair and sideburns. He dressed in jeans and a flowered shirt. He wore love beads. Dr. Landy looked more like a rock star than any of the Beach Boys.

"What can I do for you?" Dr. Landy asked.

"I have a big problem," Marilyn said.

"That's why people come to me," he said.

"My husband. My husband is my problem," she said.

"Your husband is your problem?" Dr. Landy said. "Leave your husband and you won't have a problem."

Dr. Landy's snappy answer caught Marilyn off guard, but she quickly explained that leaving me wasn't in her plans. She desired help. I was beyond anything she was capable of. For the next hour, Marilyn supplied background. She loved me but detested that I was a victim of drugs and depression. She felt it was tragic that I wasn't creating.

"What does he create?" Dr. Landy asked.

"Music," she said. "Haven't you heard of the Beach Boys? My husband wrote all their music. He's a musical genius."

"Honestly," Dr. Landy laughed, "I've never heard of Brian Wilson."

Continuing, Marilyn explained that the eccentricity she had tolerated as a part of my genius had deteriorated into a blanket fear of everything. I refused to wash, brush my teeth, or comb my hair for weeks at a time; I believed blood would gush out of the sink faucet and snakes would spring out of the shower head. I was reclusive to an extreme. I didn't talk to people, not even my own kids. She told how I slunk around our large house like a phantom, a mysterious emanation that disappeared whenever anyone looked at it.

"Does he have interaction with anybody?" Dr. Landy asked.

"Not really, he's too scared," Marilyn said. "I'm the only one he allows close to him."

"Do you have sex?" Dr. Landy asked.

"No," she said. "It's rare, if ever. Actually, never."

Marilyn revealed that I spent the majority of my waking hours in the same position that I spent my sleeping hours—in bed. I had not always been like that, but for the past several years I had withdrawn into a private world and showed absolutely no interest in leaving it. The only things that interested me, she added, were getting stoned, eating, and playing discordant sounds on the piano.

After several more appointments in which she did most of the talking, Marilyn finally spent an hour listening to Dr. Landy explain what he thought was going on. From Marilyn's description, it sounded as if I was an undiagnosed and untreated schizophrenic. I'd withdrawn and retreated into a complex, painfully scary world that made sense to me alone.

"He's generally frightened," Dr. Landy said. "He's not able to deal with 'frightened' or even have a response to 'frightened,' and therefore he lives in the area of fantasy. And as difficult as it might be to understand, that doesn't bother him. He's actually enjoying himself in that fantasy world.

"The problem is that it bothers everyone around Brian—you, the kids, the Beach Boys. He's not relating on the level we in society expect. For instance, when you pick the phone up, you expect it to say hello. If you do something different, depending on how different, you frighten people around you. And if you're frightened yourself, you simply withdraw.

"That's the kind of person you have to reach out to," Dr. Landy finished. "Brian needs help."

Marilyn knew that. But the question was *how* to help. Dr. Landy had an answer.

Born in Pittsburgh, he was the only child of a physician father and psychologist mother. Thought retarded by teachers who were unaware of his severe dyslexia, Dr. Landy dropped out of school after the sixth grade and worked odd jobs. By his late teens, he had produced a nationally syndicated teen radio show, then began promoting records. He discovered a guitar-playing shoeshine boy named George Benson, personally assisted jazz legend Louis Armstrong, and produced Frankie Avalon's first single for RCA records.

In the late sixties, he shifted gears, earning his master's and doctorate from the University of Oklahoma. After moving to L.A., he set up the adolescent drug program at Gateways Hospital, started a drug treatment program at L.A. County Hospital, and authored *The Underground Dictionary,* the classic 1974 handbook of slang. By then, he'd earned the moniker "Shrink to the Stars," having treated Alice Cooper, Rod Steiger, Richard Harris, and Gig Young—a few who've spoken about their therapy.

But mine was the most unusual celebrity emergency brought him.

Dr. Landy explained to Marilyn his method of treatment: a twenty-four-hour, round-the-clock therapy he had developed at Gateways Hospital and Community Mental Health Center. Dr. Landy believed that if the patient's behavior was changed, his feelings and emotions would change accordingly. Whether or not the patient understood that immediately was irrelevant. Often the patient was too out of it to understand his or her destructive behavior. Explanations came later, when the patient was healthy enough to comprehend.

Pleased with what she heard, Marilyn asked Dr. Landy to start treatment immediately. Before accepting, he explained she had to agree to one overriding condition. His method of treatment required him to have total therapeutic authority over the patient and the patient's environment. After all, Dr. Landy told Marilyn, his goal wasn't to make me a functioning piano player and then hand me over to the Beach Boys. His job was to get my life together.

"Brian Wilson the person is the point," he said. "Much more important than being a Beach Boy is being a whole, live, functioning person. Do you think there will be any difficulty with the band or other relatives?"

"No," Marilyn said. "The Beach Boys will not be involved—no matter what."

"Good," he said. "Brian can be a part of the group. But that has to come later, over time. You talk to everyone, explain what's going to happen, and let me know if they agree. It's important for everyone to understand that treatment is for Brian Wilson the person and not the legend. Otherwise, I won't be able to treat or help him."

By the end of her third visit, Dr. Landy had devised a plan and began teaching Marilyn how to implement it.

My method of escape was to erase myself. Mine was the world I saw when I rolled my eyes back into my head—private, dark, frightening. No one, not Marilyn and not the Beach Boys, was going to get me to venture out of that world by attacking, circling, or pushing me. Marilyn knew she couldn't scare or threaten me into doing something I didn't want to do. As frustrated as the Beach Boys were with me, they finally understood it too.

The pattern had been established a long, long time ago. It was as clear as my dominance of the Beach Boys' musical direction, as pointed out by my refusal to tour, as damaging to the group as my lack of interest in contributing musically, as frustrating as my retreat into self-imposed exile: I did only what I wanted to do. To this day I still do only what I want to do.

The trouble then was that I didn't know what I wanted to do without logic or reason. If and when I acted it was purely on impulse and instinct. My specialty was building walls around myself. Dr. Landy's forte was knocking them down. But he knew you didn't do that with a sledgehammer. It had to be done with as much guile as firmness.

"Brian literally has to come and tell me he has a problem," said Dr. Landy, "and, whatever that problem is, he has to say he wants me to help him to get better."

"But most of the time he won't even get out of bed," she said. "Let alone talk to strangers. How's he going to tell you he has a problem and wants you to help him?"

"We're going to help him help himself." Dr. Landy smiled.

My life started to change in a way that was ever so subtle and different. If you consider life like a game, somewhere, I don't know exactly where, a small rule changed and then so did the whole game of life. Ever so slightly. But it made a major overall difference.

Marilyn came home one day and began acting on Dr. Landy's therapeutic directions. She threw out all fattening foods, booze, cigarettes, and whatever drugs she could find. She also stepped up her office visits with Landy to three and four times a week, preceding each visit with a little charade specially designed for me.

For an hour or two before leaving for his office, Marilyn came into the bedroom, or wherever I was, and boasted in a singsongy voice, "I'm so happy today because I get to see my Dr. Landy. Every time I see my Dr. Landy, I feel so wonderful." If she was getting dressed, she said, "I'm going to see Dr. Landy and I'm going to tell him all my problems. I'm happier than ever, Brian, because he's going to tell me how to deal with all my problems." If I was eating breakfast, she pulled up a chair and confided, "I'm so excited about finally having somebody I can talk to about all my fears. Not your problems, Brian. *My* problems." If she saw me lying on the sofa, she sat down and, in the kindest voice I ever heard her use, said, "Dr. Landy loves when I talk about my problems. The kids are one of my problems. My mother is one of my problems. You too, Brian, you're one of my problems. My girlfriends make me crazy. My sisters and the Beach Boys and sex and everything makes me crazy. And it makes me so happy to talk about my problems to Dr. Landy. I don't ever talk about your problems, though. Just my problems, the things I'm scared about and have fears about."

After baiting me, Marilyn skipped merrily out the front door. At Dr. Landy's office, they had coffee and exchanged information. Then Marilyn went out for lunch, did errands, visited her girlfriends, and finally came home with a smile on her face and a spring in her step, ready to continue Dr. Landy's carefully scripted home psychodrama.

"Oh, that Dr. Landy, he's so wonderful. Everything is sure great after I get to see my Dr. Landy."

Two weeks later, the stakes were raised. Suddenly, Marilyn was informing me that she was taking the kids to see this wonderful Dr. Landy. Then it was her parents. Her girlfriends. Then she told me my brother

Carl, Mike, and everyone else was seeing Dr. Landy. Also my mother. Which was true. At various times, Dr. Landy met with everyone from the Beach Boys to my mother and explained what was going on and how they were to speak to me.

Looking back, that charade was one of the all-time great therapeutic moves ever played. But that's what the situation required. Soon every person who walked in the front door of our house was seeing Dr. Landy, and they all talked about him as if he was a spiritual magician. "Didn't you love what Dr. Landy said?" I heard. "Didn't he make you feel terrific? I've never felt better. Seeing Dr. Landy makes me so happy."

That went on for another couple of weeks. By that time my curiosity was more than piqued. I was constantly asking Marilyn, "Who's this Dr. Landy?"

"Never mind, Brian," she said.

"You've got to tell me, Marilyn," I demanded. "Who is this Dr. Landy?"

Marilyn had been primed by Dr. Landy. She was ready with an answer sure to heighten my curiosity.

"He's my doctor," Marilyn emphasized, "and you can't have him. Don't even think about talking to this doctor. Brian, you can see any other doctor in the city, but not Dr. Landy. He's all mine."

Dr. Landy's tactics were working. The more Marilyn kept him away from me, the more I wanted to know about him. I peppered her with questions day and night. I wanted to know why she was going to him. How come she was feeling so good. How come things were all of a sudden so wonderful. I wanted to know what this Dr. Landy did to her that made her feel so happy. And how come everybody knew him.

One day Marilyn sat in the bedroom and cried, upset because Dr. Landy was out of town. She missed her Dr. Landy. When I asked where he was, Marilyn said she didn't want to talk to me about it. She was too upset. Marilyn's depression was followed by anger. Dr. Landy instructed her to be intentionally mad at me.

"You're always in bed," she began lashing out. Then she shrugged. "Dr. Landy says I should just sort of accept that in you. But it upsets me."

That kind of talk was a jolt of reality I wasn't used to. Ordinarily, Marilyn treated me like one of the children, tolerated my weirdness like one does that of a strange relative. It had been years since she had expressed any anger toward me. She accepted everything and went on with her own life. Suddenly, though, Dr. Landy had given her permission to unleash her real feelings, and while the truth didn't hurt, it at least caught my attention.

I wondered how he knew so much about me.

A few days later Marilyn was beaming again, grinning from ear to ear and bouncing around the house, speaking in a lighthearted voice, "My Dr. Landy's back." Though the man was still a mystery to me, I distilled one obvious fact: he made Marilyn and everybody else who knew him happy when he was available and sad when he wasn't. It struck me that seeing this mysterious Dr. Landy was a good thing to do.

While Marilyn and everybody else went on with their lives, I became obsessed with Dr. Landy. Even when Marilyn wasn't talking about him, I thought about him. He was obviously full of some powerful juice that made people feel good, and I wanted to taste it firsthand.

Living in constant fright, I was like an animal in the wild, an expert at detecting any sort of sneakiness or sleight-of-hand. Nothing out of the ordinary got by me. But anything obvious or straightforward blew right over my head. Marilyn knew I was an easy mark. So when she pushed back from the kitchen table one day and exclaimed, "Wait a minute! I've got an idea," I didn't raise an eyebrow. She picked up the phone and dialed. "Dr. Landy?" she said. "I'm so sick today. Can you come over to the house? You can? Oh, I'm so glad. Okay, I won't get hysterical. What time? You'll arrive at eleven o'clock tomorrow morning. Wonderful! I'll write it down on the board beside the refrigerator."

The next morning I heard Marilyn buzz Dr. Landy through the security gate out front. I stayed upstairs when she went to greet him. I was dying to know what he looked like, yet I wasn't about to go downstairs and see for myself. Instead, I hid on the stairway and listened as Marilyn showed the doctor around. After the tour, they locked themselves in the den. I tiptoed to the door and eavesdropped on their conversation, though all I could make out clearly was Marilyn saying, "Okay, let me show you around upstairs."

That was my cue to sprint back upstairs and hide in my bed. I pulled the covers up to my nose and listened. Their voices were hushed, but I heard occasional laughter and some serious "Hmmms." Then there was a knock on the door—a dramatic moment. Marilyn announced, "Brian, I'm coming in with Dr. Landy." Frightened, I yanked the covers all the way over my head and then put my pillow on top of that for added protection.

"Brian," said Marilyn, "this is Dr. Landy."

I didn't say anything. I didn't know how. Despite my intense curiosity about this man who was standing beside my bed, I remained quiet and still, invisible in my own mind.

"Brian!" she reprimanded me in a stern voice. "I want you to meet my doctor. Brian, don't embarrass me. Say hello to Dr. Landy."

The psychology was simple. Marilyn was pushing. Landy was the catch. I had to come out of hiding and catch him.

Very slightly, almost imperceptibly, I moved the pillow from my head, creating a tiny crack through which I could see both Marilyn and Dr. Landy. But I couldn't see them too clearly; the sheets were still over my head. Then Marilyn stepped forward and pulled back the covers, exposing my head. But Dr. Landy had quickly turned around, his back toward me, so that I still didn't know what he looked like. As I scrambled to cover myself again, he walked out of the room.

From then on Dr. Landy came over every day at eleven sharp and talked with Marilyn in the den, behind locked doors. In subtle ways, the climate of our life began to change. For instance, Marilyn, who had spent years running our home the way she saw fit and never consulted me on anything, discussed every chore and decision with me. Even if I didn't respond, she ran things by me.

Jealous of Marilyn's relationship with Dr. Landy, I had many questions I wanted to ask her about this man whom I still hadn't really seen clearly. I wanted to know what they did in the den behind closed doors. They spent an entire hour in there. An hour was a long time to me then. With my ear pressed to the door, I heard laughing and giggling. During one session, I heard them having what I imagined to be so much fun that I couldn't restrain myself from knocking on the door.

"Who is it?" Marilyn asked.

"It's me," I said.

"I'm with my doctor now," she replied. "You'll have to wait till I'm through. Now go back to your room and get in bed like you always do."

With Dr. Landy's guidance, Marilyn was leading me down a path I didn't even know I was traveling. Every move, every situation, every conversation I heard was choreographed and programmed. I watched the clock. Waited for eleven to come. Listened for the doctor's station wagon to wind up the driveway and then scrambled to hear his knock.

One afternoon he stood outside the door knocking. Marilyn, who purposely left the front gate open, wasn't around and the knocking didn't go away. Dr. Landy wanted to come inside. I had no idea that Dr. Landy and Marilyn had scripted this scene, which was designed to get me one step closer to asking for help. Dr. Landy wanted us to have a face-to-face confrontation.

"But what if Brian doesn't answer?" Marilyn had asked.

"He will," Dr. Landy assured her. "If not now, then soon, very soon. Let's try."

As the knocking continued, I smelled the opportunity to see what this Dr. Landy was all about and seized the moment. In my bathrobe, I went downstairs and opened the door. I braced myself for anything the enigmatic Dr. Landy might throw my way.

"All right!" I screamed as I opened the door.

"I'm here to see Mrs. Wilson," he said calmly.

"I'm her husband," I said. "I'm Brian."

He said, "Is your wife home?"

I was so excited I couldn't really get a good look at him. A blinding sun was shining over his shoulder, straight into my eyes. It looked as if he had an aura.

"Yeah, come on in," I said, and then yelled to Marilyn, "Dr. Landy's here!"

"Well, maybe I should wait out here until . . ."

At that moment Marilyn appeared. She gave Dr. Landy a big hug. He put his arm around her. Marilyn said how much she had to tell him. Then they disappeared into the study. Dr. Landy didn't say another word to me and didn't look back.

I'd reached the point where I wanted in on the action too. I followed them to the den and banged on the door. I let them know I wanted in. Marilyn opened the door a crack and let me know that I was encroaching on *her* therapy.

"If you want therapy, you have to get your own doctor," she said. "This is my doctor and my therapy. Now, if you'll excuse me."

She started to shut the door. That ticked me off. I was accustomed to getting what I wanted. Pulling up a chair, I positioned it outside the door like a roadblock, and sat down. They knew I was waiting; after a while the door opened. Marilyn gave me a disapproving look, then went into the kitchen to get a cup of coffee. Dr. Landy sat on the couch with his back toward me so I could only see the back of his head.

"I want therapy," I said, inching into the den. "Can you give it to me?"

That was exactly what Dr. Landy's plan had been working up to for these past two and a half months. The hook was baited, the line cast, and now the fish, or in my case, whale, was biting. I wanted therapy. Now I only had to ask for it myself.

Dr. Landy told me that I could have therapy, but like every one of his patients, I had to make an appointment. He was treating Marilyn and didn't have time for me during her session. Then he upped the ante. He told me he didn't know if I qualified for therapy.

"What do I have to do to qualify?" I asked.

"Call my office," he said. "We'll talk about it."

"Okay, what's your number?" I asked.

"It's in the book," he said.

Okay. I spent a day searching for the phone book. Then I lost the paper where I wrote the number. Then I misplaced the phone book and couldn't find it. Then I couldn't find my notepad. Then my pen was gone. It was a comedy of errors. The simplest task took me a week. Finally, I put everything together and made the call. Marilyn, listening in on the extension, was excited. I was taking the bait.

Although Marilyn copied down my appointment as I made it, I had to call Dr. Landy's office several times. First I forgot what the receptionist told me. Then I lost the slip of paper on which I wrote the information down. When I got the details straight, I then had to ask Marilyn to drive me, since I didn't have a license.

Despite the anticipation, I still wasn't completely aware of what was going on when Marilyn and I arrived at Dr. Landy's Beverly Hills office. Shuffling into the waiting room, I stared at the walls, shielding my face from the receptionist. Uncomfortable with that, I tilted my head back and let my eyeballs roll back into the sockets. Suddenly, Marilyn tugged at my arm. It was time to go in.

Getting up, I lumbered into a different room. I quickly glanced around, nervous, then rolled my eyes back. Dr. Landy was sitting down opposite me. I listened to him breathe. Unsure what was supposed to happen during this brand of therapy, I just wanted to get on with it, whatever it was, and see what everyone thought was so great. Finally, Dr. Landy broke the silence, asking why I had come.

"I want therapy," I said.

"For what?" he asked.

"Well, I don't know."

"Do you have any problems?" he asked.

"I don't know," I answered.

"Then I guess we have nothing to talk about," he said. Then he got up and left the room.

Two minutes, if that, had elapsed. Dejected and confused, I went straight to the car. Marilyn got in the driver's seat and asked how it went.

"Dr. Landy said I have to find some problems," I told her. "I have to get a bunch of problems in order to have therapy. How am I going to get any problems?"

Marilyn and Dr. Landy had spent months preparing for this moment. She let me stew all the way home, where I made a beeline for the bedroom. Following me, she suddenly unloaded. Problems? If I was looking for problems, she had a list of problems a mile long. Marilyn got out a piece of paper, sat me down at the kitchen table, and together we made a list of problems that not only went from A to Z but extended from triple A to triple Z.

I couldn't have been happier. My list of problems qualified me for therapy. I made another appointment with Dr. Landy.

"There," I smiled proudly, presenting him my list. "There's all my problems."

"Right. They're your problems," he said. "Why don't you solve them?"

"I can't," I said. "I don't know how. That's why I'm here."

"What do you want me to do?" asked Landy.

"I want you to help me," I said. "Please. Will you help me?"

27

Therapy

I returned to Dr. Landy's office two days later, the soonest he could give me an appointment. I spent the time between sessions going over my problems. I didn't understand all of them. Nor could I explain them. It didn't matter to him. It was more important that I merely had them, that I acknowledged they were mine, and that I wanted to change them.

During that session, Marilyn asked if Dr. Landy could see me at home. She drove enough car pools for the kids without adding my appointments. Dr. Landy asked what I wanted. I thought it was a great idea. I wouldn't have to leave the house, *and* I could still see Dr. Landy. This was turning out to be very good.

Our first home session began in the afternoon. I heard Dr. Landy drive up the driveway, then ring the doorbell, then say hello to Marilyn, then climb up the stairs. Seated in a chair in my bedroom, still wearing pajamas I'd had on for days, I keyed every one of my senses to anticipating his entrance. Hyperexcited, the second I saw the door to my room open, I threw my head back and let my eyes roll upwards until whites were all that showed. I didn't even see him.

Dr. Landy sniffed the air.

"Are you stoned?" he asked.

I didn't answer.

"Where would you be comfortable?" he asked.

Instead of answering, I got up, walked over to the double walk-in closet, opened the door, stepped inside, and slammed the door closed. Pitch-dark inside, the closet was one of my favorite hiding places. Why? Because sane adults didn't go into closets; I usually got to be alone in there. Five seconds passed. Suddenly, the door opened. As in our first meeting, Dr. Landy was bathed in light. I shielded my eyes. Then Dr. Landy entered the closet, slammed the door shut, and sat down across from me.

For the next hour, we sat next to each other in the pitch-dark closet, not making a sound. I knew he wasn't going to attack me, just that he wasn't letting me run away. Without words, he was telling me that, like it or not, I was in for the duration. No question, we seemed to speak the same language. No one else had ever followed me into the closet.

The simple act made me consider trusting him. Finally, I mustered up the courage to answer the question he'd asked an hour earlier.

"The closet," I said.

Dr. Landy didn't say a word. He let a half hour pass before breaking the silence again.

"Good," he said.

I said nothing. Close to another hour passed before another sound was uttered.

"I have to go to the bathroom," Dr. Landy said, getting up and pushing the door open.

"Okay," I said.

There was something about him I started to trust. He seemed to understand me. Judging by the way he sat in the closet, silently, not demanding anything, I opened my eyes to him and began thinking that maybe there was something to him. Maybe he had the juice everyone said he did. The vibes were heavy but good.

When Dr. Landy came back from the bathroom, I was seated in the chair where he'd originally found me. My eyes were open, watching him reenter. Noticing where I was, he stopped in the doorway and smiled.

"This is a beginning," he said.

Under Dr. Landy's twenty-four-hour therapy, every hour of the day was planned and accounted for. For starters, I was delivered to a team of doctors for complete physical and mental work-ups. They poked, prodded, and questioned me until I felt like a medical school experiment. Medications were prescribed, psychotropics for my hysterical schizophrenia, vitamins, tranquilizers if needed, antibiotics for minor infections I was fighting, and Marilyn was instructed on when I was to take them.

In order to get into my head and know what I was thinking, Dr. Landy moved an assistant, Scott Steinberg, his bookkeeper's son, into the house. His job was to supervise my every move and write down every comment I made. He kept track of my daily activities: at 9:00 A.M., I jogged; at eleven, I spoke with Dr. Landy; a healthy lunch was eaten at one; then I exercised, washed, dressed, and participated in the family discussions that were conducted after dinner each night.

It was torture. I resisted and complained about every step that brought me into contact with reality. But for the first time in years I was out of bed.

The treatment was hard, not just on me but on the entire household. Scott was living in the house. Dr. Landy gave Marilyn a list of healthy foods she could buy and unhealthy foods that were prohibited. He had a lock installed on the refrigerator. Phone calls were monitored. Rules were devised, limits set, and all were strictly enforced. Drs. Arnie Horowitz and Lynn Turner, two interns from Dr. Landy's F.R.E.E. Clinic, a nonprofit clinic he founded to aid the poor and needy, were selected to work with Marilyn and the girls on acting, speaking, and relating in the context of a family.

All of us were learning. Carnie was an aggressive, wild, and hyperkinetic child, while Wendy was withdrawn, regressive, and scared of everything. Drs. Landy, Horowitz, and Turner devised a gamelike exercise that used poker chips to reward the girls for good behavior and punish them for being bad, and as a result Carnie quit eating junk food and began losing weight and Wendy started talking and acting more sociably. There was method to the madness.

Dr. Landy also drew up a list of people who were negative influences—my drug buddies. He prohibited them from seeing me and me from searching them out when I tired of lying in bed. Since the list included almost everyone I knew, it was quite limiting. I couldn't do something as simple as go out for coffee with various friends. When I asked why, Dr. Landy explained that I had done a lot of drugs with most of my friends.

"But that was then," I protested.

"Good point," he said. "Will you do downers or uppers if someone offers them to you?"

"Do you know someone who has them?" I asked, anxiously.

Late one night when everyone was sleeping, I slipped out of the house. Despite not having a driver's license, I drove to Danny Hutton's, where I snorted coke almost till dawn, then bought a little for myself and drove home before anyone woke up. In the morning, Scott discovered the coke.

Later, Dr. Landy called Danny and threatened to call the cops if he ever supplied me with coke again. Dr. Landy also spread the word to my connections: if anyone supplied Brian Wilson with drugs, he would have him busted.

I got sneakier. One afternoon I called Mo Ostin at Warner Records and demanded that $1,000 be delivered to my home. When he asked why, I made up an excuse and insisted that I wanted the thousand dollars delivered in a very precise manner. At a specific time, it was to be dropped in the mailbox in front of my Bel Air mansion. Reluctantly, he agreed— after all, I was still Brian Wilson, and that gave me some clout with record people.

In the meantime, I called a dealer and made the same type of arrangements. At a specific time, drive by the house and put the coke in the mailbox, where there'd be a stack of cash waiting. At the appropriate hour, I hid in the bushes, watching the transaction take place like clockwork. I managed to pull off several of these deals before Scott nabbed me and turned me into Dr. Landy.

That might've been worse than the police. Dr. Landy didn't punish me. He made me learn a lesson. He also called Ostin and instructed him never to give me money or anything else for that matter, without first checking. The record company chairman was mortified to learn that he'd been an accomplice to a drug deal. Dr. Landy was still very hard on him.

I tried other methods. I hid in the bushes along Bellagio Drive and jumped out at passing cars, waving my hands in distress. When the car stopped, I asked for any spare joints or cigarettes. The family who owned the house next door to ours, the Wymans, had several children, including a teenage girl, Betty.

One afternoon I knocked on their door. Betty answered, and I offered to trade her two Bob Seger tickets for a six-pack of beer. She refused. Dr. Landy had already notified the neighbors and the Bel Air patrol.

After about a month, Marilyn began acting territorial with Dr. Landy. Accustomed to being in charge, she started resenting that everything had to be run by him. Despite obvious improvements in me, our relationship, the kids, and everything in general, she felt the restrictions were too confining. The real reason might've been jealousy; I showed Dr. Landy more respect and attention than I showed her.

Some clash between Marilyn and Dr. Landy was inevitable, perhaps. It was Marilyn's house. She was used to running it and caring for her husband. Yet this authoritative psychologist exercised a sweeping control.

She might understandably have felt threatened, insecure, afraid of losing autonomy. She tired of Dr. Landy's willingness to go to extremes. He did things no one else would've dared. He wasn't going to give me a little candy if I was good. He wasn't going to make me just a little better. Marilyn just wanted a household that ran smoothly. Dr. Landy aimed for much more. He wanted me healthy.

He didn't let me get away with anything. One day, I woke up feeling scared and didn't want to get out of bed. Scott immediately called Dr. Landy and told him what was going on. Dr. Landy drove over. He wanted to know why I wasn't out jogging and doing my exercises. Explaining how I felt, to no avail, I finally screamed, "Get off my fucking back." Dr. Landy informed me that wasn't an option.

"Then I'll beat the shit out of you," I threatened.

"Do it, man!" he shouted, ripping off his shirt and offering me his stomach as a target. "Do it! If you're gonna do it, do it! Take your best shot!"

Holy shit! I hadn't realized what a crazy motherfucker he was. He wanted me to hit him. He dared me to. I couldn't hit him, though. With his shirt open, his eyes bulging, and his roaring voice telling me to take my best shot, he was scaring the shit out of me. Wanting him to stop, I forgot all about my original fears and jumped out of bed, promising to begin my jog around the neighborhood.

I bowled too. But one day I got to the alley and decided I didn't want to pick up the ball. Actually, I didn't want to bowl. Dr. Landy reminded me that I had said earlier I wanted to bowl. I explained I'd changed my mind. Dr. Landy said we'd brought a group of people, and they still wanted to bowl. I shrugged, tough. What did I want to do instead? he asked. Go home and go to bed.

"No," Dr. Landy said. "You made a commitment and you are learning to be sociable. Responsible people keep their commitments or they don't make them. So bowl."

"I'm not," I said.

"Okay," he said. "I'm going to rent this alley for as long as it takes you to keep your commitment. For as long as it takes you to roll the ball down the alley. If it's now, fine. If it takes a week, then we will all be here a week. A month if that's what you want. It's okay. It's your money. And it's your choice."

I knew he wasn't kidding. I rolled the ball. I even enjoyed bowling. But I still never stopped testing Dr. Landy to make sure he'd keep his commitment too. What was his commitment? Helping me. Being there for me.

Another time, Dr. Landy and I joined the Beach Boys in San Francisco for a $5,000-a-plate fund-raising dinner at Ernie's steakhouse celebrating the premier of the Joffrey Ballet's dance to "Little Deuce Coupe." Arriving at Ernie's, I was nearly doubled over by fear-induced pain in my stomach. It got worse and worse. As food was being served, I announced I was sick and had to go to bed.

"No," said Dr. Landy. "We're staying."

"But I'm gonna throw up if I don't go," I said, making my voice louder because I knew that in public I could usually embarrass people into getting my way.

But he acted as he did when I threatened to hit him. He jumped up from the table and shouted, "If you're going to do it, do it! Do it here!" He pounded the table in front of me. "Throw up! Throw up! If you're gonna throw up, do it! Do it here and now on the table! For everyone to see!"

"Here?" I asked, amazed and aware that I was again challenged and that my fears weren't able to dictate my behavior and influence anyone else's.

"Here! Do it!" he screamed. "Then we can continue dinner after you throw up."

The scene was something out of the movies. The people at our table, VIPs including Mo Ostin, the mayor of San Francisco, and Mr. Joffrey, were shocked and disgusted. Everyone in the restaurant turned toward us.

Suddenly, I was no longer sick to my stomach. I made an amazing recovery. Smiling sheepishly, I sat down and ate my dinner. Dr. Landy was teaching me a lesson. By creating a bigger scene than I had, he became more threatening to me than anything I could imagine. I knew I was crazy, but he was able to act crazier. If I was dramatic, he was more dramatic. Shocked, scared, and embarrassed, I made the discovery that was central to the rest of therapy.

Dr. Landy always said, "There's only room in each head for one crazy person," and he maintained that he could be crazier than me. When I was ready, he explained, I could be sane. I could even control Dr. Landy. All I had to do was function, be sane, responsible, and logical. Then *I* was in control. I finally understood.

After roughly two months, Dr. Landy introduced the paino. From the start of the treatment, the Beach Boys had been pressuring him to get me to a point where I could write and produce again. That's all they wanted. But Dr. Landy resisted. Becoming a Beach Boy again, he explained repeatedly, wasn't the goal of therapy. First, he was trying to make me a healthy person, physically and mentally. I began to see Dr. Landy as a protector.

I wasn't ready to return to the Beach Boys, to handle the pressure cooker again. Just playing the piano again was a big step. It symbolized everything great I had been a part of as well as everything I was trying to avoid.

Dr. Landy changed our daily meeting site from my mansion to Brother Studios, the Beach Boys' own recording studio. He booked ninety minutes of piano time for me every day. The first time I went there I didn't want to get out of Scott's little Honda. Petrified about returning to the studio, the whole idea brought back too many memories and got me down. However, Dr. Landy explained that playing was another means of communication like talking, and I should look upon it as therapeutic.

Dr. Landy made sure the studio was empty. Despite previous explanations, the Beach Boys, especially Mike, made no secret that they were anxious to put me back to work writing songs. But Dr. Landy kept them at bay. Every day he started me out on a half an hour of private time, playing the piano with the lights off, in the pitch-dark with no one else around, not even him.

It was a peaceful time that very quickly allowed me to rediscover my connection to the piano. I grabbed hold of an E-flat boogie-woogie and played till I was lost in a meditative groove.

After half an hour, Dr. Landy came in and, with the lights still off, talked to me for another thirty minutes. Our talks were always wide-ranging, covering everything from how I was feeling, how my day was going, what I was thinking, what I'd had for breakfast or lunch, and how the children were doing to favorite colors, impressions people gave me, even the weather. If Dr. Landy didn't understand what I was trying to say, or if I was having trouble thinking of the right word, he said, "Brian, why don't you play what you mean instead?"

That was the next step. Relearning how to put my thoughts and feelings down in music and words.

"You want Marilyn to use a different salad dressing?" Landy said. "Is that what's pissing you off?"

"Yes," I said.

"Fine," he said. "Put those feelings to music. Show me how you'd say that musically."

Without realizing it, I was writing songs again. They were stupid songs. Silly songs. They were songs about favorite foods, television shows, girls. Songs about my bedroom, my slippers. They were songs about pissing, shitting, getting blow jobs. Bad songs. But songs nonetheless.

In this sensitive, nurturing milieu, dark, calm, and free of pressure, Dr. Landy and I began collaborating on songs. He surprised me with his musicality. I learned about his background in the music business. He continued to get me to look inside myself, examine my emotions, and put them to music. When I didn't feel like speaking, we passed notes. Or I simply played. It wasn't easy. It was work. But Dr. Landy got me to return to something for which I had a special talent.

"You want Marilyn to stop using your part of the bathroom?" he said. "That's great. But is 'Stop using my part of the bathroom' poetic? Is there another way to say it?"

Oh God, there are boxes and boxes of tapes of these bizarre songs lying around. Quit using my toothpaste. Bring your own comb. Stop Carnie from eating so many peanut butter and jelly sandwiches around me. Strange stuff. But from that evolved more and more communication between me and Dr. Landy, more understanding, and ultimately, more songs. It wasn't good commercial writing, not by my standards. It wasn't supposed to be, though. It was therapy.

Most important, it was regular work. I sat at the piano six days a week, ninety minutes a day, and wrote.

Mike was the first to register a complaint. He said I was using the studio unproductively. Carl agreed. He said the music we were making sounded crazy. That's what they thought all right—until they recorded some of these same songs later on, such as "Johnny Carson" and "The TM Song." Both were among the many songs that appeared on various albums without crediting Dr. Landy as writer or paying him the royalty he deserved.

In addition to songs, those writing sessions also produced break-throughs that didn't concern music, like understanding, somewhat, the voices I heard inside my head. The voices were unpredictable. They might tell me to hurt myself or self-destruct. Or they might tell me that other people were going to hurt me. They were among the many reasons I didn't want to be around people.

Dr. Landy was the only person ever to take them seriously. He was the first to ask me about them point-blank. He was also the first person to offer a way of dealing with them. I had to understand and learn to manage them because they weren't going to go away.

"You've got to change the channel, man," he said.

"What?" I asked, puzzled.

"You hear music in your head too. Right?" he asked. "Music and voices, is that right?"

"Yeah."

"So when you hear the voices, change the channel by putting on the music."

I could help that process along by putting on headphones and blasting music. Or by playing music. Or by running. Or a combination. By putting on headphones and going out for a run. I could direct myself into another frame of mind, something I do now. But back then it wasn't so easy.

Interestingly, I wasn't just gaining insight into myself, I was also discovering an option to being crazy. I could hear voices, be scared, and hide from people or I could learn to deal with my problems and function in reality. I could be a Beach Boy or I could be a bedridden dropout. I could participate in life or I could waste it in solitude. The point of Dr. Landy's program was at least to be able to make the choice.

Dr. Landy told the Beach Boys I wasn't ready to cope with the pressure of making an album. I was still too fragile. They didn't see it that way and began complaining about the studio time he and I were using, time they could have been renting to other people.

"You want Brian back?" Landy asked. "Or do you want to make a couple hundred bucks a week? What's more important?"

When they saw that Dr. Landy had begun recording our piano sessions, they asked for the masters. Dr. Landy refused to turn them over. They were part of my therapy, privileged.

Privately, Mike and Carl figured that we probably wouldn't know the difference if they secretly taped us. They were wrong. One day Dr. Landy noticed a curious reflection in the glass window separating the engineer's booth and the studio and discovered that they were indeed recording me. Without saying a word, Dr. Landy found a pair of scissors and cut the wires to the microphone.

Mike was irate when he found out. He challenged Dr. Landy in one of their first confrontations. I found it interesting. I heard Landy exclaim, "Nobody makes secret recordings of me or Brian Wilson. He has rights. After all, this isn't Watergate." Caught and embarrassed, Mike slammed his fist down on the piano.

"Where the hell is Brian?" Mike asked. "Let's ask him what he wants."

Where was I? I was hiding in a large closet, what everyone referred to as the meditation room, listening to Dr. Landy and Mike go at each other. I relished the way he handled the guys, standing up to them in a way I was completely incapable of doing. He was doing just what he had promised and what I wanted. He was looking out for me and my best interests.

But that was only the beginning of war with the Beach Boys.

28

Brian Is Back!
Or Love Gone Bad

*M*arch 1976. Five months into the program. One look at me and the change was apparent. My weight was 210, down from 250-plus pounds. I was eating health foods. I wasn't smoking, drinking, or using recreational drugs. Although I wasn't outgoing, I was learning to control my fears and desire to withdraw, and sometimes I even enjoyed getting out beyond the gates of my mansion.

I was progressing in the studio as well. Dr. Landy surprised me one day when I arrived at Brother Studios for my piano time. Expecting to walk into an empty studio, I found Dr. Landy waiting for me with several other musicians. They were session players, and they seemed just as surprised to see me. Immediately, I turned and walked straight out of the studio and into the meditation closet. Dr. Landy followed.

"Why are they in the studio?" I asked.

"They're going to help us," Dr. Landy said. "One plays guitar, the other plays violin."

"So?"

"Do you play guitar or violin?" he asked.

"No," I said.

"And did you say the song we're working on needs violins?" he asked.

"Yes."

"Then we need their help," Dr. Landy said. "Let's go."

It was all part of the gradual process of reacclimating me to the studio. After months of just playing piano, Dr. Landy began having me think about more than writing a melody. He asked what other instruments I heard in my head, what else was necessary to flesh out the song and make it a potential record. For instance, if I answered violins, then he asked how many. If I said I didn't know, then he asked why I'd answered violins.

"Okay, violins," I said.

"Then how many?" he asked.

"One."

"Why'd you say 'violins' then?"

"All right. I hear two."

"How are they playing?" he asked.

I showed him on the piano what I heard in my head. The next day Dr. Landy had two violinists come into the studio and I instructed them what to play and how to play it. Soon, the same thing began happening with guitarists, horn players, percussionists. I didn't understand what Dr. Landy was getting at. The process was often irritating, as it forced me to concentrate, expend effort, pay attention to the moment. When an engineer was needed, I had to go to the booth. I hadn't worked the knobs in years. It was frightening, but I realized I hadn't forgotten anything. It was like riding a bicycle.

After weeks of dealing with a variety of session players, engineering, and mixing, everything we'd been working on made sense. The process crystallized. For the first time in four and a half years, I was producing songs.

At the same time, the Beach Boys began complaining about the bills Dr. Landy and I were accumulating. The studio time, the musicians, our own engineer (Dr. Landy didn't trust the Beach Boys' staff engineer after he'd taped us), and, of course, Dr. Landy's personal bill. As the money added up, the Beach Boys, who were footing the bill, demanded the expenses be justified. Carl and Mike were the most vocal. Their exchanges with Dr. Landy usually ended in yelling contests. Dennis couldn't understand why the songs I wanted to cut were oldies. The simple answer is I was more comfortable with them. He wanted new material. One day he burst in, stoned, and demanded I write new songs with him instead.

"Do you see your brother in there?" Landy asked, a question he had to repeat often. "He's working. Do you want him back in bed or do you want him working?"

"We like him working," said Dennis.

"You want him working?" Dr. Landy said. "Great. Then get out of here and let me work."

"Why do I have to leave?" Dennis asked.

"Because he's not strong enough to deal with being watched and manipulated," Dr. Landy said.

"But why do I have to leave?" Dennis asked again.

"Because if you stay, I'll leave," Dr. Landy said.

"But what does *he* want?" Dennis asked.

"Ask him," Dr. Landy said.

"Brian?" Dennis asked. "What do you want?"

"I want Dr. Landy to stay," I said.

In my head I had a whole list of reasons why I hated the Dr. Landy program—it scared the shit out of me, for one—but the negatives were overshadowed by the control Dr. Landy exerted over the Beach Boys. He was able to say everything that I wanted to but couldn't. He kept the guys at bay. With Dr. Landy coproducing, we worked in private and without pressure. He created an environment where I was able to play and write without meddling and second-guessing. It was very un-Beach Boys and I loved it.

Some things were impossible to escape, though. In the early spring of 1976, I began hearing the same old song. The record company, Warner Brothers, was pressuring the guys for an album. Any album. They hadn't delivered an album of new material in nearly four years, illustrating the creative bankruptcy they suffered without me in the lineup. Mike wasn't able to write songs, and neither Carl nor Dennis had the chops to fill an album with potential hits.

Dr. Landy had brought me to a point where I was working on songs with the guys, supervising both instrumental tracks and vocals, knowing that I was producing an album. By April, I accepted the fact and suggested a title, *Group Therapy*. It was nixed in less time than it took to suggest it, and the title became *15 Big Ones,* a nod to the Beach Boys' fifteenth year in the business.

I might as well have been stuck in déjà vu: all Mike and Carl talked about was how much the group needed a hit. Dennis and Al echoed their concerns, though less vocally. After a while, I began to waver under the increasing pressure. Too many memories were stirred. If not for Dr.

Landy, that LP would never have been finished because there were count-less days when in the middle of a song I dropped everything and an-nounced that I was quitting, I was too sick to continue.

"You're sick?" Dr. Landy said.

"Yeah, very, very sick," I said.

"Somebody call an ambulance!" Dr. Landy screamed.

"I don't need an ambulance," I said.

"But you're sick," he said.

"Yeah, but I don't need an ambulance."

"Then I'll drive you to the hospital to see a doctor right now," he said. "Let's get in the car."

"No, I don't need to go to the hospital or a doctor." I shrugged.

"If you don't need to go to a hospital or to see a doctor, then you aren't sick," he said.

"Right," I said.

"Then you might as well keep working," he said.

By overseeing the production of a Beach Boys album for the first time since *Pet Sounds,* I put a crimp in the group's balance of power, and as a result we spent more time around the conference table arguing than in the studio. Everyone wanted his say. After a playback, Al might say, "I'd suggest more 'dit-dits' in the background." Then Carl would say, "No, it really needs 'ah-ahs.' " Mike would demand "dit-dos." They were hilari-ous meetings.

Disgusted by the waste of time, Dr. Landy eventually spoke up and organized a regular band meeting to discuss each song individually. Al-though the meetings gave me time to work in between, they sometimes lasted as long as eight hours. Carl was disturbed when Dr. Landy took over the meetings, though he realized their usefulness. Mike was outraged. Dennis loved them. They gave him the chance to voice his opinion without everyone putting him down.

During production, Dr. Landy shielded me as much as possible from the business going on between the Beach Boys and Warner Brothers. But as we neared the end of the album, we also reached a point where I had to get involved.

One day Dr. Landy informed me of a meeting at Warner Brothers. I didn't want to go. I even tried pretending to be sick. But Dr. Landy insisted.

Both Dr. Landy and I were under the impression that the meeting at Warners was nothing more than a lunch where we could play some tracks for executives. But when we entered the Warner Records conference room, we came face-to-face with a well-prepared corporate culture. At least twenty-five people, maybe more, were seated around the enormous table, which was set for a grand luncheon. There were people from marketing, advertising, and promotion set up for a video presentation. There were stacks of T-shirts, bumper stickers, and press releases. And all of them bore the same message:

Brian is Back!

We were dumbfounded. Then angered. We'd been had.

It turned out Mike had been working for months on this huge publicity campaign heralding my return. He'd written a terrible song, "Brian's Back," and sold Warner Brothers on a publicity campaign designed to exploit the fact that I'd produced the Beach Boys' latest album. No one had mentioned a word to me. Nor to Dr. Landy. Everyone knew except us. I got frightened and turned to leave, but Dr. Landy grabbed my arm and led me to my seat.

There was nothing we could do at that point except ask what the hell was going on. That's what the whole luncheon meeting was about. One presentation after another was made to the group, the guys listening carefully, taking notes, while I tried screwing myself deeper and deeper into my chair. It wasn't enough for me to write and produce songs. Now they had to sell my illness publicly too.

Prior to the summer release of *15 Big Ones,* Dennis became obsessed with the idea of the Beach Boys doing a prime-time television special. He ordered Steve Love, Mike's other brother, who was, at the time, the Beach Boys' manager, to take care of it. Steve, who was subsequently fired in the late 1970s as manager after being accused of taking over $500,000 from the band, couldn't be trusted. But Steve prodded our agency, ICM, which secured the hippest producer on television, Lorne Michaels of "Saturday Night Live."

Everything happened fast. We got the show's title: "The Beach Boys: It's O.K." Then Michaels told us he had dipped into the "Saturday Night Live" talent pool and got one of the show's writers, Gary Weis, to direct and his friends John Belushi and Dan Aykroyd to costar. Within days, Lorne, Belushi, Aykroyd, and a small production team flew out to L.A. for meetings with the group.

In early June they set up camp at the Château Marmont on Sunset, the hotel where Belushi later died, and arranged a meeting between the Beach Boys and the cast and writers in Lorne's suite on the top floor.

Right away there were problems. Michaels was immediately put off by the guys, who showed that they couldn't make up their minds about anything. I caused Michaels severe pains. Putting me on TV was a big deal, a coup. It was contrary to my reputation as a crazy hermit. Yet whenever he looked at me, I was lost in thought.

Then Dr. Landy showed up at the meeting late. He took a seat next to me. I'd been expecting him. No one else had, though. Dr. Landy politely asked what had been discussed in his absence, then made a request. Because he knew better than anyone what I was capable of doing, he asked that my participation be subject to his approval. Michaels blew a fuse.

"Dr. Landy, this is really a meeting for the cast, just the principals," he said. "So would you excuse us."

No one said a word. The other Beach Boys were reveling in the moment. I wasn't paying too much attention because something else was occupying my thoughts. But Dr. Landy looked surprised.

"Are you serious?" he asked.

"Yes," said Lorne. "We'd like to talk to the Beach Boys alone. Just the cast."

"Brian, do you want me to stay?" Dr. Landy asked.

"Yes, I do," I said.

"Lorne, perhaps you'd better talk to Brian yourself," he said.

Lorne did. He told me that he wanted to discuss the show with the cast, period. He thought Dr. Landy was intruding, restricting the creative atmosphere. His tone was intimidating. He said Dr. Landy could wait downstairs but he shouldn't be in the room with the cast. Didn't I agree? Everyone was watching Lorne in disbelief. I shrugged. Dr. Landy then got up.

"All right," he said. "I'll wait downstairs."

Less than ten minutes later Lorne was downstairs, trying to cajole Dr. Landy back upstairs to the meeting. In the interim, everyone had begun discussing a skit, and since it involved me, they demanded I give some kind of input. I explained, however, that while I would've liked to discuss the show with them, the trees outside the window were giving off bad thoughts. Then I suggested that if everyone went downstairs and planted food under them, they'd give off better thoughts.

"How 'bout it?" I said.

It was my way of avoiding the work altogether.

Lorne quickly agreed that Dr. Landy had to give his consent on everything that involved me. He also gave Dr. Landy a script and editorial approval. I might've looked well, much better than I had in years, but I still feared performing without a great deal of support and protection. For that, I relied on Dr. Landy rather than Marilyn or the Beach Boys. Dr. Landy had a better track record than either.

In the meantime, I was downstairs, standing to the side of Lorne and Dr. Landy, who were huddled in deep conversation. I was ready to leave. Lorne threw up his hands. The meeting had started only a few minutes earlier. Dr. Landy shrugged and said that they had gotten their chance to talk with me. Lorne then explained that all they had done was listen to me jabber about some cockeyed ideas concerning trees. Dr. Landy smiled.

"By the way, I've been here an hour," he said. "Brian shouldn't be paying me for this. I presume you'll budget my fees into the show."

"What?" Lorne exclaimed.

"I presume NBC can afford them," he said.

Lorne didn't know what to say.

"Look," Dr. Landy continued, "if you'd like my participation, which I think you do, I'll agree under the conditions I've outlined. We'll get it in writing tomorrow."

At that point, Scott Steinberg and I followed Dr. Landy back up to the production meeting. Dr. Landy, whether he knew it or not, was doing for me what a manager does for an artist. Since everybody wanted me to do things and Dr. Landy knew what my increasing capabilities were, he accepted the role. He never asked me to do anything I wasn't ready for. Even those times when I thought I couldn't do things, I knew I could trust him. I knew he wouldn't put too much on me, and he didn't.

Dr. Landy was upset with the Beach Boys about the TV show. No one had talked with him about it before the fact. But the Beach Boys were upset with Dr. Landy for still being fearful and sick. They hated it when Lorne Michaels called me back in. I rather liked the fact that for the first time in my life I had someone on my side with the Beach Boys, someone making it fair, instead of all of them ganging up on me.

The show's opening as well as the highlight was a poignant sketch in which Belushi and Aykroyd, dressed as policemen, bust into my bedroom. I'm under the covers, just as I had spent the four and a half previous years. They showed me a warrant for my arrest. The charge: never having surfed. Belushi and Aykryod then escorted me downstairs into a patrol car that had a surfboard on the roof and took me to the beach, where I was supposed to run into the water and get on a surfboard.

Dr. Landy had approved the skit, and if he said okay, I figured the danger factor was minimal.

The first rehearsal was scheduled at my house, and before anything even started Scott Steinberg was making a frantic telephone call to Dr. Landy. When Dr. Landy pushed through the front door he was as incredulous as he was upset. People were smoking cigarettes, drinking beer, and pizza slices were everywhere. Worst of all, I was sitting in the corner, having downed five beers and consumed an entire pepperoni pizza myself, lighting a cig with the butt of another.

"What the hell's going on?" Dr. Landy's voice echoed throughout the entry. "Who brought this stuff?"

Belushi came immediately to the forefront.

"I did," he said.

"Why?" demanded Dr. Landy. "This man's on a diet. He doesn't smoke or drink. Who'd you ask?"

"I don't have to ask," said Belushi. "I'm at his house, so I brought it in. I thought it was a nice thing to do."

"Well, it wasn't," rebuffed Dr. Landy.

"Who the hell are you to say that?" said Belushi.

"I'm the one who's telling you that you aren't allowed to do this here," said Dr. Landy, going nose to nose with the overweight comedian. "Look at yourself. You're fat. You want to be fat, okay. But not Brian. And if you do bring this stuff here, you can get your ass out of here."

Belushi lost his head. The two men stood nose to nose, screaming at each other. Lorne ran like the fire department to put out the fire but to no avail. Dr. Landy insisted on specific conditions, and Belushi was adamant about defending his hospitable gesture. Aykroyd shadowed Belushi, and the Beach Boys were ten steps behind them, unsure of how close to the fire they should go. Marilyn stood off to the side, powerless. She might've been lady of the manor, but this maniac Dr. Landy was setting the rules. I watched the fracas from the ground while munching more pizza and drinking more beer. I knew Dr. Landy was going to win.

"The bottom line is you can't come in with the goddamn fattening pizza and expect this man to say no," said Dr. Landy. "He doesn't have that kind of self-control."

There was a quiet pause, then the famous Belushi smirk and nod of the head.

Playfully, he poked Dr. Landy in his much slimmer belly and said, "And neither do you."

From that moment on, Belushi and Dr. Landy became friends.

Meanwhile, the show went smoothly—until it was time for me to surf. The scene was shot on June 20, my thirty-fourth birthday. It had been eight months since Dr. Landy had begun working with me. Though my eyes, unfocused and zombielike, belied my still fragile state of mind, I had performed my part fine. But when we got to the beach and I stared out at the ocean, I had myriad unsettling thoughts.

In a green terry-cloth bathrobe and pajama bottoms, my pizza-filled stomach bulging like a beach ball, I became extremely scared and self-conscious. The wind blew against me, and I motioned Dr. Landy over.

"I don't want to go in the water," I said.

There was a tribal meeting of all the principals. After a short conference, Dr. Landy came over to where I was standing, which was apart from everybody else. He told me he knew the water was cold but that I had to do it. I shook my head.

"Why?" he asked.

"I'm going to drown," I said.

"I'm going in the water too," he said. "Am I going to drown?"

"No," I replied.

"But you are?"

"Yes."

Dr. Landy scribbled something on a piece of paper. Then he gave the sheet to me and told me to read it. It said, "I promise you will not drown. You will live. Signed, Dr. Landy."

"There," he said. "It's in writing. If it's in writing, it must be true."

"Right," I agreed.

Dr. Landy knew my fears were irrational in those days, and sometimes it was best to deal with irrational fears in unusual ways that made sense only to me.

Carefully, I folded up the piece of paper and stuck it in my bathrobe pocket. Then I asked what I had to do. Landy instructed them that I was only going into the water once. They had one shot. On cue, I lumbered into the waves, carrying my surfboard. With my robe wet, flapping as it came untied, I braved my fears and dove on the board and paddled into the water, getting knocked off, getting back up. It was horrible. Everybody on shore laughed and cheered. The camera rolled. When I finally came out, drenched but not drowned, Dr. Landy ran up to me.

"I'm proud of you," he said.

I was cold. I blamed Dr. Landy for it. So when he applauded my effort, I showed him my anger.

"Fuck you, motherfucker," I snapped, and headed straight for my dressing trailer.

29

My First Christmas

B rian is Back. I still wasn't clear where I'd been. What did "Brian is Back" mean?

It meant the guys all talked about me in interviews after the *15 Big Ones* was released in July. It meant I sat through two uninspired stage appearances that same month in Anaheim and Oakland, my first live performances in seven years. It meant enough PR so that by August everything worked: the LP hit number eight; the single, a remake of Chuck Berry's "Rock and Roll Music," rose all the way to number five, the best Beach Boys single since "Good Vibrations" ten years earlier; and the NBC special got huge ratings. It meant that by the time the guys departed on a thirty-two-city tour they had bought their own PR.

It almost seemed like old times. With the boys on the road, I went back to the studio, where I started work on the next album, working with Dr. Landy and continuing to show improvement under the twenty-four-hour therapy program. I was even looking forward to the holidays.

In November, I preceded an appearance on "Saturday Night Live" by going on "The Mike Douglas Show," my first-ever talk show appearance. I proved a surprise, playing two songs and conversing with a perspective, awareness, and candor I didn't have before therapy with Dr. Landy. Asked about LSD, I told how it had shattered my mind and that I then struggled to come back. "But I don't know in how many pieces," I said. Talking about my mythic reclusiveness, I painted a picture of myself as "some

Maharishi in the hills, hibernating in his bed, snorting cocaine, meditating, all these weird things."

It went over big. But since "The Mike Douglas Show" didn't air until December, my highly touted "Saturday Night Live" guest spot, without the Beach Boys, on November 27, 1976, became noteworthy as my first solo performance on television since the Leonard Bernstein special in 1967. For Bernstein I played the original version of "Surf's Up." On "Saturday Night Live" I sat at a grand piano in a sandbox and played "Good Vibrations." Reviewers lambasted the show for being insensitive.

I thought the criticism was undue. I understood and agreed with the concept, which was more than I could say about the Brian is Back campaign. Yet the Beach Boys had the most severe criticism for my "Saturday Night Live" appearance. They resented the hell out of not being there with me. Dr. Landy explained that Lorne Michaels had specifically asked for me alone.

That only intensified the bad blood between the Beach Boys and Dr. Landy. Heading into December, tensions reached new heights. Steve Love was pushing everyone, especially me, to step up the pace on the next album, the last one on the Warner Brothers contract. At the same time, Dr. Landy was trying to keep me within a therapeutic regimen rather than let the guys take over and put me to work full-time.

But there were priorities. Steve and the others wanted to get out of the Warners' contract while they could still capitalize on the success of *15 Big Ones* somewhere else. Steve wanted the new LP done no later than January 1, 1977. With several million dollars at stake in a new contract, Dr. Landy didn't exactly endear himself to the group or Steve when he told them that was impossible.

"Can you explain why?" Steve asked.

"He seems to be doing fine," Mike added.

To both Love brothers, Dr. Landy calmly said, "Brian is indeed doing better. But he's taking Christmas off and spending it with his family. He's never done that. He's never had a family dinner. He's never gone shopping for a tree. He's going to play with the kids."

"That's ridiculous to take so much time off work," Steve said.

"Look, Brian's never done Christmas," Dr. Landy said. "He's been working since he was nineteen. He's thirty-four. Don't you think it would be good for him to shop for a tree? To buy his kids some presents?"

"He needs an entire month to do that?" Steve asked.

"Yes, Brian needs an entire month," Dr. Landy said.

Steve had his own agenda in mind, and Dr. Landy's struck him as unreasonable. Tempers flared. They called Dr. Landy a "control freak." Dr. Landy responded by telling the Beach Boys it was exactly this kind of attitude that caused me to break in the first place. As this went on, I sat at the piano and played, ignoring the argument exactly as I had done as a kid when my dad's temper turned our house into a free-for-all.

"He's supposed to make records," Steve said. "What the hell are we paying you for?"

"To make him well," Dr. Landy replied. "The fact is he made one record already, more than the Beach Boys have done in four years. But he can only make records when he's well, something not one of you seems to understand."

"Listen, we want to turn in an album by January first," Steve said. "That's it. That's all I've got to say to you."

"Ain't gonna happen," Dr. Landy said.

Steve stopped in his tracks. He drew breath and shook his head, as if calming himself down. He looked at Dr. Landy.

"Okay," he said. "Okay. Whatever you say."

A couple of days later, I began hearing stories. Marilyn told me that Dr. Landy was demanding outrageous salary increases. Steve told me that Dr. Landy was requesting unheard-of percentages of tour grosses. Carl and Mike added to the reports. If, in my unproductive years, I had an Achilles' heel, it was my pocketbook. None of the stories were true, but they had the desired effect: they confused me to the point where I began to doubt the only person I trusted.

In a meeting at Dr. Landy's office, which Marilyn also attended, I let him have it. He listened. Then he laid out the facts, showing me I'd been misinformed. That got me pissed at Marilyn, and I started shouting at her for fouling me up. I was boiling over with anger, and for the first time anyone could ever remember, I was letting it out. But in the midst of yelling at Marilyn, Dr. Landy became frightened I'd get physical with Marilyn. He butted in. At that moment he reminded me of my dad. I saw my dad's face and feared getting hit.

"You can't tell me what to do. I can yell at whomever I want," I shouted, feeling as if I were speaking to my dad.

"Oh yeah," said Dr. Landy, bumping into my big belly.

Dr. Landy wanted me to explode. He was goading me. For the first time in years I was displaying anger, verbally and physically. Marilyn pleaded with him to stop, but Dr. Landy told her to step out of the way and let me express my anger and myself. Marilyn obeyed. Then Dr. Landy bumped me in my stomach again, as if that was the button that would release my anger.

"Goddamnit," he encouraged. "Get mad! Get mad at your father. At the Beach Boys. At your wife."

"Quit hitting me," I said, although he was only bumping me.

"What are you going to do about it, huh?" he continued.

I wanted to take a swing at him, but since I outweighed him by a good hundred pounds and stood about five inches taller, I decided against it. Instead, I grabbed him in a giant bear hug, lifted him off the ground, and tossed him across the room. He landed in an antique chair that splintered. Dr. Landy saw red. Huffing mad, he turned red in the face and shouted, "No fucking way you're getting madder than me."

Then he rose, lowered his head to battering-ram level, and ran straight into my gut. I stumbled back and caught myself. We were both snorting and snarling like two Brahma bulls. Dr. Landy kept encouraging me, "Good, good, good!" Frightened, Marilyn shrieked. That alerted Dr. Landy's office staff, who charged into his office and broke us apart.

Puffing hard and calming down, I stared at Dr. Landy with a mix of emotions. I still wanted to hit him. But I also felt like hugging him. Some kind of breakthrough had occurred. Although I couldn't have articulated it, I sensed that sometime in the future I might be able to handle my anger rather than fear it. Just the same, I was still amazed by this doctor.

"This guy is crazy," I said to Marilyn as she led me outside, followed by Dr. Landy. I turned to him and added, "You are fucking crazy."

"And you aren't?" he challenged.

"No, I'm not," I said.

"Good," he harumphed. "Then I must be doing a good job. You must be getting better."

30

Death at Christmas

*T*he opinion wasn't unanimous. Later that week, Scott Steinberg drove me to the studio in the morning. It was business as usual, except for two things. The other Beach Boys were already in the studio when we arrived, and several large bodyguards with no-nonsense physiques were standing cross-armed outside the studio door. They let me pass, though their menacing, unfriendly glares frightened me as I zipped through the door.

Scott didn't fare as well. The bodyguards weren't letting him in. Chicken, I went immediately to the closet. I later learned that Scott called Dr. Landy and informed him of what was happening. Dr. Landy then tried telephoning the studio. He couldn't get through. Then he tried Marilyn. She answered, and he asked what was going on.

"Well, I've talked with Carl and Steve and I'm taking Carl's advice," she started explaining, but then stopped herself. "No, actually, Brian's decided he doesn't want you to travel with him anymore and that he wants to be alone in the studio."

"Marilyn," Dr. Landy said, "we both know Brian hasn't decided anything of the kind. That's bullshit. What's going on?"

"I have Steve and Carl here," she said.

"Okay, put them on," he said.

Neither of them would speak.

"Listen, Marilyn," Dr. Landy said. "I think Brian needs to do Christmas. That's what I think. I'm sure that's what you'd prefer. Now Steve just wants to get that goddamn album made, which can wait till January. And Carl, you can tell him for me that he should stop being so jealous of his brother."

Later, Dr. Landy finally spoke with Steve, who came right out and said he was fired.

"You guys don't understand," said Dr. Landy. "If I'm not in the studio, you're not going to get anything out of Brian."

"Not true," Steve countered. "Brian's going to work. He'll work. We're all working. The group's going to finish their album."

In the meantime, I was panicking because Scott wasn't with me in the studio. He was my security blanket, my tie to Dr. Landy, who I knew could fight my battles with the Beach Boys. Without one or the other, I felt helpless. Having moved from the closet, I dropped into a chair by the console and disappeared within myself. Stan Love, who'd been serving as Marilyn's errand boy since Dr. Landy was hired, suddenly reemerged as my bodyguard and twenty-four-hour watchdog. As soon as I saw him, I got even more scared. Something weird was going on.

Finally, Steve, like a factory foreman, lied that Scott was simply detained. Everything was being taken care of. In the meantime, I needed to get back to work on the album. There was a deadline to meet.

"Okay," I said, slowly rising, looking around, and heading straight for the piano.

Everyone was delighted. Brian was at the piano. He was going to work. But I just sat on the bench, looking poised from a distance, while up close my head was tilted to the side and my eyes were rolling back into their sockets. I knew they'd started lying to me; next, I feared, they'd attack.

"What do you want to get started on?" Mike asked.

"Huh?" I snapped to.

"What do you want to get started on?" Mike repeated.

"I need to think," I said.

They understood that. The genius needed to think. But, they didn't understand me. While they all congratulated themselves on the completed coup, I pounded the keyboard as if it were a punching bag, working myself into the meditative boogie-woogie groove I had used all my life to shut myself out from the world. Twenty minutes later I quit and looked at Steve.

"I'm tired," I said. "I'm not feeling so great. I need to go home and rest."

"Okay, Bri," he said. "We'll get someone to drive you back. Tomorrow'll be better. Don'tcha think?"

"Sure," I mumbled, telling him what they wanted to hear, though it was anything but the truth.

About three or four days later the Beach Boys and Marilyn received a two-page, typewritten letter from Dr. Landy, who reiterated the serious mistake in judgment they were making. He reminded them that his original agreement with Marilyn had granted him control and final say over me and stipulated that the Beach Boys were to remain at arm's length. Predicting a tragic backslide for me if proper and reasonable care wasn't sought, he recommended contacting either the UCLA or USC psychiatric hospitals. He also kept his own door open. If they ever wanted to consult with him, he wrote, they were welcome to call.

About the same time the letter was delivered, Marilyn broke the news to me. Dr. Landy had been fired.

"Wow," I exclaimed. "That's great."

"It is?" she said, looking puzzled. "Why?"

"You know, that's a hard program," I explained. "It was really hard to do. Real rough."

In my gut, I knew life was going to be easier without Dr. Landy but not healthier. In those days, I didn't have the strength to choose what I instinctively knew was right and good for me.

Marilyn threw a big Christmas party attended by nearly 100 people. Strangely, she invited Dr. Landy. Stranger still, Dr. Landy showed up. However, if he hadn't gone looking for me, I never would've known he was there. Paralyzed by fear, I spent the entire party hiding in my bedroom. Dr. Landy made several attempts to talk to me privately, but each time he was prevented from being with me alone, either by Stan or my cousin Steve Korthof, the two babysitter-bodyguards Marilyn hired to watch over me.

"How are you doing?" Dr. Landy asked.

"You know," I said, not bothering to add anything else.

"I do," he said. "I love you, man."

Except for one brief, coincidental encounter in Lake Tahoe in winter 1981, I didn't see Dr. Landy again for six years. Looking back, I realize both of us knew I was already starting a long downhill bummer.

31

Playgirl's Man of the Year

I t took time to unravel.

Sticking to their schedule, the Beach Boys delivered a new album to Warner Brothers in early January, satisfying their contractual obligations and freeing them to negotiate a new deal with another label. Warners hated the LP, which was primarily a collection of leftovers from my exercises with Dr. Landy, including "Johnny Carson," a song Dr. Landy helped me write to tame my fear of appearing with the Beach Boys on "The Tonight Show."

Released in March, *The Beach Boys Love You* album, the group's best in years, contained at least half a dozen songs coproduced and cowritten by Dr. Landy. He still didn't receive a single credit—not even a thank-you for returning my health or returning me to the band. Both of us knew why. The Beach Boys were attempting to erase both Dr. Landy's contributions and his presence—not to mention his bill.

Dismal and lost, I began regressing, slipping back into the old patterns of staying in my room, eating too much, not exercising, and skipping the medications that helped control the manic feelings and hallucinations I couldn't handle on my own. I knew I was losing all the progress I'd made in the past year and there wasn't a damn thing I could do about it.

At the same time, the Beach Boys were ecstatic. Free of the Warner Brothers contract, Steve Love quickly finalized a multimillion-dollar, multialbum deal with CBS he had been negotiating for several months. I had no idea that the deal stipulated I write and produce 80 percent of the material. That was preposterous. I wasn't in any shape to take on that job. My head wasn't up to it—nor was my heart.

I was the soul of the group. But with me no longer able to deliver, the Beach Boys had turned into an entertainment corporation interested only in money, a far cry from a band that once put out important, spiritual music. The realization made me cry.

I didn't even know my band mates anymore. Were they family, friends, or foes? Heroes or villains? At the time of the signing, Mike was in Switzerland, studying how to levitate under the guidance of the Maharishi. Al was at his Big Sur ranch. Dennis, divorced and heavily into drugs, was working on his solo album, *Pacific Ocean Blue.* Carl was trying to get unhooked from cocaine and considering doing his own solo album. Everyone was frustrated. None more than me.

Without Dr. Landy, I had no one to talk with, no one to run interference for me, no one to help me make sense. I saw Dr. Harold Bloomfield, a nice man and a friend of Mike's, but I didn't trust him. Next, I began twice-weekly visits with Dr. Steve Schwartz, a psychiatrist. But after several sessions a colleague of his called me in for an emergency appointment and explained that Dr. Schwartz had been killed in a hiking accident. I freaked out and left in a funk that put me in bed for a week.

One morning Stan and Steve, my tenders, appeared at my bedside. I stared up at them blank-faced. I hadn't spoken a word to anyone for the past week, and I didn't plan to start.

"Get out of bed!" Stan barked, yanking back the covers.

The sudden movement scared me. I put my hands over my face.

"Don't hit me," I pleaded.

"Then get out of bed," Stan said.

Stan and Steve handled me as they would a truculent child at summer camp, threatening, pushing, and goading me into one frightening situation after another. Stan finally went to Marilyn and said he and Steve needed help. The job of watching over me, previously done solely by Scott Steinberg, was too much for this ex-pro basketballer and his ex-roadie partner. Marilyn understood.

It was spring 1977. Several months had passed since Dr. Landy was fired. I was constantly agitated. I missed appointments with my new shrink, Dr. Lee Baumel. Stan caught me arranging another mailbox cocaine delivery. Then the girls complained that I ran after their school bus one morning, a madman in an open shirt and bare feet. I thought it was a city bus in Bel Air. When the bus driver stopped, I stepped aboard and asked him for a cigarette. Then I saw the girls. Mortified, they said, "Oh, hi, Dad." Stan hired a friend of his to help.

Rushton Pamplin liked to be called Rocky. He and Stan had both been big-shot athletes at the University of Oregon in 1967. Stan was a campus basketball star, and Rocky was on the football team. Like Stan and Steve, Rocky was drifting through life, directionless. His biggest claim was that he'd modeled as the centerfold for *Playgirl* magazine and been voted by readers "Man of the Year" and "Man of Five Years."

Marilyn approved of Rocky immediately. After glimpsing him play basketball with Stan at the Bellagio mansion, she immediately called Stan to the side and drooled over his looks. A week later, Rocky was put on salary at $40,000 a year and later raised to $50,000. Clearly, Marilyn liked his qualifications.

My life became hell under these three hypermacho watchdogs. In contrast to Dr. Landy's constructive therapy, Stan, Steve, and Rocky had their own idea of care. They ordered me out of bed in the morning. They screamed at me when I wouldn't get out of my bedroom chair. They threw me into a cold shower, ignoring my cries that I was scared of the water. On good days, they bribed me to dress, wash, or go to the studio with cigarettes. On days when I was beyond control, they calmed me with cigarettes.

For the most part, Stan and Rocky intimidated me. They towered above me. Chided me for being overweight. Both screamed at me, "You goddamn fat, lazy, fucking rock star! You chickenshit! When are you going to straighten the fuck up and get your shit together? You fucking pussy!"

Against my wishes, the Beach Boys ordered them to drag me on several tour dates early that summer. Every afternoon my bodyguards took me to a local YMCA to play basketball. One time, while they were showering, I slipped downstairs to the coffee shop and ordered a couple of sandwiches. Stan discovered I wasn't in my room. He and Rocky found me in the coffee shop, finishing my meal. Stan swept his arm across the table, knocking the food and the dishes onto the floor.

"Get the fuck away from those sandwiches!" Rocky screamed, creating a scene in the restaurant.

In the elevator Stan pushed me into a corner. He clenched his fist and pushed it into my chest.

"You fucking rock star," he growled. "You goddamn, fucking obese rock star. You fucking disgust the shit out of me."

As he chided me, Stan pounded his fist into my chest, not to hurt me, but enough so that I thought he was going to kill me. Because of his and Rocky's big size advantage there wasn't a damn thing I could do but flinch and take the abuse. It brought back memories of my father.

In a state of regression and constant fear, I obeyed like an abused dog. At the end of July 1977, I accompanied the Beach Boys to London for the start of what was supposed to be a long and profitable tour. It had been arranged by the band's new manager, Henry Lazarus. Lazarus, a former drapery salesman, was Carl's find. He'd never managed before and his inexperience quickly showed. Overwhelmed by the complicated paperwork required overseas, Lazarus messed up so badly that the tour was cancelled. The fuck-up cost him his job.

In London we managed only two shows, and both were total disasters—at least from my half-drugged standpoint. In the first, a CBS convention, Mike lost his cool at me for not paying attention during a song and pushed my piano at me. During the second, at Wembley Stadium in front of 50,000 people, he noticed that I was playing songs other than what the band was performing and attempted to throw the piano bench at me.

By August, the Beach Boys nearly self-destructed. In hard-core behind-the-scenes politicking, Mike and Al formed an alliance based on their insistence in rehiring Steve Love as manager. Carl and Dennis were strongly opposed, questioning Steve's integrity. Neither faction spoke to the other for the rest of the summer.

There was a brief reprise in the fighting when the Beach Boys hit New York. On September 1, the band played a free concert in Central Park that drew an estimated 150,000 people. I spent half the show playing bass, the first time I'd ventured away from the keyboard since 1964. But more notably, everyone's family appeared onstage, including Carl's wife, Annie Hinsche; Marilyn, Carnie, Wendy, and Diane; my mother; and Dennis's girlfriend, Karen Lamm. Within the year, everyone would split up.

By that point, relations among band members had deteriorated to a point where Mike and Al seriously considered replacing Carl and Dennis, who were threatening to walk if Steve Love returned. At a gig in Providence, Rhode Island, Dennis told a *Rolling Stone* reporter that the show might be the band's last because of "a lot of backstabbing and maliciousness."

When I asked to get off the airplane at one point, Mike insisted Stan and Rocky keep me on board. In case the factions really split, Mike wanted to insure that he could intimidate me into staying with him. Despite my frailties, I was still the prize.

Two weeks later the entire group, each one accompanied by an attorney, powwowed at my house. The tension was worse than ever. Not only were they fueled by the business disputes, but Dennis's solo album, *Pacific Ocean Blue*, had been released the previous day to glowing reviews. That infuriated Mike and Al so much they strongly suggested he might want to venture out on his own permanently. I spent the meeting splayed out on the floor, asleep.

Mike yelled at me whenever an issue came to a vote. Scared, I voted with Mike and Al every time. It wasn't that I agreed; hell, I didn't understand what was being discussed. I just wanted to appease Mike, get him off my back. Outraged by the charade, Carl and Dennis stalked out of the meeting, disgusted.

Afterward, Mike assumed leadership of the band. Given the status of the group, it was fitting. Mike was the least musical of anyone in the band and the most commercially inclined. Immediately, he rehired his brother Steve as manager. Then he decided that the band's next album would be recorded over the winter at the Maharishi International University, in Fairfield, Iowa, a move as smart as Jack Rieley's sojourn to Holland.

In Fairfield, Mike demanded that everyone working on the album either meditate or be fired. Medicated and depressed, I was caught up in the old spiral of insecurity, fear, depression, and drug abuse. Pushed into the studio, I played fragments of melodies, then ran outside and snuck a joint, letting everyone else complete the songs. If forced to stay in the studio, I played Ping-Pong, batting the ball back and forth until it was time to go home.

The album was completed at the end of November 1977. Afterward, everyone's family flew to Iowa, where we made a new holiday album, *Merry Christmas from the Beach Boys*, the first LP on which Carnie and Wendy sang. But the record company had no interest in a Christmas album and never released it.

Back in L.A., it seemed the band was ready to scatter. Dennis was working on his second solo LP and getting more involved in hard drug use; Mike and Al formed Waves, a band they used to promote TM and spiritual awareness. Al also planned a solo LP. Carl retreated to Colorado. Marilyn and Diane persuaded me to produce half a dozen new Spring songs, and then Marilyn pushed me into producing two songs, "California Feeling" and "Don't Be Cruel," for, of all people, Rocky.

"What did you really think?" Rocky asked one day at Brother Studios.

"You aren't going to hit me, are you?" I said.

"Come on, Brian," he said. "I'm asking your opinion."

"I think you're a really great entertainer," I said, though he didn't realize I was putting him on. He was *awful*. "You definitely have genius."

"Thanks, man," he smiled, satisfied.

He might have been the only one of us all who felt that way.

32

"Help Me, Rhonda"

*T*he new year, 1978, began with a three-week tour through Australia and New Zealand, which Steve Love arranged to satisfy the CBS contract. The tour was promoted by Paradine, a company owned by talk show host David Frost, who made one stipulation: I had to be on the tour. More important, he also demanded the band send him a letter indicating I was healthy enough to make the tour.

It's ironic Frost was only concerned about me. At the time, Dennis was into heroin and Carl was coming off a long cocaine problem. On top of which nobody was really getting along too well.

"How are you feeling, Brian?" Steve Love asked one morning.

"I'm okay," I said, my pat answer.

"Can you handle a couple of weeks in Australia and New Zealand?" he inquired.

"No," I said.

"How 'bout it?" he asked again. "It's summer there. It'll be warm, sunny."

I had mixed feelings about Australia. I had good memories of the Beach Boys' first trip in 1964, right before "Fun, Fun, Fun" came out. The second trip had been a bummer after I got it into my head that Mike and Marilyn were having an affair. I didn't want to go back, but Stan persuaded me the trip would be all right. I didn't have a choice, though. With the tour hinging on my performing, I couldn't help but sense the pressure.

The tour was a bloody mess from the start. Dennis smuggled heroin into New Zealand, our first stop, then purchased another $100-worth in Melbourne, Australia, from one of David Frost's company's employees. I wouldn't have known of his score, except that one night I managed to shake Stan, Rocky, and Steve who continued to maintain a near-twenty-four-hour vigil over me, and snorted the stuff with Dennis. Straggling back to my room sick as a dog, I was met by Korthof.

"Brian, have you been drinking?" he asked, pissed off.

"Yeah," I moaned, dropping onto the bed.

The next day, the shit hit the fan. In a vocal meeting as volatile as an arms depot on fire, the guys insisted that Dennis be sent home, while Frost threatened to cancel the remaining dates and then sue the band if they did. Carl, trying to calm the turbulence by admitting his involvement in the purchase of the heroin, ended up getting punched in the face by Rocky.

The tour finished up, but with Dennis and Carl traveling separately from Mike and Al. They even walked onstage from separate sides. The fighting created too many bad vibes for me to handle. I stayed in my room as much as possible and waited to go home.

The night before our departure, I sensed a way out of all the tension. Summoning the hotel doctor, I complained of insomnia and stress—which was true—and got him to prescribe a bottle of sleeping pills. I promptly swallowed most of the bottle and waited for sleep to blanket me with everlasting peace. I just wanted to be alone.

The next thing I remember was Stan and Rocky holding my 240 pounds up awkwardly under a cold shower. It was the following morning. They'd broken into the room and found me in bed, unconscious. They'd also found the pills.

"Jesus Christ, where'd you get these," Stan bristled.

"What?" I asked groggily, too out of it to worry that he might hit me.

"These fucking pills, you asshole!"

"From the doctor," I said. "They're okay."

"Not when you take three-quarters of the bottle," he snapped.

From then on it was a constant battle to escape. I was sick of the band, of my bodyguards, of my life, and wanted nothing more than invisibility.

Right before leaving Australia, I swallowed a handful of pills I'd hidden from Stan, Rocky, and Steve and nearly overdosed again. Back in L.A. I immediately scored my drugs via the mailbox—cocaine first, and eventually heroin. But I didn't do the heroin right away. I let the tiny vial sit inside my desk.

*   *   *

Some days I refused to get out of my chair. I would spend up to twelve hours sitting silently. Paralyzed by stress and fear, I rolled my head backwards, took stock of my situation, and imagined myself a prisoner inside a small box that kept shrinking by painful increments, squeezing me tighter and tighter until I was gasping for air and unable to move my arms or legs. Agonizing pressure pressed from the sides of the box against my head. After several days of this I opened my desk drawer, took out the heroin, and inhaled the whole thing.

Finally, some relief.

Apparently, Marilyn found me late that night semiconscious on the bed, choking on vomit. She screamed for Stan, who cleared my throat and helped Marilyn stand me in the shower until I regained consciousness. It wasn't until I had a cup of coffee and swore that I didn't have any more drugs that Marilyn let Stan put me to bed.

I didn't have any more drugs. But when I woke up the next day, I decided drugs or no drugs, I had to get away.

I thought it would be much harder than it actually was. I didn't have a plan, a driver's license, or a car, and I'd misplaced my wallet, so I didn't have any money either. But later that day, I just opened the front door and walked out.

Without looking back, I reached the end of the driveway, turned right on Bellagio Road and kept walking, heading downhill. An hour and several miles later, I was at the Century Plaza Hotel bar, talking to a nicely dressed man who bought me several drinks.

"Do you have your own car?" I asked him.

He did.

"Do you have a driver's license?" I asked.

"Yes." He laughed.

"Are you going anywhere?"

"Yeah, San Diego," he said.

We left late that afternoon and got to know each other better on the two-hour drive south. He was a Beach Boys fan and exhausted me with questions about being a rock star. "The money's good," I admitted. "But the pressure is shit." He was a salesman, and his mom and dad had a place in San Diego where he sometimes stayed. Most of the drive, I raved about Danny Hutton's great singing voice, and it turned out that he had some Three Dog Night albums, which we listened to till bedtime.

Late the next morning my new friend had to go somewhere on business. He left me the house keys.

By the time he returned I had already set out on a new adventure. I walked to a neighborhood bar, where I started knocking back drinks people bought me and playing pool. Hours passed. Borrowing a quarter from the guy with whom I was playing pool, I studied the jukebox and punched up a Rolling Stones song, "Fool to Cry." When it finished, I asked for another quarter and played it again.

"Oh my God!" I cried out.

"What's wrong, man?" my pool partner asked.

"Listen to this song," I said. "I think it's saving my life. I mean, it's great. It's saving my entire fucking life."

"Let me buy you another drink, okay?" he said, patting my back.

It was dark by the time I decided to leave the bar. I was smashed. I'd been drinking most of the day, and my brain was a thick fog. I walked aimlessly through the dark streets, searching for a familiar landmark, someplace to squat for the night, walking, walking, walking. It never dawned on me to call home. I was content to be on my own, away from Marilyn, Stan, Rocky, Steve, and the rest. Locomoting without contraints.

Yet I was miserable, depressed by the sorry state of my life.

If I'd had the ability to take an objective look at myself, I would've seen a pitiful sight. This fat, bearded, long-haired guy in filthy clothes, plodding barefoot through dark, empty, cold streets, in an unfamiliar city, babbling strange, nonsensical thoughts out loud. I looked like the kind of person I tried to avoid.

At some point in my hike, I became short of breath and fell to the ground. I struggled to get up, then lost consciousness. The police found me lying facedown in the gutter, without any ID, mumbling over and over, "I want to die. Just let me get some rest. Let me die." They radioed for an ambulance, which deposited me at the Alvarado Community Hospital. Apparently, at some point I was cognizant enough to give my name, Marilyn's name, and my phone number. But I don't remember any of that.

A nurse was wiping dirt from my bruised face when I woke up the next day. I looked around the unfamiliar surroundings and tried to sit up. She put her hand gently on my shoulder and kept me lying down. Then she told me where I was. I relaxed. She had a pretty smile, and when I asked her name, she grinned. "It's Rhonda."

"Rhonda!" I smiled. "Help me, Rhonda!"

"Did you write that song about me?" she laughed.

That day, Marilyn was notified of my whereabouts. Right away, she flew down with Stan, Steve, and Rocky, prepared to take me back home.

I never saw them. The doctor persuaded her to let me stay and detox there. My stay lasted six weeks. I made some nice friends among the other patients and generally had a good rest.

As the six weeks neared an end, I realized that while I had to leave the hospital, I had no desire to return home. I still harbored affection for Marilyn, but I wasn't getting the care and attention that made me feel good. It seemed to me that over the years Marilyn had become a princess, while I'd become a prisoner. Although she called me at the hospital daily, it took several conversations before I had the courage to tell her what was on my mind.

"You know, Mare, the time is up," I said.

"What do you mean?" she asked.

"I think we should separate," I said. "And think about getting a divorce."

There was a gasp of surprise on the other end. Marilyn had no doubt thought the same thing. But the realization that our marriage was over was still tough to digest.

We'd grown up together. We believed we'd be with each other the rest of our lives. I remembered whispering to Marilyn that I believed we were each half of an angel and together we would be able to fly. We had been destined to share our lives with one another. But now we were destined to be apart.

That was sad.

33

The Betrayal

S eptember 1978 was loaded with action. Marilyn and I split on the fifteenth. Warner Brothers released the *M.I.U. Album,* a total flop. Brother Studios was sold. Steve Love was fired as manager of the Beach Boys for pushing the guys too hard to deliver their first LP to CBS, already months overdue, despite the record company's having advanced a sizable $2 million.

And I checked out of the mental hospital.

That day I flew to L.A. from San Diego. Stan met me at the airport and led me directly to another plane headed for Miami, where the Beach Boys were mired in work on the album they were calling *L.A. (Light Album).* The guys had been holed up there for some time, working at Criteria Studios, owned by the Bee Gees. Even before I got there, everyone knew they were in trouble. Without me, there was a paucity of songwriting ability.

My arrival didn't change matters. I said hello, then fell asleep on the studio floor.

Still, I attempted to work up several demos. The best I could manage was overseeing production on the twelve-minute disco remake of "Here Comes the Night," which had originally appeared on the Beach Boys' *Wild Honey* LP in 1967. Production-wise, the song is cool, but the Beach Boys clearly had no place on the disco bandwagon. I just did as I was told, though.

After several weeks, CBS president Walter Yetnikoff and vice president Tony Martell flew to Miami to hear what they were paying for. Mike made a big deal out of the presentation, describing what they were about to hear as one of the group's best efforts. I stood in the corner, rocking back and forth, trying to make myself invisible, as Mike continued slinging bullshit. Yetnikoff quickly realized that too, and said as much.

"We've been fucked," he said. "But it's a start."

It was obvious to everyone that I wasn't up to salvaging the album. Depressed, I spent several days lying in bed, then came up with the best idea yet.

Bruce Johnston had left the group several years earlier to run his own label, Equinox, with Terry Melcher, on RCA Records. They'd even signed me, though nothing ever happened. Their deal was about to expire. I suggested calling Bruce to skipper the album through rough waters.

Everyone agreed it was a good idea. I phoned Bruce and told him he was needed. He flew to Miami the next day and has been back with the Beach Boys since.

When the album was finished, I returned to L.A., depressed and lost, remembering that Marilyn and I had split and I had nowhere to live. For $2,300 a month, I rented a small furnished house on Sunset Boulevard in Hollywood. It was as dark and dreary as my state of mind. Stan, Steve, and Rocky continued their round-the-clock supervision, but I still spent most of my time in bed, smoking cigarettes, drinking coffee, and letting negative thoughts surge through my head.

It was October 1978, less than two years since Dr. Landy had been fired. And just as he'd predicted, I'd backslid to where everything he had accomplished was erased. I was eating, gaining weight, drugging, living in a schizophrenic nightmare the Beach Boys suspected was mostly a put-on. Forced to tour, I drank every day. At an outdoor festival in Toronto, I went onstage so drunk I lasted only several songs before I lay down on the stage, closed my eyes, and tried to sleep. Rocky and Stan dragged me off before Mike literally kicked me off.

At home, I gorged on coke. Aided by Dennis, I slipped past Stan and Rocky and began snorting prodigious amounts of the powdery substance. Dennis, my biggest admirer musically, also turned into my biggest supplier. One day he drove me around L.A. and gave me a gram for every song I helped him write. Some mornings we woke up on the floor of his dealer's Venice home. On other occasions, we didn't go to sleep for days.

One night he watched me snort six grams in an hour. My body

rebelled. According to his account, I sucked them up in rapid succession, growing more incoherent by the minute, frothing and snarling as the numbing waves of euphoria washed over me. Suddenly, I buckled. My body crashed to the floor, unconscious, then I went into a convulsive seizure. I survived only because he reached down my throat and held onto my tongue, which prevented me from choking to death.

When Stan and Rocky found out about my brush with death, they took it upon themselves to dissuade Dennis from supplying me with any more coke. Late one night, they broke into Dennis's house, found him in his bedroom, and punched and kicked him until he was lying on the ground, semiconscious. Then they tossed him through a window. Though he was bleeding, they beat him some more. Finally, they threw him across his bed, smashed his face against the headboard, and left him.

Later, Dennis pressed charges, and in court Stan and Rocky were fined and given probationary sentences. Both said the punishment inflicted was worth the price.

It was December. I lived furtively, in constant fear. I snuck to the liquor store to buy cigarettes and booze. When my caretakers weren't looking, I guzzled coffee right out of the pot. I paced aimlessly around the house, around the pool, around the perimeter of the property, devising patterns and dealing with the voices inside my head. At night, I occasionally let a groupie I'd known for years come over and relieve me sexually.

A former telephone operator from Kansas, Debbie Keil, then in her early twenties, was a pretty blond girl who reminded me of my high school fantasy, Carol Mountain. Debbie had followed the Beach Boys for years before moving to L.A., where she got a job with the band's fan club and through that finally met me. I saw her intermittently, whenever it was convenient for me. She asked nothing except to please me.

Now that I was split from Marilyn, it was easier for Debbie to take care of my needs. In addition to sex, she drove me places. She gave me cash to buy booze. She didn't even get mad when I discovered a vial of diet pills in her purse and swallowed the whole batch. Despite her devotion, mine was still a lonely, friendless, and musicless existence.

One morning I woke up with the urge to visit my old Bellagio house and asked Debbie to drop me off there. Marilyn had let me keep a key for just such a time. Unlocking the front door, I looked around. Nothing was changed. Wanting to cuddle against Marilyn, I climbed the stairs to the bedroom. Quietly, I pushed the door open.

It was dark. A few shards of sunlight filtered past the drawn shades.

I took several steps forward, until I was standing at the foot of the bed. I let my eyes get acclimated to the darkness. I noticed Marilyn's black hair spread over the pillow. She was sleeping soundly. Then I did a double take. She wasn't alone. Rocky was sleeping beside her. It wasn't the first time I'd seen Marilyn with another man.

Maybe seven years earlier, I had fantasized about watching Marilyn have sex with another man. It had to do with my own insecurity. I wondered if I was satisfying her or if another man might do better. I'd even acted on it, persuading Tandyn Almer, a songwriting friend, to have sex with her. Before that happened, I slept with Tandyn and Tandyn slept with both Marilyn and me together. But the experiment turned out to be more than I could handle.

So did seeing Marilyn and Rocky in bed together. I later found out that they had begun their affair only a month after he was hired. I can't blame Marilyn; I wasn't able to satisfy her.

I knelt beside Marilyn and touched her hand. She opened her eyes, shocked. I took her hand, kissed it, and whispered, "I love you." Suddenly, Rocky woke. The look on his face showed how startled he was to see me.

"Brian!" he blurted. "What the fuck are you doing—"

Without answering, I darted out of the room. Downstairs, the reality hit me. I was confused, hurt, jealous. Rocky found me pacing outside, agitated. Marilyn hurried out a few moments later. By then I was crushed, feeling as low as a pebble on the asphalt driveway. I didn't have a right to be hurt, but I was. I felt like a betrayed child. They asked if I wanted a ride back to my house.

"No thanks," I said. "I'm going to walk."

"Are you okay?" Rocky asked.

I looked at Marilyn. Then at Rocky. Finally, I turned and began walking slowly down the driveway.

Stan and Rocky showed up at my house later that day. I was sitting in the living room, the shades down, cigarette butts littering the floor around me. Drunk, I was mean and nasty, spitting insults that were completely out of character. Stan asked if I was planning on going to the studio that evening. I wasn't.

"Then what're you going to do?" he asked.

"Nothing," I said.

"How 'bout some exercise, get some endorphins going?"

"No."

Ticked off by my drunkenness and lethargy, Stan and Rocky grabbed my arms, forced me to stand, and began screaming insults and threats. After they explained the endorphin rush from exercising would get me high, I agreed to swim. I went inside and changed. By the time I came out, I had changed my mind. I dipped my foot in the pool to satisfy them, then I started walking around the pool. I did that regularly, sometimes making more than 200 circles. It bugged the hell out of them.

After going around thirty times, Stan suggested doing something else.

"No, I'm busy thinking," I said.

"How 'bout playing basketball?" he asked.

"I like this," I said.

I went around another 100 times, working up a heavy sweat. Stan and Rocky watched for twenty minutes. Then both jumped in front of me.

"If you continue like this," said Stan, "we're going to take you to the doctor."

"You can't do that," I snapped, irritated. "I'm Brian Wilson."

"Big fucking deal."

"You're fired," I said, and kept walking, speeding up the pace.

After another twenty minutes, by which time I was huffing and wheezing and drenched in perspiration, Stan stopped me again.

"If you don't quit walking around the goddamn pool I'll have to call the doctor," he threatened. "I'm going to have to explain that this is an abnormal situation, and I'm sure he'll want to see you."

Without saying a word, I turned and started walking again. Stan and Rocky bristled, not sure what to do. While they considered options, I did another couple of hundred circuits around the pool. Finally, Stan grabbed my arm and tried to force me into a chair, which pissed me off.

"No, I want to do this," I said, struggling to get free.

"I said you can't," yelled Stan, trying to hold onto my arm.

"Goddamnit," I bellowed, finally breaking free.

The second I realized I was out of his clutches, I ran over to the patio and kicked in a big plate glass window. It shattered into a handful of big, razor-sharp shards that luckily didn't do any damage to my leg.

"If you do that again," screamed Stan, "I'm going to take you straight to the hospital."

Without hesitating, I kicked in another window.

That did it. Stan and Rocky grabbed me, lifting my feet off the ground, and dragged me kicking and fighting into the car. They drove me straight to my internist's office. The minute I saw Dr. Ganz, I launched into a violent temper tantrum. He had been sitting behind his desk, smoking a pipe, and the pipe reminded me of my father, which triggered the outburst. I threw books and paperweights, kicked chairs over. As Dr. Ganz dodged the flying debris, his staff called the cops.

By the time the squad cars pulled up, sirens blaring, Stan and Rocky had restrained me and the doctor had given me a sedative by injection. The cops drove me directly to Brotman Medical Center in Culver City, where my psychiatrist, Lee Baumel, checked me into the psychiatric ward.

"I don't want to go here," I protested as they hustled me out of the car and upstairs into the ward.

"Brian, just be quiet, will you," Stan urged. "You're going into the hospital, and that's that."

I didn't have a chance. I was drunk, then sedated, and eventually straitjacketed. At the hospital, I was examined and locked in an isolated room. Admitted as self-destructive, I was given an injection of Thorazine as soon as the alcohol wore off.

The Thorazine was horrible. It felt as if I'd been given a shot of sulfuric acid. My whole body burned and trembled. I looked at a nurse, whose name tag said Meredith. Suddenly, I saw flames shoot out of her forehead and began yelling at the people in my room, "You fucking bastards! Let me out of here!"

At some point a nurse, whose name Mary Ross, I remember, and five other people walked into the room and tied me down to my bed. That scared me so much I quit yelling. After several hours, Mary came into my room again and asked how I was doing. By then I was quiet. I gave her a friendly smile and told her I was tired. Soon, it seemed, several attendants came into the room and untied me. However, I continued to lie there, staring up at the ceiling, and finally I lapsed into one of the better sleeps I'd had in months.

I woke up in the morning, some ten hours later. I was full of the same fear I had had the night before. Yet I felt relieved, safe. The hospital was comforting. It made me think of Dr. Landy. I hoped he'd get word that I was there and visit. I fantasized about running into him in the halls. I knew if I saw him again, I'd ask him for help. I knew I could trust him. I knew he'd help. The only thing I wasn't sure of was whether or not I'd ever get that chance.

Later on that morning, I was given another shot of Thorazine. Unlike the previous shot, this one was calming and I drifted off into another daylong sleep.

My stay at Brotman lasted three months. The first week was spent on the floor for the most severe patients. The rooms were padded, the furniture sparse. After that, I was upgraded to the level where the patients are healthy enough to be mostly on their own. I easily adapted. I ate meals in the cafeteria, met with Dr. Baumel every other day, watched TV, smoked cigarettes, and spent the rest of my time at the piano in the big social room.

One day I saw a familiar face among the patients. Dallas Taylor, the original drummer of Crosby, Stills and Nash and an acquaintance of mine, walked into the ward. He'd been on a three-day coke binge and checked himself in. He looked like used paste. Upon seeing me curled up on my cot, he remembered thinking, "Shit, that guy's in bad shape." But after he woke up from a rest, I gave him some advice.

"Don't talk to anyone here." I smiled.

"Why?" he asked.

" 'Cause they'll think you're crazy," I said in a serious tone. But I was joking.

In truth, I'd become quite friendly with my night nurse, Carolyn Williams, a large, outgoing black woman who showed me special attention after learning I was famous. She brought me extra food, sweets, and spent many hours listening to me talk. The favoritism she showed me went beyond nursing. It was a very comfortable relationship, I thought.

Insulated from the Beach Boys, I was able to put pressures, demands, and group politics out of my mind. Only once did they manage to encroach. Toward the end of the three months, in February 1979, Stan and Rocky snuck into the hospital and looked around for me. They found me in the cafeteria. Marilyn had fired both of them shortly after I entered Brotman. She fired Rocky out of guilt, knowing I was disturbed after catching them in bed together. Stan was fired for supporting Rocky.

Both wanted their jobs back. Marilyn denied several requests. That's when they decided to go directly to me.

"I'll have to think about it," I said between bites of food.

With typical manipulative insensitivity, Stan argued that he and Rocky loved me and wanted only to help. He demanded to know why I couldn't see that. I asked Stan if he thought constantly poking me in the chest was good therapy. I asked Rocky if he thought sleeping with my wife was the proper way to help. Neither answered.

"We're offering you our love and our help," Stan said.

I said nothing, and after finishing my meal I left without saying good-bye. Neither wanted to give up the $50,000-a-year job. Marilyn later testified that she had to hire professional bodyguards to prevent Stan and Rocky from appearing at our residences. When that failed to work, she notified the police.

34

The Chemistry of the Moment

S tanding backstage in Las Vegas, I wanted to drop everything and run away. It was early spring 1979, near the end of an arduous three-week tour, and I felt as if I had nothing except a bunch of memories. The past three months had been awful.

Marilyn and I had been divorced on January 23. In February, I'd gotten out of Brotman and learned that she had sold the Bellagio house and moved to Encino. Marilyn made it clear that my daughters, tired of being embarrassed by me, didn't want to see me. Marilyn's sisters wanted nothing to do with me, and her best friend, Sherrie Champion, told me not to call anymore.

Then Carl and Mike had gotten together and kicked Dennis out of the group after drugs and booze turned him into a full-time liability. In March, CBS released the *L.A. (Light Album)* to bad reviews and bad sales. The Beach Boys were a reflection of me, and now the band was a mere shell of what it had been twenty-five years earlier. That was also true with me.

"You know, people are really it," I told Carl.

"Huh?" he asked, confused.

"I said, people are really it. Don't you know?"

"Brian, what in the world are you talking about?" he asked.

"I'm talking about people who've fucked with my head," I explained. "I have a whole list of them."

"Great, Brian," he said. "Let's do the show and then we'll talk about it."

We didn't talk about it for another week. After the tour ended, the Beach Boys retreated to Hawaii for a cleansing of mind and body. Everyone fasted on broths made from vegetables. We had colonics, jogged, and lay in the sun. Everyone took roommates. Mine was Carl.

One night, while both of us were in bed, I brought up a subject that had always bothered me, his friendship with Marilyn. From the time we met the Rovell girls at Pandora's Box in 1962, Carl and Marilyn enjoyed an intimate friendship. Suddenly, I wondered how close they had been.

"You always loved Marilyn, didn't you?" I asked.

"Brian, I think Marilyn is great," he said. "Just like you think Annie is a real nice girl."

Carl and Annie Hinsche had divorced a year and a half earlier.

"But did you ever fuck Marilyn?" I asked, cutting straight to the core.

"Brian!" he said sternly. "Go to sleep."

It didn't matter whether or not it was true, I believed it was and I believed Carl was fucking with my mind. Similarly, I grew suspicious about Dr. Baumel, and when we returned from Hawaii, I told him I was quitting. I was tired of talking about my problems, I explained. But Dr. Baumel insisted I see him at least once a week.

"No," I said. "I'm not coming."

"I think you're making a big mistake," he cautioned.

Perhaps. But there was logic to my convoluted thinking. I was distancing myself from the things I felt threatening, like the Beach Boys, or things I didn't want to do, like see my psychiatrist. I'd found a protector and servant in my ex-mental-hospital nurse, Carolyn Williams. After being supervised by a four-person, twenty-four-hour team of psychiatric nurses following my discharge from Brotman, I insisted everyone be terminated except Carolyn.

Carolyn moved into the two-bedroom, Spanish-style home I rented in Santa Monica after I left Brotman and took charge. Acting more like a wife or girlfriend than a nurse, she moved in her children, stocked the house with food and booze, masturbated me whenever I wanted, but otherwise left me alone. I slept in a little guest room; she had the master suite. The Beach Boys disliked her, not for her irresponsibility as a nurse, but because of her skin color. At one concert, I overheard Al complain to Steve, "Oh Jesus! Does he have to put his arm around her?"

She shielded me, though. Carolyn was the buffer I relied on to keep me from having to deal with reality. She handled everything. Pretty soon, she demanded on attending the Beach Boys' meetings and going out on the road with me. I didn't mind, since she made my life easier. I also didn't mind that she supplied me with marijuana and anything else I wanted. However, it was clear to everyone else that she had definitely crossed the line between helping me and self-interest. I couldn't, or didn't want to, see that.

In November 1979 the Beach Boys geared up to record another album, our second for CBS. At Carl's and Bruce's urging, recording was done at Western Studios, where the Beach Boys had started. They thought a comfy environment would restimulate my interest. They were hoping for a miracle, for gold records. The only gold I cared about came from Kona and was wrapped in rolling papers. I lasted three days in the studio.

Released in March 1980, *Keepin' the Summer Alive,* an album as slick as any commercial effort, became one more Beach Boys failure. Of the five original Beach Boys, only Mike and Al toured with the band in 1980. Dennis and I were too drugged to participate even if we wanted to, and Carl split for Colorado to record his first solo album, *Carl Wilson.* After it was released in March 1981, Carl quit the Beach Boys to tour in support of his album.

Nineteen eighty-one was the Beach Boys' twentieth anniversary, and it didn't seem as if the group would survive much longer. October marked the release of Mike Love's first solo album, *Mike Love: Looking Back with Love.* Neither Mike's nor Carl's solo efforts stirred up much interest. But Carl still put everyone on notice. He wasn't returning until the band played as if it were 1961.

The odds of that happening weren't good. Although Dennis, his once rock-hard body showing the ravages of alcoholic bloatage, managed to tour sporadically through 1981, he spent a lot of time with me chasing a cocaine high—we thought nothing of dropping a couple grand a week on blow. Between binges, we also attempted to record songs, never successfully. But we spent enough time at studios that Dennis tried convincing me to start our own band.

The first day of 1982 began with Carolyn shaking me out of a deep sleep on the sofa. Finally, she smacked my bearded face. I opened one eye and looked up.

"Brian, you're a bad boy," she scolded. "You fell asleep with a cigarette in your hand. You could've burned yourself straight to hell if I hadn't come along."

Just thinking about the life I lived after Carolyn came into the picture leaves me with a cold shudder. It was a life of absolutely no self-control; I was absolutely dependent on the chemistry of the moment. Now at more than 300 pounds, I had the physique of a sumo wrestler. I consumed booze, drugs, food, cigarettes, and caffeine in grotesque quantities. I suffered hallucinations, haunted voices, mad laughter, bottomless despair. I was in worse condition than ever before.

In the midst of this bleakness, I decided to go out on the road with the Beach Boys—not because I cared about performing but because I wanted the ease of hotel living. The guys hadn't seen me for months, and they were shocked when they did. I'd deteriorated more than they'd expected. They weren't surprised when I stayed in the hotel and missed the show. Nor were they disappointed.

No one knew what to expect from me. In Salt Lake City the promoter explained the local prohibitions against drinking and smoking onstage. No booze, no cigarettes, no exceptions. Shuffling onstage late, Mike turned around during an instrumental and I knew there was going to be trouble. He dropped the microphone and ran over to the piano. For an instant, I thought he was going to take a swing at me.

"What the hell are you doing?" he snarled.

"I'm smoking a cigarette," I said.

Despite the warning, I was smoking Marlboros and sipping out of a bottle of whiskey I'd placed on the piano. In addition, I couldn't have looked more uninterested. I was more relaxed than anyone in the audience.

"Why the hell aren't you playing?" Mike fumed.

"Because I'm watching," I answered. "You're in one hell of a groove tonight. It's a great show."

"I'm glad you like it, *asshole*," Mike said.

In March 1982 Carl saw me for the first time in a year and was horrified by what he saw. He'd been getting weekly reports on my behavior. He knew I'd been hanging out with Dennis. He knew when and on whose floor we'd crashed in Venice. He'd tabulated that I'd dropped fifteen to twenty grand keeping both Dennis and myself supplied with coke. He'd heard about the three-day bender that ended with me too stoned to smoke a joint, pleading with Dennis to blow smoke into my mouth before I passed out. He knew all about Carolyn's and my wretched life-style—from the dog excrement on our floors to her condoning my drug use.

. The fact he knew all this scared the shit out of me. I knew he'd take some kind of action. I was right too. As soon as the Beach Boys returned to L.A., he had me sign a trust document, giving him control of both my money and my vote in the Beach Boys corporation, Brother Records, Inc. I didn't know what I was signing, though he assured me it was for my benefit and protection. He also showed up at my house one afternoon to discuss what he had described on the phone as very important business.

"I want you to go into St. John's," he said, referring to the private Santa Monica hospital near my house.

"Fuck you, Carl," I said.

"Listen, Brian, you're stressed out. You look terrible. You're obese to the point where I think your life is in jeopardy. Whether or not you like it, something has to be done."

At that point, I got hopping mad and tried to slug Carl. I didn't want to go back to any hospital.

"Do you know what that's fucking like?" I screamed.

"No, I don't," he said.

"It's like going to hell," I said, taking another swing at him.

Carl left the house before I got lucky. But the next day one of the Beach Boys' bodyguards rang the doorbell, then forced his way past Carolyn and told us that he was under orders to take me to the hospital. I refused, called the cops, and screamed I was being kidnapped. They didn't believe me. Defenseless, I was bullied into an unmarked van and checked into St. John's for an involuntary seventy-two-hour stay.

For the next three days, I went through nauseating withdrawals. Finally, with the help of a legal aid group, Carolyn got me out. I went home the day John Belushi died from a heroin overdose at the Château Marmont Hotel. I told Carolyn I knew him. She was impressed.

But instead of realizing I was playing chicken with a fate similar to Belushi's, Carolyn lit a joint. I stared at the TV set and remembered that almost twenty years earlier I had met Phil Spector in that same hotel. Life is really full of weird connections.

Less than three weeks later, on March 24, 1982, Carolyn and I were on the road with the Beach Boys again. We were traveling to Tampa from

Fort Myers, but the guys were letting their dislike for Carolyn show more than ever. They had tolerated Carolyn only because of the sway she had over me, but they'd decided her influence was no good. On numerous occasions, they'd strongly suggested I break up. They'd even told me so directly. Each time I refused. They'd forced Dr. Landy out. I wasn't going to give up Carolyn.

But I didn't have a choice. During a routine security check of carry-on bags in the Lee County Airport in Fort Myers, Florida, the security guard dumped Carolyn's purse out on a table. No one else's bag was given that treatment. The security guard flipped through the contents. Suddenly, he looked up, with an expression on his face that spelled trouble. Mixed in among Carolyn's billfold, charge cards, breath spray, candies, and cigarettes was a razor blade, a straw, and a paper containing a substance tests indicated was cocaine.

"Miss, I think we've got a problem here," he said.

"What are you talking about?" Carolyn asked, shocked. "This is Brian Wilson. We're going to miss our connection."

"Lady," a policeman, one of several who suddenly appeared, said, "it looks like you already made your connection."

The cops immediately grabbed Carolyn. She was too surprised and confused to resist.

"I've been set up!" she suddenly shrieked, her voice filling the airport terminal. "Set up! *Set up!*"

She might've been right about the setup. Later, when I asked Carl how they knew the stuff belonged to Carolyn and not me, he shrugged. "I guess they just figured it was hers." Nonetheless, it freaked me out to see Carolyn, my only ally, cuffed, read her rights, and then hauled off to jail, where she spent the next twenty-four hours. I locked myself in the hotel room and missed that night's show.

In jail, Carolyn received an anonymous phone call not merely warning her to stay away from me but threatening her with an "or else." She pleaded no contest to possession of a controlled substance and was released on $300 bail. The sum was charged to my credit card.

Ignoring the warning, she returned to our home in L.A., where we noted her trial date and continued life as as if nothing out of the ordinary had occurred. Clearly, the incident was intended as a warning to me as much as Carolyn.

A week after Interior Secretary James Watt prohibited the Beach Boys from playing a free Fourth of July concert at the Washington Monument because rock bands attracted the "wrong element," I bottomed out. Joining the guys in Philadelphia, I refused to come out from backstage, too stoned and scared to face the 20,000 fans. But midway through the set, Al told Jerry Schilling, Carl's manager, to bring me out for the encore. Fans were chanting my name. Jerry decided, "Why not?"

Why not? One look and that was obvious. I was slumped in a chair, drunk, stoned, and mumbling incoherently.

It didn't matter. With the crowd on its feet cheering, I was pushed onstage. Instinctively, I dumped myself behind the keyboard. Pawing the keys like a baby and singing "do-do-do" to whatever song was being played, I smiled and waved but made no attempt to follow along the music. I wasn't capable of it. The guys, embarrassed, realized they'd made a mistake.

The next morning, I missed the band's flight to St. Louis. The problem was too much breakfast. Although I was up in plenty of time, I ordered a forty-cup urn of coffee to complement my steak. I was probably working on my twentieth cup when the plane took off. I made it to St. Louis just as the guys were about to go on.

"You aren't playing?" Carl asked.

"No, I'm not up to it," I said. "I'm heading back to the hotel. Maybe I'll see the doctor."

"No doctor," he said emphatically. "Listen, Brian, we had a meeting this morning, and Al and Mike are really adamant about docking your pay. The sentiment is either you get treatment or you play."

"What does that mean?" I asked.

"It means that nobody really wants to pay you to sit in a hotel room and drink and smoke yourself into oblivion, which is exactly what's happening now."

"That's fucked," I argued. "You have to pay me. I'm trying my best."

Though my best was hardly good enough, Carl sensed I wasn't able to take hard criticism and changed his tact. He suggested I take some time off.

"Well, when can I come back?" I asked.

"Maybe on a weekend," he said. "Maybe come to Vegas. Look, you don't *have* to play. You just have to be with us, and stay off the shit."

"But I don't want to go home," I started to cry. "I *really* don't want to go home."

"Why?"

"I'm scared," I said.

Carl shook his head and left the situation unresolved. In the meantime, I flew to Miami, joining Carolyn in time to pay the $5,000 fine the judge handed her for possession of cocaine. She also received three years' probation. The legal bill for all this eventually totaled more than $100,000.

Immediately afterward, Carolyn and I jetted to Las Vegas, arriving late Thursday afternoon, in time for opening night at Caesars Palace. We went directly to our room and began ordering food and champagne. After ignoring repeated phone calls, I finally went down to rehearsal.

"You gonna play?" Mike asked.

"Yeah," I mumbled, refusing to look at him.

"The fuck you are," he laughed. "You know you aren't going to play. You aren't. More to the point, you can't."

"Are you going to beat me up?" I asked, voicing my worst fear about Mike—that his violent temper would erupt and I'd be the target.

Mike, playing one of the typical head games he knows scare me, ignored me. Provoked by the challenge, I attempted to rehearse, but it was obvious to everyone, including me, that I couldn't play. The ability was gone. My mind couldn't concentrate, didn't send out signals to which my fingers could respond.

Depressed, disgusted, and humiliated, I retreated to the safety of my room, where Carolyn and I spent the evening ordering prodigious amounts of food as well as fourteen bottles of champagne. How much we drank and how much was spilled on the carpet or poured in the sink is impossible to say. But I didn't roll out of bed until the road manager called me several minutes before show time the following night. As I traveled downstairs in the elevator, I wasn't very different from a coma victim.

"Nice shoes," Mike scoffed when he saw me.

I looked down. I wasn't wearing any shoes. In fact, I had forgotten to change clothes for several days. I wasn't aware of the stench emanating from my sweat-soaked fat cells.

"You're going on like *that*?" Carl asked.

I nodded.

"Can you be part of the band?" he implored.

I nodded.

"Are you sure, Brian?"

"No," I admitted.

"What's going on, Bri? You look like shit. What'd you do last night?"

I thought for a moment. That wasn't what I wanted to talk about. My mind was free-associating.

"Did you see Jeff?" I asked, referring to our guitar player. "He's lost a bunch of weight."

"Yeah, about ten pounds," Carl said.

"You know, I wish I could get it on with chicks," I said. "But you know, what am I going to say? Honey, look at my tremendous belly?"

"It's a problem." He nodded.

"Well, Carl," I said. "I've got some stuff to do back up in my room. I'll see you." I did not go on.

A few days later I ordered forty-four grasshopper cocktails from room service in the span of a single day. Other days I asked that convention-sized urns of coffee be sent up. Room service managed as best it could, delivering several large urns. Then it was more champagne.

On the flight back to L.A., the guys commented I was fortunate to still be alive. Someone suggested that the oddsmakers in Vegas had been offering bets against my surviving the weeklong run. If that was in fact true, they weren't too far off the mark. By the time I got home, I was suffering excruciating pain in my gut, a pain that became so severe by the next day that I checked into Brotman.

The doctors found my stomach filled with fluids, my liver damaged from the toxic combinations of booze, coke, and psychoactive pills I'd been ingesting. The prognosis wasn't too good. My mother was the first one I called with the news. I wanted her concern. But more than that I wanted to lay a heavy guilt trip on her. I wanted her to know how she and Dad had fucked me up.

"The doctor says I'm probably going to die," I groaned into the phone. "Can you come see me?"

"No," she said. "I'm making dinner for Carl and his kids and Marilyn and the girls."

Two days later, I called my mom again.

"They say I'm doing better," I told her. "I'm still pretty ill, but they say I'm probably going to live."

She sounded happy. But I couldn't say the same about myself.

35

Jumping Off the
Empire State Building

*U*nbeknownst to me, months before I was hospitalized, Carl and
Marilyn initiated the return of Dr. Landy. The process began
in April 1983. At the time, Dr. Landy was consulting on a
murder trial in an Orange County courthouse when he received an emergency call from his office. Dr. Landy was told the Beach Boys wanted to
meet immediately.

"I'm busy," he told John Branca, the Beach Boys' attorney. "The trial
is interesting. The Beach Boys aren't."

After some discussion, Dr. Landy agreed to meet with Tom Hulett, the
group's new manager, Branca, Jerry Schilling, and several others. Meeting
over breakfast at the Century Plaza Hotel, Hulett, Branca, and Schilling
gave Landy a frank assessment of my condition and wanted to know if he
could treat me again.

"I'm scared," Hulett said. "I've been through it with Elvis, and I fear
picking up the paper one weekend and seeing Brian Wilson as the next
headline."

Little did anyone suspect that within eighteen months Dennis, not I,
would be the headline.

"Well, how bad is he?" Dr. Landy inquired.

They spent the next half hour telling Dr. Landy stories. He got the
picture. He'd warned them. Landy told them to have Carl make an
appointment with his office to discuss treatment. Within a week Carl was

in Dr. Landy's office, asking how much the treatment would cost.

"About half a million dollars," Dr. Landy said. "Because it's going to take some time."

"How much time?" he asked.

"I can't be sure," Dr. Landy replied. "He's older now. I don't know how bad he is. We're going to have to start all over. But Brian doesn't have a family living with him anymore, so maybe eighteen to thirty-six months. We don't have to worry about the domicile and all the privileges that go on between the sheets. But—"

"But what?" Carl interrupted.

"But I'll need complete and total control and complete and total help again," Landy said. "This time, though, unlike the last time, I'll want a written contract guaranteeing that therapy will be uninterrupted. Because last time we had the same deal, but as soon as he started to *look* better, you guys decided that he didn't need help anymore and terminated his therapy."

"What do you mean?" Carl objected.

"You know what I mean," Dr. Landy said.

They knew each other well. Dr. Landy explained himself clearly, knowing Carl was going to take the information he got from the meeting and tell Marilyn, who had helped him through the dissolution of his marriage and now was providing him comfort in dealing with me. That made me jealous.

To insure that Carl and Marilyn would understand why he was making certain stipulations, Dr. Landy thought it best to give my brother a cursory explanation of what Freud meant when he spoke about a Flight to Reality and how it related to me.

Patients get well to a point where they appear wonderful, he said. They dispense with therapy and fly straight into reality—which they aren't well enough to deal with.

"That's what had happened to Brian," Dr. Landy explained. "The Beach Boys aided the situation by insisting he abandon therapy and make an album. But if you look back, that all-important Warner Brothers album died and your brother almost died too."

"I understand," Carl said.

"This time, Carl," Dr. Landy said, "be a musician. Don't try to be a doctor." Carl never liked Dr. Landy's bluntness and was scared of him.

Landy then added that it was going to be more difficult to bring me around this time. I was six years older. My recuperative powers weren't as good. I'd incurred a lot more serious drug damage to my brain. I'd done exactly what Dr. Landy had predicted. Carl had lots to consider.

In June 1983, two months after the first emergency phone call, Dr. Landy met with Tom Hulett and the Beach Boys' business managers, lawyers, and staff to discuss the same things he had gone over with Carl. The treatment plan he outlined met with everybody's approval, but it still had to be presented to the Beach Boys themselves. That took several more weeks to arrange.

A powwow was finally set up between Dr. Landy and the Beach Boys. Dr. Landy, accompanied by psychologist Dr. Arnold Dahlke and office manager Sally Steinberg, showed up at Hulett's office and waited. The Beach Boys were all there; they were playing an ego game. After a courtesy fifteen minutes, Dr. Landy got up and left. The Beach Boys rushed out of Hulett's office just as the elevator doors were closing. Dr. Landy waved good-bye.

Later that day they called, asking for another appointment, for which they promised to be on time. When was Dr. Landy free?

"Six months," his secretary said. "And Dr. Landy says to tell you that you haven't paid the bill for our previous meetings."

Carl and Al complained Dr. Landy's fees were outrageous. The secretary replied that Dr. Landy considered nonpayment of bills outrageous. Carl and Al hung up without an appointment.

Later Tom Hulett called Dr. Landy directly. Hulett has always been the group's peacemaker, a thankless job. He's also been my friend. Later he and Dr. Landy would become great friends. Hulett said the Beach Boys were available whenever Dr. Landy was.

Knowing Carl's hatred for mornings, Dr. Landy suggested the next morning, 8:00 A.M. sharp.

"How about two?" asked Hulett.

"You don't seem to understand," Dr. Landy said, and promptly hung up.

Eventually, peace was made and another meeting set up. This one took place on time. Mike, Carl, Al, Dr. Landy, Hulett, and the rest sat down at a large conference table. Predictably, the first thing they wanted to discuss wasn't my health, it was Dr. Landy's fee.

"Are we here to talk about my fees or are we here to talk about Mr. Wilson?" Dr. Landy asked.

"Well, what can you do for him?" Mike challenged.

"What do you mean, what can I do?" Dr. Landy replied. "I can do better than you've done. But what I don't know is if I can ever *undo* what you've done. I had him pretty much on the road to recovery, and then you took him away in nineteen seventy-six. What can I do now? I don't know. What do you want me to do?"

"We want him to get well," Mike said.

"I don't care if he ever sings, plays again, or makes one more note of music," said Carl.

"Yeah, we just want him to be well and happy," added Mike.

"Okay, that's nice to hear," Dr. Landy said. "But I don't believe any of you. So will you put that in writing?"

Dr. Landy was already fighting for me, and I hadn't even seen him yet. Within minutes, another battle arose. The one Dr. Landy expected—his fees. Al voiced the group's complaint, saying Dr. Landy's price was, in a word, exorbitant.

"I think that's how you perceive the value you're getting and how much you value the person you're trying to help," Dr. Landy said. "For what you get, I think my fee is a bargain."

"But where do you get off charging five dollars a minute?" Al asked.

"Where do I get off charging five dollars a minute?" Dr. Landy said without missing a beat. "With much more justification than you have being paid twenty-five to thirty thousand dollars to play twenty-year-old music for an hour onstage. How the hell do you justify that?"

"Would you be willing to listen to what we say about him and what we want from him?" Al asked.

"If you would be willing to play a ukulele onstage and play Beatles songs that I pick," Dr. Landy said.

"That's outrageous," Al exploded.

"No more so than you telling me how to practice," Dr. Landy countered. "Do you tell surgeons how to operate?"

With the atmosphere heating up, Al was yanked out of the room by his lawyer. Carl was also led out by his attorney. The hall was buzzing. They knew they had a fight on their hands.

Dr. Landy didn't feel he was being difficult. Just realistic. He wanted them to know what they were getting into from the beginning. Why start and then fight?

After several minutes, Carl, Al, and their lawyers returned and sat down. Al's lawyer said there would be no interference with treatment and no problem with the fees.

"I don't see why there should be," Dr. Landy said. "I'm going to save his life . . . again."

It took until October 1983 to iron out an agreement between Dr. Landy and the Beach Boys, which the lawyers had to rework again as soon as the group realized they were responsible for the bill, not me.

Afterward, Dr. Landy set up a meeting with the entire Beach Boys clan, those who were close to me, including Marilyn. Everyone showed up except Dennis, but that was okay. No one counted on him anyway. Dr. Landy used the meeting to explain his plan. It was necessary, he told them, to take me from the security of my safe little world to which I had withdrawn since he'd last seen me. That world had kept me crippled by not requiring me to function. Everything was done for me. Dr. Landy planned to put me in an environment of my own making, where I'd have to learn to live within my means. He said that would force me to function.

The philosophy Dr. Landy outlined was simple. Each person has room in his head for just one crazy person. Normal thinking is easily manipulated by craziness. If Dr. Landy acted crazier than me, then I had to either get sane or get crazier than Dr. Landy. It was no contest, Dr. Landy assured them. He guaranteed that he could be crazier than me because he was saner than me.

"You can't possibly get Brian to do something until he has to," Dr. Landy explained. "That's the point. Making him have to do things. I'll get him to choose different behavior because, figuratively speaking, he'll be traveling down a familiar street and suddenly it will have been closed off. He'll be forced to find a new route. He'll be forced out of his craziness and into dealing with reality."

Then Dr. Landy explained what was going to happen. He was going to remove me from the easiness of my reclusive home life, terminating the self-destructive avenues I'd set up for myself. My money would be cut off. The Beach Boys would fire me. I wouldn't be able to afford drugs. I wouldn't be able to afford an escape. Cut off, I'd be placed in a healthy new environment where I would find it impossible to reinforce my self-destructive behavior. There, I'd begin learning to do and think for myself.

In short, all my safety nets were going to be removed. To survive, I would have no choice but to cope. Then, and only then, could I be awakened from my long, dangerous, and unhealthy hibernation.

The next question that arose was who should kick me out of the Beach

Boys. After all, they weren't discussing Al Jardine. The person in question was the band's founder and leader, Brian Wilson.

"It should be a letter," Dr. Landy said. "Signed by everyone."

There were no objections. The letter they drew up wasn't legal, a fact that would be lost on me, but it was signed by everyone except Dennis. Had he been there, Dennis probably wouldn't have gone along with the plan, figuring he'd be next. Everyone took turns signing Dennis's name; Mike showed the most talent, and his forgery won.

On November 5, 1982, Carolyn and I showed up at the management office, where, in a meeting choreographed by Dr. Landy, I was formally fired from the Beach Boys. They gave me a letter that terminated my services.

From Tom Hulett's office, Dr. Landy listened over an intercom as the meeting unfolded. I had little touch with reality to begin with, and I had no idea what hit me. I didn't understand how they could fire me. I yelled. I argued. I slumped in my chair, confused and dazed. At home, I got smashed, while Carolyn stewed and schemed. She called my accountant and requested money.

"Sorry," she was told. "There is no cash to send. Brian is broke."

I didn't want to start treatment again with Dr. Landy. I was petrified of him and what he would make me do—stop doing drugs, stop hiding, and confront reality. I complained bitterly to Dennis and his wife, Shawn. Carolyn supported me unconditionally. She had staked her territory— me—and was willing to fight for it. I tried enlisting Carl's support too.

"Brian," he said on the phone one night, "I think you have to go to Dr. Landy. He's your only chance. It's the only way you're going to get better."

I didn't care about getting better. But I did care about the money. I had to start seeing Dr. Landy. Once I began going to appointments, the Beach Boys would pay me again. Carolyn called immediately but was told that a patient had to make an appointment by himself. I tried several times without success. She ended up dialing and I talked.

When we arrived at Dr. Landy's office for the appointment, the receptionist shook her head. We were ten minutes late. Carolyn said, "So?" Well, it was Dr. Landy's policy not to see new patients who arrived late to their first appointment. Irate, Carolyn nearly punched the receptionist.

"How in the hell are we going to live?" she railed. "If we don't see Landy, we don't get any money."

"Would you like to set up another date?" the receptionist asked calmly.

Showing up on time the following day, Carolyn literally took me by the collar and led me into Dr. Landy's office. The prospect of being with Dr. Landy again filled me with anxiety. On one hand, I knew how hard his twenty-four-hour therapy program was and didn't want a thing to do with something that difficult. However, I was also angry at Dr. Landy for deserting me the first time. Even though it wasn't his fault, I felt it was. I'd trusted him, and he let me down. I also missed him and our relationship.

Dropping into a chair, my head lolled to the side, my eyes went up, and my right leg pumped up and down uncontrollably. Carolyn said a triumphant hello to Dr. Landy. The money was just around the corner, a phone call away. Dr. Landy smiled, then turned toward me, shutting Carolyn out. Although my eyes were still rolled back, I knew Dr. Landy was staring at me. I sensed him leaning close.

"What can I do for you?" he asked.

I didn't say anything. Carolyn hit me on the leg, a not-so-gentle prod.

"Nothing," I muttered. "I don't want anything."

"Okay," Dr. Landy said. "I guess we have nothing to talk about."

He got up and started to leave the room.

"No, no! Wait a minute!" Carolyn said. "We're here for the money. We want the money. Right, Brian? The deal is, Brian sees you, then we get the money. Isn't that so?"

Dr. Landy gave Carolyn a scornful look and asked why she was in the office with me. Who was the appointment for? He asked Carolyn to leave. Defensive, she said she was seeing the deal through to completion; she was going to get the money started up again.

"Look, Carolyn," Dr. Landy repeated. "Do you want me to continue? Or should I stop? Because if you want to stay, fine, I'll leave. It makes no difference to me. I charge for the room. If I'm in it, I charge more."

Indignant, Carolyn stalked out and slammed the door behind her. With just the two of us in the office, Dr. Landy let time pass and the ruckus settle before sitting down across from me. I allowed myself a quick glance at the situation, then let my eyes roll up again. Dr. Landy was inches from me, intense, serious, caring, not going away. The same as he'd been before.

"What do you want?" he asked. "What do you want from me? I know it's not the money."

Thirty minutes passed and not a single word was exchanged. I was testing Dr. Landy, yet I was really too exhausted and disturbed to put up much of a fight. I just wanted to disappear. If not that, I wanted to turn belly-up and let whatever was going to happen happen.

"I know how scared you are," Dr. Landy said, breaking the quiet.

"I know you do," I mumbled.

"I can help you," Dr. Landy said. "But you have to want me to help. If you don't want me to, I can't. I can only do it if you ask me, if you empower me. What do you want?"

Minutes passed. I considered my options.

"Nothing," I said.

"That's okay," Dr. Landy said. "Then nothing will happen. Get up. Go. Go take care of yourself. Good luck."

He was inviting me to leave. Asking me. Telling me it was okay. Yet what I said and what I wanted were different. I didn't want to go.

"What have I got to say?" I asked.

"Nothing," he said. "You don't have to say anything."

"Well, what's going to happen?" I asked.

"You're going to die," Dr. Landy said. "I'm going to live. That's what's going to happen."

The truth. It flashed in front of me like a neon sign. I had a choice, life or death. The obviousness was blinding.

"I don't want to die," I blurted, tears starting to pour out of me. "I don't want to die."

"If you don't want to die," Dr. Landy intoned, "what do you want?"

Dr. Landy was asking if I was willing to do the equivalent of jumping off the Empire State Building. I understood the fall might kill me. But I also knew that once I hit the ground, everything about my life would be better. I started to say the words in my spongy brain, but they were drowned in tears.

"I . . . want . . . you . . . to help . . . me."

Dr. Landy put his arm around me.

"Help me. Please," I cried.

36

I Almost Die

*O*nce regular office visits had started, Dr. Landy's treatment plan required separating me and Carolyn. We were unaware of that next step, since up to this point she was included in every discussion and made to feel an integral part of my rehabilitation. Attempting to be as nonthreatening to her as possible, Dr. Landy called Carolyn to his office and explained that before he could begin intensive treatment, my health was such that I had to be thoroughly checked out in a hospital. It could take several weeks to run all the tests.

Carolyn, anxious to keep the money flowing, agreed. First, she drove me to a multitude of doctor's appointments, which covered several weeks. Then I was checked into Cedars-Sinai Medical Center for more comprehensive workups. While in Cedars, Dr. Landy began preparing Carolyn, unbeknownst to her, for the fact that she was going to lose me.

Dr. Landy felt, and everyone concurred, that if I was going to get better, Carolyn Williams was a negative influence and couldn't remain involved with me. She serviced me with joints and cigarettes. She provided whatever I wanted, showing no regard for my health. It was obvious that Carolyn would fight Dr. Landy every step of the way for control.

Carolyn had the feeling something was up, but she couldn't put her finger on it. In the meantime, she was kept extremely busy, running from meeting to meeting with Dr. Landy's assistants. They advised her on how to care for me when I got out of the hospital. She was given instructions on exercise, diet, drug withdrawal, anything to keep her occupied.

Then came the meeting where the team of doctors and Dr. Landy discussed my medical condition with the Beach Boys, Hulett, Branca, Schilling, and others. Ninety minutes into the meeting, Branca turned to Dr. Landy and asked what the hell was being said. He didn't understand a word of the medical mumbo jumbo or even why he was there.

"What they're saying is that he may not live longer than a year under the best of circumstances and conditions," Dr. Landy interpreted.

"Really?"

"Yeah," Dr. Landy said. "Without any more drugs, without anything, Brian is still in danger of not surviving. I've studied the reports. His liver's bad. He has one quarter of his lung capacity. His heart is overstressed. And he's 150 pounds overweight."

Dr. Landy had visited Cedars periodically to see me. He was there just enough to let me realize he was around. I was a miserable patient. I yelled at the nurses. I threw my food. Too obese to get up, I peed in and off the side of my bed. I wouldn't bathe. I spent most of the time chain-smoking cigarettes. Dr. Landy had to post his son, Evan, in my room at night to make sure I wouldn't fall asleep with a cigarette going and burn the place down. After checking out, I had to pay to have the room recarpeted.

I trusted Dr. Landy, though. Although I feared him as I did everyone else, I also knew him to be fair and kind. He had a good track record with me. He'd never done anything destructive to me. He'd never taken advantage of me. The worst thing Landy had done was force me into situations that scared the shit out of me. But I realized that nothing he made me do ever harmed me in any way. It was for my benefit.

So I listened when Dr. Landy planted the seed of what was going to happen to me.

"You want to get well, don't you?" he asked, sitting beside my bed during one of his hospital visits.

"Yeah," I moaned in a raspy voice.

"Will you do anything that needs to be done to save your life and get well?" asked Dr. Landy.

I nodded.

"Even if it means going away for a while?" Dr. Landy slowly said. "You might not like it and it might not feel good, but you're going to get well. That I promise. And I never break a promise."

"Okay," I said.

37

Learning to Walk

I didn't know the details, but Dr. Landy had dropped enough bla-
tant hints for me to suspect I was going away. I learned the details,
all of which had been approved by the Beach Boys, as the operation unfolded.

I was going to be sequestered at an isolated compound in Hawaii for
an unspecified period of time, long enough to complete the job. With a
team of assistants, including my psychiatrist Dr. Solon Samuels, physician
and holistic medical expert Dr. Murray "Buzz" Susser, Dr. Arnold
Dahlke, Alexandra Morgan, my future exercise coach, nutritionists, cooks,
nurses, local doctors, and hand-picked assistants, Dr. Landy was going to
awaken me from my seven-year stupor, introduce me to good health, and
make me deal with life and confront the reality I'd been dodging.

I was going to be resurrected. I was going to be given life again.

On the second Monday in January 1983, the plan that Dr. Landy and
the Beach Boys had agreed to in October was implemented. It began with
the crackerjack precision and scope of a military maneuver. At six in the
morning, a fleet of limos began picking up Dr. Landy's fifteen-person team
and ferrying them to the airport, where the entire second floor lounge of
a United 747 had been booked on the 9:00 A.M. flight to Hawaii.

I was awakened and wheelchaired outside to the waiting limo. I knew
I was leaving the hospital, but my destination was a mystery.

Somehow I knew—how I'm unsure—but I knew that this wasn't just another limo ride.

Meanwhile, Carolyn showed up at Dr. Landy's office for an eight-thirty appointment with one of his assistants, the first of a half-dozen time-consuming meetings Dr. Landy had arranged to occupy her before she was supposed to check me out of Cedars. The point was to keep her busy until I was in Hawaii. It was easy as long as Carolyn was reassured along the way that the money would start up again if all these tasks were performed.

The plane landed in Honolulu without a hitch. While the considerable luggage and medical supplies—enough to set up a mobile hospital, necessary because we were heading for an isolated location and no one knew my physical capabilities—were transfered from the airplane to several trucks, I was led to a private room, where a makeshift dental office had been assembled. Dr. Jerry Wall, who's still my dentist in L.A., had agreed to meet Dr. Landy at the airport and examine my teeth. I saw the setup and thought, What the hell? Dr. Landy explained that I hadn't had a checkup for years; he didn't want any infections flaring up.

When that was over the entourage shuttled to the interisland terminals and boarded a plane that deposited us in Kona, a small, rural town by itself but too big for our purposes. We caravaned by car for another hour, heading out of Kona and around a mountain, past several smaller villages, then some five miles down a beautiful winding road that cut down to the ocean. I was enraptured by the scenery but confused beyond all means by where we were. I kept repeating, "This is Hawaii."

Finally, it seemed we were getting someplace. We zigged off the main highway and turned onto a dirt road, which became a gravel trail that led onto a dirt path, which eventually led to the little compound Dr. Landy had found. Actually, it was a fishing outpost of six homes, and Dr. Landy had rented three of them. The point is that we were in the middle of nowhere, with nothing around us for miles and miles.

It was getting late by the time we arrived. I noticed a few people had arrived ahead of us, shopped, and prepared dinner, a sumptuous outdoor feast of fresh fish, fruits, and vegetables.

As soon as I could, I parked myself in a chair as far away from the activity as I could get and watched. At some point, Dr. Landy told me that I was permitted to eat as much of anything I wanted. I refused. I didn't want to be with people. I didn't want to be part of anything or anybody.

Dr. Landy expected that. I was alone, scared, and on my own. I was completely isolated from everybody in the world who'd ever helped me because I was Brian Wilson, the rock star. Instead, I was surrounded by this group of virtual strangers, people I knew were going to take care of me, though not in the way to which I was accustomed. I feared them, but I didn't fear for my safety.

Hunger got the best of me. I wandered warily over to the dinner table, as sneakily as possible—as if no one would notice a 340-pound smelly man approaching a buffet table. Quickly, I shoveled some bread into my mouth and then sat in typical fashion—with my head back and my eyes rolled up into their sockets so the whites of the eyeballs showed. Rocking back and forth, in wide, rhythmic sweeps determined by some inner metronome, I wanted to disappear.

Dr. Landy was surrounded by the team of doctors, nurses, and assistants. As the conductor of this talented orchestra of medical personnel, Dr. Landy was preparing his players for the most memorable performance of their careers.

Before dinner was over, I left the table and hid in my room. Up to that point, I was thinking, What the fuck have I gotten myself into?

Then I began realizing what was going on. It was a new game. I knew that. At the same time, I wondered, What am I going to have to do? How am I going to do what I have to do?

By the time I got to my room, my senses were on overload. I was beyond scared, I was petrified. I'd ceased to think and wonder about this new environment I was in and was instead living from moment to moment, involved in the more primal concern of survival. That high-pitched level of excitement was exactly the kind of emotional charge I lived on. Waiting for the worst to happen. Anticipatory death. It was horrible, but I also enjoyed every minute of how terrible it was.

It was both bad and good, positive and negative, terrifying and exciting.

The next morning I woke up to a drastically changed scene from dinner. There was no food. No coffee. No more cigarettes. No nothing. I didn't know it when Dr. Landy woke me up, but my only sustenance was going to be juice and intravenous vitamin drips.

Dr. Landy lived in a separate two-bedroom house that slept four people. My house had six occupants scattered throughout the bedrooms and sofas. In addition to the staff Dr. Landy brought over, he also employed round-the-clock nurses from Kona Hospital as well as Dr. David

Allan, a specialist in emergency medicine. Later, Dr. Landy told me he wasn't going to let an obese, drugged-out rock and roller avoid getting better by dying from a heart attack.

When Dr. Landy entered my bedroom that first morning, I was a mummy in bed under the covers. A nurse was trying to set up an intravenous vitamin drip, but I was so fat she couldn't find a vein. I wasn't helping any either. I wouldn't move. I wouldn't talk. Dr. Landy sat down beside the bed and stared into my eyes, which I promptly rolled up into my sockets. I wasn't going to give one inch. But Dr. Landy knew how to play the game.

"Let's get up, Brian," Dr. Landy said.

"I don't want to," I replied.

"Well, what do you want to do?" he asked.

"Nothing."

"Why don't we take a walk?"

"No."

"How about a ride?"

"Maybe."

"You want breakfast?" Dr. Landy asked.

That got me. My eyes opened.

"Yeah," I said.

"Okay, let's go," he said.

"Why don't you bring it here," I suggested.

"We don't have any food here," he said. "Remember, we just got here."

"Yeah, I remember."

Dr. Landy suggested going out for breakfast. Remembering the feast of the night before, I agreed. But I was too obese to get out of bed myself.

No problem. Aided by an assistant, Dr. Landy helped me up and then put a shirt and a pair of swimming trunks on me—my outfit for the next couple of weeks. Bathing and washing was too advanced for me. Dr. Landy just wanted me up and out of bed. That itself was an achievement. Though it was excruciating, I followed Dr. Landy downstairs, careful to remain a safe distance behind him and away from everyone else.

We climbed into a little Chrysler convertible, one of six cars that were parked outside. The car's compact size immediately made me self-conscious about my weight. Dr. Landy drove. I sat next to him and shook with fear. Three other people I didn't dare make eye contact with sat in the back. I didn't like the crowd, but Dr. Landy didn't want to get stranded in the middle of nowhere. He also wanted protection for himself in case I should suddenly become violent.

I was still such an unknown quantity. No reaction was predictable. Dr. Landy knew I needed more time with him before I felt comfortable with what he was doing.

We drove a quarter mile down the road—out the dirt to the gravel, down the broken-up street and so on, until we hit the beach. It was exactly a quarter of a mile. Dr. Landy pulled the car over, took out the keys, and told me to follow him. I didn't. I stayed where I was, not moving a single muscle.

"What are we going to do?" I asked.

"We're going to get out and look at the beautiful ocean," Dr. Landy said. "It's pretty. This is a nice palce. Come on."

It took me a few minutes, but I grunted my way out of the front seat and stood a few steps behind Dr. Landy, who stepped backwards so that he was next to me.

"Look, isn't this water wonderful?" he asked.

"Yeah. Wonderful," I said. "When do we eat?"

"Okay, you want breakfast now?"

"Yeah, I'm hungry," I said.

"How about some juice?" Dr. Landy offered.

"Great. Where is it?"

"We have to go get it," Dr. Landy said, and started walking back up the road on which we'd driven.

The group immediately followed. I was confused. I went to the car. Dr. Landy called for me to join the group.

"Where are you going?" I asked.

"We're going to get some juice," Dr. Landy answered.

"But I want to drive," I said.

"No, we're going to walk," Dr. Landy called.

"I can't walk," I said. "I have to drive."

It was an important moment—our first major confrontation. Dr. Landy was asking me to do something that I hated yet could accomplish even though I told myself otherwise. It was a test. I was either going to adapt or not adapt. If I didn't, he'd have to confront me at a lower level.

I didn't want to walk. I didn't know much of anything, that much I knew. I also knew that nobody else was around for miles. No people, no cars, no phones.

"You can walk," Dr. Landy encouraged. "You'd be surprised by what you can do."

"No, I can't," I said.

"Well, what are you going to do?" Dr. Landy said, finally halting his pace so he didn't get too far away from me.

"I'm going to drive this car," I said.

"You can't," he said. "I've got the keys. The car is staying here till tomorrow morning, when we'll drive it back."

"What do you mean?" I asked.

By then, I was sitting in the front seat.

"I mean we'll walk back tomorrow morning and get it," Dr. Landy yelled.

"But I *can't* walk back," I protested, my voice straining with panic.

"Then you can stay in the car," Dr. Landy answered, resuming the walk up the road. "We're going home to have breakfast. See you tomorrow."

"You're not going to come back?" I hollered.

"Not today!"

Motherfucker.

That's what he was. Raising my 340 pounds from the car seat and struggling to a standing position outside the vehicle, I stared long and defiantly at Dr. Landy. Then my resistance gave in. I took a small, difficult, and uncertain step toward him. Then another step. And another.

Pretty soon I was walking. It was waddling, really, but when you're over 340 pounds, waddling is the beginning of walking.

Little did I realize I was starting down the path of the rest of my life.

I was expending the effort only to catch the doctor, who'd lured me into the middle of this wasteland disguised as a paradise by promising me good health. Instead, he was trying to kill me. Ten steps and I was out of breath. Dr. Landy, a good twenty-five strides ahead of me, was shouting something to me, but I couldn't hear above my wheezing.

"Wait, goddamnit," I coughed.

"What?" he yelled.

Shit. I stopped, panting. I wanted to tell Landy I'd changed my mind. The walk was too much. I was going to skip breakfast and spend the night in the car. But those weren't the words that came out of my mouth.

"Wait a minute!" I yelled.

"I can't," said Dr. Landy. "In a minute, we'll be a quarter way there."

"But I can't—"

"Yes you can!" he shouted.

"But I'm gonna die if I don't stop," I said, gasping for big gulps of air.

"So stop," said Dr. Landy, backtracking a few steps, which closed the distance between us. "You're not going to die. I promise you that. You're only going to feel like you're dying."

Dr. Landy sent someone back to give me a few words of encouragement, then we started up again. Whenever I leaned on someone to make the walk easier, the motherfucker told him to stay ahead of me. He didn't want me to lean. He said, "You've been leaning your entire life." He was right. It was time I stood on my own. But that didn't stop me from complaining the entire way.

As we walked, I imagined dying. I felt my heart pounding straight out of my chest and bouncing up the road ahead of me. I stopped and rested every ten steps or so. I listened to the encouragement, chose to ignore it, and instead cursed Dr. Landy for being the king of tyrants.

However, an hour later I was trudging the last couple of steps up to the doorstep of my house, sweat-soaked, winded, slightly delirious, and extremely angry. The half-dozen people who'd been on the walk stood around the door as if it were a finish line and applauded my effort with a loud ovation. I was too exhausted to feel proud of my accomplishment. Too tired even to smile. Too tired to stop and enjoy the moment. I just kept going till I hit the dining room table and fell into my chair, a big round orange thing that reminded me of the hand of a comforting mother.

"Breakfast," I bellowed.

"It's coming," said Dr. Landy, who seated himself next to me and watched impassively as Dr. Susser, my new physician who also doubled as our nutritionist and resident poet, set two tall glasses of juice on the table.

While Dr. Landy studied his glass of blended juice, I downed mine in one breathless swallow. I then looked around expectantly for more food. Eggs. Steaks. Rashers of bacon. Bagels. Waffles. Maple syrup. Doughnuts. Toast with butter and jelly. A Sara Lee coffee cake. The stuff I normally ate.

"Where's the rest?" I asked.

"That's it," said Dr. Landy. "There is no more."

"What?" I exclaimed. "I'm still hungry."

"Sorry," he said. "But for the next week or so it's just juice and multivitamins."

"You can't do that," I protested.

"I'm not," he said. "You are."

"Well, that's fucked," I said as I tried to get out of the chair. My bulk held me down. I needed help. Scared and sulking, I managed to get up and stalked off to my room, where I sulked in anger and withdrew into my own world.

38

Starting to Listen

Not unexpectedly, during the first couple of days in Hawaii I was consumed by tremendous fear and anxiety, anger and frustration. So much so that I didn't pause to think about Carolyn. Since I was being cared for, in a manner of speaking, I no longer needed her. I tried not to pay attention to the aches and yearnings of my body withdrawing from drugs. I didn't even try to resist the torture of confronting the harsh glare of real life. I was too busy coping, just dealing with each moment. Every moment. Surviving.

Somewhere in the back of my mind I knew what was happening was for the better.

For two days Drs. Samuels and Susser prescribed Valium, a mild tranquilizer, to ease my immersion in the baptismal fires of recovery. Psychotropic medications for my schizophrenia, begun immediately, also helped ease the shock. But nothing could've prepared me for the most torturous of tasks, exercise.

The first week was experimental, since my physical capability was uncharted territory, but I plugged into a routine right away. Wake-up was at 8:00 A.M. Then my intravenous vitamin drip. There was always a struggle to start the IV with vitamin C. The same was true at night. Dr. Susser, nicknamed the Vitamin King, and the nurse gave me about 50,000 milligrams of vitamin C every day, in addition to a cornucopia of others.

The vitamins were an important part of cleansing my system and making the withdrawal from drugs easier.

After my morning vitamin drip, I set out on the quarter-mile hike down the windy dirt road to the beach. Then breakfast—juice. By week two, breakfast was upgraded from juice to frozen fruit, which we ate at the beach. That was followed by an exhausting half hour of stretching exercises led by Alexandra Morgan, Dr. Landy's longtime girlfriend.

Next, we hiked toward a church perched on top of a mountain with a picturesque view of the ocean, an ordeal measured in inches and blisters. The walk to the church was five miles round-trip, but the incline was equivalent to another couple of miles. The goal for each of us, not just me, was to make it there and back. Initially, I was able to do only a couple hundred yards before dropping to the ground, exhausted. Dr. Landy always led the way, followed by assistants. I started out in the middle of the pack. More people were always behind me, everybody shouting encouragement.

That damn mountain became a challenge to me, the first challenge I'd accepted in years.

The mountain was also a metaphor for the progress I made daily. We climbed a little farther every day. That became a rule by which to live, to survive, though I guess it took years before I really understood that idea intellectually.

The more distance I accumulated, the more confidence I developed. At the time I was without any sort of ego. I didn't have the tiniest drop of confidence in myself. Everything from fetching a glass of water to walking two miles was out of my reach.

In those early days I looked to Dr. Landy for my confidence. It was as if I were a sponge and absorbed his confidence. I used him as my backbone. When I quit on something, he was there, buzzing in my ear.

"You can get up off the ground, Brian," he said one day as I sat on a rock, huffing and puffing in a pool of sweat.

"I can't," I said.

"Yes, you can," he exhorted. "If I can go a little farther, you can do it too. I'm older than you."

"But I'm too fat."

"You won't be if you get up off your ass and walk."

I didn't want to get up. In the worst way I didn't want to. But I did. That was the difference between Dr. Landy and everyone else. Even though I didn't like what he asked me to do, I knew Dr. Landy was right. He was always fair. He didn't put me down. If I couldn't do something, he encouraged me. He taught me lessons that weren't easy, and I hated them. But I knew it was in my best interest to try to learn.

At home I did household chores, the first time since my dad made me mow the lawn. After getting up, I made my bed. After that, the jobs varied. One day it was my turn to empty the garbage; the next day I washed dishes or swept the porch. The fact that I was a Beach Boy didn't count for squat. I was no different from anyone else, except I was unskilled in the tools of everyday life and personal survival that most people take for granted.

In the past two years, I'd been sponged in the hospital and taken the rare dip in a pool, but I hadn't showered or bathed once. Knowing I was petrified about what might spray out of the shower head, Dr. Landy didn't *force* me into the stall. Still, he insisted on immediate bathing. Every day the first week, I walked over to his house, which had a pool, and took a swim. The second week I started bathing in the ocean.

Toward the end of the first month, Dr. Landy insisted I step into the shower.

I tried. I shut the door, ran the water, and came out with a towel wrapped around me.

"Your hair's not wet," he noticed one day. "Let me see the soap you were using."

"I don't know where I put it," I stammered.

"Did you leave it in the shower?" Dr. Landy asked, checking the stall. "Ah-ha! The soap is dry too."

"I guess I forgot to use it," I said.

"Get undressed," he insisted. "You're going to take another shower."

"No," I insisted. "I can shower with my clothes on."

Dr. Landy raised his eyebrows and stepped into the shower with his clothes on. He motioned for me to follow. Then he stripped off his clothes. Reluctantly, I took mine off. When both of us were naked, Dr. Landy explained he was going to take a shower with me. As always, he was calling my bluff, making it impossible for me to slip out. I was shaking, holding back tears. I didn't want the water to come on. There was no telling what might come out of the nozzle. Fire. Snakes. Blood. Acid. Bullets. Liquid death. Terrible things.

Dr. Landy ignored my complaints and turned on the water. It shot out. I darted into the corner and cowered. Dr. Landy stood under the warm stream of water. We had two washcloths, two bars of soap. He explained he was going to teach me how to take a shower. If I didn't know how to wash, I'd learn. If I was scared, he'd prove there was nothing to be scared of. He handed me a washcloth and a bar of soap.

"Now get under here and do what I do, Brian," he said. "If something's going to come out of the shower head, it's going to hurt me first. No matter how much you fear something's going to happen, believe me, it's not."

Forcing myself to move, I grabbed the door and stepped in hesitantly, standing face-to-face with Dr. Landy. I waited for something painful to happen to me. For scalding hot water to rip off my skin. For snakes to streak out of the shower head. For bullets. For blood to spray. Instead, I was given a lesson on how to scrub my body with soap and a washcloth, from my toes to my ass to my ears. Then Dr. Landy picked up a bottle of highly viscous liquid.

"It's green," I said.

"Yes. This is shampoo." Dr. Landy smiled. "Hold out your hand."

Despite the intensive daily instruction, I was still allowed time alone. I was guarded, but I was still alone. I treasured it as the time when I was able to disappear inside myself and explore the commotion in my mind, the time when I did what I described as "fancy thinking."

It was ten hours at first, then less as the weeks passed. Dr. Landy understood that alone time was necessary for my sanity. It was time for me to recharge my battery, time that helped smooth the transition from someone who had spent twenty-four hours a day withdrawn and alone to someone who participated and integrated with other people. I would've preferred to spend those hours in bed, but Landy closed off the bedroom during the day.

"The bedroom's for sleeping," he told me.

So I spread out on the couch. Or I lay on the floor. Or I sat in the closet in the dark.

As I adapted to the daily routine, the most difficult, and often most painful, part of each day became not exercise or chores but dinner. Drs. Landy and Susser always talked about the Brian Wilson Diet—"No sugar, no salt, no fat, no fun." They weren't exaggerating. I not only had to learn manners and how to eat using silverware without shoveling my food down my throat in sixty seconds but I also had to participate in the dinner table discussions. My first inclination was to devour my meal and then withdraw from the rest of the table by rolling my eyes up and rocking back and forth. But Dr. Landy prohibited such antisocial behavior.

"Dinner is a ritual when everyone talks about what they did during the day," he explained.

Fine. Whatever he wanted, that was fine with me. I focused my concentration on the layout of the table. Freshly filleted sashimi was piled on one platter. Chicken on another. Mountains of fresh fruit piled up in a big bowl. And vegetables. Lots of them. The difficulty arose when Landy forced me into the conversation and I realized I hadn't been paying attention.

"Brian, what did you think of what David just said?" he asked, referring to another assistant David Berlow.

"Uh, I wasn't listening," I admitted reluctantly.

"David, say it over again," he said. "Brian, do you want David not to listen to you?"

"I don't care," I said.

"Okay," said Dr. Landy, who stopped eating, pushed his chair back from the table, crossed his arms, and waited, bringing the entire dinner, including the flow of food at the table, to a sudden standstill. Everybody just sat and waited.

Such instances were frequent, and sometimes these pauses lasted an hour or two.

Dr. Landy didn't get angry. He didn't need to. He used affectionate gestures, lots of hugs, and spoke with kind, understanding words. It was when he stopped speaking that I couldn't handle it. Silence, ordinarily my best friend, could be unnerving too. Dr. Landy's most effective method of making me function was to stop functioning himself. If I stopped functioning, everyone stopped. Dinner came to a halt. It was only after I performed as I was supposed to in a normal, sociable manner that the eating and talking began again.

"What are we doing?" I would finally ask, my stomach growling.

"I'm waiting for you to care," Dr. Landy explained.

The conversation ran backwards. He'd ask me again what I cared about. I wouldn't know because I hadn't listened. I just wanted my dinner. But my old manipulative games didn't play in Hawaii. I had to learn new ones, how to use the other side of my brain in order to figure out what this fucker wanted so he'd get off my case.

"Okay, I guess dinner is over," Dr. Landy finally announced at a certain point after a couple of hours of silence. "We'll try again tomorrow night."

"What do you mean?" I reacted. "We're not going to eat until then?"

"If you don't care, Brian, none of us cares."

"But I care," I implored. "I want to care. Tell me what I should care about."

"Well, what are we talking about?" he'd ask.

The whole exercise dealt with discovery. Dr. Landy was making me discover things, in this case listening to conversation and thinking. Believe it or not, that was new. I'd never listened to anybody. Then I had to integrate what I'd heard and use it, as if I were learning a new word and had to use it in three different sentences, past, present, and future. Finally, the original conversation was replayed again and I was asked for my opinion on David Berlow's comments.

"I didn't hear him," I said.

"Is there something wrong?" Landy asked.

"I don't know. I mean, how would I know?"

"You'd know if you couldn't hear me," he said.

"I can hear you," I said, not realizing the trap he was leading me into.

"You can hear me. I can hear you. Both of us can hear David. David, would you repeat what you said for Brian."

The point of this madness, as Dr. Landy later explained and I came to understand and appreciate, was to get me to acknowledge that I wasn't paying attention to anything or anybody. I'd drifted into private space. It wasn't that I didnt' care or wasn't able to hear. I didn't put the information into my brain. And the minute I admitted that I hadn't been paying attention, he wanted to know what I was paying attention to.

"I don't know," I said.

"What do you mean you don't know?" he asked.

"I forgot."

"You forgot? Well, maybe we should write things down. Get a pencil and paper. When you're not paying attention to whatever's going on, you can write down what you are paying attention to."

"I'll pay attention," I promised.

I was trapped. I was trapped into exercising. I was trapped into losing weight. I was trapped into eating with a knife and fork instead of my hands. I was trapped into hygiene and cleanliness. I was trapped into making my bed. I was trapped into listening and responding to conversations.

One day the pressure of feeling trapped got to be too much and I exploded directly at Dr. Landy.

"I feel like a goddamn caged animal," I ranted. "I feel fucking trapped."

"I'm sure." He nodded. "But you want to know what your real problem is?"

"What?" I asked.

"You're starting to get well."

After six weeks, a piano was moved into my house. I was out when it was delivered. When I returned, it was at the bottom of the steps. At first glance my eyes nearly popped out. It was an upright Steinway, the first and only upright Steinway I'd ever seen, but I felt as if I were meeting an old friend. I was told I had to help lift it up the sixteen steps to the porch and then inside. It was heavy. It was hard. It was a pain in the royal ass. But it was worth it.

I sat down right away.

"It's locked," I said.

"Yes," Dr. Landy acknowledged. "It's not to be used."

"Why?"

"Because first it's necessary to learn how to talk and relate to other people," he said.

My longtime escape route was cut off. Dr. Landy explained that when I could sit and hold a conversation, when I could comprehend what was reported on the television news, when I could do such and such things, then I could play the piano for small amounts of time. All of a sudden, the piano was no longer the back door through which I disappeared but instead a much desired, longed-for reward. As always, this shrink was changing the guidelines on me.

The only person I'd really ever listened to before was my dad. I listened to him solely because he made me. He beat me. He threatened me with pain. He tortured me psychologically. I'd never cared what anyone else had to say because I was preoccupied with my own voices and with the music I heard inside my head. It was far more interesting, far more exciting.

Lo and behold, Landy comes into my life and he has the same power. He beat me too—but not physically, like my dad. He beat me at my own Scrabble game in my head. It was dumbfounding how he got inside my head, knew my thoughts. The piano was a perfect example. Until then, the instrument was my escape. Everybody expected me to play. Told me to play. My talent gave me a wonderful ability to be right all the time. I used it to manipulate people and get my way.

Now Dr. Landy was using it to manipulate me. If I fucked up, I lost piano time. If I did well, I was rewarded with increased playing time. Before I just did things; there were no consequences in life. This forced me to learn that there *were* consequences to my actions. I did things and saw how there was a domino effect. As a result, I forced myself to do things like listen. If a conversation went too fast, I learned to say, "Wait a minute! I didn't understand that."

I wanted my piano time.

Not too long after the piano arrived some corporate papers concerning the Beach Boys were delivered. I had to sign them, and they had to be notarized. The officer at the bank in town asked to see my ID. I didn't have any—no driver's license, nothing. I hadn't had any identification for years. I walked around town and was known. Dr. Landy herded some of the locals who knew me into the bank, but that wasn't any good. They had to see something on paper.

Dr. Landy suggested going to the record store down the street and buying an album with my picture on it. We purchased several and showed the banker I was the same guy. He accepted it. When we got back home Dr. Landy played one of the albums. Up until then Beach Boys music hadn't been part of the repertoire that was played in the house; Dr. Landy didn't want it around. They were the circus, the contaminated neighborhood I was running from.

I cringed when I heard the songs. Instinct told me to run into my bedroom and jump in bed—under the bed. Or lock myself in the closet. Anyplace where I couldn't hear the music. I'd killed myself for that music. I didn't want to be reminded of the pain.

Dr. Landy took the album off.

"Will you play that song for me?" he asked.

"What?" I said, puzzled.

" 'Help Me, Rhonda,' " he said. "Play it."

"I don't know it," I said.

"Who wrote it?" he asked, playing my own game.

"I did."

"When did you write it?" he asked.

"I don't know."

"Why'd you write it?"

"I can't say," I said.

"Well, how do you know you wrote it then?"

It became clear I wasn't playing a game. I'd actually forgotten how to play the songs I'd written. I'd suppressed that ability under tons of painful memories and drugs. Locked the stuff up and thrown away the key.

It was then that Dr. Landy decided I was going to start relearning how to play my own songs. I agreed and Dr. Landy flew family and marriage counselor Bill Flaxman to Hawaii. Flaxman was a kind man whose warm voice later inspired me to write a song called "Bill Sounds That Way."

We worked one hour in the morning and one in the afternoon, taking each song until I mastered the music and the lyrics again. But the playing never extended beyond the prescribed hour, no matter if I hungered to continue. Each song dredged up memories and experiences, most of them unpleasant, and Dr. Landy wanted me to deal with them. I'd spent years ignoring these emotions, drowning them in booze, drugs, and food. There was none of that anymore. Instead, we talked.

"Why do you think Mike Love's going to beat you up?" Dr. Landy asked.

"Because he hates that his name isn't on 'California Girls.' "

"Why isn't it?"

"I don't know."

"Well, who wrote the credits down?" he asked.

"My dad."

"Did he ask if Mike had written any of the song?"

"No."

"Did Mike ever tell him that he wrote some part of the song?"

"No."

"So what's the problem?"

"He's mad at me," I said.

"That's Mike's problem," Landy said. "Not yours. If he's convinced himself he wrote it, that's his problem. Not yours. He'll have to get his own shrink and work his own problems out, as you are. Do you understand?"

I was starting to. I really was.

Sitting on the beach at the end of February 1983, I finished breakfast and thought of the progress I'd made in the nearly two months I'd lived on the island. I felt like a new person. I was thinner. I exercised, talked, and listened to people. I cared for myself. I played music again. As Dr. Landy promised, I was learning to live again.

Admiring the emerald green water and postcard-pretty scenery, I drew a breath of Hawaiian air and appreciated the freshness. Even my trips up the mountain were becoming enjoyable interludes of exercise and thought.

"Do you know Einstein's theory of relativity?" I asked Dr. Dahlke as we stretched one morning.

He nodded.

"That's something," I said. "That a man could come up with something like that and be proved right. My God, that's fantastic."

Dahlke's eyes were incredulous. He didn't know I even knew about Einstein.

"Why were you thinking of that?" he asked.

"I just was," I said.

"Does it relate to your music any?"

"I don't know." I shrugged.

"You know, Brian," Dr. Dahlke said, "I've always wanted to ask how you write music. How does it come to you? How do you do it?"

"I don't know." I shrugged again. "I just hear it in my head. Everything. The instruments, the background. And I just write it down."

"That's something too." He smiled.

Several days later, I was on the beach again, watching the morning sun paint the sand a warmer hue. I was wearing a new pair of running shorts, proud testimony to having dropped more than sixty-five pounds. As a group of us stretched in preparation for our run up to the church on the mountain, I found myself anticipating the run with excitement and realized I was looking forward to the jog. The once dreaded walk, which had been so slow and painful, had become a challenging yet enjoyable jog.

"Today's the day," I announced proudly.

"Today's the day for what?" Dr. Landy asked.

"You'll see," I said.

Forty-five minutes later I was out of breath, exhausted, and enjoying the aches in my muscles. My heaving chest swelled with pride. For the first time, I'd conquered the entire mountain. Standing outside the tiny church, I was atop the mountain, gazing down on the little fishing village and the ocean below. I waited for the rest of the group to catch up with me. They arrived huffing and complaining a few minutes later and found me revived and smiling.

"I did it!" I exclaimed, holding my arms high in the air like Rocky Balboa. *"I did it!"*

Several seconds later, Dr. Landy and Alexandra chugged up the hill. All smiles and congratulations, they were struggling to hide something behind their backs. I couldn't make it out. Dr. Landy told me to shut my eyes. There was some commotion. I heard banging, digging, then muffled laughter. It took real self-control to keep my eyes closed.

"Okay, open up," Dr. Landy said.

My eyes bulged; my jaw dropped. "Oh my God!" I cried out.

In the ground they'd planted a large white sign with black letters. It said "MOUNT WILSON," and it stayed there like a monument to my improved mental and physical health another month, right up until the time we left for California.

39

Carolyn, No!

*I*t was the first week of March, the beginning of our last month in Hawaii, and time for an adventure. A group of people, including Dr. Landy, organized an outing to Kona, where they wanted to see *E.T. The Extra-Terrestrial.*

I hadn't been to a movie theater since I'd seen *Seconds* in 1966 and left convinced that Spector had persuaded Columbia to make the movie to screw up my mind. I begged not to go and see *E.T.*

"We're all going—you can't stay home alone," Dr. Landy said in a logical tone I couldn't argue with.

All of us did things together, like a family. Since popcorn wasn't on my diet, no one had popcorn at the movies. That's the way our family was. We played together, suffered together, cried together, and triumphed together. It was really the first time I'd ever felt like part of a family.

I was glad I didn't pass up the movie. Like the millions of people who saw *E.T.*, I was sucked into the story within the first few minutes. By the time I glimpsed the lovable alien, I felt a certain kinship with him. He and I were both outsiders: we had trouble communicating, being understood. I tensed after realizing he'd been left behind, applauded when the kids adopted him.

I nearly jumped out of my seat in the scene where the kids hide E.T. in their bedroom closet, a place I would've hid. As their mother, searching for whatever it was her kids were hiding, begins her snooping, I clutched the armrest and leaned forward. As she went toward the closet, I put my hand over my eyes. Finally, when she opens the closet door and looks inside, the scene where the audience sees E.T.'s head among all the stuffed animals, I bolted up from my seat and yelled, "Watch out, E.T.!"

My heart had opened up wide and I cared about E.T., evidence of the improvement I'd made. More important, though, I was able to go to the movies, follow the story, and enjoy the film without the paralyzing fear I had usually experienced in movie theaters.

Meanwhile, the now defunct Los Angeles *Herald Examiner* ran the mock-serious headline, "Brian Wilson, Please Phone Home." It was part of a story in which Carolyn claimed that I'd been kidnapped. More than two months had passed since I'd last seen or spoken to Carolyn, and in that time I'd decided that I no longer wanted her in my life. She loved me. She had satisfied my every wish. But she also indulged and catered to my most self-destructive tendencies, and now that I was involved in a battle to win back my health, I no longer wanted to be around her.

Carolyn was hurt. The rejection tore her up, filled her with rage. Asked to vacate my home, she refused, claiming it was as much her residence as mine. My attorney, John Branca, disagreed and took action. He had my furniture moved out, the gas and electricity turned off. The stove and refrigerator were even taken away. But still she wouldn't budge. She lit fires on the wooden floor for heat and burned candles for light. Eventually, the Sheriff was called in to help force her to clear out.

In early March, the Beach Boys arrived in Honolulu for a concert and Tom Hulett called to inform us that Carolyn was also lurking in town, intending to have a public showdown.

Hulett wanting to quash the story, asked Dr. Landy and me if I could make the show. I didn't know. How about a press conference? Dr. Landy answered for me. Yes.

"But I can't do that," I protested.

"Sure you can," he said. "You just answer questions the way you feel. For instance, do you love Carolyn Williams?"

"No, I do not," I said.

"When we return to Los Angeles, do you want to go back to living with her and her kids?"

"Absolutely not," I said.

Despite my feelings on the subject, I panicked at the thought of being grilled by reporters. So I practiced. Every day for two weeks Dr. Landy or Dr. Dahlke or Dahlke's wife, television producer Leslie Noble Moore, bombarded me with every conceivable question. They forced me to think

304 / Brian Wilson

and respond to questions ranging from the Dodgers to the space program to whether I was a Republican or a Democrat. I had to overcome my tendency to answer every question with a "Yes" or an "I don't know."

"What kind of time are you having in Hawaii?" David Berlow asked.

"Terrible," I answered.

"Is it really a terrible time?" he asked. "I mean, you look better than you have in years."

"Well, yeah," I acknowledged. "It isn't so bad. It's just hard. Real hard. Like I ought to get a badge of courage or something."

Indeed, those three months in isolation in Hawaii—January through March 1983—were both the worst and the best times of my life. Frightening. Hard. Stressful. Exhausting. But also worth every torturous second. The bad feelings I had about the things I had to do were overwhelmed by the enormity of my accomplishments. I wasn't perfect by any means. But I was back from the dead.

The press conference was being held in a suite at Honolulu's Kahala Hilton Hotel, the same hotel where Carolyn had been registered until Beach Boys security had her relocated. Dr. Landy and I went to Honolulu several days early and scouted the locations of the press conference and the band's show. I wanted to familiarize myself with the surroundings and eliminate as many surprises as possible. Walking onstage, I suggested to Dr. Landy that I might want to play.

"It's your band," he said. "As Phil Spector in the early sixties said, 'It's Brian Wilson and his background singers.' "

Dr. Landy and I hung around the Kahala for several days, careful to avoid Carolyn. We heard she was on the lookout, telling anyone who'd listen, "I want my Brian back. I've been saving myself for him." Fortunately, our paths never crossed. I didn't want the ugliness of a confrontation. Nonetheless, by the time Dr. Landy and I entered the Kahala suite to meet the press, she'd spoken to every reporter in town.

The suite was jammed with reporters. There were several rows of chairs. Behind them were television cameras. From outside the suite, we heard the commotion of the packed room, the jostling of chairs, discussion of how weird the situation was, a call to order by our longtime publicist, Sandy Friedman of Rogers and Cowan, the whir of motor drives winding camera film into place.

Dr. Landy faced the press first, while I ducked into an adjoining room and waited for my turn. Seated next to Tom Hulett, Dr. Landy explained I was still involved in the slow, recuperative process of regaining my physical and emotional health. Some questions allowed him to talk about the therapy, but he spent most of the time underscoring the fact that I hadn't been kidnapped. Yes, the Beach Boys had sanctioned everything. The subject exhausted, it was time to answer the most asked question, "Where's Brian?"

At that point, Dr. Landy excused himself and left the room. He came into the adjoining room and patted me on the shoulder, saying, "Go make me proud." I sauntered into the suite, awkward and nervous, then darted backwards as the reporters surged forward. There was a burst of anticipation, then everything settled down. Taking a seat, I sipped a glass of water and nodded to Sandy that I was ready.

The questions came fast and furious, and I had to ask people to speak up and repeat themselves, explaining I was deaf in one ear. Self-possessed, I acknowledged we were trying to get rid of Carolyn, that I hadn't been kidnapped, that I supported the therapy program. I admitted the situation was, indeed, weird. Some ten minutes into the Q&A session, a reporter pointed to a telephone and asked if there was anyone I wanted to call. I shook my head no.

"Can you call anyone you want?" he asked.

"Yeah," I said.

"Have you been able to up till now?"

"Yeah, I can." I nodded. "Except for my old drug dealers, and it's obvious why I can't call them."

The press conference lasted nearly an hour, and I was on my own the entire time. It was both terrible and wonderful. Nobody could question the fact that I was on my way back.

If doubters remained, Dr. Landy thought it best that I speak to them by joining the Beach Boys onstage. Sure, earlier in the week I'd wanted to perform, but by the time we got backstage and I began rubbing shoulders with the guys, I'd lost my confidence. It helped somewhat that the guys, who hadn't seen me for three months, were impressed by the changes in me. I was sober, cognizant, cleaner, and much slimmer, having gone from 340 pounds to 250. Everybody was happy. But the guys went on without me.

"Where the hell is Brian?" Dr. Landy shouted as he ran into the dressing room.

"He's still here," said Dr. Susser. "He can't move. He's frozen."

"What's wrong?" Dr. Landy asked.

"I can't do it," I said. "I can't go onstage. I'm too frightened."

"Okay, I'm going to help you relax," said Dr. Landy. He put his hands in mine and told me to squeeze with both hands. As hard as I could. I began to clamp down. Then I realized that I was much stronger than Dr. Landy. If I squeezed with all my might, I thought, I'd hurt him. I stopped.

"Why'd you stop?" asked Dr. Landy.

"I don't want to hurt you," I said.

"How do you feel?" he asked. "Stronger? Like playing a show?"

"Yes," I said, and, indeed, the act of starting to squeeze, then stopping and thinking about hurting Dr. Landy cleared my mind of stage fright.

In fact, it distracted me enough that I absorbed the energy from the large audience and felt energized myself.

Calm and centered, I walked onstage as if it belonged to me and the Beach Boys played with me every day. The guys had just started "I Get Around," but the music was quickly drowned out by the ovation I got when the crowd recognized me. Mike gave me a brief introduction—more like a nod—and then he kept on singing.

I grabbed a microphone and moved to the front. The guys looked shocked to see me singing and swaying, but not as shocked as they were when I asked them to stop playing.

"Wait a minute," I ordered. "Wait. Stop."

Carl and Al continued strumming their guitars but stared at me with faces that asked, Is he still crazy? Mike's eyes told me he wanted to wring my neck. There was no time to explain that I'd suddenly been struck by inspiration. In the din of the applause that greeted me, I'd heard the song differently and decided to act on it. I turned to the audience.

"I'm going to rearrange this song right here," I said. "For you."

The guys didn't know what hit them. They must have wondered why they even let me onstage. They probably thought, Heck, even without drugs he's still weird. I gave Carl a new harmony to sing and asked Al to play a different rhythm. I told the audience that this was how we did it in the studio. I figured it out and taught it to the boys.

"You'll like the song better this way," I said, then turned to the band and counted them down, "One, two, three, four."

The new arrangement sounded great and the audience went out of their heads. My first concert was a success for everybody, particularly me.

"What hat did you pull that out of?" Carl asked between songs. "That was really from left field."

"Surprised you, huh?" I laughed.

"I wish you'd told us at rehearsal," he scolded. "That's what they're for."

"Sorry." I shrugged. "But I didn't think of it till I came out."

Right and below: approaching my low point in 1982. I'm ashamed of how I look in these photos. Dennis doesn't look great either. *Beach Boys Archives*

FOR SALE sign in front of the home where Carolyn and I lived. *Eugene Landy Collection*

Dr. Landy's crew sitting around the dinner table the first night in Hawaii. From left: Leslie Moore Dahlke, Dr. Samuels and his wife, David Berlow, Dr. Susser, Dr. Landy, and Alexandra Morgan. The empty seat is mine. *Eugene Landy Collection*

My second day in Hawaii, January 1983, before Dr. Landy woke me for our morning walk. *Eugene Landy Collection*

Intensive therapy with Dr. Landy in Hawaii in 1983. *Alexandra Morgan and Dr. Murray "Buzz" Susser*

After three weeks in Hawaii, I still looked like I didn't want to talk to anyone. *Eugene Landy Collection*

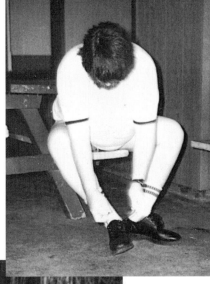

Right: in Hawaii, tying my shoes for the first time in ages, a feat made possible by my shrinking belly. *Eugene Landy Collection*

Above: during therapy, I had to do daily calisthenics, a fate worse than death... almost. Here I am doing push-ups in February 1983. *Eugene Landy Collection*

Dr. Landy showing me a picture of myself. I hated what I saw. *Eugene Landy Collection*

Above: at the summit. This was a proud moment for me. *Eugene Landy Collection*

Hiking at the end of February 1983 with (from left) Bill Flaxman, Dr. Susser, Alexandra Morgan, Dr. Landy, me, and Pam Thomas. *Eugene Landy Collection*

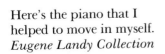

Here's the piano that I helped to move in myself. *Eugene Landy Collection*

Marilyn with Carnie (left) and Wendy, and me with Marilyn in April 1983 (below), just after I returned from three months of therapy in Hawaii. *Eugene Landy Collection*

May 1983: Five months after starting with Dr. Landy, I've lost more than 100 pounds of weight and problems. The proof is in this picture of me with Beach Boys manager Tom Hulett. *Chad Einbinder*

On the road in 1984, learning to drive outside San Francisco. *Chad Einbinder*

Finding my way around New York City. *Chad Einbinder*

Another peak scaled: Me atop the Empire State Building. *Chad Einbinder*

Gene and me in 1985.
*Eugene Landy
Collection*

Hiking in northern California in 1985. The sign was describing my past.
Chad Einbinder

On tour with the Beach Boys in 1985. Gene is giving Mike, Carl, and me healing advice. *Kevin Leslie*

Rafting the Rogue River in Oregon, June 1986. *Kevin Leslie*

Chynna, Carnie, and Wendy before they became Wilson Phillips.
Eugene Landy Collection

Proud papas—John
Phillips and I in
September 1986 on the set
of the "California
Dreamin'" video. *Eugene
Landy Collection*

Gene and Mike write lyrics for "Male Ego" in the studio in 1986. *Kevin Leslie*

Working out at home in Malibu, November 1986. *Eugene Landy Collection*

Working on my first solo album at Village Studios in May 1987 with Warner Brothers president Lenny Waronker. *Eugene Landy Collection*

Shaking hands with Prince Edward backstage at the Prince's Trust concert in England, May 1987. *Kevin Leslie*

Gene and I meet with then-Vice President Bush outside his home in 1987. *Kevin Leslie*

Above: with the guys in 1987 on a video shoot for "Rock and Roll to the Rescue." *Eugene Landy Collection*

Right: working on lyrics with Van Dyke Parks at his Los Feliz home in August 1987. *Eugene Landy Collection*

Below: playing alongside Carl with the Beach Boys in 1988. *Eugene Landy Collection*

Backstage at the Universal Amphitheater: Me, Gene, and Carl. *Kevin Leslie*

Working on the Beach Boys' 25th anniversary TV special at the Commercial Recording Studio in Miami. From left: Gary Usher, Glen Campbell, me, and Mike Love. *Eugene Landy Collection*

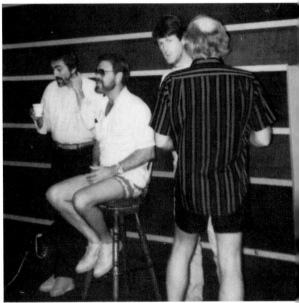

Visiting the White House in January 1988 with Gene. *Alexandra Morgan*

Taking a snorkel break with Alexandra and Kevin after just completing the writing of "There's So Many" in Hawaii in 1988. *Eugene Landy Collection*

Me with Gene in Hawaii, 1988. *Alexandra Morgan*

My personal assistant Kevin Leslie (left) and my friend Evan Landy. *Eugene Landy Collection*

With my special friend Frances Morgan in July 1991. I was playing her my new song, "Brian." *Eugene Landy Collection*

Below: Glen Campbell dropped by my studio while I worked on my second solo album *Sweet Insanity* in 1990. *Eugene Landy Collection*

Above: ex-Beach Boy David Marks in my studio, 1990. *Eugene Landy Collection*

To remind myself of how far I've come, in May 1991 I returned to the house in Hawaii where Dr. Landy had taken me in 1983. *Eugene Landy Collection*

Ghosts

T he first week of April 1983 I returned to L.A. and rented an enormous, beautiful home in Malibu Colony, an exclusive stretch of beach located behind a security-gated entrance. A six-bedroom, two-story beachfront mansion, I moved in along with the six-person support team Dr. Landy employed to help me. Despite the improvements made in Hawaii, I was still fragile, resistant, and difficult.

But there was no drifting back, Dr. Landy made sure of that. I had chores. I had to exercise. It was my job to cook breakfast for everyone. Every morning I chopped up fresh fruit and poured cereal for the entire support crew. That simple task took me a good hour and a half. The problems arose when I insisted on pouring maple syrup over the cereal and then refused to brush my teeth or shower after the meal.

But that stuff was nothing compared to confronting the ghosts of my previous life. Danny Hutton lived only half an hour away. My drug dealer's phone number hadn't changed. My craving for uppers, downers, any kind of drug hadn't dissipated. Every second, every minute, every hour, every day was a struggle. Temptation was everywhere. The difference was that I resisted. I stayed clean and healthy.

Dr. Landy knew the return to California was going to be hard. That's why he was extremely careful that my environment be isolated from the bad influences of old friends. He expected me to backslide and prepared for difficult times with a large, sensitive staff: Gordon Forbes, Pam

Thomas, Arnold Dahlke and his son, Greg, Dr. Landy's son, Evan, Scott Steinberg, Carlos Booker, Nikki Simon, Chad Einbinder, Deirdre Courtiney, Joseph Rispoli, David Berlow, and Christopher Rodgerson.

There was humor in the difficulty I had in learning to do the things people take for granted. I shopped for groceries. A charge account was set up for me at the Malibu Colony grocery store, which was within walking distance from the house. It didn't take long before I realized my shopping trips exposed me to lots of forbidden foods. With no one looking, I stole as much as I could fit into my mouth and chew without attracting attention. I'd open a jar of pickles, take one, then put it back on the shelf. I scooped out thumbfuls of peanut butter, opening and shutting the lid in seconds. I plucked out cookies, cheese. I thought I was getting away with the ruse. The store's management didn't interfere; they knew I was crazy—except in Malibu they call it "eccentric."

But their tolerance had limits. One day I recognized actress Geneviève Bujold pushing a cart up the aisle. I had a big crush on her. She was in little running shorts and a skimpy tank top. I stopped and stared. As she passed, I grabbed her butt, a big handful of flesh, and she screamed. I got very frightened and ran to the front. The manager explained that Miss Bujold didn't like what I'd done. As a result, he banned me from the store. I still didn't quite understand why.

I expected Dr. Landy to get upset. He didn't. He simply told me that I had to go to a different market. That taught me an important lesson. The next closest market was a thirty-minute walk. An hour there and back. Carrying bags of groceries. I quickly learned to economize my energy, follow my lists, clip my coupons, not steal, and resist pinching pretty women.

"I'm proud of myself," I wrote in a journal I kept. "I'm learning responsibility. I feel like a teenager. I'm learning how to be an adult. It's not easy. But I'm learning."

I had no idea how quickly I was learning. In October another contract with Columbia Records was negotiated. Again, without my knowledge, it obligated me to write and produce 80 percent of the material. But by the time I heard about it, the record company had already replaced me as producer. With little faith in my ability, they hired red hot producer Steve Levine, who had just produced Culture Club.

Levine was noncommittal. He showed interest, but he wanted to be persuaded. Carl urged everybody to fly to London to meet with Levine. They did. But before making a decision, Levine expressed interest in meeting me. He knew the Beach Boys' music came from a single source.

The calls streamed in, half a dozen a day. Through October and November. Can Brian travel to London? Can he meet with Steve? I didn't go. I wasn't in good enough shape to bash egos with the band again. I had to stay with the program. I had to get stronger. I had to work on me.

I fancied myself like a weight lifter in training, dedicated to the lonely pursuit of developing my muscles—in my case, my brain. The isolation was at times overwhelming. I wasn't a prisoner. I ventured outside, saw movies, shopped. The struggle was adapting to a completely different life-style as well as a completely new set of intimates. I can't say I was unhappy, just confused by the change in reference points.

Somehow, Dennis managed to sneak a phone call through the various layers of protection that sealed me off from potential harm. He might have been my brother, but his drug use made him a threat to me. It was early morning, and I'd been left alone to do some thinking. His voice sounded haggard, and he was dazed. He wanted to know what I was doing.

"I'm sitting here, looking out at the ocean and doing some heavy thinking," I said. "Eating some broccoli and working on the inside of my head. How about you?"

"Just hanging out," he said. "Trying to write some songs. The usual."

"That's good. It's good to work," I said.

"Hey, Bri," he said. "I was wondering if I could swing by and borrow a couple hundred bucks."

"Are you going to buy cocaine with it?" I asked, cutting through the bullshit and catching Dennis off guard.

"Yeah, as a matter of fact, I am," he snapped. "And what of it?"

I felt my body twitch with a familiar craving, a familiar sickness. I would've loved to have given Dennis the money and have him bring me back half the coke. I would've loved nothing more than for Dennis to score me a handful of uppers. A blast. A jolt. I'd rocket into fucking orbit. I fought the urge to say, "Yes, come on by, Dennis."

But I had willpower and knowledge now. I relished life. Using drugs again was out of the question. With what I had learned, it was impossible for me to do that to myself. It was also impossible for me to be a party to that kind of destructiveness to Dennis.

"Sorry, Dennis," I said. "I can't. That's against Dr. Landy's policy. That's against my life-style policy. I just cannot give you money to buy cocaine."

Before I finished, Dennis told me to take a flying fuck and then he hung up. I listened to the receiver for a moment, then set it down. I looked out at the ocean and imagined snorting a line. Several lines. The high. The euphoria. The cheap, ephemeral burst of invincibility. Instead, I chomped into a stalk of broccoli and wondered what Dennis was going to do next.

41

Dennis, My Brother

*O*nly a very few people knew that several weeks before Christmas 1983 Carl and his manager, Jerry Schilling, approached Dr. Landy about treating Dennis. They wanted him to work the same miracle he'd done for me.

Dr. Landy had been close to Dennis. He'd counseled my brother about drugs. He'd gotten him out of numerous jams with young girls. He'd paid his hotel bills for a few days when Dennis was broke.

In his own way, Dennis was jealous that Dr. Landy had gotten me to clean up. It seemed as if he was on the verge of asking for help himself.

Although willing to take the case on, Dr. Landy said he couldn't whisk him away as he'd done with me. Dennis had too much fight in him. He'd punch someone. He'd call the cops. He'd find a way to get stoned and drunk.

A week later, Dr. Landy devised another plan and promised Carl he could have Dennis cleaned up in six weeks. Whether he liked it or not.

"You almost sound too certain," Carl said.

"Look, my methods might not be orthodox," Dr. Landy said. "But I'll save his fucking life. After he's clean, then we'll talk about what happens. Remember, detox is only the first step."

That gave Carl's manager time to ask how much treatment would cost. Dr. Landy said $10,000 to $20,000 in expenses, plus another $50,000 in fees.

That discussion took place on the twenty-second of December. The next day Schilling called Dr. Landy and told him Carl needed longer to make up his mind. The price was steep, too steep, he thought, for the Beach Boys to carry.

Beyond that, Carl didn't want to upset his family's holiday plans by having, as Dr. Landy suggested, an intervention in Lake Arrowhead. Carl suggested talking after the holidays.

Dr. Landy told Schilling to tell Carl he was making a grave error. Whether he knew it or not, Dennis was on a self-destructive binge heading in only one direction.

Carl was adamant, though; he didn't want to deal with the problem until after New Year's.

I looked at the wall calendar. December 28, 1983. I still had one or two unopened Christmas presents. A couple dozen brightly colored cards decorated the fireplace mantel. But there was no use pretending. I pushed the presents out of view and threw my Christmas cards out.

With great hesitation, I dialed the number for Carl's ranch in Colorado, where he and his family had gone for the holidays with my mother. I wondered how they would sound; I suspected they'd be crying. As the oldest, I knew I had to be the strongest. I coached myself as the phone rang. Be strong, real strong.

"Carl?" I asked.

"Yeah?" he said, sounding weak.

I was right. He had been crying.

"It's Brian."

"Hi, Brian," he said softly.

"I'm okay with it," I said. "Are you?"

"I was," he said, his voice cracking. "But now that I'm talking to you . . . I've had to be the one to hold things together."

Less than two hours had passed since I'd talked with Jerry Schilling. In a somber, tearful voice, Schilling had apologized, saying he hated to be the one to have to break the news to me. What news? I wondered. But in the time it took Schilling to collect himself I knew he was going to tell me something tragic. Indeed, he did.

Dennis was dead.

I was stunned. But for some reason I accepted the news as if I'd been expecting it and calmly listened to the details. Dennis had been partying on a friend's boat in the marina. The boat was berthed in the same slip where Dennis had kept his old boat, *Harmony*. The weather was gloomy, cold, overcast. They'd been boozing it up good. Then Dennis suddenly dove into the chilly water to retrieve possessions he said he'd thrown in that area years before. I presumed he had gone looking for the glimmer of a happy life he imagined having thrown away about the same time he sold the *Harmony*.

The accounts said he surfaced once, then slipped underneath the murky waters. Forty-five minutes later, the Harbor Patrol located his body on the bottom.

"Now that I'm on the phone with you, Brian, I feel real emotional," Carl wept.

I hadn't lost it yet. I was hanging tough.

"Carl," I said. "Dennis is still with us. You've got to realize that in this life we're not God. We can't understand death. But we feel the loss. I feel the loss. I loved Dennis. I loved him and you loved him. Right?"

"I loved him so much," Carl replied, collecting himself.

"Sure you did," I said. "I did too. And that's the rip-off, isn't it?"

Although Carl avoided the news all night and managed to keep my mother away from the television, I was riveted in front of the set through the five, six, and eleven o'clock local broadcasts. They provided me with a last glimpse of my middle brother. They showed Dennis lying on the cement, covered by a large body sack. His arm and leg stuck out. I knew the picture was real, but I still hoped, expected, Dennis to get up and yell, "Surprise."

He didn't. He couldn't. I thought, My God, that's the last time I'll ever see Dennis.

All that night and the next day I cried. I moped around the house and wept, trying to deal with the sorrow. Death was impossible for me to understand. Dennis was so much stronger than me. Much more together. Despite the way drugs and alcohol had ravaged him, I still thought of Dennis as all muscle, good looks, and charm. He was one of my best friends. The loss was permanent. It made me feel strange.

I thought of the last time I'd seen him. Where? A concert. He'd stumbled out from behind his drums and wobbled to the microphone. He smiled. That never changed. Then, in a voice ruined by cigarettes and alcohol, he sang "You Are So Beautiful." As he sang, tears ran down his face, as if he knew he was singing for the last time. After the show, I'd stood backstage and watched Dennis sip from a can of soda. He wasn't much different from when we were kids, still angry and restless.

In his final months, Dennis's life was as disheveled as the clothes he wore on his back. He was estranged from his wife, Shawn, and their two-year-old son, Gage. He was broke. He bummed drinks and cigarettes from strangers. He slept wherever he dropped. He became obsessed by our old man and rambled nonstop that Murry did this and Murry did that. It was as if Dennis was trying to fight one last unwinnable battle.

He never slowed. Always on the run from the same demons that chased and tormented me. The only difference is that I had Dr. Landy. Dennis didn't.

My mom didn't want a funeral. Like me, she didn't believe in them. She didn't like the sorrow. My only wish was that Dennis not be cremated. Carl didn't know what to do. Before making any decisions, he insisted on consulting with John Rogers, a cult leader Carl referred to as his spiritual master. However, it turned out that Shawn, whose divorce from Dennis wasn't yet finalized, had ultimate authority, and she decided that he'd be buried at sea.

Although federal law prohibited sea burials, President Reagan, a friend of the Beach Boys after the James Watt incident, gave special dispensation, and three days after he drowned, Dennis was dropped back into the water that had played such an inspirational role in both our lives.

Two weeks later, January 1984. It might've been a new year, but Dennis's death continued to hang over me like a fog that wouldn't lift. Dr. Landy told me that he heard record producer Steve Levine was in Kingston, Jamaica. Suddenly, a business vacation seemed like a great idea. Dr. Landy, Alexandra, and I flew to Montego Bay, checked into the Round House resort, and spent five rejuvenating days in the sun.

As the warm Caribbean bathed our bodies and spirits, Dr. Landy received news that his mother, Frieda, had been hospitalized, seriously ill. He debated whether to fly back to L.A. but after being told his mother's condition was serious but stable, he decided to take an extra day and stay to see Steve Levine. After all, he'd come all this way. Still, we sped up our schedule and flew over the dense jungle into Kingston. Levine was working at Bob Marley's studio, Tuff Gong.

Tuff Gong was situated on a large, lushly gardened compound, protected by an imposing gate and an even more imposing guardsman. Dr. Landy and I drove up, parked our car with the others, and approached the gate. As he reached to open it, the guard suddenly jumped out from the tiny guardhouse, upset.

"Don't open the gate, mon," he ordered. "You don't have any business here now."

"Yes we do," Dr. Landy said.

"Well, what's your name?" the guard asked.

"My name's Dr. Landy," he said. "His name is Brian Wilson."

Upon hearing my name, the guard raised his eyebrows. It seemed the right words had been mentioned. He smiled and opened the gate, asking us to please wait. He then disappeared into the guardhouse and returned a second later, holding what I assumed was the local newspaper. He handed it to Dr. Landy, who looked startled by the thing's size. Suddenly, he laughed. Then the guard struck a match.

"What the hell is that?" I asked.

"Gang, mon," he said.

"That's a joint?" I exclaimed. "Gene, have you ever seen anything that large?"

"Never," he said.

"Let me try it," I asked, holding out my hand.

"Control, Brian," Dr. Landy said. "You don't smoke pot, and you don't take drugs. Exercise self-control."

I concentrated on the exquisitely beautiful grounds and put the thought of pot out of mind. Nearing the main house, the sound of reggae music drifted outside. When I walked inside, as if on cue, a dreadlocked Ziggy Marley began playing "Surfer Girl" on a grand piano. It was a touching welcome. Finally, Dr. Landy and I met Levine.

The producer showed us around the modern studio. It was chock-full of state-of-the-art equipment that had been developed while I was out of commission. With an upper-crust British haughtiness, Levine gave the impression that he was squeezing us in, explaining his schedule packed with activities, including a workout, tea break, and even a nap time. It was more rigid than my day.

"I'd love to hear some of your songs," he said.

We were in the dining room, waiting for lunch. There was a piano in the corner. Although Levine had met the other Beach Boys, I knew he was holding out for just such a moment when he could get me on a piano and hear if my chops were intact. I played half a dozen songs that I'd either written alone or with Dr. Landy. Although I was still tentative, given to pacing myself rather than playing things out, I finished and knew as soon as I saw Levine's face.

"Fantastic," he said. "Now I understand."

"But getting them on tape, I don't know if I'm up to that," I admitted.

"That's the reason we're getting Steve," Dr. Landy said. "He's going to produce. You'll study. It'll be like going back to school."

Class wasn't going to start until late summer or early fall, the soonest Levine was available. But our trip was successful, and the next day Dr. Landy and I flew to New York, where we were greeted by bad news.

Dr. Landy's mother had slipped into a coma, her condition more dire minute by minute. He dashed through the airport, barely catching the next flight to L.A. I stayed in New York with Alexandra Morgan and her mother, Frances, to handle the baggage, and the three of us returned to L.A. the next day.

Dr. Landy arrived in Los Angeles at 2:00 A.M. Calling the hospital, he reached his father, who told him nothing had changed and he should come in the morning. Falling asleep, he woke suddenly at 5:00 A.M., a chill down his back, and immediately called the hospital. His father picked up again. This time he was crying. Dr. Landy's mother had died a half hour earlier.

About a week later, I was at Dr. Landy's house for dinner. While Alexandra prepared the meal, I played the piano, normally a time when Dr. Landy would've listened appreciatively. Instead, he retreated to his study, closing the door. After perhaps a half hour, I knocked and let myself in. He was sitting on the sofa in the dark, crying.

I didn't know what to do or say. It disturbed me to see my pillar of strength in despair.

"What is wrong?" I asked, though I knew the answer.

"My mother died," he said. "I was remembering my mother and I realized that she was gone. She isn't coming back. I'm never going to speak to her again. I didn't even have a chance to say good-bye. That made me sad and angry."

"Like you were ripped off," I said. "Like I felt when Dennis died."

"Yes, Brian," he said somberly.

I put my arm around Dr. Landy and held him. Suddenly, tears started flowing from my eyes too.

"You're sad?" he asked.

"I'm thinking about Dennis," I said.

My dad had died and I hadn't felt the loss. He'd left me scared, hearing his voice.

But Dennis's death was different. With him went a piece of me. I'd never dealt with it. I'd never mourned his passing. Until now. With Dr. Landy grieving over his mother, I was suddenly consumed by the loss of Dennis, an overwhelming feeling of vulnerability and sadness.

I cried.

Dr. Landy looked at me, gave me a knowing nod, and put his arm around me. There was nothing for either of us to say. Instead, we shared our loss. It was the completion of a bond and the start of an even deeper relationship. For the first time, I realized my seemingly all-powerful Dr. Landy could be just as vulnerable and scared and as human and frail as I was. It was as much an awakening as a relief.

I needed him. He also needed me. In the dark room, we sat beside each other, holding one another, crying.

42

Outward Bound

*I*t was the spring of 1984 and I was still getting unscared. It was a slow process, and I placed my total trust in Dr. Landy.

When he began treating me I was scared twenty-four hours a day. It's difficult to convey that feeling. Imagine itching all the time, every part of the body. Then Dr. Landy shakes hands and, miraculously, that body part stops itching. That's what happened to me. I might well have screamed, "Goddamnit, touch my other arm! Touch my leg!"

Dr. Landy got me involved in situations that had to do with confronting the irrational fears that controlled me. There was little truth then; only my interpretation of reality, codes, secret meanings, inner voices. I wanted only to do whatever was required to appease a situation and then get the hell out. I wasn't brave. But Dr. Landy forced me to be. He exhorted me to develop integrity, to regain whatever truth I'd lost, and to develop more and stronger truths.

The harshest lessons came in dealing with the Beach Boys again. I started to do more shows and selected dates in major cities, where I could explore the museums and finer restaurants. Every city was a discovery, an adventure. On previous tours, I never left my hotel room. I'd traveled the world but never seen it.

Dr. Landy also called rehearsals, something the Beach Boys rarely did. During the shows, he stood beside the stage or positioned an assistant there and yelled at me to pay attention when I started listening more to the voices inside me than to the music.

I was still quite intimidated playing with the guys. They hassled, fought, and tested me onstage. Al often suggested finishing songs we'd started years earlier, like "Loop De Loop." Without the audience catching on, Mike could spend an entire show telling me about a song idea he wanted to work on with me.

"Maybe we can do it right now," he said during one show. "Or right after. But think about this."

Then he hummed a tune. Afterward, Dr. Landy was all over my case.

"Do you want to write with him?" he asked.

"No," I said.

"Then why did you say you would?" he wanted to know.

"Because I didn't want him to beat me up," I said.

Despite the progress I was making, I continued to perceive the Beach Boys as a threat. Crossing the street isn't ordinarily life-threatening—but it can be. And for someone with my thinking, that's reason enough not to cross the street. Somebody had to teach me how to cross the street or I wouldn't do it. Dr. Landy was trying to do that with the Beach Boys.

"You can work with them or not," he always said. "I don't care. I just want you to have the choice. I want you to be strong enough to say no when you mean no."

Late in the spring, Dr. Landy intensified the process of strengthening me. The only way to deal with fear, he explained, was to turn around and face it. Until I finally did that, it would always be there. That's when Dr. Landy told me I was going on Outward Bound, a program that deals with survival in the wilderness. The idea was to place me in legitimate life-threatening situations but under the safest possible conditions. Upon learning that I was going into the wild outdoors, alone, I said one word:

"Noooooooooooo!"

"You're going to hate every motherfucking second," Dr. Landy said. "But afterward, nothing will be too much because you'll be able to say, 'I got through it.' "

The weeklong program took place in the mountains outside Denver, Colorado. Dr. Dahlke accompanied me to Denver. I thought he was going too, but when he woke me the next morning and said the bus was leaving for the high country, I was hit by a terrifying reality. Dr. Dahlke wasn't going. Dr. Landy wasn't meeting me. It was the start of my own journey.

"Come on, Brian," Dr. Dahlke said. "Get up. You got a bus to catch."

"No," I said.

I refused to get out of bed. Dr. Dahlke tried reasoning with me. When that didn't work, he called Dr. Landy and put the receiver next to my ear, which was under the pillow.

"Get out of the fucking bed, Brian." Dr. Landy demanded calmly.

A fear worse than my fear of being alone shot through me. I stood up. It took Dr. Landy's ego to jump-start mine.

"Get in the fucking bus," he ordered. "You're going."

"What if the bus driver's on acid?" I asked.

"Enjoy the drive." He laughed.

Unbeknownst to me, Dr. Landy had spent weeks preparing for my excursion. He briefed the Outward Bound staff about my behavior. He instructed them on handling me. He prepared them for my perpetual complaining. He predicted I'd bitch and scream every step and refuse to do everything they asked. I might even threaten to kill myself. I didn't let him down, either.

But they were to respond as he said. If I refused to hike, they were to leave me. If I threatened to kill myself, they were to tell me if that's what I wanted, then go ahead. If I needed help, they were to say no. If I complained, they were to ignore me. They could not rescue me. Period.

Dr. Landy's instructions ran counter to everything the staff had been taught. He made them sign a contract agreeing to everything.

In theory, Dr. Landy wanted me to be the strongest one. If any of the others got scared, he wanted me to be the one they asked for help. But that was in theory.

The first day we learned the basics: how to start a fire, boil water, make a bed, locate directions, and leave tracks. Daniel Boone stuff. We also hiked and started on the rudiments of mountain climbing. None of us was even close to being an outdoors person, which made for a comical scene. One girl hadn't learned how to tie her shoes. Another was scared of the dark. Another just stood and cried.

I had many of the same feelings, but I had worked so hard to learn how to overcome and control them that I was the strongest in the group. I just didn't know it.

By nightfall, our campsite was a disaster. Everyone was cold, hungry, panicked, and, most of all, still utterly, completely helpless. If anyone asked me for help, as Dr. Landy had theorized they might, I didn't hear. I was too busy looking for someone to help me.

On day two, I refused to hike to the second campsite. One of the supervisors, buckling under the pressure of having to ignore everything he'd been taught, shrugged, loaded me into his station wagon, and drove four hours to the nearest telephone, where he called Dr. Landy. It was a mistake. Dr. Landy reminded him of the instructions he'd been given.

"Get back out there," Dr. Landy told him. "If he doesn't hike, then leave him. Despite what he says, he can do it. He's not being helped if he doesn't."

We returned and I hiked.

Later, though, it came time to rappel down the rugged side of a mountain and I refused again. I didn't want to swing on the ropes. The whole thing was making me sick and scared. But the staff obeyed Dr. Landy and called my bluff. They gritted their teeth and told me I could do whatever I wanted, but they were leaving me behind.

Faced with desertion and the prospect of being eaten by wild animals, and knowing I was totally helpless, I went down the fucking mountain. Inch by agonizing inch. At the bottom, I hiked. Then I crossed a stream. At night, I gathered wood, lit a fire, and cooked dinner.

This shit went on for three grueling days. Then it got worse.

After spending six days learning survival skills from map reading to cooking to treating snakebites and dealing with grizzly bears, the staff informed us we were ready for our solo. The solo was the pièce de résistance. The graduating exercise. The hard part: a hike from point A to point B, which required use of all the skills we'd been taught. It lasted two days. Overnight. Alone. I thought about shitting in my pants.

Having spent four days in the wilderness, I didn't think for one second that I was capable of finding a single tree. Hiking for two days? Climbing a mountain? Crossing a river? Following trails? No fucking way.

That morning, the head mountain man gave the group a pep talk. Then he spoke to me individually: he told me not to worry, that I could do it. He showed me on the map the ground I was going to cover and where he'd meet me. Then he smiled and said, "See ya in two days. Good luck," and disappeared into the woods.

I watched, paralyzed. I don't know if I've been more scared in my life.

Petrified, I did what any self-respecting, brain-damaged, chickenshit, spoiled rock star would do. I walked straight to the largest boulder I could find, a craggy mother of a rock at the base of the first mountain I'd have to climb. I kneeled beside it, and then I beat my head against the side. I knew I'd either be rescued or I'd die. I was right.

As soon as I started hitting my head, the staffer who'd said good-bye moments earlier came charging out of nowhere waving his hands, yelling at me to stop.

"What the hell are you trying to do?" he asked, hauling me upright and checking my head.

"I wanted to kill myself," I said. "I figured I was going to die anyway."

He shook his head. Then, grabbing my arm, he led me across six miles of trails, back to our original camp. We got into the station wagon we'd used on the previous emergency. Then we hurtled over rough terrain, driving four hours to the nearest telephone. Dr. Landy was on board the *Queen Elizabeth II*, in the middle of the Atlantic Ocean, when he received the call. He couldn't believe that the staffer was calling for such an idiotic nonemergency.

"Take him back out," Dr. Landy hollered. "He's got to do his solo."

"But he was trying to kill himself," the staffer argued.

"If that's what he wants, let him," Dr. Landy said. "Let him draw a little blood and he'll quit. Brian's no dummy. Give him some respect. Now get his ass our there."

"But there's not time for him to do the solo," he said.

"Make time," Dr. Landy replied. *"Or I'll sue your fucking ass off. We have a contract."*

It was two in the morning when I was dropped off again. I stared at the clouds that curtained the moon and wished it was light out. I listened to the coyotes howl. I imagined an enormous bear, saliva dripping from his fangs, as he prepared to devour me in small bites. Then I remembered my first tentative walk in Hawaii. This was no different. Slowly, I put one foot in front of the other and began covering ground.

After about half an hour, I unfurled my blanket and lay down for the night. In the morning, I chugged along again, eventually coming to the base of the mountain I was expected to climb. I looked up, studied the rugged side. I tried to guess at which spot I was going to die. I knew I was going to meet my demise on that slope. It was just a matter of where. But I didn't have a choice. I had to climb it. Otherwise I would die for sure.

It took me six hours. But with my heart pounding louder and faster than a Hal Blaine drum solo, I made it. I conquered Mother Nature. I bested fear. I stood on the mountaintop and cheered myself.

If I'd had a gun, I would've charged straight back down and emptied the cartridge into Dr. Landy, though not before thanking him for forcing me to complete the blasted program. I was pumped up, full of a pride and confidence that ranks among my biggest achievements. It was better than any Number One song because money and fame had nothing to do with what I had accomplished. I earned it the hard way. Of course, that didn't mean I enjoyed a second of it.

From Denver, I flew straight to Atlantic City, joining the Beach Boys for a July 4 concert celebration. The following morning I took a run, then met Dr. Landy for breakfast. He was already packed and checked out of the hotel. He told me he was going to Manhattan for the weekend.

"What time's the plane?" I asked, confused.

My travel arrangements should've been the same.

"In forty-five minutes," he said.

"Jesus Christ, Gene," I exclaimed, bolting out of my chair. "I can't make that. We'll have to reschedule," I said with a new confidence.

"No, no, no." He laughed. "Don't worry. You're not going to fly to New York. You're going to drive."

He set a pair of car keys on the table. I'd recently earned my driver's license. Now I was going to get a chance to use it. One of the assistants, Pam Thomas, was going to drive with me.

"But I don't know how to get there," I said. "How'm I going to get to New York?"

"Don't ask me." Dr. Landy smiled. "If you can walk halfway across the state of Colorado, if you can climb a four-thousand-foot mountain at night, then don't you think you can get to New York?"

Normally, the drive from Atlantic City to Manhattan takes a little more than two hours. Pam had been instructed to say nothing helpful, and I drove through the Lincoln Tunnel eight and a half hours after leaving the Boardwalk. My final destination was the Parker Meridien Hotel, whose address—56th Street and the Avenue of the Americas—I had memorized for the past seven hours. I knew it was south of Central Park. Unfortunately, I couldn't figure out how to get to Central Park South. I ended up lost in Harlem.

After spending too much time weaving blindly past burned-out tenements and dimly lit, dangerous-looking side streets, I spotted a nicely dressed woman on the sidewalk and pulled over to ask directions. I commented to Pam on the woman's red dress. I thought it was pretty.

"Excuse me, Miss," I called.

The woman stopped walking, turned, and approached the car. But as she leaned into my window, a street lamp illuminated her features and, to my utter amazement, I saw that she was actually a he. With a mustache, short beard, and long red hair! Unnerved, I covered my eyes tight with my hands and froze in that position.

"What's wrong, baby?" he cooed, amused.

"I thought you were a girl," I said, peeking through a crack in my fingers.

"Oh, baby, I only wish," he said. "Now what did you stop me for? Did y'all want to party or something?"

"No," I said. "I'm trying to find the Parker Meridien Hotel. Do you know which way to go?"

"You go down," he said.

"What?" I asked.

"You don't get it, do you, hon?" He laughed. "No, I can see you don't. Well, listen, you drive yourself downtown, headin' toward the money, and then you ask some rich white bitch where this Parker Meridien is and *she'll* tell you."

Following his advice, I finally pulled up in front of the hotel. Thoroughly exhausted, I had enough strength to relay my adventure to Dr. Landy before dropping off into a deep sleep. The rest of the week was the same. No limousines or taxis were allowed. I walked everyplace or caught the subway. That meant I was at least an hour late to everything. But as cruel as Dr. Landy's methods appeared, I got New York down, and now I tackle the streets like a native.

From New York we flew to Chicago, rejoining the Beach Boys for a couple of shows. On the morning we were departing, I was packing when Dr. Landy came in. I asked if I was late for the airplane.

"No," he said. "I was just wondering if you'd ever seen the Grand Canyon or the Painted Desert?"

"As a matter of fact, Gene," I said, "I haven't. Why?"

"Because," he said, "you'll be driving by on your way home."

I groaned. Another test. Another challenge. It was going to be hard. But I knew it was going to build character. I accepted it as a matter of course. Dr. Landy didn't even have to give me a pep talk about reading maps or fending for myself. The payoff came several months later when I discovered how much stronger I'd become.

I used Henry Edwards, the former *New York Times* rock critic, for comparison. A friend of Dr. Landy's, Henry is the stereotypical New Yorker. Urbane, literate, and unathletic, he smoked cigarettes and exercised by walking to restaurants. Dr. Landy had invited him to go on Outward Bound, but Henry said no after reading in the brochure that they recommended spending a month just to break in the hiking boots. But he agreed to accompany me and my assistant, Kevin Leslie, and trainer, Michael Whitis, on a rafting trip down the Rogue River in Oregon.

I was in good shape from my Outward Bound experience, and navigated easily, but Henry's mishaps made the trip. As we got instructions on paddling, the instructor took one look at him, heard his nasal tone, and decided he would be a passenger and float down the rapids like a blue-blooded pasha. Standing on the shore, Henry watched as everyone got into rafts, which were positioned in a little pool of still water, and practiced strokes.

"How is it, Brian?" he asked.

"Easy," I called. "Real fun."

Deciding it couldn't be that hard, Henry slipped into an empty raft and tried to imitate the stroke. He couldn't. The more he tried to master it, the more feeble he looked. Then, suddenly, his raft was seized by the current and he was carried backwards down the rapids. Water poured over his head. He screamed. Everyone watched, stunned, as he went roaring down the white water. We were just three minutes into the trip.

There was panic on the shore. I grabbed Kevin. The guide was already in his boat, maneuvering into the current. We followed, paddling frantically, though we had just learned the stroke. The guide was shouting. We were shouting. Both of our rafts were equipped with an extra life preserver. But we didn't see Henry. Ten minutes later, we reached the eddy where the rapids emptied. The water was as calm as a bathtub. Henry was floating in the middle, grinning.

"Hi, guys," he said. "I did it. Now what?"

It was more of the same for three days. At the end of the trip, our touring party went for a hike through a beautiful, dense woods. For someone who was not an outdoors person, Henry was the most enthusiastic of the bunch. He rhapsodized about the forest, the wonders of nature, and then, quite suddenly, he whipped off all his clothes and began prancing naked among the trees, laughing and enjoying himself, while the rest of us looked on, amazed.

"I'm dancing with the primitive spirits!" he called out. "Come join me!"

I'd experience a lot over the past few months. I climbed mountains. I read maps. I drove from one end of the country to the other. I saw the Grand Canyon. I learned how to handle adversity. By the time I'd finished traversing the Rogue River, I sensed there wasn't anything I couldn't do.

But then I saw Henry dancing naked in the forest and I knew there were still a few things that were beyond me.

In the fall, Eugene, Alexandra, and I accompanied the group to London, where Steve Levine finally made time to record the Beach Boys' album. Digital was a long way from the Duophonic sound I'd recorded with at Capitol in the early sixties. Then I did everything live. Everyone sang and played together. In London, every single note we sang and played was programmed, digitized, and run through a computer. When we heard it played back, it was perfect. The sour notes had been made sweet, the offbeat notes had been pushed back into line. Every sound had been blended into seamless perfection.

"Digital recording?" I said.

"That's right." Levine nodded. "Blows your mind, doesn't it?"

The technology was impressive—awesome, in fact. I'd always strived for clarity of sound. *Pet Sounds* had been my breakthrough, and I'd spent all my energy afterward trying to top it. But while working with Levine on *The Beach Boys* I learned the lesson that so many people who made albums in the eighties missed: no matter how perfect technology made the sound, an album still boiled down to great songwriting and a spiritual investment in the music.

The Beach Boys never got the combination right with Levine. I collaborated on five songs in all, including three written with Dr. Landy.

"You don't like the lyrics, man?" said Dr. Landy to Mike one day when we were doing "Male Ego." "Fine. Let's redo them."

I sat at the piano. Dr. Landy stood to the side. Mike refused to move from the engineer's booth.

"I need Brian alone," he protested. "I can only write if I'm alone with him."

"We wrote the song," said Dr. Landy. "If you want to add your thoughts, let's do it now. Here."

"Sorry," he said.

"Brian," said Dr. Landy, "do you want to go write with Mike or do you want to write here?"

"I'd prefer to do it here, Gene," I said.

Even though Mike was eventually given a third songwriting credit, there was no compromise to the conflict, which, coincidentally, was overshadowed, at least that day, by a run-in with Levine at the same session. The Englishman's tedious, dictatorial work habits were driving everyone crazy. None of us were kids; we'd been around twenty-five years. On top of that, I complained that Levine was preoccupied more with the technology than the music. I saw lots of computers and blinking diodes, but I didn't hear any human qualities in the music.

How could I? Levine recorded each voice individually and ran them all through computers, which squeezed out every imperfection until they all sounded alike. Later that day Dr. Landy persuaded Tom Hulett to take Levine out of the studio so I could take a crack at producing. As soon as they went out to eat—or so we thought—I put Al, Mike, Carl, and Bruce in the studio, lined them up around a solitary microphone, as we used to do, and had them sing the harmonies on "I'm So Lonely."

"What the hell's going on?" exclaimed a surprised Levine, who'd returned to the studio to get his address book.

"We're working on this song," I said from the booth.

Both Levine and his engineer were amazed. Neither had seen anybody record a group all at once.

"That's really not what I had in mind," he said.

"It's *not* what you have in mind," said Dr. Landy. "This group was made because of what's in *Brian's* mind."

The eponymously titled LP *The Beach Boys* was released in June 1985. With the short-lived success of the single "Getcha Back," which peaked at twenty-six, the album managed to reach number fifty-two on the LP charts. Not great but not bad either.

The highlight of my year came six months later. After my usual morning swim at Pepperdine University in Malibu, I stepped on the scale and weighed in at a lean and fit 186 pounds. I hadn't been in such good shape since high school.

43

Little Children

*I*n the dressing room area at the Universal Amphitheater in Los Angeles, I was greeted with compliments about my improved appearance. It was as if people didn't expect to see me, and now they couldn't believe I was trim, nicely dressed, clean, and smiling. It was the summer of 1984, over a year of rehabilitation and reacclimation since my return from Hawaii.

Joining the Beach Boys for a local performance, I waited in the backstage area for Dr. Landy to return with an all-access pass to use during the show. When I performed, I preferred that he station himself in front of the stage, right in the center, where I could see him during the show. It helped keep me on track in case I began to drift, especially in L.A., where everyone I knew would turn out to see if I was going to play or be crazy.

Although the Beach Boys had been playing for nearly twenty-five years, a hometown show was still a big deal, and I'd been working on my new social skills for several days. Dr. Landy outlined and directed me. I'd never looked people directly in the eye when I spoke. Now I rehearsed saying, "Hi, I'm Brian Wilson." I memorized the conversation starters Dr. Landy taught me—What's your name? Where do you live? What do you do?

When I was young and successful, I never needed skills like these. It's a sad commentary, but the truth. Though simple to others, these short statements and questions were a lot for me to coordinate. Silence had always been my ally in situations where people expected conversation but I had nothing to say. Now I wanted to feel adequate when talking to people. Rather than feel frustrated or awkward, I wanted to talk like everyone else.

With only a few minutes left till we went onstage, Dr. Landy and I began walking through the preshow party toward the backstage entrance, shaking lots of hands, smiling, saying hello, and nodding. He stopped to talk with someone, leaving me to continue on my own. As I neared the stairs that led up behind the stage area, a young, overweight girl with shiny cheeks and a bright smile came toward me. As I'd practiced, I reached out my hand and said, "Hi, I'm Brian Wilson."

The girl stopped dead in her tracks. Her smile turned into a look of shock. I wondered what I'd done wrong.

"Daddy!" she exclaimed, aghast, "don't you know me? It's Carnie."

Before Carnie finished, I realized my mistake. Panicky, I broke into a sweat. My own daughter, and I hadn't even recognized her!

My heart sank. I tried to explain and apologize at the same time, but my tongue tripped over my words and everything came out gibberish. What could I say? Nothing. The fact was, I *hadn't* recognized my own daughter. It hurt me, but I knew it hurt Carnie even more.

Why did that happen? I hadn't been paying attention. I was too absorbed in my own thoughts, which ironically were practicing how to be sociable. Then I'd been startled. I lost it. Dr. Landy and I had been working to prevent just that type of situation. I had to conquer my own chemistry and stay on top of my emotions.

But I'd fucked up. Goddamnit.

Suddenly, Dr. Landy came sweeping around the corner and saw Carnie and me face-to-face. I was disturbed, she was crushed. Dr. Landy took each of us by an arm and ushered us into my dressing room. Then he located my other daughter, Wendy, and brought her in there too. Wendy had no idea what was going on. She looked frightened and confused. What a scene. What a family!

Over the past couple of months, there had developed a serious rift between Dr. Landy and Marilyn. She demanded I be reintegrated back into the family. She wanted me to become a dad to the girls. Do the whole number, visits, dinners; the phrase used was "quality time." I had a lot of lost years to make up for. She called to set up dates. She had the girls call. When I failed to return their repeated calls, they just assumed Dr. Landy wasn't giving me the messages.

Their assumptions were without foundation. The truth was I hid behind Dr. Landy. I used him as an excuse for not doing things I found unpleasant. "Dr. Landy won't let me" became my favorite catchphrase. Everyone thought he kept me from family functions and seeing the kids. Wrong. He tried encouraging me to do family things, but he didn't insist. The choice was mine, and I chose not to see anyone. To me, family meant bummer time. All I had were bad memories and bad feelings.

As time passed, Marilyn's misunderstanding turned to hatred. She accused Dr. Landy of holding me hostage. Marilyn even brainwashed Carnie and Wendy into believing that it was true, not ever considering I might be responsible for the estrangement.

The truth was as difficult for me to confront as it was for everyone else, perhaps more. But it reached a new level of difficulty as I stared into my daughters' confused and troubled faces in my Amphitheater dressing room. The room filled with the tension of anticipation. Shaking myself, I sensed the girls' nervousness too. Carnie was bravely holding back tears; Wendy was emotional without knowing what was happening. I desperately fought the urge to sprint out the door.

"Brian," Dr. Landy said, breaking the silence. "I want you to tell Carnie and Wendy what you feel about being their father."

I heard his words. I understood them. I'd even given the subject glancing thought on occasion. Just one more thing to feel guilty about. However, the myriad thoughts and emotions that suddenly flooded my brain confused me.

"What do you mean?" I asked.

"Tell them how you feel at this exact moment about being their dad," he reiterated.

I turned toward Carnie, sixteen, and Wendy, fourteen. Their big eyes, as deep as wells, looked at me so expectantly. At that moment, an intenseness built up inside me. I thought of my dad, who was at the root of this mess. He'd fucked me up. I wondered if the girls knew about him. I'd never talked about him; Marilyn probably gave them background. I was still trying to figure him out myself.

Looking at the girls, I felt empty, awkward, and inept. A lifetime of failures engulfed me. I wanted to say something to make Carnie and Wendy feel better. I wished I had an explanation. But I didn't have the slightest clue of what to say. I tried to imagine what they would've wanted to hear. That I loved them, that I'd made terrible mistakes in my life. Perhaps they hoped I'd open up my arms, invite them into my life, and give them a hug.

I wasn't capable of that. In dealing with emotions, I could understand my own, but I was years and years behind both girls when it came to relating to others. I knew I had to say something. I couldn't run forever. I'd made that much progress in the therapy program.

"I'm going to tell both of you something that I'm sure both of you already know," I said, speaking clearly and slowly. "I'm not a very good daddy. Your mommy has had to be both a mommy and a daddy. I love you, in my own way. And I support you. With money and with my heart. I take care of all your needs. But that's about as much as I'm able to do. I'll show you that I care for you. I'll write a song for you. But that's as good a daddy as I can be."

Both girls were silent.

"Tell them why that's as good as you can be," said Dr. Landy, once again cutting through the long, uncomfortable silence.

"Because I never had a good dad myself," I continued. "And I don't know if I'll ever know how to be a good daddy. I don't want to be the kind of dad to you that mine was to me. I'm sorry. I'm sorry you've not had a good daddy. Your mommy's been a good mommy and a good daddy. I didn't have either. You've been lucky that way. If I had known how to be a good daddy, I would have. It's not that I didn't want to. But I can't. And that's really all I have got to say. I love you, and I'll prove it to you. I'll write you a song someday."

I was drained. Neither girl moved a muscle. They sat shocked: shocked at my honesty and my directness. Shocked that I wasn't going to play games and make believe things would get better. They didn't know how to respond, and I can't say I blame them. But I felt too uncomfortable sitting there, facing them, and fortunately the band was about to go on.

"Now, if you'll excuse me," I said, getting up and starting to walk out the door.

"Daddy!" Carnie, a lot more talkative and outgoing than her sister, called after me. "Don't you want to know anything about us? Don't you want to hear about what we're doing?"

"Oh, yes," I said. "What are you doing?"

Carnie attempted to fill me in on a year's worth of stories concerning everything from her friends, schoolwork, afternoon escapades, and movies she'd seen. But I was too distracted by what had just taken place to pay attention. I was already concentrating on the show. The only bit of information of Carnie's that I caught was something about making an album with Wendy and their friend Chynna Phillips.

"Good, good," I muttered. "If I can help you in your music in any way, I would love to."

That said, I split.

In fall 1986, I was recording "Let's Go to Heaven in My Car." Dr. Landy and I had written it together, an extension of the songwriting we did as part of therapy. It was being used on the soundtrack of the film *Police Academy 4*. In the course of putting together the tracks, Gene suggested getting my daughters to sing the background vocals.

"It would provide you and Carnie and Wendy something to talk about," he said. "They could talk with you about music. You could talk to them about what you do."

"Great idea, Gene," I said.

Dr. Landy called Marilyn and told her the idea. Without a moment of thought, she said no. But Dr. Landy didn't give up. He asked Tom Hulett to call Marilyn. She said no again. This time she mentioned that the girls were working on their own album with producer Richard Perry. Dr. Landy phoned Perry and asked him. He also turned us down. Then Hulett called Perry, who now said he'd ask Marilyn. But her reply was the same as before.

That's just one example of how Dr. Landy tried to keep up my ties with my family, which he thought was important. When Carnie was in the hospital, he took her flowers and told her they were from me. He sent the girls birthday gifts and signed my name to cards. He gave them suggestions on how to get together with me. But Carnie and Wendy, soured by Marilyn's opinion of Dr. Landy as evil incarnate, said no to anything that had the slightest connection with my therapist.

Nobody had to tell me I was the real loser because of it. I knew all of us were losing equally.

It's too bad that everything in my life has had to be a struggle. Wouldn't it be nice if it were different?

Early in 1986 Carl threw his weight into the war against Dr. Landy, a move that triggered everyone's long-simmering acrimony and distrust toward my friend and therapist. The Beach Boys loathed the independence Dr. Landy was giving me. They hated that I was beginning to be able to say no to them and act on my own thoughts. They resented that I wrote songs, not with Dr. Landy, but *without* them. They accused him of being a Svengali who was holding me captive.

The struggle suddenly escalated when Carl began withholding my paychecks and money. That authority was his through The Brian Wilson Trust of 1982, which he'd had me sign prior to Dr. Landy's beginning treatment again. As trustee, he controlled both my corporate vote in the Beach Boys corporation Brother Records Inc., and all my money, property, and stocks.

In Carl's opinion, the trust was supposed to protect me from Dr. Landy, but as I got saner, I began questioning my brother. I couldn't remember signing the document in the first place. I was too incompetent at the time to know what I was signing. As I got saner, Dr. Landy began questioning me to see what I knew about the trust. What kind of trust was it? I didn't know. Why don't you know? I don't know. Wouldn't a responsible person know? Don't you think you should? Yes. Then why don't you ask?

That's when the money stopped. By making it impossible for me to pay my bills, Carl figured he could drive Dr. Landy away. He assumed my therapist was only interested in the money. Typically, he miscalculated. Dr. Landy's and my relationship extended way beyond money. Gradually and naturally, we had become a team. I thought of us as a work in progress. We devoted as much effort to living life as we did to making music.

I was disturbed by what was said about Dr. Landy. Like any two creative people, we didn't always agree. But I trusted him with my life and career. After all, I wouldn't have a life if it were not for him. It made sense that he wouldn't build me strong just to knock me down the way my dad and the Beach Boys did.

If I'd felt otherwise, I would've said something. I'd have told Carl or Marilyn or my mother. Someone.

For six months, Dr. Landy paid my bills. In February 1986, acting on the advice of independent legal counsel, I wrote a letter to Carl informing him I wanted the trust dissolved. I complained about not having access to my money, to my corporate vote, and about not being able to make any choices. In May, The Brian Wilson Trust of 1982 was officially dissolved.

But that was also the start of an intense PR battle in which the Beach Boys publicly denigrated Dr. Landy and called me a prisoner. The truth was anything but. I jogged daily along the Pacific Coast Highway. I worked out at Pepperdine University. I saw movies, shopped for groceries, attended concerts. I even played a handful of shows with the Beach Boys every year. I was more accessible and public than ever before. I was really growing up.

*   *   *

"You want to go to New York and present an award at the Rock and Roll Hall of Fame dinner?" Dr. Landy asked before Christmas.

"For whom?" I wanted to know.

"Leiber and Stoller," he said.

Jerry Leiber and Mike Stoller were heroes of mine. Among the best and most influential of rock's early songwriters and producers, they wrote "Hound Dog" for Big Mama Thornton, which Elvis turned into a smash. They wrote "Searchin'," "Yakety Yak," and "Charlie Brown" for the Coasters. Peggy Lee recorded "Is That All There Is?" and the Drifters had a hit with "On Broadway." Gary Usher turned me on to them originally. Later I learned Phil Spector had been their protégé.

"Definitely," I said. "I'll do it."

Held in January 1987, the Hall of Fame ceremony required me to make a speech, a fact I didn't realize was terrifying until the plane ride to New York. Seated behind a piano I was fine. I only had to rest my hands on the keyboard and I'd relax. But I wasn't a public speaker. Dr. Landy asked Henry Edwards to help prepare a speech, and I spent two days practicing my lines. By the night of the dinner I had the speech down.

It was my first glitzy public outing since leaving Hawaii, and I felt a lot of warmth and camaraderie in the room, especially from my table mates Atlantic Records chairman Ahmet Ertegun and Sire Records president Seymore Stein. Seymore and I spent the dinner talking about how nervous we were making speeches. I followed him in the lineup and told him I'd watch how he did.

Seymore finished, and I gulped. As I walked up to the dais, I received an emotional standing ovation. If I hadn't been prepared for one, I would've been thrown off and blown my speech. Fortunately, Dr. Landy told me to expect the thunderous applause. He also instructed me to let the people in the banquet hall show their affection and admiration.

"Even though you don't enjoy it," he told me, "stand there and look like you do. That's why they call it *show* business."

I put my hands up. I smiled. The crowd slowly quieted.

"Thank you." I smiled. Then I veered off the prepared script and added, "Thank you from the bottom of my heart."

That did it. The audience stood up again and clapped and cheered. Dr. Landy hadn't prepared me for a *second* standing ovation. My timing was thrown for a loop. Fortunately, though, I'd practiced my speech enough that I got through it fine. Midway through, however, I decided to ad-lib a bit. In trying to emphasize how much I admired Leiber and Stoller's "On Broadway," I began to sing parts of the wonderful melody, and as I hit those wonderful, soaring high notes, "On Broadway," the audience broke into a roar and applause once again. That reaction, as an entertainer, I understood and enjoyed.

When I got back to the table Seymore Stein was speaking in a hushed voice to Landy, ignoring Leiber and Stoller onstage as they accepted their Hall of Fame plaques. After several minutes, Seymore left the table and Landy turned to me. As it turned out, Seymore went and called his trusted A&R man, Andy Paley, in London and asked him who I was beyond just a member of the Beach Boys. Seymore wanted to know if he should sign me. Paley told him I was the soul of the group, the brains, and if he had a chance to sign me to a solo deal to do it.

"You'd be getting something special," he said to Seymore.

In the meantime, Dr. Landy asked if I would like to make a solo album.

"Yes, Gene, I would very much like to," I said. "But I don't have a deal. In music, you have to have a deal before you can make an album."

In my naiveté and simplistic manner of thinking, I assumed Dr. Landy didn't know anything about the music business. I forgot that he had worked for RCA before becoming a clinical psychologist. But in that one sentence, I told him almost everything I knew about the business end.

"Well, you know this man who's sitting next to us, Seymore Stein," he said. "He's president of Sire Records. He just asked me if you'd be interested in making a couple of solo albums for his label."

I didn't even have to think about the answer.

"Let's do it," I chortled.

What a trip!

44

Demos

I t wasn't until spring 1987, three or four months after the Hall of Fame handshake with Seymore, that contracts for the record deal were finally signed. During that time, Dr. Landy and I expressed enthusiasm for the project, but both of us, deep down, sincerely hoped that the prospect of my branching out would compel the Beach Boys to ask me to do an album for them. As much as I wanted to make a solo LP, I would've liked nothing more than to make an LP for the band.

The Beach Boys were still my group.

But neither Mike, Carl, nor Al asked. They wouldn't as long as Dr. Landy was involved. They ridiculed his qualifications every chance they got. I responded, "What's anybody's qualification for writing a song?" Nobody ever asked why I wrote with Roger Christian, a disc jockey. Or Tony Asher, who worked in an advertising agency. Or Mike Love, who pumped gas in a filling station and wrote with me because he was my cousin.

Ironically, Carl was then writing songs with his manager's wife, but no one thought that odd. Their only concern was who wrote with me.

The guys congratulated me on my solo deal, but I think they also worried I might be successful. I sensed they were jealous that I was writing and producing an album-worth of songs for someone other than them. It wasn't as if they'd never done solo albums. Carl and Mike had each done two unsuccessful albums, and Al had tried but failed to complete one.

I thought, Screw 'em.

Talking about making an album and signing the papers was one thing. Actually doing it was another. I hadn't made an album, actually written and produced and dug my heels into the ground, since, well, since *Smile*, in 1967, when I was twenty-five years old.

In the days when I was on a roll, I used to approach album making as if it were an athletic contest. The process was natural, the songwriting feverish. Now I looked down the field and wondered, Where to start?

Dr. Landy supplied the answer.

One morning he had me come to his office. I walked in and he was sitting next to a table. On it was a stack of studio tapes, rising several feet in the air. All of them were labeled with Brother Studios.

"What's this?" I asked.

"Homework," he said. "Your homework."

Dr. Landy had collected all the old Beach Boys masters and various outtakes he could find. The tapes captured me producing and instructing everyone what to play and sing. They were evidence against potential insecurity. For the next months, I booked time at different studios and listened to the tapes, reliving the way I used to work and absorbing the feel of being in a studio every day. It became part of my daily schedule, like working out.

"What do you think?" Dr. Landy asked when I neared the bottom of the stack.

"I think I was a bear to work with," I said. "I was really tough and demanding. It's kind of a shock to hear."

"Can you be that way again?" Dr. Landy asked.

"Well, I don't know," I said. "I mean, I was twenty-one, twenty-two years old. I had gasoline in my veins then. Jesus Christ, I'd love to be that age again. I can't, though. Can't go backwards. However, I can work hard. You know that. I'm in pretty good shape."

"Good," he smiled. "That's what I want to hear."

But I went through a number of head trips getting started. I had to convince myself I still had the touch, that my talent wasn't gone but rather dormant, and I spent too much time looking for a sign that would let me feel that. Dr. Landy and I had written a number of songs. I'd written some myself. Alexandra Morgan's writing helped enormously on a lot of songs, but especially on one of my favorites, "There's So Many."

The few people who heard the songs at this early stage gave me high marks.

But compliments were one thing, confidence another, and I had trouble believing in the song. I doubted everything. The doubt turned into frustration; the frustration became the source of constant complaining about every studio I worked in. Dr. Landy and I changed locations every couple of days, and by the end of the first two months, I'd made demos in fifteen different studios, including my old haunt, Western.

"I haven't found the right studio yet," I protested.

"What's wrong with the ones we've tried?" he asked.

"They're too hard," I explained.

"There are no easy studios, Brian," he said. "There is no magic formula."

"Well, they're too threatening," I said. "I get in there, and I feel threatened with pressure."

"Sure you do," he told me. "All studios are threatening. It's like looking at a blank piece of paper and wondering what the fuck to write."

"But it's just not the same," I said in a childish whine.

"No, it ain't the same, babe," he said. "And it isn't ever going to be the same. But that doesn't mean you can't still make great music. Now what do you want to do? Sit around and bitch or try to make an album of great music?"

Despite having watched Steve Levine, I realized I still had a lot to learn about making modern records, but I was hungry, interested, and willing. Dr. Landy proved to be a hard taskmaster. I gave him songs I thought were finished, and he handed them right back. He often told me what I'd done would've been great in the sixties, but it was the late eighties and I had to bring it up to snuff.

I was still discovering synthesizers. There was a gap between what was in my head and what got on tape. The reason was my lack of familiarity with the technology, but I blamed myself. I figured my ability had withered. That got me terribly depressed. I didn't have to be told I wasn't the same guy who wrote "Good Vibrations." I knew. Any forty-five-year-old knows he's no longer twenty-four.

That didn't mean I was washed up. I still had the desire to express myself that makes all artists do what they do, but I didn't have the ferocious intensity I did twenty years earlier. I suppose that's unavoidable. I think many artists feel that loss as they get older, and that realization is a bitch, a serious reckoning with mortality. I spent hours every day talking about this with Dr. Landy.

"Describe what you're feeling," he said.

"I'm frustrated, really frustrated," I said.

"By what?"

"I'm not twenty-four anymore," I said. "I can't be in my twenties again. And that's bugging me."

"So what?" he asked. "Think of the alternative. You could be a dead twenty-four-year-old forever. Or you can be alive. And if you're alive, you've got something that you didn't have when you were twenty-four."

"What's that?" I asked.

"Experience. Wisdom. You're smarter," he explained. "You've lived life. You made mistakes and you've learned from them. Haven't you?"

"Yes, I have, Gene," I said, encouraged. "But I don't know about putting it on record."

"Do you hear music? Can you still play the piano? Can you still sing?" he asked.

"Yes," I said.

"Then you can make records."

I needed those pep talks, but being in the recording studio every day eventually produced its own results. Despite a plethora of reservations and self-doubt, despite my continued frailties, work made me feel vital and validated again. The studio was my place, as much my room as my old bedroom I'd written about in "In My Room."

Doing something as simple as pulling my car into my reserved parking space was an upper. Getting out of the car, I used to tell myself, "I'm going to be making music here. That's my thing."

And I'd get a good feeling.

One day in June, Gary Usher, my first songwriting partner, called Dr. Landy. It was out of the blue. I couldn't even remember how many years had passed between conversations. Gary knew about my troubles, he'd read about my recovery, and he'd heard I was recording again. He said he wanted to help. Despite some successes after we split, Gary was going through some hard times too. He figured we could help each other.

Dr. Landy suggested the three of us might work on some songs together, but he really saw Gary as another step in returning me to working order. Gary was a good sparring partner. He and I were well acquainted, comfortable, and I wouldn't be intimidated. After working several days at my house, Gary said he had an eight-track in his garage, a simple setup, but it was still a lot more than I had. We switched workplaces.

At Gary's the pace picked up. I felt a homey sort of déjà vu sitting across from him. We'd been teenagers when we started writing together. We'd gotten drunk together, shared our most intimate thoughts. He'd known me better than my own family. He'd been tormented by my dad. He'd introduced me to Marilyn. We'd done some great work together, and now some twenty-seven years later we were at the piano again.

"I liked how you handled yourself in the studio yesterday," I said at the start of one of our workdays.

"Thanks," said Gary.

"But you know you're a genius, don't you?" I asked. "You're an absolute genius. Like attracts like. So maybe we got two geniuses working together. It ought to be a great combination. We're going to make some great music."

When Gary greeted me the next day, he was more serious than I remembered. He came right out with it. He wanted to let bygones be bygones. Whatever broke up our friendship was history. Nothing could be changed. No hard feelings. The past was just that. We could begin creating a new future right now. Clearly, Gary's words had an emotional effect on me. I wanted to hug him. I wanted to thank him for being understanding. I appreciated his friendship.

"You know I was a member of the big three-forty club," I said, trying to catch Gary up on my life.

"What's the three-forty club?" he asked.

"I weighed three hundred forty pounds," I explained. "I didn't care. I was paranoid, eccentric. But I kicked all that."

"Yeah, I can see," he said, encouragingly. "You've done a great job. You look great."

I really did look like new. Dr. Steven Zax, my plastic surgeon, fixed my crushed cheekbone from where my father had hit me as a child. But I didn't always feel as good as I looked.

"But you know I'm a goddamned prisoner," I yelled, suddenly growing dramatic. "I have no hope of escaping."

Gary was stunned, puzzled. He didn't know what I meant and asked me to clarify. I launched into an emotional tirade against Dr. Landy. I explained that Dr. Landy was teaching me how to be responsible and how to function in the world. But I railed about how difficult the regimented program was.

"I hate being told everything," I ranted. "I hate being watched. I'm a goddamned prisoner."

"And that's Landy who's telling you what to do?" asked Gary.

"Yeah," I said. "Landy."

In those days I talked literally, and Gary took me at my word. But I was really expressing my fear about the record, and it was safe for me to get mad at Dr. Landy. He and I argued, made up, shouted at and admired one another. He was family. In many ways, he'd become my family. If I got angry, for whatever reason, I directed it toward him. That's what I knew, and that's what felt safe and comfortable.

Spending time with Gary was giving me insight into the way I felt about myself. Despite my friend's professional disappointments, Gary still looked happier than me. Even with all my money and fame, I didn't think I was as well off as him. At least, that's the way it looked to me then. The more I analyzed the situation, though, the more I found it difficult to ignore the admission I'd been reluctant to make.

Although healthier, more competent, and more productive than I had been in years, I was still ill. Mentally ill. Finally admitting that to myself was depressing as all hell. But I came to grips with the fact that, at that time, I wasn't responsible enough to live by myself. I knew I needed psychiatric care. I knew I needed some type of supervision. I knew I couldn't be trusted yet not to slip back into a behavior that was self-destructive. I knew all this only because I was healthier than I had been for most, if not all, of my life up to that time.

The moment I accepted this the more I got angry, and Gary was the first person I told. I wasn't mad at Dr. Landy. Getting upset with him was how I showed my anger at myself and my new awareness of life situations.

"Pain is sometimes a necessity," Gary offered. "Think of it as a privilege to have pain. Only through pain do we learn and grow."

"Yeah, yeah." I sighed, calming down. "Like the sign at my chiropractor's office says, 'No pain, no gain." Dr. Leroy Perry has always been there to relieve my back pains, as has Dr. Arnold Ross with his orthopedics.

There turned out to be a fair amount of pain in working with Gary. Although he and I and Dr. Landy all collaborated on songs, Gary submitted a whopping $14,000 bill for his time. It came out of the blue. Then he got to Sire and Warner Brothers presidents Seymore Stein and Lenny

Waronker and tried cutting a deal for himself as producer of my solo album. I didn't know what was going on with him.

"Gary, why are you doing this to me?" I asked.

We were at the studio. It was two days after Dr. Landy and I had mastered "Let's Go To Heaven in My Car." Gary, who had helped write the song, had missed the session.

"I'm trying to help," he said. "I can help you make music *and* get away from Dr. Landy."

"But I don't need that kind of help," I said. "And I don't want to leave Dr. Landy."

It turned out that the whole time I was working with Gary, he kept a journal, recording everything I said. After I told him Dr. Landy and I were going to push ahead on the solo LP without him, he gave his journal to the attorney general's office, which had begun an investigation of Dr. Landy.

It made me realize that even paranoids have real enemies. There was reason for me to watch over my shoulder.

By spring 1987, I had put Gary behind me and was going full-blast on writing songs and making demos. Dr. Landy and I had recorded tracks for a dozen songs. We were getting along swell. Then the record business intruded.

An album is nothing if not a personal statement, a postcard of an artist's vision at that point in time, but suddenly Dr. Landy and I received word that we needed help. It was news to us, but we wanted the album to succeed and accepted Warner Records vice president and staff producer Russ Titelman when we learned he wanted to assist us. I knew Titelman from twenty-five years earlier when he was a skinny kid hanging around the studios in L.A. Now he was an executive with enough power to get what he wanted, and he wanted to work with me.

Titelman, who lived outside Manhattan, wanted to work in New York. Being open and cooperative, Dr. Landy, Alexandra Morgan, my long-blond-haired assistant Kevin Leslie, and I went to New York in June. The fighting started immediately. First, Titelman banned everyone except me and the musicians from the studio. Then he refused to messenger Dr. Landy tapes of the work. It was maddening, and for nearly two weeks nothing substantial was accomplished, except that Andy Paley, the A&R man Seymore Stein gave us, and I discovered we made a better team than me and Titelman.

The overriding problem was the record company didn't believe Dr. Landy was capable of coproducing with me. Seymore and Waronker both refused to accept him in that role or any creative role. Andy Paley could coproduce, that was all right. It seemed like anyone could coproduce, except Dr. Landy. Like the Beach Boys, the record company argued, "He's a doctor, not a producer."

The record company's limited understanding and sensitivity led to one hassle after another. Dr. Landy and I, trying to keep moving forward, were forced into making too many compromises. We were frustrated at every opportunity. I understood what was happening, though. Everyone wanted to take credit for the return of Brian Wilson.

But, I was going nowhere in New York, and the experiment fell apart one afternoon when Paley told Kevin that he smelled marijuana smoke coming from the bathroom. Titelman was inside. Kevin made a notation. After Titelman left the bathroom, Dr. Landy and Kevin sniffed the air. Titelman realized what happened and freaked. He ordered the studio cleared.

"Wait a minute," Dr. Landy said. "This is not your studio. More important, do you know that Brian has had a drug problem? Do you know it's not appropriate to be smoking marijuana anywhere around him? Do you understand what a threat you and your drug smoking present to him?"

Watching from a chair I rolled into the corner, I despaired that the solo album was slipping away as easily as it had come.

"There's not enough room here to do any work, not with that fucking Surf Nazi watching," Titelman said, referring to Kevin.

"Fine," Dr. Landy said. "Then we won't work here. You're the expert. If you say there's not enough room here, then we'll go back to Los Angeles."

In L.A., Lenny Waronker got into the act. The Warner Brothers president began coming to the studio. One day he brought Fleetwood Mac's ace guitarist Lindsey Buckingham, who wrote a song with Gene and me. Another day he brought Jeff Lynne. Lots of artists wanted to work on the album. I was honored and flattered, but the point was, Who asked?

It even got other artists pissed at me. One day I ran into Prince outside the studio. I introduced myself, but he refused even to look at me. He told an associate to tell me he didn't want to know me. What the hell had I done to him? Prince, it turned out, heard Waronker was in the studio with

344 / Brian Wilson

me and assumed that was why Lenny was unable to listen to his album.

By December 1987, we were making progress. It was slow but steady. The process brought to mind my experience at Outward Bound. Dr. Landy had been right to make me go on that godawful trip. If I could survive that experience, I had no doubt that I could ride my first solo album to a successful conclusion.

45

The Love You Make

I t was January 1988, and I was with the Beach Boys backstage at the Waldorf-Astoria Hotel in New York. Having finished talking with the press, we were waiting for the third annual Rock and Roll Hall of Fame awards dinner to start. Work on my album had been consuming, so this was the first time in months I'd seen the guys.

"So I hear the album's gettin' done," said Al Jardine. "Is it any good?"

"Oh yeah, how's the album going?" chuckled Mike Love sarcastically.

Before I could answer, Mike turned his attention back to former world heavyweight boxing champion Muhammad Ali, his special guest. Al walked off with his wife. Carl said a chilly hello but avoided Dr. Landy altogether.

"What's with Mike?" I asked. "He's got a funny look."

Carl didn't answer. Later, at our table, I found out. Mike had been fasting. As part of his TM practice, he hadn't eaten anything for nearly a week. That explained the frightening look in his eyes, the manic temperament. Next to Ali's glass façade, he looked like a severed electric wire, spitting sparks every which way.

I picked up Mike's vibe and got nervous that he would attack me. It was an irrational fear, but a fear nonetheless. Dr. Landy reassured me that he would not hurt me, he might do something crazy, but not to me. I felt better. As we moved to our table—the Beach Boys' entourage took up two tables—he told me to concentrate on my speech. As he did the previous year, my friend Henry Edwards wrote another great speech and helped me rehearse it until I got it right.

The Beach Boys were among the stellar field of inductees. Headlined by the Beatles and Bob Dylan, the list also included Leadbelly, the Supremes, Woody Guthrie, Motown founder Berry Gordy, guitar great Les Paul, and the Drifters. The Waldorf's banquet room was filled with the most impressive turnout of rockers I'd ever seen—Dylan, Neil Young, George Harrison and Ringo Starr, Bruce Springsteen, Paul Simon, and Little Richard.

The only star missing from this rock and roll galaxy was Paul McCartney. Through a publicist, he stated that unresolved business differences with George and Ringo made a reunion imprudent. It was too bad, but I understood that problems like that happen between group members. I have had the same problem myself.

Elton John introduced the Beach Boys, paying tribute to our harmonies and the music I had written, even mentioning that in the earliest days of his career he'd been a Brian Wilson fan. His speech sent me on a nice memory trip. As he finished, I was reliving the night Danny Hutton had brought an unknown songwriter named Elton John up to my house to play his stuff.

"Brian"—Dr. Landy nudged me—"get up. It's time to walk up there."

The guys were already up on the stage, standing around the microphone and drinking up the applause when I lumbered onstage, causing the applause to crescendo. The hall could've filled with smoke. Someone could've yelled fire. None of it would've mattered. I'd prepared myself for the applause and was concentrating on my speech.

Taking my time, I put on my glasses, smoothed the piece of paper my speech was written on, and cleared my throat. My concentration was so intense that I ignored the fact that the microphone was too low and, rather than adjust it, I bent down. However, just as I was about to utter the first word, I was interrupted by Mike, whose bald pate was topped by a nonformal UCLA Bruins cap.

But nothing mattered. I let Mike say his piece and then resumed my speech. "Who could've known twenty-seven years and more than thirty albums later, we'd be standing before you," I said. "I only wish my younger brother Dennis could be at our side tonight—" Suddenly, Mike interrupted again. He reached directly in front of me and said, "Here, let me adjust the mike for you." He couldn't stand I was doing so well and had the spotlight instead of him.

"When I was a teenager, I listened to the Four Freshmen and Frank Sinatra, and they got me through high school and that's what this is all about," I continued. "All of us in this room have the privilege of making music that helps and heals . . ." I paused and looked across the hall. "Don't forget, music is God's voice . . ."

Over the years the Beach Boys have been in style and out of style and in style again. But what's kept me going is the same thing that got me to write 'Surfin'' all those years ago. I wanted to write joyful music that made other people feel good. That's what I've tried to do for the past twenty-seven years."

I finished by saying, "The surf's up tonight. Let's all work together to keep it up forever. Love and mercy to everyone." There was a rousing cheer, then a standing ovation. By that time, however, Mike had interrupted me three times. Unperturbed, I still couldn't believe his rudeness. Jealous, he couldn't stand not to have the spotlight.

As I moved to the side, Al said thank you, Carl nodded, and bandleader Paul Schaffer struck up the band. Carl, Al, and I held our statues high and thought, as did everybody, that we were done.

Not quite. Mike leaned toward the microphone. Looking out at a front row of tables that included Harrison, Starr, Yoko Ono, Springsteen, Jagger, and Dylan, he exhorted the crowd to "Stop, stop, stop!"

I thought, uh-oh, what now? I'm sure Carl and Al bit their tongues too. Judging by the scowl on Mike's face and his furrowed eyebrows, there was no telling what he was about to do or say. Fasting made his behavior volatile and completely unpredictable.

No one could've imagined the venomous diatribe that Mike was about to deliver. Puffing out his forty-six-year-old chest, he boasted with blue-collar bravado that the Beach Boys were about harmony and that all McCartney could do was hide behind a high-priced attorney. "We do a hundred and eighty performances a year," Mike sneered. "I'd like to see the Mop Tops do that. I'd like to see Mick Jagger get onstage and do 'I Get Around' rather than 'Jumpin' Jack Flash.' " Then he challenged "the Boss"—Springsteen—to "dare climb onstage with the Beach Boys and jam. I wanna see Billy Joel see if he can tickle the ivories." He ranted on and on.

It was horribly embarrassing, and I felt awful. As Mike spoke, Seymore Stein raced up to the stage, took me by the arm, and pulled me off. Al and Carl stood there. Then Seymore turned to Schaffer and instructed him to play, hoping to drown Mike out. Not a chance. Mike kept on talking. The room resonated with boos and hisses and calls of "Get off the stage, schmuck."

Later, Springsteen introduced Dylan, who began his speech by pointedly thanking Mike for not mentioning him in his mean-spirited monologue. "I play a lot of dates every year too," Dylan said. "Peace, love, and harmony are important indeed, but so is forgiveness."

Mike didn't get it. Six weeks later, the spectacle was brought up among us for the first time during one of the group's corporate meetings. Mike listened stoically to everyone assess the damages his comments had wrought. He then explained how it had been the highlight of the Hall of Fame ceremony. The newspapers had all spelled his name right, and as far as he was concerned his remarks had made the Beach Boys the evening's biggest stars.

"I think it's the best thing that could've happened," he said. "I wanted us to stand out and we did, didn't we?"

Dr. Landy pointed out that Lee Harvey Oswald stood out too. But what you stand for is more important than just standing out.

Fortunately, I was able to put the incident behind me and return to my solo album. With Dr. Landy, I worked on "Child, Adult and Parent," a suite that mirrored, in music, the transitions my own life had undergone since Landy and I had restarted therapy in 1983. The collaboration was among the most fascinating I'd ever engaged in, involving nearly constant analysis and discussion of the past five years. It was beautiful.

The eight-minute suite was an ambitious project, especially since it had no chance of becoming a single. It was an exercise in pure imagination and artistry, and with great expectation we played a near finished tape to Lenny Waronker.

"No, no, that's not it," said the record company president. "No, what I want from this is cowboys and Indians. I loved "Cabin Essence." I loved "Cool, Cool Water." I want something with an all-American type of feel. Cowboys and Indians. None of this intellectual therapy stuff—get it?"

"Yeah, I get it," I said, still in the mode of an appeaser, but I couldn't believe it. "I know what you mean."

I liked what we had written, but I didn't want Lenny angry at me and agreed. Then he suggested that I work with Andy Paley on a Western-theme piece. I was anxious to appease and please. I wouldn't do that now. Stronger, I've gotten to the point where I can to stick to my gut instincts again. Pressed, I can say no. I wish I would've been able to say that then and kept the piece as it was.

But Dr. Landy and I were still letting ourselves be pushed around by the record company. Suddenly, Dr. Landy's contributions to the piece were erased, along with his name. Suddenly, Paley was cowriter and, lo and behold, he had his own publishing deal set up at Warners. It was a business of favors, not music.

As a result, "Child, Adult and Parent" was transformed into a western travelogue called *Rio Grande*. Lenny and Seymore, loved it. Dr. Landy and I went along with it.

In the midst of work, Beach Boys manager Tom Hulett called Dr. Landy and me at the studio. We were nearing the finish of a ten-hour session. He explained that the guys were in the last stages of recording "Kokomo," a song Terry Melcher, John Phillips, and Mike had written that was going to be on the sound track of an upcoming Tom Cruise movie, *Cocktail*, a celebration of booze and babes. The only reason Hulett called was because the Beach Boys' corporate bylaws stipulate that each group member had to be notified of any recording session, though how far in advance was unspecified.

"When is it?" Dr. Landy asked.

"Tomorrow," Hulett said.

"Yeah?" Dr. Landy said, playing it cool. "Where and when?"

"Two o'clock," he said.

"In the afternoon," Dr. Landy said, speaking loud enough for me to get what was going on.

"Oh yeah," Hulett added. "The session is in Atlanta."

"Georgia?" Dr. Landy asked, surprised. "It's six o'clock now. We're supposed to drop everything and catch an airplane in two hours? Brian, did you hear that shit?"

"Yeah, Gene," I said. "We can't do it."

The gamesmanship was unending.

Soon after the "Kokomo" session, Seymore suddenly expressed unhappiness with Gene's and my entire album after months of diligent work and compromising and attempts to please everyone and his cousin. The Sire president complained that there weren't any radio hits. Well shit, I thought, how did he know? How did anybody know? I thought "Love and Mercy," which Warners later refused to put out the way I wanted, and "Walkin' the Line," were both singles.

A weeklong discussion ensued. Seymore and Waronker were on the phone with us constantly. Their solution: Seymore wanted Paley to write another song, "a big radio hit," he said. The song, "Meet Me in My

Dreams Tonight," wasn't even released as a single. Waronker insisted Titelman return. Dr. Landy only requested that Titelman change his attitude. He agreed and returned to L.A.

In the meantime, Dr. Landy and I were hit by a bombshell that severely darkened the already long shadow in which we stood. In February 1988, the Board of Medical Quality Assurance (BMQA), California's custodian of the medical professions, charged Dr. Landy with ethical and licensing code violations that threatened his ability to practice psychology in California. The public witch-hunt Carl, Marilyn, the Beach Boys, and Carolyn Williams had pursued and always hoped for began.

One morning after my workout, Gene broke the news to me. He had spent the morning with his attorney, Mark Meador. Gene described how, while Meador had explained the legalities, he'd sat on the floor, depressed and paralyzed. I told him I knew how he felt.

My first reaction was distress. What if we were split apart? Everything we'd achieved, from my health to my burgeoning solo career, would crumble. What if I was handed back over to the Beach Boys and my family? I'd wilt. I'd die. I was certain of that. After discussing the situation, I became angry and slammed my fist down on the breakfast table so hard my silverware jumped off the tabletop.

"Gene, these charges, I want you to know, are bullshit," I said, trying to console and support him. "They're inaccurate. Whoever made them, my whole family, they're untrue. I can't imagine being more upset in my life."

"Thanks, babe," he said wearily.

"Not long after we first started working together, you told me everything that had happened to me," I said. "You were brutally honest. You told me what had happened to my body and my brain. And I couldn't hear it. I just wouldn't let myself hear it."

"Yeah, but it was the truth," he interjected.

"Exactly," I said. "I couldn't hear it. I didn't want to hear it. But one night in Hawaii, while I was lying in my bed, I said to myself, 'Here I am, Brian Wilson, the freaked-out druggie. A real case study.' And you know what? It hurt my feelings. It got me down. But even though it hurt, it also made me see the truth. And that's gotten me through all this."

"I deeply appreciate your saying this," Dr. Landy said.

"I know what's being said and written," I continued. "That was a tough program. A motherfucker. Five years ago I told myself that I couldn't take another day of it. Five years have gone by and I'm still saying the same thing. But now I ask myself, 'What do you mean? You took five years of this, you can take another day.' My point is, it's going to be real tough on you, but you've got to hang in there."

"Hey, man," said Dr. Landy, slapping me on the back, "I must've done a good job on you. I don't know which one of us is the shrink."

Filed by the attorney general's office, the BMQA's charges originated with a complaint filed by Carolyn Williams in 1984. They were then fueled by the journal Gary Usher compiled while we wrote songs together the previous year and pressed by Marilyn and Carl. But the real reason the BMQA brought charges had to do with Dr. Landy's unorthodox treatment of me.

The papers filed by the BMQA detailed his roles as my executive producer, coproducer, business manager, cosongwriter, and business adviser. The charges implied that Dr. Landy took advantage of me, even though at the time they were filed I was in the best physical, emotional, and financial shape I'd been in since the Beach Boys' inception. Not only had Dr. Landy saved my life, he'd returned my career to me.

But the state had its canon of ethics. It maintained that during treatment a therapist should not enter into any nonprofessional relationship with a patient.

My situation had presented extraordinary circumstances, and Dr. Landy by reputation was an extraordinary therapist—the reason he'd been contracted originally.

At a certain juncture, he was faced with a dilemma created by the state's canon: Is it ethical to take a patient to a certain point and then leave him there because the ethics say not to go any further? Should he depart from his traditional therapeutic process and enter into another role in which he could help me or should he not help because of an ethical process? Should he stop at a certain point because ethics imposed restrictions, or should he throw ethics to the wind and continue to improve my life? I feel the ethics should fit the circumstances, not the other way around. In my opinion, I'm able to write these words only because of the choice he made.

More than a month before the BMQA levied charges, Dr. Landy and I ended our formal doctor-patient relationship. For treatment, I saw Dr. Solon Samuels, a gentle, wise man. Dr. Landy became my friend, partner, and manager. If he and I were going to collaborate, we had to have equality.

A year later, the BMQA affair reached a quiet conclusion. After a discussion between Dr. Samuels, Dr. Landy, and myself about how I would hold up under the scrutiny of a trial, everyone decided a trial would be devastating to everything we'd accomplished. So rather than fight for his license to practice psychology in California, Dr. Landy decided to admit to administering legally prescribed drugs, essentially asking me questions like "Have you taken your medicine?" In taking the heat off me, he agreed to surrender his license for two years, after which he could reapply.

The whole thing disgusted me. Dr. Landy was being punished for saving my life, and I was being humiliated for having responded only to treatment that was outside what was considered ethical, a type of therapy that had never worked for me anyway. In the end, Dr. Landy and I were both stronger.

Dr. Landy may have surrendered his license, but he didn't surrender the fight. Neither did I.

By the end of February 1988, Dr. Landy and I, and everyone at the record company, decided we were ready to mix the eleven songs selected for the solo album. Without consulting anyone, Titelman hired Hugh Padgham to mix. Padgham, whose credits included hit records for Phil Collins and Sting, was good, but he had a sound of his own and I wanted the album to sound like me.

Mixing began at A&M Studios. The atmosphere started off badly and soon became volatile. One day Titelman, Padgham, and I were working. My assistant, Kevin, entered the studio and sat down on a sofa behind us. Titelman abruptly stopped everything and ordered him to leave. Kevin called Dr. Landy, who arrived at the studio within the hour.

"Look, Gene," Titelman said. "We can't work with you or Kevin in the room."

"Hugh, is that true?" Dr. Landy asked. "You can't work with me in the room?"

"Well, it does make us a little tense," he admitted.

"I understand," said Dr. Landy. "So, Russ, why don't you leave. Maybe it'll be less tense. Because if Brian's here, I'm here."

Titelman and Dr. Landy, both furious, were unyielding, and every day from then on all of us showed up. Instead of working, I fretted the album was going to fall apart at the finish line. With the fights and hassles, we didn't need someone to mix as much as we needed a referee.

The situation reach a critical point one day when I asked if I could hear more horns on a particular song. I might not have been mixing, but it was my album.

"No, there's plenty already," Titelman said.

"Okay," I said, leaning back in my chair.

"Not okay," Dr. Landy snapped. "Russ, did you hear what Brian said? He'd like to hear more horns."

"But it's okay as it is," Titelman said stubbornly.

I braced for the showdown I knew was imminent. Padgham and Kevin also became spectators in this studio equivalent of a barroom shootout.

"Listen, Russ, let's get one thing straight," Dr. Landy said in a controlled tone of voice. "I think your intentions are admirable. Even good. I want to thank you for spending so much time and effort on this project. And for all the organizational ability you brought to it. However, I don't think you understand the music or the songs. Intellectually and emotionally, I don't think you're grasping what we're trying to do or say . . ."

After this saccharine-sweet dressing-down, Titelman phoned Lenny Waronker, who also received a call from Dr. Landy. Eavesdropping on the conversation, I heard Dr. Landy tell the record label president in no uncertain terms that we were going to have to finish the album ourselves. Lenny pleaded with him not to kick Titelman out. It would look bad. He had promised Titelman there wouldn't be any problems.

"But he's mixing things Brian doesn't want mixed," said Dr. Landy.

"I'll make you a deal," said Lenny. "Let him finish, and if there's anything you don't like you can go back into the studio and remix it. I'll even go back to the studio to remix with you. Also, Warners will pay for it, and I'll give you up to ten days to remix—free. The studio, engineer, anything."

"Ten days might not be enough to undo everything Titelman has done," said Dr. Landy.

"All right. Two weeks," said Lenny. "Just please let Russ do his thing. Please. Do it for me, okay? Don't make trouble for me here at Warners.

"Okay, Lenny," said Dr. Landy. "I don't want to, but I'll do it for you. But know that I'm doing it for you. Because we really have no reason to continue working with Titelman. All he's going to do is spend our money and hassle us."

As Dr. Landy returned to the studio, my right leg was nervously pumping up and down with the speed of a jackhammer. All eyes turned to him. Strangely, Dr. Landy was smiling. Titelman, who had also spoken with Lenny, seemed ready for a truce too.

"Russ," said Dr. Landy, his smile a figment of a misconstrued moment, "you're fired."

"What?" exclaimed Titelman, shocked.

"I just promised Lenny I wasn't going to do that," he said. "But now I've done it. And it felt great. You're fired, Russ. So get your ass out of here."

"Fine, but I'm taking Padgham," he said.

"No, Padgham has a contract with me," he said. "He stays."

"Well, I can't stay without Titelman," said Padgham.

"Then you will be in breach of contract," said Dr. Landy.

By that time, I had risen from my chair and was pacing back and forth zombielike by the door, not hearing anything but the voice in my head that was saying, "It's all fucked. The album is never going to happen." There was screaming. Titelman was yelling he could do the album without us. Wanting the final word, he told Dr. Landy that he was fired. Then he looked at me and in an out-of-control rage shouted, *"That includes you too, Brian. You're fired. You're all fired."*

There was an unbelievable, surreal silence. Dr. Landy and I were in shock. We looked at each other in disbelief. Russ Titelman had just fired me from my own album!

"Well, if we're all fired, let's get out of here," Dr. Landy said. "Kevin, get all the tapes."

"You can't have them," a studio employee told Dr. Landy.

"Why not?" he demanded.

"The bill hasn't been paid," the man said.

"Then fuck it," Dr. Landy said. "And fuck you, Russ."

We did go back and remix the album. But Lenny went back on his promise and refused to pay.

46

Love and Mercy

*O*nly the weather was true to form in my niche of Malibu on June 15, 1988. The blanket of gray coastal fog that kept the summer heat at bay didn't burn off until shortly before noon. By that time I'd gone for my jog, showered, and fixed lunch. Sitting on my balcony, I was transfixed by a group of long-haired surfers doing their thing in the waves. On the sand, their suntanned girlfriends held their places. I looked at my watch.

Seven hours until the first single from my album was going to be played on the radio.

It seemed as if eons had passed since local radio stations vied for the chance to debut a new Beach Boys single. I remembered Tony Asher, my collaborator on *Pet Sounds,* once told me how he used to drive around, waiting for Sam Riddle, Wink Martindale, Gene Weed, or some other local DJ to cue up the new record. "Then I'd hear those first few bars," recalled Tony, "and think, Damn, Brian did it again."

Eons.

"Kevin," I said to my assistant, who with his shoulder-length blond hair and swimmer's body was like the surfers I was watching, "you're twenty-four, right?"

"Yeah," he said, adjusting his chair in order to soak up maximum rays.

"Tell me what it's like," I said. "Tell me how it feels to be twenty-four."

"I don't know, Bri." He said.

"That's the problem," I said. "I do."

By nightfall, I was resting in my dimly lit living room and leafing through a magazine. The stereo played softly in the background. I'd been tipped that "Love and Mercy," my album's first single, was going to be played by Deirdre O'Donoghue, a DJ at KCRW, sometime after 8:00 P.M. I waited with the anxiousness that had interrupted the flow of the entire day. My stomach churned.

I tried to create a calm mood by opening my french doors to let in the sound of the breaking waves outside and lighting candles. My last and only single, *"Caroline, No,"* had been released twenty-two years earlier. Those days, the glory days, were long gone—not forgotten, not unappreciated, but gone. I harbored no rancor or sorrow. A lot of regrets, like my drug abuse. But no bitterness.

I saw myself poised on the cusp of a new beginning—a nice place to be for a forty-six-year-old man.

I took a call from Dr. Landy.

"Yes, Gene, I'm waiting. I have the radio on," I said. "I don't know how I feel exactly. Excited. Nervous. I think my layoff has created quite a bit of tension. People are interested in hearing what I've done. I just hope they like it."

After a string of several songs, Deirdre's wispy, sandpapery voice returned. Her voice had the perfect sound for radio. It made you feel less lonely. She spoke poetically about the spiritual power of music and cued the next song. A moment later, I heard my voice—not the 1960, precigarette model but the present-day, postcigarette version—flower gently out of the stereo speaker.

> I was sitting in a crummy movie
> with my hands on my chin
> Oh the violence that occurs
> seems like we never win
> Love and mercy, that's what you need tonight
> Oh, love and mercy
> to you and your friends tonight . . .

My eyes were closed when the song finished, the music still playing in my head. Deirdre began speaking again. The three-minute song was brand-new, she explained, but if it sounded like an old friend, it was for good reason. The man who wrote the song, sang it, and played all the instruments was the same man who'd handled similar chores for the Beach Boys for so many years. He was the same man who'd created the sound track to so many people's growing-up.

I liked the subtle drama she created by withholding mention of my name, though eventually she did say it:

"Brian Wilson."

Growing up with only one good ear, I was always sensitive to the tone of people's voices. As I got older, the sensitivity increased. Deirdre's voice was soft, romantic, and, above all else, loving. I let her pronunciation of my name linger, silently inhaling the aroma of appreciation.

The album, titled *Brian Wilson,* entered the charts in the low seventies and did a slow and steady climb skyward. Reviews in the *New York Times* and *Rolling Stone* glowed. The Los Angeles *Times* review, which gave the LP four stars, began, "The long-awaited solo debut by the mastermind behind the Beach Boys' hits is not only the comeback of the year, it's a strong case for the argument that genius isn't a perishable commodity." An accompanying profile in the *Times* was headlined: "Brian Wilson—Back From the Twilight Zone."

That said it all. Radio was playing the album. The reviews were good. The stage appeared set for the comeback few people, including me, ever expected.

The only dark cloud then was that Elektra Records had, on the same day "Love and Mercy" came out, released "Kokomo," the Beach Boys' latest single. Elektra was spending much dough on promotion and MTV had it in heavy rotation. Several weeks earlier, Dr. Landy and I had taken an advance copy of "Kokomo" to Seymore Stein and Lenny Waronker. In order to compete, we asked to make a video, which our contract called for, and to have independent promotion.

"Don't worry," they both said. 'Love and Mercy' is a sure bet."

They never did release a video, and anybody will tell you that without a video you can't introduce a new artist, which as a solo artist I was. After everything, Warners and Sire didn't support the album the way they said they would. We believed them. That was a mistake.

In August 1988, I set out on a promotional tour of radio stations across the country, a throwback to the Beach Boys' earliest days. But then I hated the travel and the handshakes. On this tour, I savored the contact I made with people and enjoyed how much my music was a part of their lives.

Walking into radio stations in Chicago and New York, I was hit by a sense of belonging to a community I'd left behind.

At a party held at the Hard Rock Café in New York City, I was surprised by an unexpected fan, Joan Rivers. Dragged to the party by her daughter, Melissa, Joan and I hit it off. I'd always been attracted to blond women. She lived in California. Joan fit my image of a California Girl. In fact, I asked her to sit down beside me on the piano bench and then serenaded her with "California Girls." A few nights later, I saw her perform at a club.

The tabloids had a field day with us. *The National Enquirer* linked us romantically and ran our photos on the cover. We shared lots in common. Joan was recovering from the death of her longtime husband, Edgar, and I knew plenty about loss and pain. We had that in common. Joan's great, and we still keep in touch.

The tour was nonstop, a parade of images and emotions that I didn't want to lose. In my Detroit hotel room, I grabbed a notepad and jotted down a few thoughts on my comeback: "Having started at square one, I went through a hell of a lot of changes. I was in a headspin the whole way, but I'm proud at how I refused to allow my spooky thoughts to slow me down. I changed the channel in my head. I was involved in a heavyweight album and my will to succeed kept pushing me forward.

"I did what I thought was truly impossible, but it shows you what happens when you put your mind to something. The rewards of all that work have been made sweet by the chart position. However, the best feeling in the world for me is to do what I know best, which is music. God has given me a new start, and I'm most grateful."

At the end of September, with things exceedingly smooth, too smooth, in fact, I went to London to work the international press. I began the trip by showing up as the surprise guest to the Stomp Convention, a gathering of 300 to 400 Beach Boys fanatics. I strolled out on the dark stage and sat down at a piano. A spotlight cast a small circle of light on the keyboard. Then it broadened to reveal me. Someone screamed, "Oh my God, it's Brian!" and the place became unglued.

Screams are nice, but that people remember is even better. I opened by singing "Surfer Girl," giving the choruses a soft, spiritual feel, and then did "Love and Mercy" and "Nighttime." The crowd reacted with a tremendous outpouring of emotion. After nearly three decades of playing music, this might've been one of the most memorable ovations ever. I was onstage by myself. There was no one to lean on, nowhere to hide. Just me drinking up the love of appreciative fans.

The bubble was burst. Within several weeks, "Kokomo" was Number One—the Beach Boys' first Number One single since "Good Vibrations." The Beach Boys were beside themselves. I thought it was fucked.

Radio, which used to consume my songs the way I consumed coke, now had room for only one Beach Boys–sounding song, and mine wasn't it. While "Kokomo" soared, "Love and Mercy" disappeared from radio playlists across the country. The facts of life hurt a lot. Through good times and bad, I'd given the Beach Boys some of the most enduring songs in pop music history. I never left any of them out of a song.

We were flying to Spain. I still couldn't figure out the Beach Boys. The hurt from being left off "Kokomo" was slow to go away.

"It's an ego trip, isn't it?" I asked Dr. Landy.

"I mother-henned them for too many years, and now they have an opportunity to jump out from under my shadow, to sneak behind my back," I said.

"I don't know if they have what it takes." Dr. Landy, suffering a bad cold, smiled. "You cast a big shadow."

It was the middle of October 1988. The night sky was cloudy and dense, an impregnable soup. I looked out the plane window and saw nothing. That was exactly how I imagined the future. No landmarks. No boundaries. A slingshot ride into the unknown. It was gruesome or great, depending on your head. Either way, you rode your vehicle until it gave out.

"But I've been wracking my brain about why they did this to me," I continued. "Maybe because I did a solo album. But Mike, Dennis, and Carl all did solo albums. Al knew he couldn't do one. Maybe it's because you're my teacher and I'm unwilling to denounce you. But that's stupid. The guys all have their teachers and gurus. So what gives?"

"You tell me," said Dr. Landy.

"They're hypocrites," I said.

"I would've used a stronger word," said Dr. Landy. "But I guess that'll do."

Lying in bed that first night in Spain, I realized that the success of "Kokomo" had a more emotionally damaging effect on me than I'd thought. Surrounded by darkness, I couldn't prevent my mind from getting hung up on a lot of negative thoughts. By the next day, I was riddled with psychological bullet holes. Everything bothered me, from the sound of my voice to the way my hair crossed over my forehead to the limitations imposed by fear.

Though Dr. Landy's cold kept him down until late the next day, he caught up with me at rehearsal, noticed that I was too nervous to concentrate, and set out to dismantle the matrix of evil and weirdness I'd created. Like a coach giving a pep talk, Landy sat with me in a café in Ibiza and spoke for several hours, the same kind of back-and-forth that we'd started during the early days in Hawaii.

Eventually, he helped me realize that my entire career was one colossal—and mostly successful—effort at overcoming self-consciousness, insecurity, and fear, and there was no more dramatic evidence than my solo LP. I'd started at square one and fought one hell of a battle in getting eleven songs on an album, and a few excellent B sides. I'd been in a headspin most of the way. I'd battled creepy thoughts the entire time. I'd been down as far as a man could go without dying—yet I'd pushed forward.

If ever there was living proof of the old maxim "You can do anything if you put your mind to it," I was it.

That night I drew a psychic deep breath and entered into my journal this thought: "Life is a puzzle that needs constant figuring out."

True to my theory, the next day brought another problem—the weather. All day rain poured from the dark sky. Arriving at the Ibiza 92 venue, a prelude to the 1992 Olympics, I learned that because of the inclement weather the outdoor stage had been made much smaller than it had been in rehearsal, which bummed me out—but only temporarily. My spirits were buoyed by a determination to make up for the lackluster showing of "Love and Mercy" on the charts by performing it with greatness.

I gave Dr. Landy a thumbs-up sign as I climbed onstage and took my place at the piano. While noodling an improvised intro to "Love and Mercy," which allowed the band to make last-minute adjustments, I noticed several television cameras zeroing in on me from the side of the stage and suddenly remembered that the concert was being televised live to more than sixty countries around the world. It was a moment in which most people would've expected me to be unnerved. I rose to the occasion.

Most people spend a lifetime searching for an answer to the most elusive of questions, Why do I exist? and never find an answer. I'd spent virtually every day of my forty-six years mulling over that question. I wanted an explanation for why I'd endured so much pain and torture. I wanted a reason for my extraordinary talent. Fate and luck didn't suffice. There had to be an answer. I obsessed over it. I wanted to know. I was *desperate* to know.

I didn't see myself as any different from the people who couldn't find an answer. At least I didn't until I looked out at the crowd of people standing in the rain and stared into the TV cameras. In the time it took to draw my last deep breath before singing, I realized the answer to my question.

"Brian," I told myself, "you're going out to sixty countries, and this is the time to do the best living you can. Be alive and sing with the consciousness of God."

Forty-five minutes later I left the stage, feeling as if I'd accomplished exactly that. My performance didn't include the athleticism of Springsteen, the wit of Paul Simon, or the sophistication of Sting, but I knew I'd affected people with my music. I'd watched the crowd sing and dance and sway to the songs. I was sure that the people who watched from other countries were also moved. I'd felt a spiritual oneness with the audience.

I had the ability to touch people's souls in a positive way with the music I wrote, and that was what my life had been, and would continue to be, all about. If I hadn't been able to see that obvious fact before, I saw it clearly from onstage in Ibiza, Spain. To make sure that I wouldn't forget, I wrote a brief note later that night to myself. It said:

"Observations of life. A mother takes care of her baby. A man looks after his business. A performer takes care of his audience. An artist takes care of his art."

My problems didn't suddenly disappear, but from that day on I didn't have to ask myself why I'd been put on Earth.

47

"Water Builds Up"

*O*n September 19, 1989, I filed a lawsuit against A&M Records and Irving Almo Publishing and the law firm of Mitchell, Silberberg & Knupp to reclaim the copyrights to the dozens of songs my dad had sold in 1969. The suit was instigated after one of my attorneys, while supervising an audit of Irving Almo's books, requested copies of the songwriting agreements between me and Sea of Tunes, the only way to find out if the royalties I was being paid were correct. What he discovered instead was a paperwork mess.

A year earlier attorneys from Mitchell, Silberberg & Knupp, the firm representing Irving Almo, a subsidiary of A&M Records, replied. They said there weren't any songwriting agreements from Sea of Tunes other than a letter of transfer purportedly signed by me and dated August 20, 1969. The existence of songwriters' agreements should've been standard procedure. The fact that there weren't any caused Jim Tierney to investigate.

Without much effort, Tierney uncovered a number of curious revelations which led to the allegations in the lawsuit I filed, among them that the law firm of Mitchell, Silberberg & Knupp, which represented the Beach Boys at the time, failed to disclose that they were also legal counsel to Irving Almo; there were no receipts or documents showing that I received payment of any kind for either the sale or transfer of copyrights to Irving Almo; that my signature was forged to various papers including the 1969 letter of transfer; and that since I owned the copyrights for the songs in Sea of Tunes, my dad couldn't sell them without my consent.

As I alleged in my lawsuit, a month before the suit was filed, Irving Almo suddenly produced copies of the songwriters agreements it previously failed to produce. According to the 1969 letter that bore my dad's and my signatures, these agreements had all been executed "in accordance with normal practice in the publishing business." Clearly, though, that wasn't the case. There were a number of songs that were transferred to Sea of Tunes before they were even written. For example, according to the documents, "Caroline No" was transferred on May 1, 1962, but I didn't even write it until early 1966.

When Dr. Landy and I were going over this material prior to my filing the lawsuit, he asked me, "So what does all this make you think?"

"I think that the lawyers are right," I said. "There's a lot of funny business here. I think there's a case."

"A good case," Dr. Landy said.

"But there's one problem," I added suddenly.

"What's that?" he asked.

"I don't want anyone to be mad at me."*

In the months that followed, I acquired a golden retriever, purchased a two-story office building, and began remodeling it into a recording studio. I also spent December in Hawaii, where Gene, Alexandra, and I began writing songs for my second solo album. Working with Alexandra, one of the few women with whom I enjoyed a comfortable rapport, I opened up a little more than with other collaborators, perhaps because I wasn't threatened or competitive as often happened when I worked with guys or as frightened as I have been around other women. Alexandra became the sister I never had.

But most of my life was consumed by lawyers. The anguishing hours I spent with them were painful, unrelenting, and exhausting. Never did I think I'd understand the difference between a plaintiff and a defendant or a complaint and a deposition. However, by early 1990 I almost felt qualified to take the Legal Scholastic Aptitude exams.

The most interesting part of the process was that it forced me to play detective and investigate my own life, an odd experience in which I tried to reconstruct all the bleak, painful events I'd blacked out from memory.

---

*As this book is being written, the lawsuit is pending and the defendants are contesting my allegations.

The attorney referred to everything as "the facts," but reading over the legal briefs, a text as dry as desert sand, it was impossible to be dispassionate. The facts offered as evidence composed my life, nothing less than my flesh and blood.

In 1961 I'd formed the Beach Boys and written the hit song "Surfin'." In 1962 I'd put my name on my first professional recording contract with Capitol Records. That same year my dad set up Sea of Tunes Publishing Company, which made us 50 percent partners in the publishing company but stipulated that I would own 100 percent of the copyrights. In 1969 my dad sold Sea of Tunes, then a corporation, for $700,000. By then I was incapacitated, mentally ill, a casualty of drug abuse.

"This is tough stuff," my attorney said after one eight-hour day of questioning in his office. "How're you holding up?"

"You know, when I was little, my dad took out his glass eye and made me look into his empty socket," I said. "It was disgusting, red, and scarred. It fucked me up for the rest of my life, you know?"

He nodded.

"Compared to that shit, this isn't so bad," I mused.

"Think about how nice it would be to get your songs back if we win this case." He grinned.

I did, and it was a nice thought.

The first time I walked into my new studio I felt a strange sense of déjà vu. It was late February 1990, and renovations on the building I'd bought weren't completed yet. But the forty-eight-track recording studio Gene and I had designed and built to work on my new album, and subsequent ones, was finished. I found myself giddy with excitement. For the first time since the Beach Boys owned Brother Studios in the mid-1970s, I had a studio where I could go and work at any hour of the day.

It was close to noon, and workmen were trudging through the rooms with equipment. I went immediately into the little soundproof room where I'd put the grand and an upright Young Chang piano and closed the door. The light was off, which made it darker than night and quieter than a deserted island. I started to play; the room overflowed with music. It was dense with sound. The chord changes lingered above me, hanging close to the ceiling like billowy clouds.

I'd worried about spending the money to buy the building, but it suddenly became clear that I hadn't made just a good investment. I now had a place where I could go and, like the song I had written nearly thirty years earlier said, "tell my secrets to." I had a sanctuary from the world that had so perplexed and troubled me. My room. My womb. I played for hours that afternoon, played and discovered the room's acoustics, an exercise which was, for me, an exploration through the emotion-packed folds of my brain.

Barely a day has passed since that February afternoon when I don't seal myself off in that room, turn off the light, and pound away at the piano. It's like taking medicine or drinking a rejuvenating elixir. If I don't play the piano or write a song at least once a day, I don't feel right. I didn't play or write during those years I spent in my bedroom and snorted cocaine, and that was as good as being dead. Given a choice, I prefer a good shuffle to death.

Gene, Alexandra Morgan, and I had been writing songs like mad in preparation for my second solo album. Given the disappointing sales of my first LP, though, and the fact that my forty-eighth birthday was only four months off, I doubted whether I could still make music that mattered. Was I too old to rock and roll? I spent many a tortured day searching for an answer, until I realized that my question was like a Zen riddle.

I asked myself, What was it about rock and roll that made it such an important part of people's lives? What made it so important to my life?

The problem worked itself out for me in the place where I did my best thinking—at the piano.

The more I labored in the new studio, the more I realized that, like any good music, rock and roll's most powerful attraction is its ability to liberate the soul. If the groove was good and the moment was right, rock and roll freed you from the world. At least that's how it had affected me at age sixteen, at age twenty-five, at thirty, and it still had that effect on me in my late forties. That thought alone convinced me that what I had to offer was still viable.

There was just one problem. There always seemed to be at least one problem.

Seymore Stein and Lenny Waronker, Warners and Sire Records' presidents, didn't want to shell out any money for my second solo even though my contract was for two albums. They were still reeling from the migraine headaches the first one generated as well as its $1 million bill. That was beside the point. My contract stipulated that if my first record sold more than 250,000 copies, which it had, they had to pick up my option.

Several weeks passed during which my lawyers and the record company's lawyers were like sharks in a feeding frenzy. I was discouraged by how miserable the record business had become for me.

"It's not like the old days," I moaned to Gene one afternoon when I was supposed to be working on basic tracks for a song called "Someone to Love" but couldn't concentrate.

He knew what I was talking about.

"I discovered George Benson and took him into the studio to cut his first single," said Dr. Landy. "He was just a kid on the corner, playing a ukulele. Now you need a team of fucking lawyers, agents, managers, accountants, psychics, nutritionists, and a dozen other people just to sneeze in a studio."

"You know what bugs me, Gene?" I said. "When the Beach Boys were starting out, we made an album in a couple of weeks. We played the instruments live on four-track, I lined the guys up around a single mike. Boom-boom. That was it. And those goddamn things sold millions of copies! What we have to go through now, I don't know if it's worth it."

The upshot of that conversation was Gene and I both realized that we didn't have to go through all that annoying bureaucratic bullshit on my second solo. We had our own studio now. We could record when we wanted, hire whom we wanted, essentially make an album that we liked without consulting anyone. It was damn exciting to think that way. I almost felt like a kid walking off the street into Western in the early sixties, a song under my arm and a point I needed to prove.

Seymore's and Lenny's actions and reticence told us they didn't want to work with us, either. So Gene sent a note to them, saying that we'd deliver a completed album between six to ten months from then. They agreed.

It was a clean break, and, I thought, a good one, though it wasn't the most political move we could've made. But record making is risky business. Sometimes you have to throw caution to the wind and say, "What the fuck."

"Fortunately, I have my health," I said to Gene and Alexandra one night at the studio as we struggled through "Water Builds Up," a song we'd written about anger.

It was the third day of May 1990. I'd gone for a three-mile run along the beach that morning, spent the afternoon with my psychiatrist discussing my disturbing estrangement from the Beach Boys and my family, talked to my mother about getting some pictures from her of me as a child, and polished off a sushi dinner earlier in the evening. Midnight had come and gone, and I was still going strong.

"Can you imagine what it would be like working this hard and not feeling one hundred percent?" I asked.

"I can imagine," said Dr. Landy. "I remember when you weren't healthy."

I didn't like to dwell too much on the process of making an album as much as I preferred to just jump in and do it. I shouldered a tremendous burden whenever I entered the studio—my past. Expectations ran extremely high. My only aim was to make good, spiritual music, but everybody else judged what I did against once-in-a-lifetime songs like "Good Vibrations" and "Help Me, Rhonda," which I would've loved to duplicate if there was some kind of blueprint for writing classics.

There isn't. Inspiration is fleeting. It comes and it goes and you hope to God you're paying attention whenever it comes a-knocking.

Between Gene, Alexandra, and myself, I felt as if we were on a pretty good creative roll. As a collaborator, Alexandra wrote lyrics that mirrored exactly what I wanted to be saying. Additionally, her one-act play, *Daughter DeLuxe,* had just won a drama award in L.A. So I felt confident the work we were doing was on the right track.

The hardest part was chosing which songs to work on. Gene and I pared a collection of sixty songs, collaborations between the three of us, down to a more manageable fifteen selections. With the basic tracks to most of the songs already on tape, we were working on lyrics, which was what we were doing on "Water Builds Up."

"I can't believe that I'm going to have another solo album," I thought out loud. "I mean, when I think about it, I'm completely blown away. You know, the Beach Boys had a Number One with 'Kokomo,' but they haven't put out an album since nineteen-eighty-nine. Even then they had to use some of my old songs, which killed Mike. That's goddamn amazing. It makes me wonder why they won't let us help them produce an album."

"We've offered, Brian," Gene said. "You know we have. Too many times to remember. It's their egos."

"You're right, Gene," I said. "They're too insecure to let us produce. That would be way too heavy for Mike's ego. Whenever they think they can do it by themselves, they like to reject me. But, Gene, I don't understand why they keep turning out such tired retreads like 'Still Crusin'.' "

Even that ended. The 1987 LP was the last one the Beach Boys put out. Even after "Kokomo" went Number One, the band couldn't get a record deal unless I was writing and producing the material. Interestingly, Gene and I offered to do just that. But the guys asked me to make demos and submit them for their approval. No way. I'd write, make tracks, then have them come in and sing. It was the original formula or nothing.

In many respects, the Beach Boys' negative feelings toward me hadn't changed a single iota from when I decided to quit touring in 1964, except they resented me even more because I was now keeping the songs I wrote for myself.

I've never lost hope for a reconciliation. I've always figured we'll reach a truce some day, hopefully before we get too old to carry a decent tune.

On May 5, 1990, my optimism was put to its most severe test ever. It was a Saturday. That morning Gene received some alarming news when a reporter friend informed him of a press conference scheduled the following Monday afternoon, May 7, at the Greater Los Angeles Press Club. My cousin and former bodyguard, Stan Love, was announcing he'd filed suit in court that morning to have himself appointed my conservator. As soon as Gene told me, I began to panic. I asked for an explanation.

"It seems they're out to get you," said Gene. "Stan Love thinks he should control your life."

"Can he do that?" I asked.

"Sure. Anybody can petition for conservatorship."

"Are the Beach Boys behind this?"

"That remains to be seen. In the meantime, I think you should get packed. The Beach Boys are playing in Oakland tonight and you're going up. You and Kevin. And we'll have your attorney go too."

"Why my lawyer?" I asked.

"Years ago people carried guns into fights," he explained. "Nowadays, they take lawyers. I'll talk to you."

The entire flight to San Francisco I wrestled with the hell I seemed to be in. One hour I was working on my album, trying to be creative, the next hour I found myself gripped by fear and unable to control the terror of existence. There was no peace. Turmoil inside and out. If I closed my eyes I heard voices and saw apparitions. I faced the evil of my family. And why? Because I'd started a band and had written songs that made millions of dollars.

No, no, no!

That's not what I'd wanted, I told myself.

All I'd ever wanted was to write songs, which gave me peace of mind.

But I'd created a monster instead. I felt as if I'd traded my soul to the devil in exchange for the ability to create beautiful music in the voice of God. I hadn't, of course. But that's the way I felt.

By the time I strode into the backstage area of the Circle Theater in

Oakland, I'd talked to Gene and he'd informed me that, from what he'd been able to learn, the Beach Boys said they were not involved in the conservatorship matter. Carl and Al claimed surprise, and Mike refused comment on the situation. But neither of us believed any of them.

I hadn't seen the guys for several months, so I didn't know what kind of reaction to expect. I hoped warm. I was disappointed. I should've trusted my instinct. Entering the dressing room, I saw Carl talking to his wife, Gina, the daughter of entertainer Dean Martin. Glancing up at me, Carl quickly turned away, then moments later got up and left the room, avoiding any chance of a confrontation. We didn't see each other again until we walked onstage.

Mike and Al were involved in conversations, though when I caught them watching me I decided to act boldly and approach them first. Al shifted his weight from one foot to the other, nervously asking how I was doing, how my album was coming along. He reminded me of "Loop De Loop," a song we had started to write in the mid-1970s but never finished.

"Say, Brian," he then said in a mocking smart-ass tone of voice, "what are you doing here?"

"I came to work," I said. "I'm going to perform."

"With the Beach Boys?" he asked sarcastically.

"That's my job, Al," I said. "I'm going to sing."

"You aren't going to embarrass us tonight, are you?" he asked. "I mean, don't sing as if you were a lounge act in Vegas. Know what I mean?"

"Sure, Al," I said. "I know what you mean. But I'll never embarrass you as much as Mike did at the Rock and Roll Hall of Fame."

"Where's Gene?" he asked.

"He's not here," I said. "I don't know where he is. I manage myself without him quite nicely."

Then Mike sauntered up in white pants and a flowered print shirt. He stood inches from me, knowing that the closer he got the more frightened I became that he'd throw a punch or try to hurt me in some way.

I understood that Mike enjoyed being a physical threat.

"Hi, Brian," he said in his smarmy, whisperlike voice.

"Hello, Mike," I replied.

He looked me up and down slowly, sizing me up in a creepy, condescending manner. He fixated on my shoes—stodgy, conservative black lace-ups.

"Those are the most hideous shoes I've ever seen," he said, flashing an evil grin.

I didn't know how to reply, and Mike turned away and slipped out of the room before I could think of something. Gene was right, I supposed. Around these guys I was a sponge who absorbed the punishment without fighting back. I didn't know how to fight. It wasn't in me. If they had wanted to make me feel like shit, they'd succeeded. It had taken minutes.

I wish I'd had the balls to tell them off. The proper thing would've been to remind Mike that if not for me, he'd still be pumping gas, Al that he'd be a medical supply salesman, and Carl that he'd be running errands for me. If the Beach Boys had come along twenty-five years later, I probably would've been a solo artist, like Prince, a guy who could write, play, produce, and sing all by himself. The hell with the rest of them.

But that wasn't the way it had worked out.

We did two uninspired shows that night. Nobody said a word to me about Stan Love or anything else. I didn't bring up anything with them, either. But I knew even though they denied it.

On the plane back to L.A. that night, I was unsettled by the Beach Boys' ragged musicianship. The songs should've filled the small theater up with a richness of sound, the harmonies should've soared, the texture of the music should've invoked a stirring sense of a time when cars and girls were all that mattered and life itself was simple.

A Beach Boys show should be a good time. But the guys were flat, and I didn't feel as if anything carried past the first row. It made me think of a radical idea I'd raised in meetings several times—hiring younger musicians to sing the songs. The music was youthful. Why not the singers? But the idea was always vetoed. The guys understood that if they let it happen, they'd be forgotten in lieu of the music, and I'd be remembered as the one who'd written the songs.

There was one bright spot to the performance, but even that almost didn't happen. It was the anniversary of my father's death. I suggested to Carl we sing "Their Hearts Were Full of Spring," a Four Freshmen song that had been a favorite of mine and my dad's. Carl didn't want to. Not without rehearsing the band. I argued that we could do it a cappella.

"We don't know it," Carl said.

"I'll get everyone together," I said, "and I'll teach it to you."

For once I stood up. And I made it happen.

I told Gene about it the next morning. I also mentioned that no one had spoken about the conservatorship suit to me. He had found out that the Beach Boys had met with Stan the previous week between shows in San Diego. The Beach Boys were playing it cagey as usual. They might've been claiming neutrality, but we figured it was only because they weren't about to support Stan before they knew whether or not he had a chance to win. No sense betting on a team you know is going to lose before the game even starts.

Although I was extremely anxious, I was too mad to allow myself to come unglued. Wanting to underscore my good health, I flew back to San Francisco that night, Sunday, for another show. The Beach Boys were playing a private show at the Cow Palace and I wanted to prove to everyone that I was anything but incompetent. For the first hour or so, Mike, Al, and Carl avoided me like the plague.

Then I decided to take action. I found Carl in his dressing room and asked if he wanted to talk about what was going on.

"I can't, Brian," he said. "I've got to take care of some business I've got going in Colorado."

"You have to do that right now?" I asked.

"I've been planning to make a few calls," he said. "I guess that's what I'm going to do. I'll catch you later."

It was clear they were shutting me out. I don't know why I expected anything more.

48

Family Fighting

I
t was close to 1:00 A.M. when I settled into the back of the limo that picked me up at LAX. At that hour, the freeway was empty and it didn't take long before the driver was speeding along the Pacific Coast Highway, heading toward Malibu. It was a clear night, and I saw the moon's reflection spread across the waves like streaks of yellow paint. The sky was deep, full of twinkling stars, and through the limo's skylight I could see all the way to infinity. My family, my band, my friends had turned against me. Staring up at the enormity of the universe, I suddenly felt quite small and very much alone.

I didn't sleep well that night. Later that morning, I made a call to Gene.

"We have to fight, Gene," I said.

"You bet your ass you have to fight," he responded. "Are you going to let that son of a bitch get away with saying you need a conservator?"

Stan's press conference was scheduled to begin at 2:00 P.M. at the Greater L.A. Press Club. Although it was supposed to have surprised us, by noon we had gotten an advance copy of both the statement he was going to read and the conservatorship petition his attorney had filed in L.A. County Superior Court that morning. It didn't make us feel good.

Stan claimed I was incompetent to care for myself. In his petition, he alleged that I was unable to provide for the most basic personal needs, including physical health, clothing, shelter, and food. He also claimed I was unable to take care of my finances. But the crux of his case centered around the allegation that I was unable to resist undue influence or fraud, a direct assault upon by relationship with Gene, who, Stan charged, had "brainwashed" me.

Sitting in the studio, where we should've been working on my album instead of sifting through legal documents and statements full of lies, I considered a counterattack. Stan needed to be discredited, and we could do this by revealing him as the same ex-bodyguard who dealt with my drug and psychological problems by threatening to beat me up, bribing me with cigarettes, who covered up his partner's affair with my ex-wife, and who Marilyn finally had to tell to stay away or she'd call the police.

At two-twenty, I sat in the front seat of my car outside the Greater L.A. Press Club, studying the statement I had written half an hour earlier. In a tiny briefing room a few steps away, Stan and his attorney were standing in front of two dozen print and television reporters. "The first thing we want to make clear," Stan's attorney said, reading from a prepared statement, "is that this petition does not claim that Brian Wilson is crazy. This petition is filed soley for the benefit of Brian Wilson."

What was that benefit? A few minutes later, the short, suntanned lawyer explained.

"We hope that in a short space of time, we will make some positive moves toward assisting Brian to become a productive member of the Beach Boys family again . . . Stan Love has had considerable discussion with Mike Love, who is anxious to be cowriting songs again with Brian . . ."

Naturally. What could be better for me than to be writing songs with Mike again? It had nearly killed me several times before. If the judge ruled in Stan's favor, perhaps they could finish the job this time.

Then Stan got up to speak. Wearing a gray business suit, he walked confidently to the podium and ran down his list of allegations about my competency. He also detailed his agenda of treatment, which included setting up a household in which I'd live while he oversaw a program designed specially for my personal care. Hadn't he done that before? With Rocky and Steve Korthof? Stan also said he missed playing basketball with me. He complained that his numerous phone calls over the years went unreturned. Beyond that, he claimed he missed his cousin.

Stan also charged that Dr. Landy prevented me from having a relationship with Marilyn, my daughters, Carnie and Wendy, and, of course, my cousin Mike. Stan finished up by expressing his hope that one day soon I'd be back writing songs with Mike just as we did when the Beach Boys were turning out hit after hit.

Was I the one who needed therapy or was everyone else in need of treatment? It seemed that Stan and whoever was backing him were all suffering from delusion and denial. Marilyn and I had been divorced for more than a decade; there wasn't any law that said I had to see my ex-wife. My children knew how I felt about being a dad; I'd told them personally. Mike would get the help he needed by signing up for piano lessons or learning how to play an instrument.

Stan looked quite satisfied when he finished, like a peacock displaying his feathers. Then he asked for questions. Hands shot up. He was in the middle of answering one of them when, suddenly, a look of shock flashed across his face. Noise from a small commotion in the back of the room caused all the reporters to turn around. Then the cameras jostled. Finally, Stan realized what was going on, then raised his long arms into the air in astonishment and exclaimed, "There! There in the back of the room is my cousin!"

Too late. Almost everyone knew. Those who didn't whipped around and saw me standing in front of the door. The surprise worked perfectly.

"I haven't seen him for years," Stan sighed, futilely trying to regain everyone's attention.

At that moment, twenty-nine years of performing experience paid off. I stood in place for several moments, allowing the photographers and television cameras to get a good look at me in my double-breasted Armani blazer, slim, in control, healthy, and calm. I didn't smile; it wasn't a situation that called for a happy face. I'm certain I didn't look like a man who couldn't care for himself.

A path was then cleared and I walked to the podium. Staring at the roomful of surprised reporters, cameras flashing in my eyes, a dozen television cameras bearing down, I put on my glasses and unfolded a brief statement. In a matter-of-fact tone that covered up my anger, I stated I'd "never felt better, never been healthier, and I've never been happier. I take care of myself, make my own decisions, and live an independent life." I hoped the message was getting through. "Do I look like I need a conservator?" I asked.

Less than two years before, I'd released a solo album and had been interviewed and profiled by virtually every magazine in the country. I'd spent time with dozens of reporters. Surely, if I was crazy or incompetent, that would've come out already. I felt silly having to make such a public statement.

"Brian, will you answer any questions?" a reporter asked.

"No, I'm sorry," I said. "I don't think there's any more to say."

There was a chorus of "But!" Reporters yelled my name, trying to catch my attention. I'd said my piece. I just wanted to split. The pathway I'd followed up to the front of the room was now blocked. The room was congested. People were crowding toward me. I motioned to the bodyguard I'd brought along as protection. I wanted him to come up and get me out. Even he had trouble.

As I waited, a pleasant-looking female reporter thrust her tape recorder in my face and asked what I thought of this situation.

"Honestly?" I asked.

"Yes," she said seriously.

"I think it's really fucked," I said. "That's what I think about it."

I felt strong. I was fighting for myself for the first time, not just giving in.

49

Sweet Insanity

I'm used to fighting. An abused child, I turned myself into a boy wonder piano player and wrote the Beach Boys into rock and roll's Hall of Fame. Dismissed for years as a drugged-out psycho, I spent five years struggling back to good health. At a time when critics wrote me off as a relic, I put out a solo record that evidenced my return to form at forty-five years old. In May 1990, when my cousin Stan decided to challenge my competency in a court of law, I was left with only one option.

Fight.

Ironically, eight weeks after Stan filed suit, I received a letter from the Beach Boys requesting that I join them on tour for a week around July 4. Mike was spending a week at a TM convention in Iowa, studying how to levitate—yes, levitate—and during that period the band was contractually obligated to produce four Beach Boys onstage. Although my brother and cousin alleged that I was incompetent and brainwashed, suddenly, with money at stake, I wasn't too incompetent or brainwashed to help them out.

Assuring Gene that I'd be just fine on the road without him, I joined the Beach Boys in Calgary, Canada, for the first of ten shows. I had a good time onstage and between shows. I visited museums, including a Salvador Dalí retrospective. I even exercised with Paula Abdul, who was staying at the same hotel. My brother Carl, on the other hand, stayed in his room and drank. I felt like asking him if he needed a conservator.

Late one night at the hotel in Montreal, I commandeered a piano behind the stage of an empty banquet room. With Bruce Johnston and actor John Stamos sitting in with the Beach Boys on drums, I ran through what seemed like every song written. I played Spector, Elvis, the Beatles, and even the Beach Boys, including rarities like "Sherry, She Needs Me," "Wild Honey," "Little Honda," and "Honkin' Down the Highway."

The scene was reminiscent of the old days. Neither Bruce nor I could remember the last time that I'd sat around a piano with any of the guys. He kept remarking how energetic and together I was. Bruce goaded me into playing one song after another, then told me how he'd love to find a symphony orchestra to perform the entire *Pet Sounds* album. At one point, he sat down at the piano and began playing "Lara's Theme."

"Isn't that from a soap opera?" I asked.

"Yeah," he said. "But listen to this. I remember once I went over to your Bel Air house. You weren't there. But I walked in and there was Carnie, at the piano, playing this song. She was about seven years old."

"Did you say she was seven inches high?" I asked, not hearing him clearly.

"No, no," Bruce laughed. "She was seven years old. But Carnie was playing this song. Slowly, methodically. She turned to me and, without missing a beat, said, 'You know, Bruce, my daddy owns the Beach Boys.' "

Laughing, I supposed it was true. But the times had changed since then.

The Number One single that first week of July belonged to my daughters' group, Wilson Phillips. Earlier that day, Bruce had showed me a copy of the latest *Billboard,* the first time I'd seen their name atop the charts.

"Well, I'll be goddamned!" I exclaimed.

"That's terrific," Bruce said.

"It freaks me out." I laughed.

Caught between joy and jealousy, I've followed Carnie and Wendy as closely as anyone. As soon as their LP hit the stores, I bought a copy. I took it home and stared at the cover for hours before listening to a single cut. When I finally played it, I knew right off that the first two singles, "Hold On" and "Release Me," were knockouts. The songs were good, but the voices had a special quality.

From then on, I opened up *Billboard* every week and followed their progress, remembering what I went through thirty years earlier when my first songs were charting. I watched the girls on MTV and swelled with pride.

Despite our relationship, or lack of one, their music let me believe that

I wasn't a complete failure as a father. They'd inherited music. The love of music. A talent for making beautiful music. The voices for harmony. For me, music is like beauty or happiness or love. I couldn't have given them anything greater than that.

In Montreal, the Beach Boys headlined a lineup at an outdoor festival located about a two-hour bus ride outside the city. Being so far north, the sun was still shining at 9:00 P.M. The stage was beside a lake. People were barbecuing, the tantalizing smell of grilled hamburgers and hot dogs wafting up to the stage. The atmosphere, made for the Beach Boys' music, infused the band's playing with a nice warmth, and as I stood in front of the stage and sang "Wouldn't It Be Nice," I knew I was in one of those bubbles in time, a moment that was perfect.

Like all bubbles though, it popped. On the ride back to the hotel, I asked Carl if he had time later to come up to my room and talk for a few minutes. The request stunned him. He looked petrified and gave Gina a questioning look.

"What do you want to talk about?" he asked.

"Good vibrations," I said, referring to the song and not our poor relationship.

"Yeah, I'll come up, I guess," said Carl with a reluctance I couldn't miss.

A half hour after we got back to the hotel, Carl phoned my room and said he was coming up. I left the door open and several minutes later he wandered in, looking left and right suspiciously. I had a suite, and my brother found me in the living room, stretched out on the sofa, in my pajamas. He still had on the clothes he'd worn onstage.

"Hey, Bri," he said, sitting down in the chair opposite me.

"Look, I'm not going to ask you anything about the conservatorship thing," I said. "That's not why I asked you to come up here."

"Good," said Carl. "Because, honestly, Brian, I don't know where I stand on that issue."

It was the perfect opportunity for me to press the issue. After all, I was in Montreal. Dr. Landy was in L.A. I was performing on my own, making my own decisions, even venturing out to art museums and restaurants while Carl was holed up in his room, avoiding the outside world, still drinkingly heavily, blind to his own problems. Yet I was the one who needed a conservator? I should've asked Carl about that. But I didn't.

Even though he hated Gene, I knew he was telling the truth. He still hadn't decided where he stood on the conservatorship issue. But then Carl had trouble making even the simplest decisions. He had always needed to consult with numerous people—his wife, lawyers, his spiritual master, John Rogers.

"I just wanted to say hi, you know," I said. "I don't see you that much. We don't really talk. I just felt like I wanted to see how you're doing."

"Pretty good," said Carl, who was so uptight his arms and legs were crossed, like he was tied up in a knot.

"Gina looks nice. How are the kids?"

"They're good," he said. "Jonah saw Wendy and Carnie recently, and they're doing real good."

"Yeah." I nodded. "Do you want to ask me any questions?"

"No. No," he said, caught off guard. "No, you look pretty good. In good shape."

"I run and work out," I said. "I try to do three to five miles every day. And you?"

"I was on the bike this morning," he replied. "You know, you're nothing if you don't have your health."

"But you still got a big belly," I said, trying out a bit of honesty.

"A couple extra pounds," he said, shifting uncomfortably.

"It looks like twenty-five, maybe thirty pounds," I said.

"So did you want anything specific," said Carl, changing the subject. "On the bus, you said something about 'Good Vibrations.' "

"Oh yeah," I remembered. "I was thinking that it might be nice if the band played 'Good Vibrations' real slow. Slowed it down, since it's real fast the way you play it now, and that way you'd turn it into a real message song. A real spiritual song, which it is. I mean, good vibrations is really a powerful message to send out to people. What do you think?"

"I don't know," he said. "I'd have to sleep on it."

"I was also thinking how we could liven up the show. Maybe take out the medley of car songs and oldies. Mike does that corny, fifteen-minute routine beforehand, which takes away any momentum and undercuts whatever viability the band still has. It's stupid. And it has nothing to do with the music. The Beach Boys started with music. If there's going to be a future, it's going to be with music, not a monologue. Maybe we could add some rarities like "Little Honda" and "Girl Don't Tell Me." Maybe we could even come up with some new stuff."

"Gee, Brian," said Carl, who by that time had risen from his chair and begun pacing, "I don't know. That would take rehearsal, some real work, and I don't know if we have the time. Everyone has things to do. You know how it is."

"Yeah, yeah," I said. "It was just an idea."

I could tell that he wanted to leave. I was much too direct and honest for his taste.

"Hey, Carl," I said. "Before you go, I wanted to ask you a question."

"What?"

"Well, I'm writing my autobiography," I explained. "My life story."

"That's great, Brian," he smiled. "You've certainly had quite a life."

"Well, it's not done yet, thank God for that. But I wanted to know if you would talk to the guy who's helping me write it. Tell him about when we were kids. How Dad used to beat the crap out of me. And about when I was all fucked up. Stuff like that. I think it might be interesting. For me, I know, it's been like a detective story, uncovering everything I did."

Carl paused and scratched his beard. He gave the proposal a moment of thought. I saw his answer in his eyes. He was too chicken.

"You know what, Brian," he said. "Let me talk to my lawyer first. I'll get back to you. Okay? Have a good sleep."

Then he was out the door.

Six and a half months passed before I heard from or spoke to Carl again. It was January 1991, and he was giving his deposition in the conservatorship suit Stan had filed against me. By then, Carl had decided to throw his support and money behind Stan. Unbelievable! My own brother taking the same side with that jerk. Carl and I said a strained hello in the attorney's office right before the questioning started, and both of our lawyers immediately went on record as objecting to that brief and simple exchange.

Gene and I got the same type of reception from Seymore Stein and Lenny Waronker when we played the Warner execs an unmixed version of my second solo album. Before they even heard a single note of music, they were disposed not to like it. As they listened, I knew that we weren't getting a fair reading. It was obvious Seymore and Lenny didn't care about the music. They didn't appreciate me. They were more concerned with politics and credits, everything but the music.

"The music is okay," Lenny said. "The lyrics are horrible. I can't stand them."

"But I like 'em," I replied. "I think they're great. They say exactly what I feel."

"I want you to redo them," he said. "I think you need to redo all the lyrics. I particularly hate the song"—he shuffled through the lyric sheets—

"what do you call it, the song called 'Brian.' That's painful."

He hit the play button on his tape machine, and the song came out:

> All my life I've been running scared
> Feeling shut out, no one cared
> Not my mother, not my brother
> Crazy beatings by my father
> Ah-ouuu.
>
> Music's been my saving grace
> Been my ticket to a better place
> Brought me riches, brought me fame
> Many people know my name
> Ah-ouuu.
>
> My old friends who knew me when say
> Brian, you've come a long, long way
> Thank you, thank you.
>
> My cousins say I ain't the same
> Criticize I've changed my game
> They're not happy, 'cause I'm different
> More creative, independent
> Ah-ouuu.
>
> I've decided to change and grow
> Face the new and release the old
> Those who love me, they know I'm trying
> Living brave, instead of dying
> Ah-ouuu.

"That hurts," said Lenny. "It's painful to listen to."

"It was worse to live," I replied.

"I don't want you to even think about putting 'Smart Girls' on the album," he continued.

I knew he wouldn't like my rap song. Like most executives, Lenny was against any type of risk, and "Smart Girls," a prowomen rap song written as a humorous send-up of all the old Beach Boys' songs that championed the dumb-blonde stereotype, was very much a risk. But my whole career was about taking chances, trying something different, which was how the song came to be in the first place.

One day Alexandra Morgan and I had happened to turn on MTV's "Yo Rap" show. After tuning in several days in a row, Alexandra remarked that all the rap songs seemed to put women down. They were demeaning. I agreed and said we should try to write a positive rap. Maybe that's why Lenny said it didn't sound like an authentic rap song.

In any event, Gene and I explained that we weren't trying to make an authentic rap song. Neither of us exactly had the credentials to do that. We were just trying to make a statement and have a laugh at my past in the context of a rap song.

"So what?" Waronker said.

"I don't think you see Brian as he is," Gene said. "Like most people, you see him the way you want to see him. That's not unusual. Many people have problems seeing change."

By mid-December, the album remained in limbo while I entered lawyer hell, spending every day with attorneys who either prepared me for depositions in my lawsuit against A&M or briefed me on the conservatorship case. The days were excruciating. I thought acid fucked up my mind, until I spent my tenth eight-hour day with an attorney. That was truly mind-addling. It was difficult to fight a corporation. It was even harder to fight my family.

Stan now had unanimous support. My entire family had turned against me—Mike, Marilyn, Carnie, Wendy, my mother, and especially Carl, who had taken over from Stan behind the scenes and was exerting whatever muscle he had. I felt alone, estranged, a tiny balloon floating in the sky, waiting to pop. With attorney's fees approaching the total of what it cost to record all the Beach Boys' albums in the sixties, I implored Gene to find some way to stop this craziness.

Communication between the various camps was virtually nil. Still, Gene fired off a letter-cum-birthday-greeting to Carl:

"The purpose of this letter, at this time and especially this season, is to attempt to avert what I perceive as a negative and destructive collision between two brothers," Gene wrote. "I personally know all the family and both of the brothers Wilson and I cannot believe that either of you wants to hurt the other, yet that is what's happening.

"Therefore, I take it upon myself to attempt what's [been impossible] to do, and that is to personally invite you and anyone you might wish to bring, perhaps other family members, or John Rogers, to sit face to face with Brian and anyone he might wish to bring in an attempt to start some form of communication that will halt what appears to be the Wilson family equivalent to the crisis in the Gulf."

There was no response. A week later Gene penned another letter to my brother. It expressed surprise, consternation, and the facts:

"Over the last five years every invitation Brian has extended to come to his home has been rejected by every member of the family. Carl, you refused two of his invitations; Brian's children refused lunches, dinners, and Thanksgiving dinner at his home; and your mother was never feeling well enough to accept several invitations to come to dinner, despite Brian's offer to send a limo to pick her up . . ."

As before, there was no response.

Fed up, I continued working with my attorneys and thinking about the album, while Gene and Alexandra spent the days after Christmas and New Year's in Hawaii, getting away from the intensity of finishing the album. Alexandra called from Hawaii to tell me that her book of short stories had just won an award from the University of Southern California. Delighted by hearing good news for a change, I promised to celebrate when they returned to the mainland.

Three weeks later, Gene, Alexandra, and I reconvened at the studio, refreshed. The three of us had spent enough time away from the album to bring a new outlook to the project. Perspective. Anxiously, I settled back on the couch while Gene put a cassette in the DAT player and punched the play button. None of us said a word until the entire album had finished, and even then it took several minutes to break the silence.

"I'd like to change a few things," I said finally. "There are a few lines that can be improved."

"There're a couple of lyrics I want to tighten up," Alexandra added.

"I agree," Gene said. "With both of you. How's that?"

"And then we're done," I said.

"It's a beautiful album," Alexandra said. "Congratulations, Brian."

"You bet," Gene said emphatically. "To hell with all the opinions. We're the writers, the producers, and the artists. If we like it, that's what counts."

"This time, I agree with you." I smiled.

"You know what, Brian?" he said. "In the context of what's going on in the world today, we've got to remember this: It's only rock and roll. It's not life or death."

"No, Gene, by God it's not," I said. "When it comes to life and death, we've already earned our gold albums."

50

Wouldn't It Be Nice

*I*t was one of those moments. Gene and I had each put in a long day. Work on the album. Consultations with various attorneys. It was nonstop. Finally, around midnight, we were in the studio, packing up. For the first time since eight-thirty that day, we were alone. The phone wasn't going to ring. We weren't going to do any more work. Although we still had a lot on our minds, it was quiet. Both of us sat back and gave a weary sigh of relief.

"What's going to happen?" I asked. "I want to know what's going to happen to me. To us. To you and me, Gene."

"You want to know what's going to happen to you and to me?" Gene asked rhetorically. "You *really* want to know what's going to happen? I want to know what's going to happen too. But you know what? Nobody knows. Nobody knows what's going to happen to either one of us.

"But we can guess. We can make a fairly educated guess, I think. I mean, based on what's going on and how much it costs to fuel an army of lawyers, I think we can make a fairly accurate guess and say that someday, perhaps in the not too distant future, you and I will no longer be partners. Not in music. Not in business. Not in life."

"We'll always be connected, Gene," I interrupted. "We'll be connected spiritually no matter what."

"Right," he said. "But make no bones about it. You and I will go our separate ways. We will do our separate work. But until that day, it is your job to make you strong enough to stand up for yourself. Your goal is to make Brian Wilson strong enough to look into Mike Love's eyes and say what you've been too frightened to say but have wanted to say to him for years: 'Fuck you.' And to Carl: 'Fuck you.' Then, Brian, you will be emotionally free to do whatever it is that you want to do."

I hated hearing what Gene said, but I knew every word was true. I couldn't think of a reply. Nothing I thought of made any sense. At least nothing I thought of *saying* made any sense.

Then I thought of a way to respond in which I didn't have to say anything. I would show Gene how strong I was. I would prove it in a way that made sense to me.

I'd heard of the Monday night jams at the China Club, a small nightclub in Hollywood. Elton John, Bruce Springsteen, Sting, John Fogerty, and Little Richard, among others, had all made surprise appearances on Mondays and cranked out old-fashioned, no frills rock and roll. My turn was going to come on January 28.

The Friday before I jotted down the list of songs I wanted to play: "Surfer Girl," "California Girls," "Johnny B. Goode," "Be My Baby," "Good Vibrations," "Melt Away," "You've Lost that Lovin' Feelin'," "Help Me, Rhonda," "The Spirit of Rock and Roll," and "In My Room." I rehearsed all weekend.

In recent years, I'd played three or four songs by myself at benefits and charity events here and there, but never in my career had I performed a solo set as long as the one I planned for the China Club. After thirty years, I thought it was about time I proved to myself that I could go onstage by myself and entertain a crowd as well as the Beach Boys had done. I also wanted it to be my reply to Gene.

By performing, I could thank Gene and say my personal "Fuck you" to Mike and Carl at the same time.

Although the show was unannounced, word spread swiftly at the American Music Awards being held across town the same night. The music industry has always lived on two things—money and gossip. By show time, the club was packed. My friend Danny Hutton was there as were other friends and supporters, including Lou Adler, Jon Bon Jovi, Los Angeles Lakers owner Jerry Buss, Chubby Checker, rapper Young M.C., superstar producer Don Was, and one of my favorite singers, Toni Childs.

It still wasn't going to be easy. By my estimate, at least half the audience were kids into heavy metal or rap. Most probably weren't born when I'd started out. They'd come to drink and get laid. They'd probably never played a Beach Boys record in their lives. They'd probably never heard of me. They probably couldn't have given a damn that I was playing. It was probably the toughest audience I'd faced in thirty years, since the Beach Boys' first show at the Long Beach Civic Center in 1961.

Unfortunately, Gene succumbed to the flu and wasn't able to make it. He waited as long as possible before telling me, reaching me finally on my car phone as I was on the Santa Monica Freeway, heading toward the club. I knew he was sick, I heard it in his voice, but I think he also wanted me to know I could perform without him, all alone. It was another test in bravery. I told Gene it wasn't a problem, that I could handle it. But at the last minute, I wasn't so certain. The nerves started getting to me and I began to wonder if it was such a good idea.

But I really didn't have a choice. I had to do it. For Gene. For the Beach Boys. For myself.

The house band was already playing when I climbed upstairs from the dressing room. In the wings, I said hi to the two musicians I'd invited to play with me, San Francisco bassist Rob Wasserman, who appears extensively on my second solo LP, and Don Was, who I knew would get a kick out of playing bass on some of the Beach Boys' oldies. Rob was introduced first, and he set up onstage. My cue was going to come about a minute later, after Rob warmed up a bit. Grinning at me from behind his sunglasses, Don was amused by how nervous I was, bouncing up and down without control.

"You'll do fine," he said.

"Yeah, but I might fuck up," I replied.

"Nah, you won't."

A half beat later, I heard my cue. The bandleader leaned into the mike and said, "Earlier today I met this kid who's gonna come out now and play some piano . . ."

The reviews were terrific, mentioning my strong voice, the quality of the songs, the emotion of the set, the standing ovations. One reviewer noted how being onstage filled my spirit with an unexpected ebullience, comparing my grin between songs to a Cheshire cat. Gene was extremely proud of me. Well-wishers sent congratulations Tuesday and Wednesday. The Beach Boys were the only people I didn't hear from.

But what I realized is that all of that paled in comparison to the joy I felt being onstage, playing and watching people, strangers, sing and dance to my songs. The China Club's crowd had made me feel loved, which was nice. I didn't often feel that way.

More than that, I realized that I fell in love at the China Club. I fell in love with my songs and the healing power of music all over again.

The experience should've been a springboard into everything that Gene and I had been working toward over the past seven years. Everything was set. My second solo album, *Sweet Insanity,* was ready to be mixed. We were planning a fall tour. We were negotiating for a television special. The bases were loaded. I was looking at a fastball coming in belt high. I smelled the home run. I could hear the crowd cheering. I could picture the victory celebration.

Then reality intruded.

In the first week of March Carl suddenly accelerated the conservatorship case. Claiming to have "proof" that Gene brainwashed and bankrupted me, he threatened to have the court appoint a temporary but immediate conservator. He wanted Dr. Landy once and for all, preferably, he told people, in jail. Carl never once tried to talk to me personally. He showed absolutely no sensitivity that I was being stripped of my dignity and rights as a human being.

That night in the studio, after an entire day of listening to explanations, I finally buckled. I pulled my chair into a corner and started to cry. Gene stood behind me, his hand on my shoulder, feeling the pain.

"I know I'm a little brain-damaged," I said. "Goddamnit, I know. But I'm not unfit."

"No, you aren't," Gene said.

"And I'm capable of caring for myself," I said.

"Yes," he agreed.

"I'm healthier and in better shape than ever," I said.

"Yes." Gene nodded.

"Then why is Carl doing this to me?" I asked. "Why? Why the fuck is he doing it?"

"Why?" Gene said in a voice that was soft and calm, a voice that was in sharp contrast to my anguish. "I think it's because Carl's been jealous of your talent and fame all of his life, and this is his chance to get even."

I let that sink in. He was right. But his next comment made that seem beside the point.

"And," Gene added, "because your brother hates me more that he loves or cares about you."

I wasn't with Gene when he signed the separation agreement, but we talked that night by phone and I heard the emotion in his voice. Caving in to the pressure and exhaustion of having battled for our lives for nearly a year, Gene sacrificed himself for me again, as he did when he surrendered his license to practice psychology. He agreed not to talk, see, or interact in any way with me for ninety days. During that time, our joint business interests would be dissolved and I would see a psychiatrist who'd evaluate me and determine whether or not I was competent or brainwashed.

In exchange, Carl agreed to postpone the conservatorship suit and there would be no immediate temporary conservator appointed for me.

I could continue living on my own, independently, making my own decisions. It was just going to cost me my business partner, teacher, adviser, manager, protector, voice of sanity, collaborator, and closest friend. Gene Landy was all of those to me, and more.

Several days after Gene signed the agreement, I put my name on it too, making it a done deal. The date, appropriately enough, was April 1. Who was the real fool?

Gene and I never spoke about the end. Never. Our doctor-patient relationship had long ago melted quite naturally into a song and equally natural friendship. Despite countless disagreements throughout the years, neither of us ever had a reason to consider the end of that friendship. Even if we had, I'm positive we wouldn't have imagined it occurring within the sterile walls of an attorney's office.

As ludicrous, far-fetched, and surreal as it still sounds to me, most of our final days as partners in business and, more important, in life were spent inside the wood-paneled confines of our attorneys' offices. After all we'd been through together, I couldn't imagine saying good-bye.

Legally, the separation is supposed to last just ninety days. If, at the end, the psychiatrist concludes that I'm not brainwashed, then in theory I should be able to tell Carl, Stan, and everyone else who has been meddling in my life to go fuck themselves.

In any event, it seems that Dr. Landy's and my relationship is coming to an end.

And then what?

Borrowing one of my own lines, God only knows.

But more than likely, one of two scenarios will play out.

After a couple of weeks, I'll start getting calls from Carl, Mike, Marilyn, and the girls. They'll have been watching, waiting for signs of weakness, slippage, circling like vultures. They'll say hello, ask a few innocuous questions. Then everyone'll want to come over, talk, and visit. Suddenly. Where have they been for the past five years?

The next step will be to write together. Then the guys'll take me to the studio. Gradually, I'll be finagled back into the Beach Boys. The guys will

be happy as pigs in mud. Finally, they'll have their songwriter and producer back, and for the first time in five years they'll be able to get an album
deal. The new contract will stipulate that I write and produce 80 percent
of the material.

It's a familiar déjà vu.

But what will the cost be on me?

If I turn out not to be as strong and independent as I think I am, or
as Gene hoped to make me, I'll begin to deteriorate. It'll be slow at first,
almost imperceptible. I'll quit brushing my teeth, washing, changing
clothes. I'll start eating, drinking, then even doping. I'll want to be alone.
I'll get scared. I'll set up walls to protect me and slip into the same isolated
fantasy world from which Gene forced me to exit before I killed myself.

On the other hand, I might be strong enough to hold out. I don't
know. But I'm going to try.

By the middle of April, with everything unfolding in a way that was
beyond my meager ability to control it, I could be certain of only one
thing: I was scared and I was angry and I was full of uncertainty.

Rather than a teary, emotional farewell, Gene and I decided the best
way to part company was to remember this moment of departure as it was.
He brought me back from the dead. I had a life. I was enjoying it like never
before. That by itself was more important than any of the songs I had
written, more important than the album we had coming out, more important than anything.

I haven't had the kindest life. Or the easiest. But I've given my life a
great soundtrack, and Gene gave me the ability to enjoy it.

After a long discussion that seemed to cover everything but our separation, Gene and I made our way to the parking lot behind the studio.
Standing between our matching yellow Corvettes, we paused awkwardly,
unsure of what to say, and then gave each other a big hug that said it all.

Then he pulled out in his car and I drove off in mine, like two
gun-fighters riding into separate sunsets. With my radio blasting, I drove
up the Pacific Coast Highway, fighting the urge to dial Gene on the car
phone.

Twenty minutes later I was home. I wandered out to the balcony.
There was a time, I suppose, when all the pressures that I was shouldering
would've tempted me to think about jumping off. But now I gazed up and
down the beach and cleared my mind by humming a melody that was in
my head, a melody I titled "What's Going to Happen Next." It struck me
as ironic how complicated the life of a very simple man had become.

My whole life, since I discovered music, has been about only one thing: about experiencing the sheer, pure, unencumbered, liberating happiness of the creative moment. That special moment. Of flight. Of running in an open field. Of beauty. Of happiness. I tasted it. Then I spent a lifetime chasing it. Like an addict. Again and again and again. Until the very chase became my life.

It was a beautiful day in Malibu, one created for enjoyment rather than worry. I breathed the salty air and studied my palette. The blue, whitecapped water, the sandy beach, the sky dotted with pillowy white clouds, surfers cutting across the waves, and girls on the beach. Beyond the breakers, two dolphins poked through the water. A sign of good luck.

Then I went downstairs to my piano. It was time to go to work.

Index

Throughout this index, "BW" refers to Brian Wilson.